ON THE AFRICAN WATERFRONT

On the African Waterfront

*Urban Disorder and the Transformation of Work
in Colonial Mombasa*

FREDERICK COOPER

Yale University Press
New Haven and London

331.592
C77o

Designed by James J. Johnson
and set in Baskerville types.
Printed in the United States of America by
Thomson-Shore, Inc., Dexter, Michigan.

Library of Congress Cataloging-in-Publication Data

Cooper, Frederick, 1947–
    On the African waterfront.

    Bibliography: p.
    Includes index.
    1. Strikes and lockouts—Stevedores—Kenya—Mombasa—
History—20th century.   2. Trade unions—Stevedores—
Kenya—Mombasa—History—20th century.   3. Mombasa
(Kenya)—Economic conditions.   I. Title.
HD5440.5.L8C66   1987   331.89′281387164′0967623   86–13171
ISBN 0–300–03618–3

10   9   8   7   6   5   4   3   2   1

To Jane

Contents

Tables, Figures, and Maps

Preface

This book emerged from a vain attempt to escape an obsession with the coast of East Africa that has lasted nearly fifteen years. When I started research on labor history in coastal Kenya, I had no intention of writing a trilogy on the subject; when I returned to Kenya in 1978 I aimed, almost literally, to move up the railway from the coast. My project was to be a history of railway workers that focused on the changing nature of work and the labor force since the beginning of this century.

What I found in the archives of the Railways and Harbours Administration not only made such a task difficult but suggested a different way of thinking about African labor history. The railway administration knew virtually nothing about its workers until nearly 1940. Then, suddenly, it became obsessed with its need to understand and to use its knowledge to transform the nature of work. The discovery of workers as something more than a quantity of labor power—as social beings—was thrust upon officials by a series of strikes in Mombasa between 1934 and 1947. The critical transition in Kenya did not occur in a particular industry or line of work but in the complex social field of a city; movements of African workers spread through the city and twice shut it down in general strikes. The strikes in turn provoked a crisis of ideas among colonial officials and businessmen that encompassed their overall perceptions of African labor, and indeed of African society.

The sharpness of the break and the fact that the events of Mombasa were echoed at the same time in several other African cities—among workers in a great variety of occupations—forced me to rethink conceptions of labor history which I shared with most Africanists. The pace and direction of change did not appear linear, as was implied by the frequent use of words like *proletarianisation* or by attempts—as in my original project—to see workers' consciousness growing along with experience in the workplace.

These thoughts called for new plans. The railwaymen of Kenya still have their history, and it is an interesting one; but my notes on them remain for the moment in a file cabinet. The changes in railway work and in workers' organization that became more rapid in the 1950s, it seemed to me, could not be understood without first deciphering the turning point of the 1940s. And that break took place in Mombasa. The vanguard of those social movements and the focus of the state's effort to regain the initiative were not railwaymen but dockers. However, the key questions concerned relationships: to colonial officials, the dockers were particularly dangerous because they were simultaneously vital to the colonial economy and part of a mass of humanity moving into and out of casual labor, idleness, criminality, and other economic activities about which officials knew nothing. The cure to the crisis of the 1940s, they came to think, was to break up the mass into a differentiated, stable labor force.

This is not a history of labor policy or of trade unions; nor is it an attempt to reconstruct the world of the Mombasa dockworker, although it touches on all those themes. It is a history of what might be called a conjuncture, a turning point, a break, a rupture. It is about connections—between the ways in which capital organized work and the ways in which workers organized themselves, between specific struggles in a city and perceptions of society in an empire.

The conjuncture of 1935–50 cannot be described equally well from all points of view. The official sources are rich. The evidence about dockworkers is necessarily uneven, but is in a sense rich—by its absence as well as by its availability—in the most important respect, in permitting the reconstruction of what aspects of workers' lives were accessible to officials and managers, should they have chosen to interpret them. The transcripts of hearings at which tribunals heard African witnesses and the reports of several sociological investigations reveal much of what officials wanted to ask workers, and what workers chose to tell them.

My objective in this context was not to evoke the daily lives of dockworkers. I did not set out to do an oral history. Such a project would be a natural complement to this one and would certainly add to, and perhaps modify, some of the points developed here. Since my year in Kenya, during the gestation period of this book, I have been working on the other side of the nexus discussed here—the labor question as part of an ideological crisis of imperialism in the 1940s and early 1950s, an investigation that also adds to and modifies research focused on a single city. Yet the experience of working in Mombasa—including a number of interviews—suggests some considerations for anyone doing the kind of oral labor history that would be the next step in studying this topic, or indeed many other related ones.

The basic problem is this: "dockworkers," like many other categories of workers, are a logical unit of analysis, but not necessarily a reasonable unit for research. To study dockworkers through fieldwork in Mombasa would be to use a biased sample. Only some have stayed in Mombasa, and not necessarily a random selection. To understand the diverse meanings that dockwork had, one must do research not just in Mombasa, but in western Kenya, in Kwale, in Kilifi, in Taita, and in central Kenya, for that is where many dockers originated and where many who experienced the transformations of the 1940s and 1950s have since returned. Locating ex-dockers scattered in rural Kenya would be time-consuming, but might yield interesting memories of the 1947 strike or the restructuring of work gangs during the 1950s. Much better would be to explore the place of dockwork in the lives of people who at times did other things, and in the wider context of family, village, and regional life. To do urban labor history, in other words, is also to do rural history.

That likely takes more than one investigator. One may well learn the most about the history of dockwork—or railway labor, or factory work—not by setting out to study that subject, but by incorporating questions about urban work into a series of local studies. The academic world, the world of historians above all, is not very well organized for such efforts. This book is an individual's contribution to a task which I hope others will join or take up in their own ways.

My research in Kenya was made possible by a fellowship from the National Endowment for the Humanities, and a subsequent trip to England to look more closely into London's view of the labor question was made possible by a grant from the Joint Africa Committee of the Social Science Research Council and the American Council of Learned Societies. My time in Kenya was made more stimulating by my colleagues at the History Department of the University of Nairobi. I am especially grateful for the openness, generosity, and insight of my fellow Mombasa specialist Karim Janmohamed, who has now made two stays in Kenya more pleasant and enlightening. I have benefited as well from participating in the lively community of Africanists in the Boston area and more recently from the intellectual stimulation of my colleagues in the History Department and the Residential College of the University of Michigan. I would like to thank John Lonsdale, Luise White, and Geoff Eley for the very detailed and insightful readings they gave to an earlier draft. And a final word of appreciation goes to Jane Burbank, whose own book emerged from the same personal computer on which this one is being written almost exactly a week ago, and who shared the machinery and the anxieties of authorship with generosity and thoughtfulness. In the midst of writing a book that largely concerns conflicts over how resources were allocated and time employed, I was able to observe every day that such conflicts are not a universal characteristic of human nature. Explanations for them must lie elsewhere.

Abbreviations

ACJ	Arthur Creech Jones Papers, Rhodes House, Oxford
Ag	Acting
AR	Annual Report
AWF	African Workers Federation
CME	Chief Mechanical Engineer, Railway
CO	Colonial Office files, Public Record Office, London
CP	Coast Province records, Kenya National Archives
CS	Chief Secretary, Kenya Government
DC	District Commissioner
DO	District Officer
DWU	Dockworkers Union
EAR&H	East African Railways and Harbours Administration
EAS	*The East African Standard*
EST	Establishment files, Railway Archives
FCB	Fabian Colonial Bureau Papers, Rhodes House, Oxford
GM	General Manager, Railway
HBR	Harbour files, Railway
IRO	Industrial Relations Officer
KFRTU	Kenya Federation of Registered Trade Unions
KL&S Co.	Kenya Landing and Shipping Company
KUR&H	Kenya and Uganda Railway and Harbours
LAB	Labour Department files, Kenya National Archives
L&S Co.	Landing and Shipping Company of East Africa
LC	Labour Commissioner
LD	Labour Department, Kenya
LO	Labour Officer
MT	*The Mombasa Times*
PC	Provincial Commissioner, Coast Province
PC's Archive	Provincial Commissioner's Archive, Coast Province, Files LAB (Labour), L&O (Law and Order), PUB (Public Relations)
PEA	Port Employers Association
PLO	Principal Labour Officer
PLUB	Port Labour Utilisation Board
PM	Port Manager, Railway

RASU   Railway African Staff Union
SPG   Railway Archives, Nairobi, files from 1930s

Note: Thanks to interterritorial amalgamation within British East Africa, the Kenya and Uganda Railways and Harbours Administration became the East African Railways and Harbours Administration in 1948, and the Kenya Landing and Shipping Co. became the Mombasa branch of the Landing and Shipping Co. of East Africa in 1951. To avoid confusion, I have referred to "the Railway" and the "KL&S Co." throughout the text, but in the notes refer to sources as they appear on the documents.

ON THE AFRICAN WATERFRONT

ETHIOPIA

UGANDA

KENYA

SOMALIA

Luhya

Luo

Gulf of
Kavirondo Kisumu

Kikuyu

Nairobi

Lake Victoria

TANGANYIKA

Kamba

Lamu

Malindi

Indian
Ocean

Railway

Taita

Mombasa

Digo Mijikenda

0   100

miles

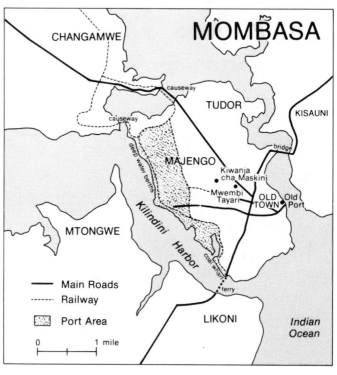

MOMBASA

CHANGAMWE

causeway

TUDOR

KISAUNI

causeway

bridge

MAJENGO

deep water berths

Kiwanja
cha Maskini

Mwembi
Tayari

OLD   Old
TOWN Port

MTONGWE

Kilindini Harbor

coal wharf

Main Roads

Railway

Port Area

ferry

LIKONI

Indian
Ocean

0   1 mile

1 Introduction

In the five hundred years in which Europeans and Africans have known each other rather well, no element has been more central to their relationship than work. Slave traders from Europe took Africans away to work; imperial powers later came to Africa and built their empires with the help of African arms and backs. The colonists, like the employers of slave labor before them, made clear their obsession with work by placing the Africans' supposed laziness among the most important features that distinguished them from civilized people. Yet this very stereotype should be a clue that Europe has not completely dominated this relationship, even at the height of the colonial era. Labeling the African worker as lazy was a way of acknowledging the limits of dominance while attributing these limits to the basic nature of the dominated, rather than to the contradictions of exercising power. However far-reaching the political, economic, and psychological mechanisms through which imperial powers tried to make colonized peoples play their part in empire, they ultimately had to penetrate inside a plantation, a dockyard, a locomotive cab, or a factory where there were workers, bringing to the encounter their own conceptions of labor, their own interests, and their own wills.

This book concerns the efforts of a colonial state and of a group of employers to reassert control over a workplace, faced with an orchestrated challenge from African workers. It examines a turning point, a moment when the old ways of organizing work and thinking about work proved inadequate, when questions that had long been set aside had to be faced. The strike wave that passed through major cities and mining regions of Africa from the mid-1930s through the early 1950s required more than adjustments in industrial relations. It helped to create a crisis of ideas, undermining conceptions of African labor and African society widely held in the colonial situation, and with it governments' confidence that they could in fact control the social and economic forces they had unleashed.

African workers had long been a worry to planters, mining corporations, and governments, but most often in a quantitative sense—frequent laments about labor shortages. The problem of how to get more work out of the African surfaced in more particular circumstances before the late 1930s, and most clearly of all in the mining economies of South Africa or

1

the Belgian Congo. Nonetheless, even employers with a direct interest in the results of work frequently approached the labor question with a notable degree of complacency, asking little more than how many workers could be obtained for a low wage.

Such was the case until the late 1930s with the largest employer in East Africa, the East African Railways and Harbours Administration. The files of the Administration reveal quite literally a conception of labor power as anonymous and interchangeable. Even in East Africa's leading port of Mombasa, where all the exports of Kenya and Uganda had to pass through the hands of a few thousand dockworkers, the shipping companies and the Harbour Administration hired each day as many hands as they needed, and did not so much as know their workers' names.

Suddenly, around 1940, official attitudes changed. Commissions were impaneled to study the labor question in Mombasa; a succession of social investigators was inflicted on the city's population; files on labor became fatter. The workers in the port, in the city, on the railway, and eventually throughout the colony ceased to be anonymous embodiments of labor power, but social beings, whose culture, welfare, and relationships with each other and with employers were vital determinants of order and productivity.

This sudden desire to understand stemmed directly from a series of strikes in the port city. It was in Mombasa that the Kenya Government discovered the dangers and complexities of the existence of an African working population. By 1945, official documents were referring to an "urbanized working class" and pondering the twin problem of getting that class to work and preventing it from endangering social order. The dock strike of 1934, the general strikes of 1939 and 1947, the strikes that spread from one Mombasa firm to another in 1942, and the barely averted general strike of 1945 had their echoes during this same period throughout Africa, and in British colonies in the West Indies and Southeast Asia as well. Two widespread mine strikes in Northern Rhodesia in 1935 and 1940; the South African gold mine strike of 1946 and the Gold Coast mine strike of 1947; general strikes in Nigeria in 1945, in Dakar in 1946, in Dar es Salaam in 1948; and several railway strikes in West Africa, most dramatically, the one that affected all of French West Africa for five months in 1947 and 1948, were notable not only for their effectiveness but for the way they spread beyond a single enterprise and cut off much colonial commerce at its most vulnerable points. The strike wave, the likes of which had never been seen before in British or French Africa, raised questions about the most intimate details of work and of the lives of workers—how a particular group of workers could be shaped to its task and its milieu. At the same time it broached the broadest of questions in an imperial context: whether colonial officials could understand, let alone control, the social tensions of the postwar era.

In Mombasa, as in other African cities and mine-towns, striking workers confronted the colonial state with the consequences of the creation of an anonymous mass of workers. In the general strikes of 1939 and 1947, a working class acted with a unity and discipline that elicited shock and later gruding admiration from officials and local businessmen. The dim anxiety that had occasionally surfaced in official reports about the dangers of the "floating population" of African towns quickly became an acute concern. Once the behavior of African workers triggered the large set of experiences and ideas associated with European working classes, officials diagnosed the problem with little delay: as in Europe, workers needed to be integrated into a stable and differentiated structure of institutions capable of giving them a stake in society, providing outlets for grievances, and hopefully influencing their values and expectations in ways that were, at least, predictable.

The diagnosis pointed to the importance of casual labor to the most vital and vulnerable of Mombasa's industries, dockwork. And it logically led to doubts about the entire system of migrant labor so important to Kenya and most other African colonies. By the late 1940s, officials in Kenya were convinced that casual labor in the docks had to be eliminated and were facing the question of whether migrant labor in general should be suppressed throughout the urban economy. Casual labor in the port disappeared with remarkable rapidity, far faster than it did in Great Britain itself. By 1954, the port of Mombasa had established a corps of regular dockworkers, each of whom was required to appear for work at least twenty days each month. By decade's end, daily hiring had been abolished.

With these changes in hiring went an equally profound transformation of the nature of supervision and discipline in dockwork, an attempt to strengthen the top-down control of management at the expense of the self-discipline of the work gangs constituted by the dockers themselves. It was more difficult for most employers and many government officials to bring themselves to accept African trade unions, but they eventually did that too, recognizing the Dockworkers Union, encouraging a bureaucratized system of industrial relations, and slowly working out a modus vivendi with organized labor. These were essential steps to keeping labor disputes within acceptable boundaries and putting an end to the danger of the general strike. But the state and the employers could not entirely control either the workplace or the bargaining table: the reforms encouraged union militancy, without ending unofficial work stoppages by dockers vigorously seeking to preserve some of their long-accepted prerogatives in the workplace.

Least successful of all were the state's attempts to reshape the city as it reshaped the port, to create an orderly and hard-working city, free from the dangerous masses who had threatened social and political order in the

1940s. In seeking to replace a mass of workers who circulated into and out of urban jobs with a compact, efficient, and stable corps of urban workers, the state was trying to recast the relationship of city and country. Its assertion of control in the city reflected in large part its inability to control the countryside—underscored in the early 1950s by the so-called Mau Mau revolt in central Kenya—but isolating the city from the seemingly atavistic currents of rural Africa proved to be beyond the capability of the Kenyan state.

To understand the transformations of work and urban society—and the limits to those transformations—is thus to peer into the intimate details of working life, and it is to look beyond the workplace to wider questions about African society and its place in the modern world.[1] This book is as much about ideas of work and society as it is about labor disputes in an African city. It begins to explore the interrelation of social action in a particular place and social analysis in an empire.

The labor crisis in Mombasa was—and was seen at the time in these terms—a part of a profound malaise in colonial society. The central political problem of the postwar era was not simply a problem of politics, a question of evolution toward self-government. British officials—and French as well—rarely separated the question of what kind of government was needed for the colonies from the question of what government was to do.[2] The postwar era was one of economic crisis for the imperial powers, painfully recovering from war, burdened with an immense debt in dollars to the United States, yet expecting that postwar conditions in world markets would provide unprecedented opportunities for selling tropical, particularly African, raw materials in hard currency markets.

The danger of crippling strikes could hardly have arisen at a more dangerous moment: as the colonial powers hoped for a breakthrough in the level of production in Africa, their control over the workforce was being challenged for the first time by collective action. Exacerbated by the very upturn in production that imperial governments awaited, the crises of inflation, urban crowding, and deteriorating conditions for African workers inexorably led to disorders that threatened to interrupt the imperial program and in the long run led officials to doubt their ability to control the contradictions of their new production drive. The problem was not just how to keep political control over the African or to ease the

1. I have written elsewhere on the theoretical and historiographical aspects of the study of labor and urban society. Frederick Cooper, "Urban Space, Industrial Time, and Wage Labor in Africa," in Cooper, ed., *Struggle for the City: Migrant Labor, Capital, and the State in Urban Africa* (Beverly Hills, Calif.: Sage, 1983), pp. 7–50.

2. By isolating the problem of self-government, some recent studies have given a rather misleading view of the debates over the future of the colonies. For example, see R. D. Pearce, *The Turning Point in Africa: British Colonial Policy 1938–1948* (London: Cass, 1982).

transition to a new political relationship, but how to get the African to work. The labor question in the late 1940s and 1950s was one of a number of social problems—soil conservation and agricultural development were others—whose intractability helps to explain why colonial regimes cast about so vigorously, if not desperately, for new governmental structures capable of getting something more than grudging acquiesence out of African workers and peasants. It was a problem that neither the colonial governments nor, by and large, their successors solved.[3]

For all the importance of the labor question throughout the period of European intervention in Africa, and for all its acuity since the 1930s, work is one of the least examined aspects of African history, even of African labor history. Rarely have scholars asked what people do when they work, why they do it, and how workers and managers alike try to shape the pace, intensity, and quality of what gets done. The flurry of anxious introspection into which colonial officials and corporate managers fell during the 1940s and early 1950s had its influence on academic research, by no means all of it in the service of extracting more work from Africans.[4] But the new direction in social research did not give rise to a school of work studies, as it did to a long and rich tradition of African urban anthropology. The value of several sociological studies of work and workers in factories and elsewhere does not negate their rarity.[5] Trade union studies have been vastly more popular.[6] Historians, for their part,

3. In my final chapter, I will draw out some of the implications of the labor question for a wider crisis of imperialism. That chapter is as much preface as conclusion, underlining the need to develop connections between research at a local level, as is done in this book, to research at the global level, an approach that I, among many others, hope to pursue.

4. Two early entries in international debates on the labor question are *Présence Africaine*, special issue on work, no. 13 (1952), and UNESCO, *Social Implications of Industrialization and Urbanization in Africa South of the Sahara* (Paris: UNESCO, 1956). For an analysis of managers' views of the sociology of work, see Belinda Bozzoli, "Managerialism and the Mode of Production in South Africa," *South African Labour Bulletin* 3, no. 8 (1977): 6–49, and, more generally, a fine review article by Bill Freund, "Labor and Labor History in Africa: A Review of the Literature," *African Studies Review* 27, no. 2 (1984): 1–58.

5. Margaret Peil, *The Ghanaian Factory Worker* (Cambridge: Cambridge University Press, 1970); Bruce Kapferer, *Strategy and Transaction in an African Factory: African Workers and Indian Management in a Zambian Town* (Manchester: Manchester University Press, 1972); Adrian Peace, *Choice, Class and Conflict: A Study of Southern Nigerian Factory Workers* (London: Harvester, 1979); R. D. Grillo, *African Railwaymen* (Cambridge: Cambridge University Press, 1974). For reviews of the literature, see Michael Burawoy, "The Anthropology of Work," *Annual Review of Anthropology* 8 (1979): 231–66, and Carol S. Holzberg and Maureen J. Giovannini, "Anthropology and Industry: Reappraisals and New Directions," ibid. 10 (1981): 317–60. See also a collection of studies emphasizing the diverse cultural meanings of work edited by Sandra Wallman, *The Social Anthropology of Work*, ASA Monographs 19 (London: Academic Press, 1979).

6. William Friedland, "African Trade Union Studies: Analysis of Two Decades," *Cahiers d'Etudes Africaines* 14 (1974): 575–89.

have so far done little to examine how ways of working have changed before, during, and after the colonial period. As sensitive a study as Charles van Onselen's book on gold miners in Southern Rhodesia focuses much more on what workers did in the compounds than on what they did inside the mines.[7]

The increasing size of the wage labor force in colonial Africa and the nature of labor markets and patterns of labor migration have been studied far more than work itself: what gets Africans into workplaces has received more attention than what they do in them. This tendency has often made African labor history appear in a linear form. Economic historians trained in the neoclassical tradition have looked at the development of wage labor as a self-propelled movement of people from an area of low productivity to one of high—the nature of work in the modern sector of an economy was taken essentially as a given.[8] Radical critics of this approach have most often replaced it with an equally linear one, only they call it proletarianization. These writers stress how the growth of a wage labor sector, its concentration in key industries, and the experience of work itself led to a growth of workers' consciousness of themselves as a class, most often expressed by the growth of trade unions and strikes.[9] Whether termed the "development of the work force"—and hence a natural part of the modern world—or "proletarianization"—hence an aspect of capitalism—the processes by which capitalists and workers tried to shape what work would be like remain unclear.

The experience of Mombasa—and the pattern into which it fits—suggest that change did not so much proceed along lines but in bursts, through moments when long-standing forms of organization and ide-

7. Charles van Onselen, *Chibaro: African Mine Labour in Southern Rhodesia, 1900–1933* (London: Pluto, 1976). The most influential collections on African labor are notable for how little they say about work. Richard Sandbrook and Robin Cohen, eds., *The Development of an African Working Class* (London: Longman, 1975); P. C. W. Gutkind, Robin Cohen, and Jean Copans, eds., *African Labor History* (Beverly Hills, Calif.: Sage, 1978). But the importance of struggles over the nature of work has been stressed in a growing and stimulating body of literature by Marxist labor economists. See, for a beginning, David M. Gordon, Richard Edwards, and Michael Reich, *Segmented Work, Divided Workers: The Historical Transformation of Labor in the United States* (Cambridge: Cambridge University Press, 1982); Harry Braverman, *Labor and Monopoly Capital: The Degradation of Work in the Twentieth Century* (New York: Monthly Review, 1974); and Michael Burawoy, "Toward a Marxist Theory of the Labor Process: Braverman and Beyond," *Politics and Society* 8 (1978): 247–312.

8. See the classic study of W. A. Lewis, "Economic Development with Unlimited Supplies of Labour," *The Manchester School* 22 (1954): 139–91.

9. The approach is exemplified clearly in the title of an influential collection, and in most (but not all) of the articles. Sandbrook and Cohen, *The Development of an African Working Class.*

ology cracked and new departures were made. These critical moments came about not only under the pressure of titanic clashes, but through an accumulation of minute and subtle struggles in the workplace, as both capital and labor tried to bend their relationship with each other.

Workers' consciousness of themselves as a class did not grow linearly with longer experience in the workplace, but the boundaries of collective relations, identity, and action shifted in complex ways. The Mombasa strikes revealed the action of a working class in the most general sense of the term—the collective action of the sellers of labor power. They were not united by the common experience of a single workplace or a single occupation, but by the fact of being workers. That some of them, at various times during their lives, also farmed small subsistence plots in nearby or faraway villages was in these circumstances no obstacle to class action in the city. Nor did the overlap of workers with petty traders, self-employed artisans, criminals, and job seekers deter common action at this time. In the course of two general strikes and a period of agitation in between, the state was confronted with a complex social force consisting of people for whom the act of selling labor power was an essential, if not exclusive, dimension of economic life. To officials, not understanding the social and cultural forms in which relationships among such people were articulated, the problem seemed to be that of an amorphous, dangerous, seething urban mass. Only with time did British officials begin to pose the problem in different terms: the unexpected, unwanted, but very real presence of an African urban working class that had come to the city to sell its labor power and had proved capable of acting in accordance with this broad commonality.

In the aftermath of the strikes, the state sought to fragment this unity into occupational and sectional components, while purging the idle and the criminal from the city. At moments, the wide class unity seemed about to coalesce again, as when the dock strike of 1955 spilled for a time beyond the docks. But the postwar reforms had had their impact: the dock-workers had indeed become a group set apart from the rest of Mombasa, no longer moving into and out of port jobs, having gained their own—much improved—pay structure and their own job expectations, and finding themselves in the midst of the dispute caught up in a newly developed organization of industrial relations geared specifically to the docks. The dockers' victory in achieving—for themselves—a major wage increase did not diminish the state's victory in having brought about a parting of the ways among the city's workers.

This study, then, is as much about the fracturing of a working class as it is about its increasing experience and developing traditions. It focuses, to take a phrase from Adam Przeworsky, on class struggle not just as the struggle *of* classes but as a struggle *about* class.[10] Workers have frequently responded to the growing power of a capitalist class and the growing importance of wage labor by doing all they could not to become a class, to be something more than anonymous labor power. Capital has, in varying ways, confronted the contradiction of its need for a class of people whose labor is freely available in the market and the danger that such a class may begin to act collectively.

The relationship of dockers to other workers in Mombasa—and the relationship of dock work to the totality of workers' economic lives—was thus of central importance. The crisis of the 1940s developed among workers who, throughout the city, came irregularly to work from unknown parts, bringing unknown motives and values into their places of work. They had, officials emphasized, little fear of the "sanction of the sack," nothing to lose but a day's work. If casual labor allowed port firms to avoid paying the full social cost of labor, it also denied them the possibility of training—and above all socializing—workers into the habits of steady, regular work. If they could hope that the transience of migrant workers—casual workers in the extreme—would inhibit labor organizing, they discovered to their chagrin that migrants could in fact act coherently and effectively in a labor struggle.[11] The instability of the work force and the absence of formal organization was more an obstacle to settling a strike, transforming workers' dissatisfactions and anger into a negotiable set of issues, than to starting one.

Mombasa became one of the two great laboratories in British Africa—the Copperbelt was the other—for experiments with the transition from a rapidly circulating labor force to a stable one rooted in urban residence and an urban way of life. The transition implied a fundamental break in the conceptions that colonial rulers had of African society. Rather than taking an African briefly from his village and returning him to its presumed tranquility once his stint was over, the new concept of society implied permanently extracting him and reeducating him in the ways of urban life and labor. The village life to which colonial officials wished to return workers was as often as not a fantasy, a myth of an unchanging and conflict-free Africa that had never existed, but it provided scant comfort during the wave of disorder that unurbanized Africans fomented in the

10. Adam Przeworsky, "Proletariat into a Class: The Process of Class Formation from Karl Kautsky's *The Class Struggle* to Recent Controversies," *Politics and Society* 7 (1977): 343–401.

11. The contrary has often been assumed. For other instances of the militancy of migrant or casual workers, see David Hemson, "Dock Workers Labour Circulation and Class Struggles in Durban, 1940–59," *Journal of Southern African Studies* 4 (1977): 88–124, and Richard Moorsom, "Underdevelopment, Contract Labour and Worker Consciousness in Namibia, 1915–72," ibid., pp. 52–87.

cities where they temporarily resided. While, in the early colonial era, profit and order seemed to require re-Africanizing the African, in post-war Mombasa, productivity and urban order appeared to demand that the African worker cease to be African at all. His nutrition, his family life, and his attitudes toward labor, career, property, and achievement had to become those of the modern working man.

The crisis of the 1940s in turn reflected the limitations of a previous attempt at systematic change. In the case of East Africa, the transforma-tions of the final decade or two of colonial rule and those of the first years of colonialism were in some ways the same transformation attempted twice. The problem was how to seize control of the labor power of African societies. As Marx wrote of the capitalist, "He must begin by taking the labour-power as he finds it in the market and consequently he must be satisfied with the kind of labour which arose in a period when there were as yet no capitalists."[12]

But in Africa that kind of labor power was not necessarily for sale in markets. Africans had long seen labor power as part of complex and multifacted relations between user and supplier, from kinship to clien-tage to slavery. Europeans, in the days of the slave trade, had bought laborers, not labor power, and establishing work discipline stemmed in large part from the act of taking slaves away from their own societies. At a later date, European powers, having rejected the slave trade and seeking new commodities from Africa itself, faced a new problem: getting Af-ricans to produce what colonial states wanted in acceptable quantities in the context of Africans' own societies and of a colonial state with limited material resources.[13]

But transforming the structure of African society proved to be a far more daunting task than people convinced of the inevitability of eco-nomic progress had realized. In coastal East Africa, the British tried to transform slave plantations that had successfully adapted to the new mar-ket opportunities of the nineteenth century (at the expense of leaving a wake of destruction in the slave catchment areas) into a form of agrarian capitalism. But even slaves resisted being made into wage laborers, using their legal freedom to seek access to land as tenants, squatters, or small-scale owners. The development of capitalism—commodity production based on the alienation of land from its cultivators and the division of society into a class of owners of the means of production and a class of wage earners working for them—required an immense and systematic effort by the state and white settlers in, most notably, South Africa; its

---

12. Karl Marx, *Capital*, trans. Ben Fowkes (New York: Vintage, 1977), 1: 291.

13. The argument of this and the following paragraphs is developed in Frederick Cooper, "Africa and the World Economy," *African Studies Review* 24, no. 2/3 (1981): 1–86.

triumph was more problematic in other white settler colonies. Efforts to develop, on the cheap, agrarian capitalism with African landlords and African workers in coastal East Africa, Uganda, or Nigeria failed. Else-where—most notably in the cocoa belt of West Africa—colonial states were happy to take the commodities Africans produced in their own ways, but it was not so often that produce arrived steadily, bountifully, and painlessly. As long as peasants had their own land, their ultimate defense was the nonproduction of marketable commodities. Even where African commodity production expanded, colonial states were frequently drawn into the contradictions and limitations of the social organizations that did the producing; and where Africans simply did not grow the crops colonial officials thought they should, awkward, brutal, and prolonged attempts to force them often ensued in the territories of all colonial powers. British and French archives, outside of strikingly limited areas of successful peas-ant or capitalist production, are replete with tales of disappointment.[14]

After a half-century of colonial rule, officials still faced a problem not all that dissimilar from the one they had faced at the end of the nineteenth century: could the demands of a rapidly expanding world economy in the period after the Great Depression be met by adding another layer of bureaucratic pressure to a variety of indigenous production systems, or did the state still have to penetrate what Marx called "the hidden abode of production"? The contradictions of this renewed period of interven-tion—the "second colonial occupation" of Africa—were not resolved by the colonial powers.[15]

If remaking African agriculture proved an elusive goal, fitting the African wage laborer into the image of wage labor that colonial officials brought with them from their industrial societies was equally difficult. The language of Victorian class society had been directly applied to the East Coast of Africa: transforming slaves into a steadily working, self-motivated, orderly proletariat had been an explicit goal of British aboli-tion policy. Some scholars have argued that part-time proletarianization was even more profitable and an intrinsic characteristic of capitalism in a peripheral or colonial context.[16] It is not clear, however, that capital had

14. That some scholars see the Depression years as a key point in colonial states' triumph over their peasants itself suggests the limits of this triumph. African economies were capable of meeting a low demand cheaply; but coping with an expanding demand was far more problematic. Catherine Coquery-Vidrovitch, "La Mise en dépendance de l'Afrique noire: essai de périodisation, 1800–1970," *Cahiers d'Etudes Africaines* 16 (1976): 5–58.

15. D. A. Low and J. M. Lonsdale, "Introduction: Towards the New Order 1945–1963," in D. A. Low and Alison Smith, eds., *The Oxford History of East Africa* (London: Oxford University Press, 1976), 3: 12.

16. Claude Meillassoux, "From Reproduction to Production," *Economy and Society* 1 (1972): 93–105; Harold Wolpe, "Capitalism and Cheap Labour Power in South Africa: From Segregation to Apartheid," ibid., pp. 425–56.

any choice in the matter: African labor power was only for sale in small units. Workers, a variety of recent studies suggest, strove to meet the indirect and direct demands of colonial states and the pressures of a new and restrictive economic order by combining wage labor with vigorous— and occasionally violent—efforts to maintain their access to land and other elements of village or domestic based production. Not infrequently, periods of wage labor were used to restore or expand the capital resources of local agriculture.[17]

So, in an era of recovery from depression, war, and the postwar commodities boom, colonial states faced anew the implications of the fact that they had not remade African economies in their own image. In Mombasa, the limitations of a labor system based on the rapid circulation of labor into and out of the city were faced in an extreme form: casual labor moved in and out of the job day by day. Capital paid for exactly what it got, adjusting its labor force to the coming and going of ships, and did not pay directly to house and feed its workers. The strikes and agitation between 1934 and 1947 changed the situation: the lack of distinction between the working classes and the dangerous classes rendered the entire city impossible to control. Forced by collective action to raise wages, fearing that adding more workers—the only feasible way to respond to expanding commerce within existing structures—would compound the threat to urban order and increase pressures for still higher wages, port firms and the state eventually saw that the only possibility for regaining the initiative lay in a radical departure. They looked to the creation of a permanent labor force in the docks, paid enough to enable workers to live in the city and raise children there, and thus to form over generations a class of workers habituated to a life of labor. At the most vulnerable points in the colony, a respectable African working class had to be defined, nurtured, acculturated, and protected from the contamination of the dangerous classes.

The state's new vision of time and authority was successfully imposed on dockwork, although workers continued to struggle to bend the system at its edges and emerged from this period with an improved standard of living and with institutions capable of defending their interests. But it had been the workers who had thrust the need for radical change on capital and the state, shaking them loose from decades in which complacency in

17. Frederick Cooper, *From Slaves to Squatters: Plantation Labor and Agriculture in Zanzibar and Coastal Kenya, 1890–1925* (New Haven: Yale University Press, 1980); Shula Marks and Richard Rathbone, "Introduction," *Industrialisation and Social Change in South Africa: African Class Formation, Culture and Consciousness 1870–1930* (London: Longman, 1982), pp. 15–20; William Beinart, *The Political Economy of Pondoland* (Cambridge: Cambridge University Press, 1982); Gavin Kitching, *Class and Economic Change in Kenya: The Making of an African Petite Bourgeoisie, 1905–1970* (New Haven: Yale University Press, 1980.)

regard to casual labor had exceeded anxiety. They had forced the state not to consider them as so many interchangeable units of labor power, but as people for whom work was part of life and whose experiences over their life cycles affected the way they worked. The initiatives of workers to gain control of their own lives and those of the state and capital to remake the workplace and colonial society shaped each other.

The need to act in a situation where the state had lost control led officials not only into specific concessions and reforms, but into recasting their conceptions of African society. Their image of casual labor and casual living had concealed the web of social connection, shared problems, and shared goals—expressed within the milieu of coastal culture— that had in fact enabled Mombasa's workers to do their jobs or to leave them as a collectivity. But even in combatting a form of social anomie that did not actually exist, the state began to reshape the socially specific patterns of relationships that existed within the docks and the residential neighborhoods of Mombasa into another vision, a universal image of modernity, rational industrial organization, and planned urbanism. The state was better able to impose that image on the workplace than on the city as a whole, and was least successful of all in reconciling the new vision of society with its own continuing political control. When we look closely at one city at a point in its long history when basic social structures were in question, as the colonial state, port firms, and African workers developed alternative conceptions of society and opposing demands, the dynamics of colonial society in its final decades begin to emerge.

2 Casual Labor and Its Critics

When colonial officials periodically expressed anxiety about casual labor throughout the colonial era, and when they seriously began to tackle the problem in the late 1930s, the language they used was reminiscent of the language in which their predecessors had discussed African slavery in the late nineteenth century. Beneath the parallels in language lay a problem unresolved in the interim: to control work, to improve productivity, and to maintain order was to encounter workers as people with their own expectations, values, and relationships, shaped both inside and outside the workplace. That officials in 1940 posed the problem in similar terms to the way it had been posed in 1895 is an important clue to the limitations of social change under colonial rule. A half-century into the colonial era—in what proved to be its final decades—the state still faced the problem of creating the conditions that fostered steady work and internalized discipline among African workers; it had not accomplished what had been achieved by then with great difficulty in England itself, the formation of a "respectable working class," with a stable place in society and distinguished from the "dangerous classes" of criminals, casual laborers, and the chronically unemployed. The importance of the transformation of work in the late colonial era was a consequence of the incompleteness and inadequacies of the changes that began the colonial phase of African history.

CAPITALIST WORK DISCIPLINE AND EAST AFRICAN SOCIETY

The Problem of Slavery in a Capitalist World

The problem of slavery and the slave trade in nineteenth-century East Africa had given both high officials in the British government and humanitarian groups a framework to articulate their conceptions of work and African society. Especially after David Livingstone's famous voyages of the 1860s, the horrors of slave raiding and trading in East Central Africa became a metaphor for the savagery of African society, and Africa was portrayed in England as a far more slavery-ridden continent than it in fact was.

The indictment of slavery had emerged during the most critical era of capitalist development in England in the late eighteenth and early nineteenth centuries.[1] In those years, the virtues of free labor in England itself were far from obvious to the workers who experienced the extension of free labor as a loss of rights to resources and an eclipse of a variety of social relations that had long tempered the harshness of life for the poor. The attack on slave labor was an important element in making a case for free labor in a period when the advance of capitalism was being strongly contested in England. It defined as immoral deviations from free wage labor, in the name of paternalism as much as tyranny. In later years, the critique of slavery as practiced by Africans on other Africans came to be a means of explaining the complex crises that had developed in Africa during a period of commercial expansion and a way of posing the case for a more radical restructuring of African society.[2]

On the East African coast, the new colonial masters faced a problem more subtle than whether slaves could produce crops or not. At that level, a problem did not exist: the plantations of Zanzibar and what became coastal Kenya were more productive on the eve of the colonial takeover than ever before. The difficulty lay in the violence and chaos that the need to reproduce the labor force through continual importation of slaves induced in a much wider region of East Central Africa, and in the consequences the deeper failings of slavery had on the structure of coastal society itself. The indictment of coastal slavery focused on the fact that discipline, relying as it did on personal dependence and coercion, was necessarily unpredictable and impermanent, and it made evolution toward other forms of work discipline impossible, debasing the value of work. Socially, the consequences of slavery were equally deleterious: accepting only the stern authority of their masters, slaves otherwise tended to be unruly at best and rebellious at worst. The unfortunate corollary of this assessment of slavery was that the slaves themselves were tainted by slavery, leaving them—as missionaries and officials at the time expressed it—without "moral character," and possessed of a "slave instinct to sit down and 'rest.'" Responsive only to physical punishment, slaves were, if left to their own devices, "apt to break loose, loot shops and shambas [farms], and commit all sorts of excesses."[3]

Later, the belief among officials that slavery had made slaves unfit for economic and social life was used to explain much of the economic failure of the Kenyan coast. As the East Africa Commission put it in 1925: "It

1. David Brion Davis, *The Problem of Slavery in the Age of Revolution, 1770 to 1823* (Ithaca, N.Y.: Cornell University Press, 1975).

2. Frederick Cooper, *From Slaves to Squatters: Plantation Labor and Agriculture in Zanzibar and Coastal Kenya, 1890–1925* (New Haven: Yale University Press, 1980), chap. 2; David Brion Davis, *Slavery and Human Progress* (New York: Oxford University Press, 1984).

3. These phrases from Quaker missionaries in Pemba (1902) and a British official in Kenya (1895) are cited—along with a fuller analysis of the issue—in Cooper, *From Slaves to Squatters*, pp. 38–39.

should always be remembered that one of the principal curses of slavery, apart from its immoral character and its economic failure, was the production of the slave mind. A human being accustomed to slavery, when freed, seems to have lost all incentive to work." As late as 1945, Lord Hailey thought it relevant to the chapter on labor in his survey of Africa to point out that "the heritage of slavery is irresponsibility and lack of forethought."[4]

Officials had to think explicitly about a question that the more enthusiastic abolitionists most often preferred not to face: who would manage free laborers? For most officials, the need for a class of managers and landowners was self-evident: that slaves in East Africa could become peasants was not even considered. The only eligibles in coastal society were the slaveowners themselves, and however much they could be faulted for their record of tyranny and oppression against the very people they were supposed to manage—and despite the fact that they were not Christian or even white—the need for a stable class structure to maintain work and order outweighed any prejudices against a particular set of landowners.

Officials were correct in seeing that they were facing a coherent and complex social system from which the legal—let alone social—fact of slavery could only with great difficulty be detached. If anything, they underestimated the delicacy of the social system of the coast. Slavery had long been sanctioned by the Islamic law of coastal East Africa, but it acquired a new meaning during the nineteenth century. Toward the early part of the century, Arab immigrants to Zanzibar built on the already developed commercial system of the western Indian Ocean region to create a plantation economy. Buying slaves from distant parts of central Africa, and producing cloves for markets in India and other faraway lands, the planters acquired a near monopoly of the clove market. The largest plantations had hundreds of slaves.[5] The plantation system spread to the mainland coast, including Kenya. The Malindi region became the site of vast plantations growing millet and other grains for export to drier regions to the north. On other parts of the coast, grain and coconut estates varied in size from a family farm supplemented by one or two slaves to enormous plantations with over a hundred laborers. Not only immigrant Arabs but members of the Muslim, Swahili-speaking African communities of coastal cities became involved in slave-based agriculture.

Labor discipline in plantation slavery had a dual basis. On the one hand, slaves in large estates were organized into gangs and kept in line by

4. East Africa Commission, Report (London, 1925), p. 37; Lord Hailey, *An African Survey*, 2d ed. (London: Oxford University Press, 1945), p. 636.

5. Frederick Cooper, *Plantation Slavery on the East Coast of Africa* (New Haven: Yale University Press, 1977).

a hierarchy of supervisors, whose authority ultimately depended on the whip. On the other hand, slaves were integrated into coastal society as dependents. Coming from distant parts of Africa—often as children— slaves had no social identity beyond what they acquired in coastal society. Given the relative weakness of state authority even within the Sultanate of Zanzibar, any individual needed the protection of a group to be safe. Slaveowners provided not only protection but small plots of land on which slaves grew their own food when not working on the owners' land. Islam reinforced the dependent social relations of the system: slaves were converted through the agency of their owners, but their masters—re- moved from the drudgery of material life—could think of themselves as more contemplative, knowledgeable, and pious Muslims.

The most significant danger to relations of dependence was that slaves might develop closer relations with each other than with their owners. To a significant extent they did, evolving forms of expression, of dance, and even of religious doctrines that subtly balanced the cultural aggression of Arab and Swahili-speaking slaveowners with the counterthrust of a par- tially autonomous culture shared among slaves. Resistance could also be more direct; but to be successful it had to have a collective element: slaves fled plantations, sometimes to join the militarized, dependent entourage of a rival potentate, sometimes to found colonies of runaways on the fringes of the plantation zone; while after the advent of Christian mis- sions in the latter half of the century, flight to this new sort of community became another option. Faced with the challenges of flight and internal autonomy, slaveowners had to reaffirm the primacy of the ties of pater- nalism, conceding special privileges to long-time slaves if they assimilated some of the ways of their owners and obeyed orders. Second-generation slaves—the people who could provide continuity to a slave subculture or slave consciousness—were frequently manumitted. This implied that the labor force could only be reproduced by the continual importation of new slaves, regardless of the birth rate of local slaves. The delicate order within the slave plantation required the violence of slave raids and kid- napping outside it.

The Problem of Casual Labor in a Capitalist Economy
How difficult it would be to transform the relationship of master and slave into that of employer and employee would slowly and painfully become clear to colonial officials. But to understand both the ideological context in which decisions about emancipation were made and the im- plications these ways of thinking had for future attempts to transform labor systems, it is important to look more closely at conceptions of the lower classes in the political discourse of England before the turn of the century, and to sketch briefly how this discourse was applied to the prob- lem of casual labor in England's docks. As Gareth Stedman Jones shows in

his study of *Outcast London,* the attitudes of a broad spectrum of the political leadership, reformers, and the middle class generally underwent a significant transformation from the early years of the industrial revolution.[6]

The early political economists had been pessimistic about the motivations and values of the working class. But in the latter half of the century, a new generation of economists were willing to acknowledge evidence of increasing thrift, sobriety, and rationality among a portion of the working class. The assault of capitalism had been cultural as well as economic, attacking notions of rights to resources that had been considered the rights of Englishmen and attacking the ways of life of preindustrial peoples—Irish and English—which were inconsistent with the time-discipline and sobriety that an efficient working class required. By mid-century, the struggle of many workers to preserve the autonomy of their various trades and avoid submergence in a class of sellers of labor power was essentially lost, although it was not over, and the equally important pattern of the later years was to struggle *as* a working class both for new rights and for respectability within a cultural framework that acknowledged the ideological power of capital even as workers militantly opposed its dominance of the workplace.[7]

But if the making of a respectable working class appeared to be an encouraging possibility, those workers' fragile hold on respectability was threatened by disease, crime, and radical politics emanating from other segments of the working class with whom they lived cheek by jowl in congested urban areas. Victorians called the threatening elements the "residuum." Urban researchers from Mayhew onward developed intricate classification schemes to define the separation of the respectable and unrespectable portions of the working class and to explain the debilities of the latter. The main distinction was not between rich and poor but between civilized and uncivilized; poverty was a cultural condition. The implications of this explanation, above all, was that the respectable working class had to be protected from the contamination of the residuum.[8]

6. Gareth Stedman Jones, *Outcast London: A Study in the Relationship between Classes in Victorian Society* (Oxford: Oxford University Press, 1971).

7. Gareth Stedman Jones, "Working-Class Culture and Working-Class Politics in London, 1870–1900: Notes on the Remaking of a Working Class," *Journal of Social History* 7 (1973–74): 460–508. In reprinting this essay, Stedman Jones qualified his two-stage conception of working-class politics and culture, emphasizing the overlap and complexity of different forms of struggle. "Introduction," *Languages of Class: Studies in English Working Class History 1832–1982* (Cambridge: Cambridge University Press, 1983), pp. 1–24. The outstanding work on this process remains E. P. Thompson, *The Making of the English Working Class* (New York: Vintage, 1963).

8. Stedman Jones, *Outcast London;* Gertrude Himmelfarb, *The Idea of Poverty: England in the Early Industrial Age* (New York: Knopf, 1984), esp. pp. 366–67.

In fact, the poverty and casualism of a major portion of London's population reflected complex changes in the structure of production in England. Although London had once been a center of artisanal production and small-scale manufacturing, it could not compete with other regions in large-scale industry. The decline of its old industries made possible the flourishing of new ones that depended on an impoverished and abject work force—the sweated trades. But the contradictions of the situation were strongest in the dockyards of East London.

In the 1810s, merchant capital had been eager to "create a permanent, sober, and responsible work-force, and to guard against the possibility that dock labour might become in any sense a residual occupation."[9] The dockyards regulated casualism and gave workers with good records a privileged status or permanent jobs. But when the monopoly privileges of the London docks broke down in the 1820s and competition and changes in the nature of shipping depressed profits, employers moved to take advantage of the wide-open London labor market and increased the casualization of port labor.

Capital's interest in stable, reliable dock labor resurfaced in the 1880s, in the midst of depression and a radical revival. To panicky politicians and key elements of the middle class, the threat that the increasingly dangerous residuum would eliminate the gains made with the respectable working class became more severe—the contamination theory flourished.[10] Some social theorists advocated establishing labor colonies in England where the residuum would be set to hard work and isolated from the rest of the working class. And some even welcomed the rise of a dockers' union in the great dock strike of 1889 as a sign that dockers were at last interested in taking themselves seriously as workers, as well as in self-improvement. Perhaps the labor unions could do what charity had not—wean the residuum away from casual labor and a casual life.[11] The anxieties about radicalism and about the threat of contamination in all aspects of working-class life were important to the growing critique—from the right as much as the left—of laissez-faire and the slow movement by reformers and the state toward regulating and "moralizing" capitalism and planning neighborhood development, transportation facilities, and social services in the city in ways that would socialize and contain a working class, even if this meant putting limits on capital's pursuit of low wages and high profits.[12]

9. Stedman Jones, p. 111.

10. Ibid., pp. 222, 225, 242, 284–89.

11. Ibid., pp. 197, 304, 307, 316–18. See also John Lovell, *Stevedores and Dockers: A Study of Trade Unionism in the Port of London 1870–1914* (New York: Kelley, 1969).

12. Damaris Rose, "Accumulation versus Reproduction: *The Recurrent Crisis of London Revisited*," in Michael Dear and A. J. Scott, eds., *Urbanization and Urban Planning in Capitalist Societies* (London: Methuen, 1981), pp. 339–81.

In London, the hoped-for tendency toward decasualization in the docks met strong obstacles in the particular interests and traditions of both employers and workers. The positive trend was given powerful impetus by the startling, if short-lived, unity of dockers in the strikes of 1889 and 1911 and by the ability of labor leaders to articulate the evils of casualism from another standpoint: that it made the workers bear the entire burden of the fluctuation in work, while capital encouraged and profited from the availability of a vast supply of laborers left permanently at the margins of capitalist society.[13] At a famous commission hearing in 1919, the labor leader Ernest Bevin made it clear that the culture of casualism among dockers was a consequence, not a cause, of the economic structure of the industry. The commission agreed that "the system of casualization must, if possible, be torn up by the roots. It is wrong."[14] But the companies countered that causal labor was necessary, and the need for steadier work that had swung the struggle in the dockworkers' favor during World War I slackened during the 1920s and 1930s, and much of their gains were eroded.[15] Rank-and-file dockers were more skeptical than their leaders about decasualization for two reasons: their traditions of solidarity made them concerned that decasualization would be used to exclude many of their number from the industry and hence from even a meager and irregular income, and the complex relationships that existed between particular groups of men and particular foremen and employers gave these influential men access to more desirable jobs.[16] Both objections were based on fears of what management might do with more centralized control over hiring and supervision.

Only in World War II—under the pressure of war and while Bevin was Minister of Labour—did the government seize the initiative, make registration of employers and employees compulsory, begin maintenance payments to all dockers who attended call-on regularly, and institute joint worker-management boards to administer the scheme. The scheme survived the war but gave rise to a period of frequent and intense disputes, often over issues of control of the labor process on the docks, which revealed considerable tension between the dockers and a union leadership that had become enmeshed in the state. The scheme did not end

13. Lovell; David F. Wilson, *Dockers: The Impact of Industrial Change* (London: Fontana, 1972).

14. Wilson, pp. 74–78; Michael P. Jackson, *Labour Relations on the Docks* (Westmead, Eng.: Saxon House, 1973), p. 13.

15. Jonathan Schneer, "The War, the State and the Workplace: British Dockers during 1914–1918," in James Cronin and Jonathan Schneer, eds., *Social Conflict and the Political Order in Modern Britain* (New Brunswick, N.J.: Rutgers University Press, 1982), pp. 96–112; Wilson, p. 91.

16. Schneer, p. 98, Wilson, pp. 113, 187; Vernon H. Jensen, *Hiring of Dock Workers and Employment Practices in the Ports of New York, Liverpool, London, Rotterdam, and Marseilles* (Cambridge, Mass.: Harvard University Press, 1964), p. 186.

the issue of casualism: registration rolls stayed large, hiring practices remained decentralized and irregular, work patterns and income were highly uneven, and public perceptions of dockers as a breed apart—demoralized and dragged down by men who shunned regular work—persisted.[17] Only after the inquiry led by Lord Devlin in 1965—itself encouraged by the companies' concern in an era of technological change and intense competition to assert power over the myriad customs and work rules that had grown up in dockwork, as well as by the workers' fears for job security—did decasualization policy at last go beyond registration and maintenance payments and toward hiring men on a permanent basis with a full range of rights, obligations, and benefits.[18]

By 1965, dock labor in Mombasa had been effectively decasualized for nearly a decade. As in England, the assertion of state power during and after World War II had been critical to imposing a new order on both shipping companies and workers. The state, even in the context of colonialism, did not exercise power in a vacuum: earlier attempts by the state during World War I and in 1930 to make dockers work more regularly had failed. But the port companies' influence on colonial politics was not enormous, and the workers only formed a union in 1954, so that the workers' attachment to casual labor—if anything stronger than that of their British fellow-dockers—did not receive as articulate an expression (see chapter 5).

The most important difference, however, was in the relationship of dockers to society. In England, a working class had been made long ago: the dockers of the late Victorian era and after did not have access to means of subsistence or alternative sources of income. The irregularity of their work separated them from the rest of the working class and shaped their inward-looking, distinctive work culture. The opposite was the case in Kenya, even as late as the 1940s. The dockers' work patterns were, from the state's point of view, all too typical of African workers generally, and the dockers appeared to be fully immersed in the working-class society of Mombasa: the two great strikes for which dockers received much of the blame had in fact been city-wide general strikes.[19] The problem of

17. Peter Weiler, "British Labour and the Cold War: The London Dock Strike of 1949," in Cronin and Schneer, pp. 146–78; Jackson, pp. 39–58; Jensen, pp. 134–54, 290–98.

18. Wilson, pp. 172–91, 278–307; Jackson, pp. 78ff. For comparison with the struggle over the control and regularity of hiring in other ports, see Jensen, and Lawrence Max Kahn, "Unions and Labor Market Segmentation," Ph.D. diss., University of California at Berkeley, 1975.

19. Thus, if the militance of Mombasa's dockworkers seems consistent with the finding in the famous article of Clark Kerr and Abraham Siegel that dockworkers generally are strike-prone, the reasons are quite different. Kerr and Siegel saw the isolation of dockers from the institutions of the wider society—which left them alone in confrontation with employers—

casualism lay not in the fact that Kenyan dockers were at the mercy of the port employers for their livelihood, but that they had too many alternatives, that their continued access to precapitalist forms of production in rural Africa gave them a certain immunity to the discipline of regular work. The English dockers were the victims of a structural anomaly in an advanced capitalist society. In the late nineteenth century, the main danger they posed was that of contaminating the respectable working class; by the twentieth, as the state began to make adjustments to ease the various structural problems of capitalist society, the problem of casualism could be isolated and eventually—very eventually—solved.

The problem of the casual dockers in Mombasa, however, was the problem of labor in general. In the 1940s, a respectable African working class had to be created. The dockers of Mombasa, far from being left on its fringes, came to be its vanguard.

For this reason, the Victorian language in which London's dockers were discussed at the end of the nineteenth century remained all too applicable to Mombasa a half-century later. The workers seemed to be choosing their life of casualism; only by forcing regular work and regular habits of life upon them could they be tamed; and the infant African working class that showed signs of emerging had to be protected against contamination.

The Problem of Emancipation in Coastal Kenya
The transference of the discourse on English class structure to East African society first took place in the 1890s in relation to the question of slavery and abolition. George Curzon, a leading Foreign Office official, described the class structure of Zanzibar as "an Arab aristocracy," a "trading class of British Indians," "a middle and lower native trading and artisan element; and the residuum, estimated at 140,000 slaves."[20] The problem behind his choice of words was that the residuum was hardly residual: most agricultural production lay in its rough and unreliable hands.

---

as critical to their propensity to strike. "The Interindustry Propensity to Strike—an International Comparison," in Arthur Kornhauser, Robert Dubin, and Arthur M. Ross, eds., *Industrial Conflict* (New York: McGraw-Hill, 1954), pp. 189–212. Edward Shorter and Charles Tilly find the pattern of strikes in France closer to my interpretation of Mombasa than to Kerr and Siegel's generalization; they reject the isolation thesis and argue that strike rates reflect complex political and economic processes involving society as a whole (*Strikes in France 1830–1968* [Cambridge: Cambridge University Press, 1974]). See also Raymond Charles Miller, "The Dockworker Subculture and Some Problems in Cross-Cultural and Cross-Time Generalizations," *Comparative Studies in Society and History,* 11 (1969): 302–14.

20. George Curzon, "Slavery in Zanzibar," 29 December 1896, CAB 37/40/58 (Public Record Office, London). See the similar analysis in Charles Euan-Smith to Lord Salisbury, 3 January 1896, FO 84/2146.

The analysis of slave labor in East Africa stressed the combination of negative traits that characterized London's residuum: they were both lazy and disorderly. The logic of control implied that abolition was both an ultimate necessity and an immediate danger, and the thorny problem was not to *abolish* slavery but to *develop* capitalist relations of production, making slaves and peasants into a disciplined working class.

Slavery in coastal Kenya was abolished in 1907. But the experience of Zanzibar, the center of the sultanate from which the British had obtained the coastal strip of Kenya, had already formed the key test of free labor ideology in East Africa. The British government ended slavery in Zanzibar in 1897, just after it had consolidated its grip, and abolition was accompanied by a series of measures designed to retain the authority of the landowning class and to transform slaves into an agricultural proletariat. As Curzon put it, "free labour, paid labour, is not indigenous to the place—it is an exotic, it would have to be imported, it would have to be carefully tended and watered to enable it to grow."[21] The Government recognized ex-slaveowners' land titles but not ex-slaves' rights to the subsistence plots they had farmed as slaves. Officials insisted the ex-slaves contract with planters to work on clove trees throughout the year to have access to subsistence. Meanwhile, the state vigorously prosecuted a series of crimes—theft, assault, drunkenness—that were taken to be characteristic "slave" crimes, much like the characteristic criminality of the rookeries of East London. It was particularly vigorous in prosecuting vagrancy and the theft of agricultural produce, for it needed to establish very clearly that ex-slaves had no right to live off the fruits of the land but had to earn their keep.

The state overestimated the power of the law. Ex-slaves took advantage of their new mobility to move from plantation to plantation, deserting planters who enforced contracts to find lax planters or vacant land. Casual labor in the port or migration to other parts of East Africa became other alternatives to the one that the state had hoped would redefine the work system. Meanwhile, the pax Britannica meant that the slaves' need for protection and membership in a social group lost much of its relevance, while the effective ending of the slave trade around 1890 had already thrown awry the delicate mechanisms of social reproduction on which slave society had depended. With so many slaves withdrawing their labor from plantations, those who remained could bargain down their obligations, and soon planters were willing to allow them to squat on non-clove-bearing land on their plantations without specific labor obligations, and

21. Curzon, speech to House of Commons, 27 March 1896, reprinted in *Anti-Slavery Reporter* 16 (1896): 101. The following paragraphs are based on Cooper, *From Slaves to Squatters*, chap. 3.

with only the expectation that they would pick their landlord's cloves first during the harvest, in exchange for piecework wages.

Short-term labor for cash wages, combined with squatting, undermined the state's attempt to instill the time-discipline of capitalist society, even if they brought in clove harvests. "Steady, regular work is just what your slave or free slave dislikes very much," lamented an official three years after abolition.[22] Their schemes to make supervision more rigorous, to control wages, to enforce contracts, and to criminalize ex-slaves' access to subsistence resources all foundered on the ex-slaves' mobility and their ability to resist labor demands, as well as on the planters' willingness to concede access to land to the legally landless in the face of their competition for workers who were willing to sell only part of their time.

Unable to create a steady, full-time agricultural proletariat out of ex-slaves, the state had to accept the fact that labor time in Zanzibar was for sale only in small units. The plantation economy survived through the willingness of new groups of people to work according to rhythms they could partly control. Villagers from non-clove areas of Zanzibar began to participate intensively in the harvest, earning some cash during a few weeks while carefully guarding their rights to land in their own villages. Migrants from distant parts of the mainland, willing to stay for a year or longer and work steadily to build up a sum of money to take home, began to do the year-round chores of weeding and cultivating. The planters and the state had not wanted these distinct forms of part-time and migrant labor, but they had to learn to adapt to labor as it came forth, in bits and pieces, in different forms from peoples of different origins. The standoff between squatters and planters held more or less steady until the era of decolonization in the 1950s and 1960s, when the threat that planters might take over the state and use it in a more vigorous drive against squatters, or else that squatters might seize the state and use it to terminate planters' property rights, led to a spiral of conflict and eventually to revolution.

The awesome difficulties of creating a proletariat in an African colony had sunk in by the time the British had secured their position on the coast of Kenya and were ready to abolish slavery. They were by then less prepared to prop up an Arab and Swahili-speaking planter class, but more eager to create the legal infrastructure for what they hoped would be a more promising initiative in developing capitalist agriculture, by white settlers and plantation companies. This never came to pass on the coast— and the center of gravity of Kenya's economy shifted inland—but it left to

22. Vice Consul O'Sullivan, District and Consular Report on Pemba, 1900, p. 12.

the coast a legacy of carefully surveyed land boundaries and a registry of titles.

Turning lack of property into an imperative to work proved to be an even more difficult task on the mainland coast than on the islands, and squatters did rather well for themselves. In most cases, landowners could only extract a modest rent and a share of the harvest of tree crops; they could not control production. Squatters grew and directly sold modest surpluses of grain, and the growth of more balanced exchange among different parts of the coastal region was the other side of the decline of the plantation-dominated grain export economy of the nineteenth century. Landowners could eke out a living from harvesting coconuts or tapping palm wine through arrangements to share the crop. But the tensions over land were exposed by the paralysis over planting new coconut and other trees. Landlords lacked the cash to pay laborers for an investment that would not immediately pay off and did not want tenants to plant for fear that, under Swahili land law, the tenant would acquire rights to the tree; squatters, meanwhile, feared that making permanent improvements in the land would only encourage landowners to evict them. As in Zanzibar, the stability of social structure depended on economic stagnation, a situation which persisted until it came apart in an escalation of tensions in the 1950s.

Mombasa, by the turn of the century, was already a critical element in the picture. Its expansion as a colonial port, draining all of the hinterland of Kenya and Uganda, gave ex-slaves another alternative that they could use to break away from their dependence on their ex-masters. The availability of casual jobs meant that squatters could use the port as a means of earning cash without jeopardizing their access to plots of land that could provide for subsistence, if not a surplus. Ex-slaves squatting on coastal land that had once been the basis of plantation production thus built a degree of autonomy by combining urban casual labor, small-scale farming, and occasional day labor, coconut picking, or palm wine tapping on a sharecropping basis on those portions of estates that planters still cultivated. They avoided contract labor for European companies, for that would make them lose control over their time for the three or more months of the contract, and these companies had to bring in contract workers from upcountry Kenya. Ex-slaves were joined in this pattern by Africans from the nearby hinterland—the Mijikenda—who had been kept off the more fertile coastal zone by the strength of the plantation economy, but who moved coastward and took to squatting and casual labor when the planters' control collapsed.

The state was trapped by its own ideology. Unwilling to acknowledge that squatting was truly working, it deliberately undermined alternatives to a capitalist farming sector that was virtually moribund. In 1914, the

Government undertook a brutal campaign of evicting squatters from the Malindi area and trying to drive them back into a reserve, only to give rise to a major rebellion and a famine. Within a year, the state had backed off and squatters were returning to their coastal lands, bringing with them a modest revival of grain production and exports and a social structure that was to persist more or less unchallenged until after World War II.[23]

The urban manifestations of this unsuccessful transition from slave to wage labor once again echoed the language of the causal labor debate in London. In 1898, the Administration issued a vagrancy decree for Mombasa,

> aim[ed] at checking, not only the influx into the town of Mombasa of idle and criminal runaway slaves, but also of disreputable free people of all sorts, who come to get an 'odd job' on the railway, then throw up their work when tired of it, or are discharged, and take to drink and rioting, thus augmenting to an undesirable extent the disorderly floating population of Mombasa.[24]

These words are revealing. Idleness, criminality, disorder, and casual labor were all conflated, linked specifically to ex-slaves who left the plantation, and more generally to urban migrants who were not serious about a life of labor in the city. The residuum embodied social and cultural values incompatible with capitalist time discipline and urban order. Colonial labor legislation—criminal sanctions against breaking labor contracts, registration ordinances, and so on—was implemented in Mombasa with a rigor not comparable to that in rural districts of the coast.[25]

But the fundamental contradiction, as in London, was that the residuum was very convenient. With shipping irregular, having to pay workers only as needed saved money for port companies and shippers. At the same time, urban casual labor was a far more successful way of affecting a transition from slave to free labor than the means advocated by the state, for ex-slaves were willing to accept wage labor on such terms. Ex-slaves and Mijikenda became the mainstay of the docks, taking to urban casual labor and rural squatting at the same time. The two activities were complementary, allowing the squatter-laborer to avoid too much dependence on any one landlord or any one job while providing both cash and food.

In the period before World War I, the contradiction provoked occa-

---

23. Cooper, *From Slaves to Squatters*, chap. 6; Cynthia Brantley, *The Giriama and Colonial Resistance in Kenya, 1800–1920* (Berkeley: University of California Press, 1981).

24. Consul and Administrator General Arthur Hardinge to Salisbury, 16 January 1898, Foreign Office Confidential Prints 7024, p. 122.

25. Cooper, *From Slaves to Squatters*, pp. 240–41.

sional comment but no action. The state had not fulfilled the images of antislavery ideology: it had not affected what one official in Zanzibar had hoped to direct, "an orderly evolution for them, from slavery to freedom, from license to law. . . ."[26] Too many laws, like the Mombasa vagrancy act of 1898, had had little effect; ex-slaves still had too much license. In rural coastal Kenya, the failure to control work had led to the demise of a plantation economy, replaced by a less export-oriented pattern in which squatters did the producing but without the security to innovate or to venture very far from their emphasis on crops they could eat as well as sell; ex-planters lacked the labor to seize the initiative, but could only skim what they could. As in Zanzibar, the standoff between ex-masters and ex-slaves was uneasy, and a serious impediment to the confidence necessary for either party to take the kind of economic initiatives that the state hoped would come with the end of a labor system it deemed archaic. By seeking to build an economy based on rigid control of property and wage labor, the state had unwittingly strengthened the essentially precapitalist character of the relationship between landlord and tenant.

MOMBASA BEFORE THE STRIKES

The Mombasa Job Market and the Ambiguities of Casual Labor

Just as the roots of what was to become the critique of casual labor lay in antislavery ideology, the roots of Mombasa's casual labor system lay in slavery. In the nineteenth century, shippers hired slaves to load and unload vessels, and the slaves in turn paid their owners half their daily earnings. This kind of work—day labor—was then known as *kibarua* labor, from the word for the chit or letter which slaves were supposed to take from their employer to their owner to indicate what they had earned. "Kazi ya kibarua" became the Swahili term for casual labor in the twentieth century. The pool of urban labor on which shippers drew consisted both of slaves kept specifically for this purpose and others who were hired out when agricultural or domestic tasks were less pressing. The relationship of ownership often lost the connotations of protection and deference intrinsic to agricultural slavery on the coast—as well as its connection to supervision on the job—and many urban slaves acquired substantial autonomy, living in the huts they built on rented land and limiting their contact with their masters to the payment of the expected share of their earnings, or less if they could get away with it. Kibarua labor attracted freed slaves as well, plus a polyglot collection of people from many parts of the Indian Ocean commercial system—Hadrami Arabs, Comorians,

26. Farler, Report on Pemba, 1898, PP 1898, LX, 559, p. 60.

and so on—who arrived on dhows and worked for a time, at least until they could set themselves up in trade, smuggling, or some other sort of independent enterprise.[27]

The other side of the collapse of agricultural slavery in the 1890s and 1900s in coastal Kenya was the relatively smooth adjustment of kibarua labor to the new situation, even before the formal abolition of slavery. Urban labor in Mombasa became an increasingly attractive alternative to a life of toil and subservience on plantations as the city's position in world commerce shifted. Mombasa changed from being the link between caravans of porters and Indian Ocean sailing vessels to being the point where railway met steamship, the major link between British East Africa and Europe. It was the terminus of the Kenya-Uganda Railway, which reached Lake Victoria in 1901. The principal harbor of Mombasa shifted from the Old Port to the opposite side of the island, Kilindini, where deeper vessels could enter. A lighterage wharf was begun there in 1896, and the first of many deep-water berths in 1921.

As the tonnage of steamers entering Mombasa doubled between 1903 and 1913, as the railway hired menial laborers, and as officials and trading firms in the city demanded laborers and servants, urban labor at least provided slaves with a choice. During World War I, when an abortive scheme to register dockworkers (see below, pp. 29–31) provided the first remotely plausible statistics, almost 2,000 workers were signed up, although no more than 500—more like 200 to 300 on the average—officially worked at one time. The workers' desire for day labor at that time was at least as irregular as the demand: in 1911–12, port workers received Rs 1/25 (Rupees) per day and could earn in ten days as much as unskilled contract workers could get in a month.[28] The work was hard, the hours long, but as long as casual workers could get enough days of work per month, they had a flexibility in their working lives that neither slaves nor contract laborers possessed. Urban ex-slaves, Hadrami Arabs, and other Mombasans provided the core of kibarua labor, but they were joined on the docks by nearby farmers—above all Mijikenda—who worked for a few days to raise cash, or for longer during seasonal slack periods.

These workers got the job done; an administration that was prone to complain of labor shortages had little complaint about the quantity of dock labor before World War I. Even the increased level of shipping by World War I amounted to an average of under two arrivals per day, and the irregularity of the ships' schedules and the seasonal slowdown from

27. Cooper, *Plantation Slavery*, pp. 184–87.

28. Seyidie Province, AR, 1911–12. In 1920, Kenya converted its currency from rupees to shillings at the rate of Shs 2 to each rupee. The statistics from the war era may be found in CP 38/611 and CP 39/629.

approximately June to October accentuated the port firms' desire for flexibility, a prerogative that port companies guarded even in busier ports, including London. The anxiety implied in the 1898 legislation regarding the "floating population" was temporarily laid aside.

The high labor demands of the growing city were met not by making its old slave population into full-time wage laborers, but by the distinct patterns in which workers from different parts of Kenya came to sell their labor power in varying units of time. Mombasa developed a split labor market: coastal people—Swahili-speakers, ex-slaves, Arabs from the Hadramaut, other immigrants, and Mijikenda—sought casual work, plus a limited range of permanent jobs, as in the police or domestic service. Various attempts by the state to get coastal people to work more steadily produced meager results. Ex-slaves or Hadrami Arabs who had settled more or less permanently on Mombasa island over the past decades formed the core of kibarua labor. They were joined by many people, ex-slaves, Mombasa Swahili, or Mijikenda, who lived and farmed nearby and could work in the port in the daytime and return home at night. Migrants from more distant parts of the coast frequently left their casual jobs during the harvest season. Such workers, as one informant expressed it, "used to come and work here during the off rainy season, just to get money to get them support. But when it comes about cultivating period, some of these people used to go away and help their families cultivate the land, to prepare for planting maize and other things. And then they'd come back and work. During the harvest they'd leave again and go back to their place, that's what they'd do."[29]

Where continuity in employment was highly desirable, especially in railway yards or in municipal service, workers were hired on long-term contracts and paid by the month—"kazi ya mwezi" (monthly work) became the Swahili term. The first reliable statistics, from 1925, indicate that there were 7,555 such workers in Mombasa, and the large majority of them were migrants from upcountry Kenya. People from the western part of Kenya, Luo and Luhya (lumped together by officials as "Kavirondo"), Kikuyu or Kamba from central Kenya, or Taita from the interior part of Coast Province, had to pay substantial costs of migration and were attracted to Mombasa by somewhat higher monthly wages than were available upcountry: Rs 10 to 15 compared to Rs 4 to 8 upcountry in 1903. Not being able to blend, on a day-to-day or even a seasonal basis, cultivation and wage labor, upcountry migrants tended to seek a steady income during their period in Mombasa. The 1925 statistics indicate that 26

29. Interview: Mohamed Shallo, currently welfare officer for the East Africa Cargo Handling Service. For a discussion of the Mombasa labor market and its relations to coastal agriculture in the early decades of the century, see Cooper, *From Slaves to Squatters*, pp. 242–47.

percent of the registered, regular workers were Luo and Luhya, 20 percent were Kikuyu, and only 17 percent were from the coast (including both Mijikenda and Swahili-speakers). Only in the 1940s did officials realize that many of these "monthly" workers in fact stayed in Mombasa for years.[30]

The docks relied almost entirely on casual labor. For employers and employees, the system worked satisfactorily only in specific circumstances, and the better it worked for the one, the worse it was for the other. The employers needed a pool sufficiently large to give them an adequate work force on peak days; workers wanted to have a job available whenever they chose to work. From the point of view of the shipping firms and the state, the experience of World War I revealed both the risks of irregular labor and the difficulty of getting coastal workers to labor more steadily.

During the war, the escalation of demands for African workers—above all the brutal roundups for the Carrier Corps—led to heightened competition for workers in civilian service. Merchants and military supply officers in Mombasa suddenly found that the port was becoming congested owing to lack of labor to unload ships at a fast enough pace. The problem was not numbers but work habits. A military transport officer insisted on a radical solution: "In my opinion the only way to recruit further is to take over and organize Port Labour, so that men working at the port may be given systematic labour (without days off whenever they feel inclined) while any man not working at the port would be available for work elsewhere."[31] The Inspector General of Communication for the East African Forces elaborated that port congestion was

> due to the refusal of the Hamali [port carrier] and Shihiri [Arabs from the Hadramaut] class to work other than as they pleased, e.g. having worked for say three days and earned some Rs 9, they elect to lapse into leisure for two or three days, even though the ships on which they are working might be but partially cleared, then work for three or four more days with another rest, and so on. It is clear from this, that if the class of labor, on which the mercantile firms have to rely, is permitted to do as it pleases in such critical times as these, the whole Commerce of the country is liable to serious disorganization, even to the extent of a complete breakdown.[32]

---

30. Native Affairs Department, AR, 1925, p. 81; Cooper, *From Slaves to Squatters*, pp. 243, 249–50.

31. Captain O. F. Watkins, Carrier-Section, DADT, to General Staff Officer, 21 December 1915, CP 38/603.

32. Inspector General of Communications, East African Forces, to CS, 5 May 1916, CP 38/611. The terminology in this quotation is imprecise. *Shihiri* is an ethnic term (pejorative) for Arabs from the Hadramaut, many of whom were manual laborers or petty traders,

The two officers' recommendations ranged from registering dock-workers and fixing wages to creating a militarized corps of dockers—500 to handle cargo on ship and 500 to work on shore—working for a fixed monthly wage. But the local administration was worried that such reforms might cause workers to leave the docks rather than work longer: "we have no great control over this very independent class."[33]

Indeed, daily labor was doing so well for itself that the porters employed by the Government on monthly terms gave notice in September 1916, telling officials that they could do better working by the day and demanding as an alternative a wage increase from Rs 25 per month to Rs 30, and transportation officials had to recommend accepting their demand, for they could not get enough porters.[34] Meanwhile, daily wages for port-carriers were rising and—even after various schemes to tame the casual laborers—went from Rs 1/25 to Rs 2/55 per day during the course of the war.[35]

The answer officials came up with in August 1916 was a registration scheme for casual workers, requiring each to wear a badge, to come to a government office for assignment to various employers in the port, to receive a set wage, and to be subject to deregistration for not working. The scheme, as officials noted after a few months and again at the end of the war, may have had some effect on stabilizing wages but little on the structure of work.[36]

The plan ran up against the social realities of work in Mombasa. The various stevedoring, shipping, and warehousing firms in the city hired workers through intermediaries (see below, pp. 37–38). The firms were presented with entire gangs and developed long-standing arrangements with them. The registration scheme had been intended in part to undermine the power of the gangs by centralizing hiring, but the gangs proved the stronger contender in this struggle. The Port Labour Committee complained in December 1916, "The labour has not been freed to all employers and agents still hold the men in gangs." Wages were not being

---

although well-established families from the Hadramaut were among the leading old landowning families of the coast. Hamalis are port carriers, who could be ex-slaves, Mijikenda, Swahili-speakers, or for that matter, Arabs from the Hadramuat.

33. PC to DADT, Carrier Section, 26 November 1915, CP 38/603.

34. Acting Director of Transport to CS, 2 September 1916, CP 38/611.

35. Native Affairs Department, AR, 1918–19, p. 23; PC to Atty. Gen., 9 January 1919, CP 38/611. War gave dockers certain advantages in their struggles with capital in England as well. The registration schemes introduced in London and Liverpool reflected the companies' acute need for more regular performance from dockers in a time of labor shortage. Schneer. "The War, the State, and the Workplace."

36. DC to PC, 5 December 1916; Meeting of Port Labour Committee, 19 December 1916; PC to Acting CS, 9 January 1919—all in CP 38/611.

held to fixed levels.[37] The companies were too anxious about their relationship with gang leaders, too well aware that the intermediaries could "hold up labour which might otherwise be engaged directly by the Merchants handling the Cargo," to tamper with existing arrangements. Although the new hiring rules provided for payment at the Labour Office, companies still paid their gangs privately or gave gratuities outside of the Labour Office.[38]

The registration scheme's figures reveal how little the Labour Office had seized control of port labor. Of 1,800 registered dockers in 1917, only 171 worked over fifteen days per month, and the average docker worked only five days. An average of 279 were being paid off each day by the Labour Office, but 52 firms were also paying workers. The actual rate of employment was no doubt nowhere near as low as these figures suggest: the port firms, the gang leaders, and the workers were ignoring regulations, and most often working or not working without regard to the registration scheme. Officials accused Asian subcontractors of responsibility for its failure, but it was clear that the old methods of port working had to be attacked far more directly and decisively than the registration scheme allowed. Some European merchants and officials wanted to beef up Government controls, but others—notably the General Manager of the Railway and the Military Commissioner for Labour—were skeptical about the possibilities of altering the relationship of shippers to gangs. The scheme continued in its halting way.[39]

At war's end, the Provincial Commissioner concluded that the effort "had only been partially effective owing to the fact that although a hamal was registered there was no obligation on him to ply his calling."[40] The port had been kept going by adjusting the daily wage upward, not by getting workers to work more frequently at a controlled price, and as the registration scheme was allowed to lapse after the war, casual labor remained the predominant form of port work. It persisted not only because it adjusted wage bills to the daily needs of business, but because it had become deeply entrenched in a set of economic relationships.

Whereas the wartime crisis of port congestion disclosed the vulnerability of the employers of casual labor, the sharp growth of the labor supply after the war years revealed that of the workers. Migrants from

37. Meeting of Port Labour Committee, 19 December 1916, CP 38/611.
38. DC to PC, 5 December 1916, CP 38/611.
39. PC to CS, 19 February, 1 August 1917; CS to PC, 2 March 1917, CP 38/611.
40. PC to Acting CS, 9 January 1919, CP 38/611. The registration scheme failed for the opposite reason that the British registration schemes proved disappointing after the war. In Mombasa, the men would not work often enough. In London and Liverpool, too many men wanted to work (and the dockers were unwilling to deny a livelihood to their fellows), so the lists became so long that they proved little protection. See Jensen, *Hiring of Dockworkers.*

western Kenya, affected by increasing pressures in that part of the colony to leave the land to earn cash, flocked to Mombasa. They pushed coastal people out of their old niches in domestic service, dominating more completely than before the market in monthly labor, and even moving to some extent into casual labor. By 1922, what officials had recently bemoaned as coastal people's dislike of steady work was termed "unemployment."[41] In the mid-1920s, some coastal people were working for three months on sisal estates—the kind of job they had previously rejected—while the urbanized ex-slaves and other Swahili-speakers who had staked their lives on the once favorable casual labor market were often driven to what officials called "living on their wits."[42]

The riots that broke out between upcountry and coastal workers in 1923 fit a common pattern of "faction fights" characteristic of situations where regional differentiation leads ethnically distinct peoples into distinct kinds of jobs. A new challenge to an established bailiwick can evoke a violent response, directed more at rival workers than at the structure itself. There were fracases with apparent ethnic dimensions in 1936 and 1937, but over a fifteen-year span of job competition and depression, the extent of faction fighting was not remarkable. A District Commissioner seemed baffled that his own stereotypes of a disorderly floating population were not in evidence: "it is amazing how very peaceful the inhabitants are."[43]

Faced with limited agricultural development on the coast and increasing competition in the labor markets of Mombasa from upcountry migrants who were being pushed into wage labor at a faster pace, the casual workers from the coastal region saw the irregular organization of work that had helped to liberate them becoming the constraints of a new economic system. Daily wages in the city remained between Shs 2 and Shs 2/50 during the 1920s, equivalent to Re 1 to Rs 1/25 in the pre-1920 currency. That is, wages had fallen to prewar rates, although prices had not. When the Depression struck at the end of the decade, wages paid to the casuals who worked on the shore were cut from Shs 2 to Shs 1/50, while stevedores—the men who worked on the ships themselves—received 50 cents more.

Most important, the reduced traffic in the port meant fewer days of

41. Mombasa District, AR, 1922; Native Affairs Department, AR, 1925, p. 81.
42. Mombasa District, AR, 1923.
43. Mombasa District, AR, 1923, 1936, 1937. The 1937 disturbance was by far the most serious: twelve died in several days of fighting between Hadrami Arabs and Luo. For comparison, see Ian Phimister and Charles van Onselen, "The Political Economy of Tribal Animosity: A Case Study of the 1929 Bulawayo Location 'Faction Fight,'" *Journal of Southern African Studies* 6 (1979): 1–43.

work: daily labor during the Depression frequently meant working one day in five. Regular work was in short supply too, and the District Commissioner thought—without saying how he could measure or even define unemployment—that one-third of Mombasa's population in 1933 was unemployed. But the hardships did not change fundamentally the structure of the Mombasa labor market: firms using contract labor experienced labor shortages in a period of urban unemployment, and people left jobs on coastal plantations to come to Mombasa.[44] Meanwhile, conditions of housing, sanitation, and health in the working-class areas of Mombasa remained poor, if not worse than they had been.[45]

Even during the 1920s and early 1930s, when wages stayed low and labor supplies remained abundant, the English distrust of casual labor surfaced from time to time, above all in a concern for the urban social order. A meeting of the principal Native Affairs officers in 1926 noted the influx of upcountry migrants to Mombasa, some of whom became casual laborers. The officers feared that such people were "living under no discipline and are becoming somewhat intractable and truculent." The officials thought of applying to Mombasa the rules which required all casual laborers in Nairobi to register and which made proof of registration, or else a definite job, legal prerequisites for any upcountry native to reside in Mombasa.[46]

Much the same language appeared in the District Commissioner's report on Mombasa for 1927: the old inhabitants of the city were being joined in the crowded native quarters by more upcountry Africans, a process which "resulted in an almost featureless mass of humanity living together more by necessity than by choice." This was a "growing and more dangerous problem. The many attractions of a port, the large wages and temporary emancipation from tribal obligations are forming a spirit of truculence and undesirable independence among many of them; in particular the Kikuyu and Kavirondo, who predominate numerically." Two years later, the District annual report contained the same warning about the migrant laborer: "Devoid of any tribal control and having come into contact with all the evils of a Port Town, he is inclined to shun his legal

44. Mombasa District, AR, 1932, 1933; Report on Native Affairs in Mombasa, 1930, Political Record Book, DC/MSA/3/3; Report of the Commission of Inquiry appointed to Examine the Labour Conditions in Mombasa (Nairobi, 1939) (Willan Report), p. 22. For more on changes in these years, see Karim K. Janmohamed, "A History of Mombasa, c. 1895–1939: Some Aspects of Economic and Social Life in an East African Port Town during Colonial Rule," Ph.D. diss., Northwestern University, 1977.

45. Janmohamed; Anthony Clayton and Donald Savage, Government and Labour in Kenya, 1895–1963 (London: Cass, 1974), pp. 216–20.

46. Notes of discussion between Chief Native Commissioner and Senior and Resident Commissioners from the Coast, 17 October 1926, LAB 9/1049.

obligations and to lose his sense of discipline." The theme of loss of rural traditions of obedience was, of course, a common one in British Africa, but it was unclear whether it could be resolved by keeping people out of cities or in them, subject to new forms of urban discipline. The housing situation compounded the dangers, for people congregated together. The District Commissioner noted the growing number of African inhabitants in the area between Makupa Road and the railway, which housed a "large number of the floating population."[47]

But the usefulness of all this labor, the inertia of coastal administration, and the belief that Mombasa was inherently a "native town," unlike the settler capital of Nairobi, sapped the initiative to intervene actively to tame the dangerous classes.[48] So the casual labor system changed little.

In 1930, the *Mombasa Times* editorialized about the "Casual Labour Problem." Its greatest fear was that workers "in virtue of the very casual nature of their job, relapse into that crime that is so easily absorbed from surroundings which are as casual as the labour itself." But if a stable job and supervised housing could be both provided and required for all workers, "The cleaner life, the discipline, the counter attraction of a well-ordered existence, in contradistinction to the loose living and evil associations of casual home life, would inevitably serve to restore some of the original sturdy character possessed by the natives, prior to their absorption in the pool of Mombasa."[49]

The conflation of casual labor with casual living reflects a long obsession with the need to exercise direct control by supervisors and state officials over all dimensions of working life. This obsession was expressed most completely in the compound system of southern Africa and was developed in Kenya in the *kipande* (pass) system and the urban location, both attempts to place residence and movement under watchful official eyes. Mombasa was frightening because none of these mechanisms applied. The kipande laws were applied with little vigor in Mombasa, and most important, the employer who hired an African for less than twenty-four hours did not have to examine his kipande; nor did he have to provide housing, as was legally required of employers of permanent la-

47. Mombasa District, AR, 1927, 1929. Rather similar language was used by French officials in reference to Dakar. Casual workers were subsumed under the rubrics of "population flottante" or "vagabondes de l'embauche." See Monique Lakroum, *Le Travail inégal: paysans et salariés sénégalais face à la crise des années trentes* (Paris: Harmattan, 1982).

48. Town Clerk, Memorandum on the Draft Casual Labour By-Laws, 11 November 1930, LAB 9/1052. Later an official wrote: "This town may be more wasteful of labour than elsewhere in the Colony. It has always presented an extremely difficult problem as it is a native town with problems peculiar to itself." Labour Commissioner Wyn-Harries, Labour Review, 15 February 1944, CO 822/117/7.

49. MT, 29 January 1930.

bor. Too much urban property was owned by Arabs, Indians, or Swahili-speaking Africans to make feasible the introduction into Mombasa of the supervised native locations or the residential segregation found in Nairobi.[50] The African casual worker lived in private housing and emerged from it at irregular and uncontrollable intervals to work a day at a time.

What upset the city fathers was the danger of the urban masses, not their poverty. A more sensitive observer who knew Mombasa well, the physician, health official, and critic of the Kenyan regime Norman Leys, saw how overcrowded and unsanitary were the residential areas of Mombasa where workers lived. He emphasized an economic disjuncture: commercial development and land speculation had sent urban land values to heights that bore no relation to the rent-paying ability of African workers. Landlords could only afford to house workers by packing them into the Swahili-style houses of the sections of the city that became known as Majengo.[51] Only later would it become clear that making the dangerous classes less dangerous could not be separated from making them less poor.

The anxieties of the *Mombasa Times* were shared by officials, but they were careful not to undermine the economic advantages of casual labor; they aimed, an official told a meeting with employers, "not to curtail casual labour but to control it." Unemployment, meanwhile, was posing a very similar danger to that of casual labor. As the District Commissioner put it, "Large numbers of unemployed natives on whom no check can be kept must necessarily be a danger and such a life is undoubtedly demoralizing." The Town Clerk feared that Mombasa was suffering from an influx of "criminals and deserters" and becoming "a haven of refuge from the up-country police." The anticipated disorder did not materialize—the District Commissioner later wrote, "there has been very little trouble of any kind and the town has remained quiet and orderly."[52] Only later would officials realize that the danger was not so much the amorphous disorder associated with their image of casual labor, but disciplined strike action by workers whose developing organization and sense of common interest were hidden from officials beneath their mythology of "casual living."

But for now, one of officials' worst fears was contagion, that the way of life of the casual worker would spread into portions of the working population upon which a fragile regularity had been imposed by contract law and managerial supervision. The Labour Officer worried that contract

50. Willan Report, pp. 42–44.

51. Norman Leys, *Kenya*, 4th ed. (London: Cass, 1973; orig. publ. 1924), pp. 289–90.

52. Mombasa District, AR, 1930, 1931; Town Clerk, Memorandum on the Draft Casual Labour By-Laws, 11 November 1930, LAB 9/1049.

workers might desert their employers and get by on kibarua work, some-times leaving in the lurch an employer who had paid a worker's fare from western Kenya; or workers might take a day off from an employer who paid a monthly wage and earn an extra Shs 2 in the port. Even toward the end of the 1930s, the Labour Officer claimed, "at the coal wharf it is not an infrequent sight to see a house boy in a clean kanzu [cloth robe] come down, take off and roll up his clean clothes and carry coal in the interval between serving his master's lunch and tea."[53]

Confining casual workers to a municipal location was one possibility, but the Town Clerk thought that "Mombasa is too poor and too oriental to allow of our starting such locations."[54] More promising was registration: requiring casual laborers to present themselves and their kipandes, pay a fee, and obtain a certificate and a badge. Only casuals possessing the badge and certificate could then be hired. This procedure would not only separate casuals from monthly workers—making it possible to trace des-erters from the latter category—but would separate the "true casuals" from urban riff-raff.[55] Such a system was enacted into municipal law in 1930.

But it was never enforced, officially "owing to lack of staff and accom-modation" on the part of the Municipality.[56] More important, the By-laws of 1930 offered no more serious approach than the registration scheme of 1916 to transforming the social basis of port labor. The actual hiring of individual workers was done by gang leaders, who then presented their entire gang to the port employers. These leaders were often unable to read certificates and had no desire to let external criteria interfere with their own relations with workers. The companies—who were now em-ploying up to 1,700 casuals a day—had no more desire to tinker with a system that at least got the workers into the port. They did not know who their workers were and had little reason to want to know. The Kenya

53. Notes of a meeting of the Town Clerk, Labour Officer, and representatives of em-ployers, 12 February 1930, LAB 9/1049; Mombasa District, AR, 1929; LO, Mombasa, 1940, quoted by Karim K. Janmohamed, "African Labourers in Mombasa, c. 1895–1940," in B. A. Ogot, ed., Hadith 5: Economic and Social History of East Africa (Nairobi: Kenya Literature Bureau, 1976), p. 161.

54. Memorandum on the Draft Casual Labour By-Laws, 11 November 1930, LAB 9/1052. The control of housing—restricting casual workers to supervised barracks—was critical to the ability of authorities in South Africa to maintain casual labor on the docks while checking the workers' militancy and maintaining control over their time. David Hemson, "Dock Workers, Labour Circulation and Class Struggles in Durban, 1940–59," Journal of Southern African Studies 4 (1977): 88–124.

55. Labour Officer, Mombasa, to Principal Labour Inspector, Native Affairs Depart-ment, 29 January 1930, LAB 9/1049.

56. Town Clerk to Chief Registrar of Natives, 29 September 1931, LAB 9/1052; Mom-basa District, AR, 1932.

Landing & Shipping Company (KL&S Co.) had one European supervisor who was in charge of hiring six hundred workers, who were all to be checked in by 6:45 A.M. each day. Moreover, the badges could be sold, and unless careful records were kept of who actually worked, they would only legitimize "vagrant residence."[57] Nothing was done, and the worries about criminals, vagrants, and deserters breeding in the pool of Africans who moved in and out of work in Mombasa continued to gnaw at officials' minds.[58]

Another Kind of Order

To a significant extent, officials could not seize control of hiring workers during World War I and the 1930s precisely because the social organization of work was not as anarchic as the image of casual labor implied. The companies did not face a mass of workers directly, but through headmen, known as *serangs*. The division of labor in the port was fairly clear-cut by the late 1920s. Three firms—The East African Lighterage Co., The African Wharfage Co., and the Tanganyika Boating Co.—all licensed by the government, took charge of stevedoring, and each had regular arrangements with the main shipping lines. In 1927, these firms and the Railway jointly formed the Kenya Landing and Shipping Co. to take charge of the then chaotic situation in shorehandling—moving goods between pier, warehouse, and railway. Each company tried to establish its own stable of serangs, giving them presents, but the serangs—not bound by contracts—had substantial autonomy. The serangs organized gangs of workers, often twenty to twenty-five in number, in turn relying on their own intermediaries (sometimes called tindals). The serangs collected the workers, supervised them on the job, and received and distributed a sum of wages representing the earnings of the gang as a whole. One official as much as admitted that the concept of casual labor behind the recent registration scheme was off the mark: "In so far as the port casual labor is concerned the systems adopted are satisfactory owing to the fact that labour, though casual, is constant and the same gangs turn out regularly."[59]

But the regularity did not stem from the dominance of capital or the state over work: the serangs were crucial and powerful figures both in recruitment and in the work process itself. Particularly as work in the port became more scarce, they could demand bribes, or at least personal loy-

57. PLO to CS, 25 April 1940, LAB 9/1835; DC, Mombasa, to PC, Coast, 23 December 1938, and LO, Mombasa, Labour Report No. 1, 20 October 1931, LAB 9/1049.

58. PLO to CS, 23 July 1938, Chief Registrar of Natives to CS, 17 November 1938, Town Clerk, Mombasa, to DC, Mombasa, 5 April 1939, LAB 9/1049.

59. Mombasa District, AR, 1932. On the organization of the port in the 1930s, see Willan Report, pp. 3-4.

alty, from workers in their gangs.[60] Yet the serangs were not, in important ways, company men. The companies lacked the complex hierarchies
typical of modern corporations, possessed small supervisory staffs, and
relied on informal bonds to the most critical of all the supervisors, who in
turn had personal and informal ties to their men. The hiring center of
Mombasa, significantly, was not in the symbolic center of the shipping
industry, the port, but several miles removed, in the marketplace known
as Mwembe Tayari, whose importance will be explained later. The centrality of the semiautonomous serangs to the daily hiring process had
made it very difficult for the companies to change the way they dealt with
labor in 1916 and 1930. The serangs could withhold, if they chose, entire
gangs of men, each a preconstituted work group. They were to be sus-
pected of doing just that in the first strike that hit the port in 1934, and an
important aspect of the postwar reorganization of port labor would be an
attack on their bases of power in both hiring and supervision.

If a work-seeker had to come to a serang in order to obtain a job, the
workers collectively could exert pressure on him, for they—as a body—
were what he had to offer to the company. Since gangs were relatively
stable and worked and were paid together, their members constituted a
social group with a common relationship to a patron. They were far from
the anonymous and ever-changing units of labor power suggested by the
term *casual labor*.

The gang as a social unit took on a double meaning in the intense milieu
of coastal culture in the working-class districts of Mombasa. Among the
most important social institutions in pre–World War II Mombasa were
Beni dance societies, whose wide distribution in east and central Africa
has been made clear by Terence Ranger.[61] Competitive dance societies
were a form of recreation, vehicles for exercising talent, energy, and
leadership, and a way of coming to grips with political and cultural domi-
nation. The leading Beni groups of Mombasa were Kingi, Scotchi, and
Settla, all taking their names and the motifs used in their displays and
parades from various aspects of the colonial experience. Each was led by a
king, a prime minister, or a field marshal. In Mombasa, these societies
were not specifically working-class organizations, but they had a particular significance to workers. In the estimate of the District Commissioner,
200 of the 500 members of Scotchi who participated in parades were
dockworkers; Settla was even more closely associated with dockers, and its
motifs were naval. The officers of Settla included an admiral, a vice-
admiral, and a captain. The admiral, as of 1934, was chief serang for the

60. DC, Mombasa, Memorandum on the Port Strikes, 7 July 1934, LAB 5/25.
61. Terence Ranger, *Dance and Society in Eastern Africa, 1890–1970: The Beni Ngoma*
(Berkeley: University of California Press, 1975).

KL&S Co.; the other leaders were also dockworkers.[62] Leaders of sections within the major bands were frequently serangs.

The key to success in the competitive dancing held each Sunday, as each society paraded to the Mwembe Tayari market and danced, was the number of dancers the leader could muster and the enthusiasm with which they danced. Having noted with some anxiety the emergence of these organizations of Africans in Mombasa in 1919, District officials were happy to report after an investigation that their object was merely "to produce a better dressed or more original *ngoma* [dance] than its competition."[63] But whatever its object, Beni cemented relationships whose significance would only emerge with experience: serangs used their work gangs as a nucleus of support in establishing themselves as Beni leaders.[64]

Once again, serangs could exercise power over workers: if they failed to show up on Sunday, there might be no work on Monday.[65] But workers, together, determined the prestige that the Beni leaders-cum-serangs acquired. The overlap between work groups and dance groups—and the evidence does not permit us to elaborate on just how tight it was—points to the complexity and ambiguity in the social organization that lay beneath the image of social chaos in English visions of casual labor. Though serangs provided companies with ready-made work gangs with little effort on the companies' part, the serangs could also withdraw the gangs. Though gang members depended on the leader for their daily jobs, the leader depended on the men for his position as an intermediary, and for his prestige as a leader of Beni dance societies. In this personal system of labor mobilization, the social power of the intermediaries cut both ways.

It may well be that the double relationship of serang and worker also contributed to maintaining the social composition of the dock work force and the nature of docker culture in the face of increasing migration from upcountry. Beni, in Mombasa, was enmeshed in a Muslim, Swahili-speaking milieu. In 1919, the District Commissioner's brief investigation into Beni concluded that membership in Beni bands was open, but they in-

62. DC, Memorandum on Port Strike, 5–7 July 1934, LAB 5/25; Interview: Salim Ferunzi, now Welfare Officer of Mombasa Municipality, who remembered Beni from his boyhood in Mombasa.

63. Acting DC, Mombasa, to Acting PC, 1 December 1919, CP 52/1319. On the concern behind the investigation, see Chief Native Commissioner, circular to PCs, 22 October 1919, ibid.

64. Interviews: Salim Ferunzi and Hussein Ramadan, a Mombasan of Digo origin, now a labor official for East African Cargo Handling Service. Similar personal relationships, with a certain ambiguity to the power dimension, are described among dockers in Tunis. M. A. Hermassi, "Sociologie du milieu Docker," *Revue tunisienne des sciences sociales* 7 (1966): 153–79.

65. Interview: Salim Ferunzi.

cluded practically no people from upcountry. In 1934, when Beni groups
were thought to have been involved in organizing a strike, the names of
the dockers/Beni leaders that appear in reports were characteristic of ex-
slaves, Hadrami Arabs, Digo (Muslim Mijikenda), plus a sprinkling of
non-Muslim Mijikenda.[66] It would be hard for non-Swahili speakers, or
indeed for anyone not familiar with life in Mombasa, to establish relationships with serangs, whether in the hiring or the dancing side of the
activities centered in Mwembe Tayari.

In the absence of reliable statistical evidence before the 1940s, it is hard
to know just how much the social composition of the dock labor force
changed after the beginning of upcountry migration. There is little doubt
that coastal people perceived themselves as threatened: riots as early as
1923 and as late as 1937 reflected the coast-upcountry tension, but upcountry people did not in fact shake the coastal people's predominance in
the dock labor force. Statistics from the early years of registration indicate
that 58 percent of casuals were coastal Africans and another 12 percent
Arabs (including Hadrami immigrants and probably Swahili-speaking
Mombasans); more detailed evidence from the 1950s confirms the pre-
ponderance of Mijikenda and Swahili-speaking people in casual labor.
During the 1937 riots between Luo and Hadrami Arabs in Majengo, the
police noted that the stevedoring companies hired few Luo: The East
African Lighterage Company reported that its Swahili headman did the
hiring, and he hired coastal people whenever possible. Luo did make a
dent, however, in the KL&S Co.[67] Whether the recent creation of the
company meant that the gang structure was less tight or whether the fact
that shore labor (involving stacking warehouses and moving goods between warehouses and trains) fluctuated less widely than shipboard labor
better suited upcountry workers' preference for steady work is not clear,
but Luo became a more significant factor in shorehandling than in stevedoring. Even so, Swahili serangs and Beni leaders were powerful in the
KL&S Co. gangs.[68]

66. Acting DC, Mombasa, to Acting PC, 1 December 1919, CP 52/1319; DC, Mombasa,
Memorandum on Port Strikes, 5–7 July 1934, LAB 5/25. This emphasis on the cultural
character of Beni is confirmed by my two best informants on the subject, who are both from
different subgroups within this Islamic and Swahili-speaking culture: Salim Ferunzi and
Hussein Ramadan. Further research could illuminate other forms of association that created a dense network of social and cultural relationships among coastal Muslims.

67. Inspector of Police to PC, 17 September 1937, PC's Archives, L&O, 16/2. The inspector found no trouble between Luo and coastal Arabs in the port during the period of
disturbances between those groups in Majengo. For later statistics, see Mombasa District,
AR, 1946, and tables 4.4 and 4.10 below.

68. The leaders of Settla included the KL&S Co. head serang, another serang, and a
laborer, respectively of Swahili, ex-slave, and Digo origin. DC, Mombasa, Memorandum on
Port Strike, 5–7 July 1934, LAB 5/25.

So the Luo workers had to come to grips not only with what happened on the docks, but also with what went on in Mwembe Tayari—the center of hiring and of Beni. Few Luo in Mombasa became Muslim; they retained their distinctiveness and eventually formed large and powerful social organizations of their own. Their distinctiveness was not simply a matter of preserving their aboriginal parochialisms, but of the partly successful defense of the workplace by coastal people. Patterns of association and recreation were part of that defense. Coastal people were not defending urban turf in general but specific portions of it. Casual workers, most decisively stevedores, generally remained coastal people, yet Luo and other immigrants found other niches in urban life and urban labor. Eventually, upcountry and coastal—casual and permanent—workers would cooperate in a struggle for higher wages. They did not find their unity in a single workplace; perhaps they only found their unity because each group became closely associated with different kinds of work and came to recognize each other's legitimate place in the structure of work. They found their unity in the city, in the very broadly defined common experience of being workers in Mombasa.

3 Dockwork and Disorder, 1934–1947

If the British in the early colonial era were troubled by the apparently anarchic nature of casual labor, they soon discovered that the problem was not caused by a disorganized mass but a kind of organization that they did not understand. Soon after the first disorders rocked the port, complacent ignorance turned into an obsession to discover what went on in the working-class districts of Mombasa and to do something to break up the menacing unity of the urban mass. Even with the first two port strikes in the 1930s, officials jumped to the conclusion that at the root of the problem were the casual labor system and the serangs. The transition from suppressed anxiety about casual labor, to bewilderment at the first organized action taken by workers, to examination, and finally to a reassertation of managerial control followed directly upon the initiatives of the workers themselves. This transition has left a rich set of material on labor in the 1940s, whose very existence—in stark contrast to the paucity of official data on workers in earlier periods—is as revealing of changed conceptions as its contents.

THE EARLY STRIKES

The First Dock Strike, 1934
In a sense, the problem that officials first faced on 4 July 1934 was similar to that faced by the historian trying to reconstruct events. The immediate cause of this first dock strike in Mombasa's history is obvious enough: the stevedoring companies decided to cut the wages of their stevedores by Sh /50, effective 1 July, belatedly copying the wage reductions imposed on shorehandlers by the KL&S Co. at the beginning of the Depression. What is hard to explain is how the strike was conducted so effectively in the absence of any visible trade-union organization or any prior experience with industrial action.

On the morning of 4 July, a Wednesday, gangs of workers armed with sticks congregated near the entrances to the port, intimidating people who tried to enter. There was some stone throwing at the police. Police got them to go home, but the next day most stevedores stayed away from work. A mass meeting took place in Mwembe Tayari, the center of both hiring and Beni dance competitions. The shorehandlers were kept from working. On Friday, the stevedoring companies met with serangs and elders and agreed to rescind the wage cut for one month, pending investigation and negotiation. The stevedores went back to work. But on Saturday, the shorehandlers left work, demanding that the wage cut they had suffered two years previously be rescinded as well, and the rest of the port went out in sympathy. The workers returned on Sunday after negotiations and concessions that are only vaguely described in the reports. The violence, police admitted, had been minimal; only twenty-two arrests were made, and officials commented on how cheerful the strikers had been.[1]

The stevedores, although competing with one another for daily jobs, had struck as a body. They had cooperated with shorehandlers, despite differences in pay, employers, the nature of the jobs, and the composition of the work forces. Somehow, people had been told on which day to strike; meetings had been held and negotiations conducted; and a return to work—concessions in hand—had taken place smoothly. It was to be twenty years before dockers had a trade union, yet they had pulled off a strike.

The momentum of the strike, however, could not be sustained after the month-long hiatus. The shorehandlers gained nothing—their wages stayed at the Shs 1/50 to which they had been cut in the Depression—but stevedores preserved the principal of Shs /50 per day premium for their more arduous and dangerous job on board ships for two decades. Wages were to remain (with some changes in hours after the 1939 strike) at Shs 2 for stevedores and Shs 1/50 for shorehandlers until 1942, when both figures rose in the midst of a city-wide strike scare. Various supplements for extended shifts and night work pushed typical earnings into the range of Shs 1/75 to 2/50, in some cases more.[2]

The dockers had also forced officials to think. Some kind of organization had to exist. It is perhaps less important whether the explanations of the District Commissioner and the police are correct than that they were made, that officials realized something had to be explained. Their explanation, however, is plausible and consistent with elements of another strike in a distant part of Africa the following year, the Copperbelt strike of 1935.[3] Officials thought that the strike had been organized through the Beni dance bands, especially the docker-dominated Scotchi and Set-

1. Inspector of Police to Asst. Supt. of Police, 10 July 1934, DC, Mombasa, Memorandum on Port Strike, 5–7 July 1934, LAB 5/25; Mombasa District, AR, 1934.

2. Report of the Commission of Inquiry appointed to Examine the Labour Conditions in Mombasa (Nairobi, 1939), p. 4 (hereafter Willan Commission); W. G. Nicol, Memorandum on the Labour Commission Report, 2 February 1940, LAB 9/1835.

3. Ian Henderson, "Early African Leadership: The Copperbelt Disturbances of 1935 and 1940," *Journal of Southern African Studies* 2 (1975): 83–97.

tla. Their weekly competitions in Mwembe Tayari had given way to mass meetings in the same location, and the mobilization of strikers had been organized by the band leaders, who were also the serangs, and thus in a position to bring all hiring to a halt. There were also somewhat vague references in reports to an organization that had grown out of Beni. Abdur Rehman bin Naaman, a former dockworker, Prime Minister of Scotchi, and a Hadrami Arab with close associations to ex-slaves and "detribalised natives," had founded a Coast Labour Association in 1932. This organization, the District Commissioner thought, had three to five hundred members, especially serangs and dock laborers, and its other leaders were also dockers with prominent connections to the dance groups. During the strike, this organization kept serangs and their followers informed of what was going on. The Inspector of Police also mentioned a stevedores' club, with three hundred members, but his description is that of a Beni dance society.[4] How these mechanisms worked in that first week of July 1934 we do not know: the official reports only suggest how the conjuncture of work structure and social groups could have created mechanisms to transform the grievances of a large proportion of dockworkers into concerted action.

This transformation was, as always, the most difficult part of organizing industrial action, reflecting not simply the relations of people on the job, but a wider process of communication, feelings of identity, and patterns of social interaction. The quick strike of a localized work group—for example, railway ballast workers or construction workers at a single site—disgusted by low pay, cheated in some way, or angered by arbitrary punishments, was becoming fairly common in the mid- to late-1930s, and such strikes would continue to be an irregular but frequent backdrop to the larger-scale events of the decade to come.[5] The port strike of 1934 had involved different categories of workers in a system of docks, considerable problems of coordination, action over several days, negotiations, and an orderly return to work. The experience no doubt contributed to the events that were to come.

By 1936, officials in Mombasa were noting that employment and prices were both rising.[6] These pressures of economic expansion—combined with the growing experience of work and conflict on the docks—slowly

4. Inspector of Police to Asst. Supt. of Police, 10 July 1934, DC, Mombasa, Memorandum on Port Strike, 5–7 July, 1934, LAB 5–25.

5. For descriptions of such a strike at the Shell oil facility in Mombasa in 1937, and for others on the railway in Kisumu and Gilgil in 1934 and 1937, see Supt. Engineer, Shell, to Manager, Nairobi, 15 January 1937; DC, Mombasa, to PC, Coast, 21 January 1937; LO to Principal Labour Inspector, Native Affairs Department, 17 December 1934, PLO to GM, 13 August 1937, all in LAB 5/25.

6. Mombasa District, AR, 1936.

began to have an effect. In May of 1936 came a short strike at the KL&S Co. that echoed the relationship of dockers and headmen two years previously. The company had some sort of dispute with the headmen, who "thereupon marched their men off the wharf. Forty-five Natives then went and interviewed the Arab headmen and threatened direct action. The Headmen gave them excellent advice and immediately reported the position to the DC." Several meetings between officials and the different categories of headmen produced an "amicable understanding." In January 1937, a strike at the Shell Oil plant in the port area revealed that the details of life in the workplace were not going to be passively left for management to decide. All Shell workers struck on 14 January, complaining that they had to sign in each day, but if there was no work they were not paid. The work rules prevented them from seeking casual labor elsewhere that day. Officials admitted that "their grievances had justification," and the company gave in. The next month, there were "a few small strikes" in Mombasa, which the District Commissioner attributed to "the increase in the cost of living."[7]

But in 1938 there were no African strikes in Mombasa (only a strike of Indian artisans). The Principal Labour Officer (PLO) of Kenya, P. deV. Allen, reported, "I consider the Native Labour in Mombasa to be far better off than the upcountry native in employment."[8] But it was in Mombasa that the colonial state discovered the working poor, not because they were worse off than the poor of Nairobi, but because they shut down the city in a general strike one year after Allen's letter.

The First General Strike, 1939

We know even less than in the case of 1934 how the general strike of 1939 was organized. What happened was in fact a series of short strikes in late July, affecting one employer after another and ending in concessions to the workers, and culminating in an effective dock strike from 1 to 3 August. Official correspondence and the report of the investigation are silent about the role of Beni, not necessarily because it was irrelevant, but perhaps because of official ignorance, exacerbated by the rapid turnover of officials that was later cited as a cause of the state's loss of control over the work force.[9] The PLO spoke of agitators but failed to produce any.[10] There is at least a hint that the serang-based system of hiring that had been critical to the 1934 strike was again relevant. An official of the KL&S Co. testified that most of his monthly labor had not struck, but that the

7. Mombasa District, AR, 1936, 1937.
8. PLO to CS, 28 July 1938, LAB 9/1049.
9. Willan Commission, pp. 40–42.
10. PLO, in Willan, p. 73. The commission was unimpressed.

trouble came with "contract boys," half of whom had gone out. These were the workers recruited as gangs through a serang and paid as a group.[11] The casual worker, as before, was at the center of things.

But this time he was not alone. In Dar es Salaam, the casual laborers in the port, but not the monthly staff, had struck for higher wages and better treatment by supervisors on 17 July. They had drifted back over the next eight days and had gained little, failing to enlist even other dockers in their effort. It would have taken very little time for Swahili-speaking sailors and travelers to take the news over the social networks of the coastal region, and it found a receptive audience in the city of Mombasa as well as the port.[12] The dock strike in Mombasa began on 1 August, but it took place after a series of rumblings in the work force of the city as a whole. The urban context was critical. The specificity of different categories of workers within the labor process of the port did not isolate them in the city: workers of all sorts lived in the Majengo quarter, and the prominence of dockers in the social life of the city, including Beni, did not amount to exclusiveness. Few employers in Mombasa provided either housing or rations; workers faced overcrowding and inflation together. The distinction between permanent and casual laborers, basic as it was, did not necessarily translate into distinct interests, a theme that runs through the subsequent decade.

In July, the Port Manager heard rumors that workers were meeting to discuss grievances.[13] The first phase of the strike began among workers of the Public Works Department on 19 July. It was a "very orderly" sit-down strike. Only 105 of these 360 workers were housed, and the rest received no housing allowance; jobs were not graded, and so experienced workers did not necessarily get higher pay; and these largely upcountry workers were being paid daily, although they were not in fact casual workers. Many had served for years. The Public Works Engineer listened to the grievances of the striking workers and promised to consider them. The Public Works laborers returned to work and were quickly granted a Shs 3 per month housing allowance.

On 22 July, Municipality workers set forth formal demands, and they too were conceded a housing allowance. But by the twenty-fourth, the strike had spread to the laborers of the Mombasa Municipality, the Electric Light and Power Company, the oil companies, and the Post and

11. Testimony of J. J. Stephen, 21 September 1939, reported in EAS, 25 September 1939.

12. On the Dar strike, see John Iliffe, "The Creation of Group Consciousness: A History of the Dockworkers of Dar es Salaam," in Richard Sandbrook and Robin Cohen, eds., *The Development of an African Working Class* (London: Longman, 1975), pp. 49–72. The interport communications network is cited, with some concern, by CS, Tanganyika, to CS, Governors' Conference, Nairobi, 3 April 1944; LC, Kenya, to CS, 6 May 1944, LAB 9–59.

13. Mombasa District, AR, 1939.

Telegraph Department—all of which employed predominantly monthly labor on more or less standardized terms—and to the mostly Indian-owned vegetable farms and dairies, where periods and conditions of employment were highly irregular, but usually bad.[14]

On the twenty-fourth, police discovered notices posted in the port calling on dockworkers to quit work and demand better pay, overtime, sick pay, and railway passes for return home. Police pulled down the notices, threatened to arrest any nonworkers, and worried about the repercussions of the Dar es Salaam dock strike. The Port Manager tried to convene meetings of employee representatives in each department within the Railway's port facilities, but failed. He complained of the "men's lack of self-expression." Rumors circulated about the general strike planned for Monday, 31 July. Officials tried to talk to port workers on that day, but the workers refused to appoint a small delegation to negotiate, although they talked long enough to demand higher pay. "The crowd was in a very excited mood."[15] The port strike broke out on 1 August, as the casual work gangs failed to report to their jobs and "large gangs" picketed the port. The port shut down. The next day, "bands of strikers" circulated all over town and 150 people were arrested for "mass picketing." The port's monthly labor did not appear, because of "intimidation," officials insist-ed. Police reinforcements arrived that day, and officials thought they were instrumental in bringing about a return to work. By 3 August, workers began to trickle back, and on the fourth, the port was "practically normal again."[16]

During the strike, the police observed strikers armed with sticks form-ing themselves into processions and marching around Majengo "in their peculiar 'job trot' chanting as they went." The marchers agreed with the police to stay in Majengo, and armed groups were broken up or arrested when they ventured too near places of work. Majengo and Mwembe Tayari were placed under an 8 P.M. curfew.[17]

Perhaps the police were observing workers using their traditional, ap-parently recreational, patterns of processions and music to a new end in their struggle against employers. Perhaps this was a glimpse of an embry-onic working-class culture, developing in an ethnically diverse work force and being used by workers in ways not fully understood by the Europeans who were observing it. The descriptions of strikers in action does fit a

14. Dairy workers often were reduced to sleeping in the sheds with the cows. Willan, pp. 36, 72; MT, 27–29 July 1939.

15. Inspector of Police, Port, to Supt. of Police, 24 July 1939, and PM to GM, 28 July 1939, SPG 35/6; Mombasa District, AR, 1939.

16. PLO to CS, 9 August 1939, LAB 9/1835; Mombasa District, AR, 1939.

17. Supt. of Police to Comr. of Police, 3 August 1939, PC's Archive, LAB 10/1; Mombasa District, AR, 1939.

picture that centers on Majengo, a place where people from different parts of Kenya lived and left each day for different sorts of jobs around Mombasa. The strike spread across the divide between the casual jobs that were generally held by coastal people and the monthly jobs in which upcountry workers were more prominent. The investigating committee's statistics on the Mombasa work force included five to seven thousand coastal people, five to six thousand people from the Lakes region, seven to eight thousand Kikuyu and Kamba from Central Kenya, and three to four thousand from Tanganyika: the strikers had included substantial portions of each category.[18]

Equally significant was the fact that Mombasa's 2,240 railway workers—80 percent of whom were housed by the Railway and hence did not live amidst the vibrant world of Majengo—did not join the strike, although the majority of them received basic wages just as meager as those paid to other monthly workers.[19] The Railway, nonetheless, quickly moved to increase the cash allowance it gave workers in lieu of rations and to consider raising the housing allowance for workers not in its accommodations, although it waited to see what the Municipality would do about the city-wide housing question.[20] What distinguished the railwaymen from the rest of the work force of Mombasa was not that their grievances were less serious: the railwaymen met among themselves and sent deputations to management in the midst of the turmoil, and the basic issues of low pay and inflation were the focus of their concern.[21] The linkage of housing to job for 80 percent of the railway work force implied that striking entailed a double risk, loss of a place to live as well as of a job. Casuals were at the other extreme: by staying away from work, they lost a day's work but did not risk either access to living space in the city or jobs with employers who did not even know their names.

Hardly had the PLO got off the overnight train from Nairobi on Monday morning, 24 July, during the Public Works Department phase of the strike, than he decided that housing was the central issue. The Railway was nearly alone in Mombasa in housing the majority of its employees, even though Section 31 of the Employment of Servants Ordinance required that employers make provision for housing. Allen persuaded the Public Works Department to grant Shs 3 per month to each worker in lieu

18. DC, Notes, in Willan, p. 60.

19. Willan, p. 74; Port Manager to GM, 2 August 1939, SPG 35/6.

20. GM to PM, 28 July 1939, SPG 35/6.

21. In meetings held on 18, 21, and 25 July, railwaymen demanded a raise and threatened a strike for 29 July, demands that were to a small extent met by the railway's concessions on rations and housing. Insp. of Police, Port, to Supt. of KUR&H Police, 24, 25, 27 July 1939; Report of meeting of Railway Committee, 27 July 1939; GM to PM, 28 July 1939—all in SPG 35/6.

of housing, and as the strikes spread, so did this general formula for getting the workers back. No doubt this strategy contributed as much to inspiring new strikes as to settling earlier ones.[22] But with casual workers, such a concession solved nothing. The stevedoring and shorehandling companies lopped an hour off their nine-hour shift, which might have pushed the number of workers needed each day up a bit; but the most important changes in working conditions that arose from the workers' activism would come more slowly. With these concessions, the workers returned. At the same time, repression by the state had been minimal—a few workers were repatriated and some arrests for violence and mass picketing had been made.[23]

The strike quickly crystallized the fears for urban social order that had lain beneath the surface for the past four decades. It made it clear that the issue of labor was not confined within the working day: the strike re-kindled the state's concern with the need to maintain some authority over all dimensions of workers' lives. In their first city-wide encounter with collective action, employers, civic leaders, and state officials acknowl-edged that low wages and poor living conditions lay behind the protest. But they were less interested in taking any major steps to alleviate these problems—basic wages remained the same—than in tying reform to an assertion of control in the two most fundamental locations of the working life, the workplace and the residence. The corollary of such control would be to purge the city of those people who did not fit into the regularized structure that officials wanted to erect for urban workers. Over the next fifteen years, ideas for remedying the dangers of poverty within the city would involve expelling the poor as much as alleviating the poverty of those who remained.

The strike was still on when the *Mombasa Times* editorialized about the connection of casual labor, housing, and disorder. It worried about men "sleeping in odd sheds and even in cow sheds and other crudely made shelters, these natives are a source of crime, ill-health, and economic discontent." It recommended not simply that housing be improved, but that it be supervised: a "native location" should be created. It complained that unemployed Africans were allowed to stay in Mombasa, while in Nairobi they were expelled to the Reserves.[24]

The Principal Labour Officer, Allen, suggested only days after the strike that "the regular worker should be substituted for the irregular worker"; that "compounds and good housing" be provided by large em-ployers and that private lodging houses, as far as possible, be abolished;

22. PLO to CS, 9 August 1939, in Willan, p. 70.
23. Willan, p. 4.
24. MT, 2 August 1939.

and that local natives be given preference as regular workers, while the unemployed should be expelled from the island and returned to their Reserves. After a few months reflection, he remained convinced that civic order required the cleansing of the city: "serious trouble will occur unless something is done at once to remove from Mombasa Island a large number of unemployed and unemployable [natives] and not only remove them but prevent them from returning." He cited a port official's concern that if employment dropped, hunger rioting might develop.[25]

Similarly, the Inspector of Police at the Port was convinced that "idlers and stiffs" in Mombasa were at the root of the unrest, and that the way to regain control was to register casuals, build a compound to house them along the Railway's model (with its own police station), and to expel idlers, who—not being registered—would be denied access to housing. The District Officer was equally direct: "casual labour is the danger point." It should be replaced by workers who were registered, guaranteed a mini-mum number of working days per month, and housed in a labor loca-tion.[26]

Reactions: Urban Poverty and the Casual Labor Problem
London was both frightened and angered. One of the first reactions had the most far-reaching implications. Minuting a despatch sent before the strike had reached the port, Frederick Pedler, a bright young star in the Colonial Office, commented, "Before very long East Africa will have to change over—probably very suddenly—from low grade labour and very low wages to something much nearer the standard of European manual labour and the European labourer's wage." Shortly after things calmed down, another Colonial Office official, J. T. Chadwick, minuted that the Mombasa strike "reveals a disgusting state of affairs and one which is reminiscent of the Trinidad strike."[27]

This precedent—the massive strikes and riots in Trinidad and Jamaica in 1935 and 1938—greatly influenced official perceptions, and the on-going disorders in Kenya and elsewhere seemed to form a disturbing pattern.[28] The most worrisome aspect of the pattern was a breakdown of

25. PLO to CS, 9 August 1939, LAB 9/1835; PLO to CS, 16 November 1939, LAB 5/30. Another coastal official thought that repatriation would be expensive and ineffective, since expelled people would drift back. He did not say that expulsions were undesirable. PC to CS, 9 January 1940, LAB 5–30.

26. Inspector Overton, testimony to Willan Commission, in MT 9 October 1939; DO to Willan, 19 September 1939, in Willan, p. 75.

27. F. J. Pedler, Minute, 18 August 1939, to Brooke-Popham to MacDonald, 31 July 1939, CO 533/513/38397/2; J. T. Chadwick, Minute, 8 September 1939, to Governor to Secretary of State, 29 August 1939, CO 533/507/38091/6.

28. Ken Post, *Arise Ye Starvelings: The Jamaican Labour Rebellion of 1938 and Its Aftermath* (The Hague: Nijhoff, 1978). The place of Africa in this pattern is discussed below, in chapter 6.

order that transcended strikes in individual firms or industries, spreading throughout a locality or even a colony. In wartime, such a threat to empire was particularly frightening.

The confrontations with labor forced officials to make clear, if only to themselves, that the mission of the Colonial Office was not to maintain a low-wage economy for the benefit of capital; wages in Mombasa, Chadwick minuted, were "indefensibly low." The Colonial Office's leading pundit on the labor question, Major G. St. J. Orde Browne, minuted that the problem of casual labor in Mombasa was made more difficult by "indifferent employers and ignorant unorganized workers," and was made no better by the Kenya Government, which told London little and probably knew little more itself.

But Orde Browne became convinced that casual labor itself was the heart of the problem, and two years later, noting little progress since his first remarks, he wrote, "Reduction and control of casual labour in the port is an essential for good order." Otherwise, there was a "prospect for serious difficulties" in all East African ports after the war.[29]

The concern with order, urban structure, and casual labor went to the top of the imperial hierarchy. Malcolm MacDonald, Secretary of State for the Colonies, wrote the Governor of Kenya after the reports of the strike had been digested in London, that cities like Mombasa were "unnecessarily crowded by large numbers of persons who are only intermittently employed. A policy of grading up wages and performance concurrently might so far reduce the number of African employees as to make it possible to ease the housing situation, through the return of large numbers to the native areas."[30]

In Kenya, the Government did what it was to do many times in the next decade: appoint a commission to investigate. This body, under H. C. Willan, was "appointed to examine the labour conditions in Mombasa." It heard evidence in September and October and reported on 3 December 1939. Willan's report put housing at the center of the urban problem. It agreed that housing in Majengo was not only bad and expensive relative to wages, but that the reliance on private, unsupervised housing in Mombasa was a dangerous idea compared to the compounds and supervised locations provided by the railway, and few other employers, in Mombasa.

29. Chadwick, Minute, 8 September 1939, CO 533/507/38091/6; Orde Browne, minute, n.d. [September 1939], ibid.; Orde Browne, minute, 12 November 1941, to Governor to Secretary of State, 30 September 1941, CO 533/526/38091/6.

30. MacDonald to Governor, 18 November 1939, CO 533/513/38397/2. A similar line had been taken by another lower-level official in the Colonial Office right after the strike: J. L. Keith minuted that African cities had "too many cheap and inefficient workers." A few housing projects would only divide workers into an "upper class" and a "lower class living in slum conditions." More economic use of labor was needed to solve the housing crisis. Minute, 2 September 1939, to Brooke-Popham to MacDonald, 16 August 1939, ibid.

A considerable market in housing had grown up since the early colonial days, and Europeans had joined Indians and Arabs in buying up the parts of Mombasa Island that later became Majengo and the other centers of working-class housing. The typical pattern was for the landlord to rent out land in small units only to individuals, including Swahili-speaking Africans as well as Arabs and Indians, who built houses—the ownership of which was thus separated from the ownership of land—and rented them out by the room, or indeed by the bed.

The housing market in Mombasa, it would seem, was the paradise of the petty capitalist, but the system did not get the approval of the Commission—the extent of private ownership was in fact considered an obstacle to developing municipal locations. Faced with large-scale employers unwilling or unable to provide housing and the reality of the pressing needs for it, the Commission acknowledged that African workers had genuine grievances over the rental cost of bed space which had to be met even before the chaotic world of the small-scale housing market could be reorganized. It recommended that unhoused workers in Mombasa be given a housing allowance equal to the market rent of a bed space in the city, about Shs 5. But it was equally clear that the provision of controlled housing in compounds and locations was the ideal solution, and it had to be accompanied by the repatriation of all upcountry Kenyans who could not "show good cause why they should remain in Mombasa."[31]

It was this central concern with the need to rationalize housing that led the Commission to one of its principal indictments of casual labor. A casual work force could not be put into controlled housing. On the contrary, the port companies stuck to casual labor in part to avoid their responsibility to provide housing; and to ensure that this system provided sufficient labor, they had to create a large surplus labor pool in the city, which in turn created the pressures of a large mass of largely idle, discontented men on the strained housing resources of the city.[32]

The Commission, and others who wrote at the time, did not complain so much about casual *work*, but about casual *workers*. They faced a social crisis in the city, even if the dockers' work seemed to be getting done. Thus without considering questions of efficiency or productivity in the port, the Commission reached the conclusion that the port should move

31. Willan, pp. 27–28, 42–44. The Municipal Board of Mombasa in 1935 had changed its mind about an eight-year-old plan—the village layout schemes—that encouraged Africans to build their own houses in controlled spaces. It believed that these areas were becoming slums. Construction of Swahili-style houses was also frozen. Richard Stren, *Housing the Urban Poor in Africa: Policy, Politics, and Bureaucracy in Mombasa* (Berkeley: Institute of International Studies, 1978), p. 133.

32. Willan, pp. 18, 23.

away from the use of casual labor. It should replace its large pool of
workers by registering the employees it needed and expelling all others
from the city, sweeping the idle and the dangerous from Mombasa. It
realized that the smooth distribution of a pool of registered workers close
in number to the actual demand for labor was impossible given the existence of three rival stevedoring companies and a shorehandling firm. But
it was so convinced of the desirability of decasualization that it suggested
that the three stevedoring companies be amalgamated, enabling a single
pool to serve all and flattening out the fluctuations of labor demand
caused by the uneven flow into the port of ships contracted to particular
companies.[33]

This ideology of control was closely linked to an ideology of welfarism.
The Commission—and the PLO before it—frankly admitted that the
strikers had legitimate grievances: their pay was too low relative to the cost
of housing and other essentials of life, while unemployment was too high.
The Commission did not provide statistics to demonstrate the impact of
post-Depression inflation, but it was convinced that this inflation was
severe. The Willan Commission began the Battle of the Budgets, a process that would recur whenever labor unrest arose and which transformed social conflict and workers' demands for an improved standard of
living into technical questions, as nutritionists and experts on poverty
were asked to establish minimum standards of living for urbanized Africans that would form the basis of the wage awards.[34]

African workers were to be caught up as well in the political need to
justify wage demands in the form of hypothetical budgets for workers or
families, but in 1939, unofficial attempts to present a budget figure were
limited to those of the Indian labor leader, Makhan Singh, whose estimate
the Commission felt obliged to mock. At the same time, the Commission
lamented the fact that there was no "reasonably-minded trade union
official" who could contribute to labor's side of the Battle of the Budgets.
The Commission turned instead to the Medical Officer of Health and the
District Commissioner of Mombasa, who showed them various model
budgets, illustrating how much people from different ethnic groups,
living alone or with various numbers of dependents, spent on food, fuel,
and other bare necessities. The Commission decided that Shs 18/50 per

33. Willan, p. 20. In England, the decentralization of hiring—London had over two
hundred call-on stands—was considered one of the worst obstacles to a less wasteful use of
dock labor or to schemes for reducing casualism. See Vernon H. Jenson, *The Hiring of
Dockworkers: Employment Practices in the Ports of New York, Liverpool, London, Rotterdam, and
Marseilles* (Cambridge, Mass.: Harvard University Press, 1964), p. 201.

34. That same year the Colonial Office had published the First Report of the Committee
on Nutrition in the Colonial Empire, Parliamentary Papers 1938–39, X, 55. This document
defined the inadequacy of urban laborers' diet as an empire-wide problem.

month, plus housing allowance, was "a reasonable, not minimum, monthly living wage for an adult unmarried African."[35] When establishing new minima later failed to quell labor unrest, future commissions and Labour Department officials were to search more earnestly for their reasonably minded trade-union official. But meanwhile, welfarism took the form of pronouncements by experts who would not have dreamed of living the life for which they were budgeting. Their calculations of how much the model African—who was of course adult, male, and single—needed to buy maize meal, fuel, potatoes, a bit of meat, and very little else shaped the definition of a legitimate wage.

The emphasis on the minimum wage in these years reflected a belief, essentially accurate, that most of the work force of Mombasa shared that end of the spectrum. The Railway probably employed the most differentiated and long-term work force, but 52 percent of its workers received the minimum wage of Shs 15 per month, and many others received not much more. Dockworkers, on the other hand, were the least regular of workers, but if estimates of how often they could get work—one day in five—were accurate, their monthly income would be around Shs 12 to 18.[36] Similar figures emerge in the evidence about other employers. With the exception of railwaymen, most workers faced similar rents, along with the same shopkeepers in Majengo.

The work force of Mombasa was not homogeneous. But the large majority of them were bunched near one end of the wage spectrum, and most were thrown into the same living situation. Above all, the categories of the casual worker and the unemployed overlapped; the casual laborer was inevitably both in the course of each month. A certain degree of wage sharing undoubtedly blurred the line between workers and the idle still further.[37] This social situation gave great significance to the contention of the police, district and labor officials, and the Commission that "idlers and stiffs" could bring about a work stoppage. For there was something of the idler and the stiff in every worker in Mombasa. If the "general worker" and the "undesirable"[38] could not be separated, danger would remain. The contagion theory of labor unrest, influential since the Victorian era, had been pushed to the fore in Kenya by the workers and nonworkers of Mombasa.

After the Commission reported, Kenyan labor officials again took up themes they had helped to place on its agenda. Clearly defining the legitimate worker and protecting him from contagion was at the center of

35. Willan, pp. 31–33. For the model budgets, see ibid., p. 58.
36. Notes to DC on Labour in Mombasa, n.d. [1939], LAB 9/1835; Willan, pp. 64, 74.
37. PLO to CS, 25 April 1940, LAB 9/1835.
38. EAS, 9 August 1939.

plans to avoid future labor troubles. As the Labour Officer of Mombasa put it, most port work was done by "a class of native and Arab who may be described as professional daily labourers whose livelihood, precarious at the best of times, must be protected as far as possible." The threat to their access to work came from upcountry migrants with questionable motives for being in Mombasa, people who wanted to avoid registration ordinances, and moonlighting contract workers. The PLO, Allen, endorsed these views, and the Provincial Commissioner used much the same terms, arguing that the state should protect "a definite class of Arab and native professional daily labourer" by registering them and excluding anyone else from the city. For Allen, registration of legitimate casuals seemed the most practical and desirable way "to raise the standard of living of the labourers concerned" and pointed to a coherent goal for urban and labor policy: "The ideal position would be that every labourer in the island should either be employed on a monthly (or longer basis), be a registered casual or in Mombasa on a pass if he is not a native of the Coast area."[39] Every alternative would specify the authority to whom the African would have to look.

Officials got as far as holding a meeting at the Governor's house which concluded that registration should be implemented as soon as badges to label the legitimate casual workers were ready, although they did not envision limiting the number of registered casuals at first.[40] Actually, nothing was done until 1944, largely because the stevedoring companies had not yet been sufficiently frightened (see below, pp. 76–78).

The KL&S Co., however, had taken a quiet and modest step almost immediately after the strike. It signed 150 pieceworkers onto monthly terms, guaranteeing them a Shs 40 per month fallback against their piecework earnings. This had been done explicitly to improve labor conditions. The other port firms were awaiting the results of the Willan Commission.[41]

The most concrete accomplishment stemming from the post-strike anxieties and the Willan Report was the upgrading of Kenya's labor officials to department status in 1940. The Principal Labour Officer became Labour Commissioner. London had long been pushing colonies to make this kind of step, and Kenya had been notable for its slowness in following directions. Malcolm MacDonald, the Secretary of State for the Colonies,

---

39. LO, Mombasa, to PLO, 21 February 1940, PLO to CS, 26 February 1940, LAB 9/1049; PC, Mombasa, Memorandum on the Report of the Commission of Inquiry, 23 March 1940, LAB 9/1835.

40. CS to Chief Registrar of Natives, 7 May 1940, LAB 9/1049.

41. Asst. Supt., Railway and Harbour Police, to Comr. of Police, Nairobi, 10 August 1939, SPG 35/6; Mombasa District, AR, 1940.

made clear that the Kenya Government deserved "severe criticism" for letting the labor situation in Mombasa get out of hand, and he used his new leverage arising from the strike to try to create institutions capable of handling "industrial disputes." He pressed local officials to remedy the housing situation too.[42] But the more far-reaching recommendations of the Commission sat on the shelf, and two years later, another Secretary of State wrote another Governor that the 1939 report should be given attention once conditions returned to normal after the war.[43]

But any change in the organization of port labor still had to face the opposition of the port companies, especially the stevedoring firms, whose daily workloads fluctuated even more than those of the shorehandlers, and whose concern with profits had not yet been enough shaken by the imperatives of order to reexamine labor policies. A vehement response to the argument against casual labor came from W. G. Nicol, Director and Chairman of the Mombasa Board of Smith Mackenzie & Co.—the leading shipping agent—and Director of the African Wharfage Co. and the KL&S Co. Involved in stevedoring, shorehandling, and shipping, Nicol had a dual interest in minimizing costs: as operator of profit-making cargo handling companies in the port and as a consumer of their services. Nicol distinguished between stevedores, whom he regarded as "the aristocracy of labour," and "the unemployable or very casual labour class with which Mombasa abounds and who promote the basis of all labour and social problems." The true stevedores received "good and generous pay," and their conditions of life were evident in their "exceptionally fine" physiques. The stevedores were, of course, casual laborers, but he insisted that port labor throughout the world was casual "and must always be so." Like officials, Nicol wanted to rid Mombasa of undesirables; but for him, undesirables were evidently casuals employed by someone else. He opposed all the measures suggested by officials to make the distinction between true stevedores and the dangerously idle more clear. The idea of amalgamating the stevedoring companies to make feasible the operation of a single labor pool appalled him: it was a dangerous interference with business, and one of the three companies was not even British. The suggestion that stevedoring companies, like other Kenyan employers, should provide housing and other amenities to their workers was "Socialism at its worst." The Manager of the East African Lighterage Co. chimed in more crudely: reliance on casual labor was "natural and necessitous"; the pro-

---

42. MacDonald to Governor Moore, 7 March 1940, CO 533/518/38091/6. MacDonald at the same time was using the disturbances in the West Indies as his most telling argument for the urgency of several types of reform, especially for expenditures on social services and economic development. See Post, *Arise Ye Starvelings*.

43. Cranbourne to Governor, 3 August 1942, LAB 9/1835.

posal to amalgamate the companies was "stupid"; and the idea that the tenure of workers should be made secure was also "stupid."[44] Faced with opposition like this, the Government backed away from even the most modest attempt to register and license casual labor and to separate the "aristocracy of labour" from the dangerous classes of Mombasa.

THE WAR YEARS

With the general strike of August 1939, the workers of Mombasa began their war. The disorders of these years were so widespread in Africa that they cannot be explained in purely local terms. Nor can they be solely attributed to the war: the era of strikes in Mombasa—like the Copperbelt—began in the mid-1930s, and it extended to 1947, as did the era of intense strike activity in West Africa. The most general characteristic of this era was the growth in export production that began as the world slowly recovered from the Depression, the productionist ethos of the war years, and the commodities boom of the postwar era, lasting until the mid-1950s. In Mombasa, this meant that the six hundred thousand tons of cargo that the port handled in 1932 became 1.3 million in 1938, 1.7 million in 1945, 2.3 million in 1948, and 2.9 million in 1952. The Kenya and Uganda Railway chalked up 430 million goods-ton-miles in 1939, just under 636 million in 1948.[45] The registered Kenyan labor force had bottomed out in 1932, and it doubled in the next fifteen years, as table 3.1 shows.

The course of expansion in Mombasa is difficult to chart, because the colonial state had not bothered to collect precise statistics there until faced with the realities of social problems during the war itself. The Willan Commission admitted that it had only the roughest idea how many workers there were in Mombasa, blaming the extent of the "floating" population for its uncertainty; the lack of enforcement of registration ordinances also made statistics on Mombasa poor even by Kenyan standards.[46] The Native Affairs Department thought there were about 40,000 Africans in Mombasa District in 1939, 63,000 in 1945. A variety of data from surveys, tax records, ration records, and censuses from 1945 to 1948 suggest that there were between 55,000 and 65,000 Africans in

44. Memorandum on the Labour Commission's Report by W. G. Nicol, 2 February 1940, LAB 9/1835; Manager, East African Lighterage Co. to PM, 2 February 1940, SPG 35/6A. The Port Manager, however, favored amalgamation and registration. PM to GM, 6 February 1940, ibid.

45. East Africa Statistical Department, Statistical Abstract, 1958, pp. 51, 53; EAR&H, ARs, 1949ff.; Irene S. van Dongen, The British East African Transport Complex (Chicago: University of Chicago Research Paper No. 38, 1954), pp. 81–82.

46. Willan Report, p. 60.

TABLE 3.1

REGISTERED ADULT MALE AFRICANS REPORTED IN EMPLOYMENT

(From Monthly Labour Returns)

1930	157,000
1931	141,000
1932	132,000
1933	141,000
1936	173,000
1937	183,000
1938	183,000

(From Labour Censuses)

1941	208,000
1942	247,000
1943	248,000
1944	245,000
1945	256,000
1946	248,000
1947	260,000

SOURCES: Anthony Clayton and Donald Savage, *Government and Labour in Kenya, 1895–1963* (London: Cass, 1974), p. 200; Kenya, Special Labour Censuses, 15 December 1942, 15 December 1943, 30 November 1944, 30 November 1945, 28 November 1946; African Labour Census, 28 November 1947.

Mombasa (out of around 100,000 people, including Europeans, Arabs, and Indians). About half were adult men.[47] Labor force data—significant mainly for registered or contract workers—indicate that there were 8,140 such workers in 1933, at the bottom of the Depression, and 21,000 in 1946. The Willan Commission had guessed 20,000 to 25,000 workers of all types were in Mombasa in 1939. Toward the end of the war, when the Government at last began to register casual workers, over 4,000 signed up, and when the rolls were allowed to rise to 7,000, they were filled up. One official thought that after allowing for legitimate casuals, there were another 5,000 Africans in Mombasa living on their wits. And a commission studying the labor situation in 1945 decided that there were 24,000 workers on monthly terms in the city and 4,653 registered casuals— although only an average of 1,600 or so worked each day.[48] If there were

47. Native Affairs Department, Report on Native Affairs, 1939–45 (Nairobi, 1947), p. 60; H. S. Booker and N. M. Deverell, Report on the Economic and Social Background of Mombasa Labour Dispute (cyclostyled, April 1947, copy in LAB 9/1847); *East African Economic and Statistical Bulletin* 7 (1950): table A7.

48. Karim K. Janmohamed, "African Labourers in Mombasa, c. 1895–1940," in B. A. Ogot, ed., *Hadith 5: Economic and Social History of East Africa* (Nairobi: Kenya Literature

25,000 to 30,000 adult male Africans in Mombasa by war's end, as many as a third might have been something other than regular workers. Despite the inadequate data, there is little reason to doubt officials' belief that urbanization had been rapid during the war, and that the growth of regular employment since the Depression had done nothing to diminish the irregular army of the partially employed.[49]

More workers meant more pressure on limited resources. The data for a thorough analysis of this phenomenon in Mombasa do not yet exist, but the argument that Michael Cowen and J. R. Newman make for Nairobi may apply to other cities as well.[50] The welfare of urban workers had less to do with the international terms of trade that swung against Africa after 1913 and worsened in the Depression, only to jump upward after that, than with local terms of trade. These often moved in a contrary direction. In Nairobi, the Depression lowered the price of export crops and cheapened the food products that fed urban workers. Despite wage cuts, the real income of Nairobi workers rose during the Depression. The sufferers were not so much those who worked as those who could not find a place in the diminishing labor force, and they were shunted into the already overstrained "social security" system of the Reserves. There, they were conveniently hidden from view and spread out over a wide geographic area. The crisis of the Depression was above all a rural crisis, and while tensions and disturbances occurred in various parts of Kenya, they followed distinct patterns.

These patterns were reversed during the recovery. In Kenya, a single railway linked a single port to a central city, concentrating communications facilities, administrative offices, and the workers that serviced both. The space where the most vital activities necessary to the smooth operations of commerce and government took place was located in close proximity to the places where workers lived. Residential space and work space were hard upon each other, and tensions that erupted in the one necessarily threatened to disrupt the other. In the post-Depression era, capital and the state—needing workers in the narrow channels through which all

---

Bureau, 1976), p. 161; Municipal Affairs Officer, AR, 1946, CP 106/53; Willan, p. 60; Report of Committee of Inquiry into Labour Unrest at Mombasa (Nairobi, 1945), pp. 1–2 (hereafter Phillips Committee).

49. Some Africans would have been petty traders, a category that in official eyes overlapped casual laborers and people living by their wits. The more regular positions in commerce were largely monopolized by Indians and Arabs, and the official perception of Africans as either workers or potential workers was a largely valid, if self-perpetuating, conception of society. See Karim K. Janmohamed, "A History of Mombasa, c. 1895–1939: Some Aspects of Economic and Social Life in an East African Port Town during Colonial Rule," Ph.D. diss., Northwestern University, 1977.

50. Michael Cowen and J. R. Newman, "Real Wages in Central Kenya," unpublished paper, 1975.

goods flowed—could not deal with social tensions by dissipating them across a large and complex spatial system, as they could during a depression. The ramifications of a crisis in living would be felt in and out of the workplace, in the dense spaces where workers in diverse jobs were thrown together.[51]

With recovery, the working poor of Kenya began to get poorer. Food—most of it Kenyan grown, especially maize—and housing were the crux of the matter. Officials estimated that the cost of living for Africans in Mombasa, already inflated by 1939, rose 100 percent during the war. Rents went from around Shs 5 per month for a room, to around Shs 10 or 15. Housing suffered not only from the inelasticity of supply caused by the slow process of construction, but from the fact that land for housing in Mombasa was concentrated in a few hands and limited to a few areas.[52] Food prices were sent up by the more than 40 percent expansion of the African laboring—and hence food-buying—population in Kenya: maize price controls were instituted by the state in July 1942 at a level acceptable to white settlers, rather than to the cheaper African producers who supplied much of the domestic market.[53] Imported goods were directly affected by the war: Kenya's imports of cotton piece goods in 1942 were 37 percent of their volume in 1938–39. This not only directly hurt workers, but did so indirectly as well, by rendering nearly unavailable the main commodities that African food-growers bought, and hence discouraging production.[54] One of many investigating committees concluded in October 1942, "At current prices the greatest essential of life, an adequate diet, is beyond the purses of very many lower paid Government African servants." The diets of the Railway and the Public Works Department, in particular, "do not provide the resistance to disease and the essential alertness which Government should expect from its servants."[55]

51. The problem of analyzing the spatial dimension of conflict in colonial Africa is discussed in Frederick Cooper, "Urban Space, Industrial Time, and Wage Labor in Africa," in Cooper, ed., *Struggle for the City: Capital, the State, and Migrant Labor in Africa* (Beverly Hills, Calif.: Sage, 1983), pp. 7–50.

52. Phillips Committee, p. 87; Booker and Deverell Report, p. 7; Willan Report, p. 9. A Government price index, specifically constructed for Africans in Mombasa and weighted heavily toward food, stood at 192 in October 1947, from a base of 100 in 1939 prices. Colonial Office, *Digest of Colonial Statistics* 24 (1956): 81.

53. John Lonsdale, "The Depression and the Second World War in the Transformation of Kenya," in Richard Rathbone and David Killingray, eds., *Africa and the Second World War* (London: Macmillan, 1984); Kenya, Report of the Food Shortage Commission of Inquiry, 1943, p. 24.

54. Inflation in the Colonies, 1949, CO 852/1052/1; Food Shortage Commission, pp. 23, 29–30.

55. Report of the Committee Appointed to Inquire into and Report Whether the Essentials of Life Are Beyond the Economic Capacity of Officers of the Government and the Kenya and Uganda Railways and Harbours (European, Asian and African) in the Lower Grades (Nairobi, 1942), p. 9.

The Rolling Strikes of 1942

In 1942, things were at their worst; they got somewhat better in large part because of serious agitation in Mombasa, a series of Government investigations, and pay raises. The pinch affected most workers. Casual workers in Mombasa, in fact, were not at the center of the wartime unrest, although they were never very far from the center of officials' ideas of how to solve the problems. The most likely explanation for their lack of militancy compared to 1939 is that they could work more often if they chose. Although statistics on working are scanty (see chapter 4 for a fuller discussion), the Government of Kenya considered that the market in casual labor during the war tilted toward the laborer. A shift apparently occurred during 1940, which began in Mombasa with unemployment remaining a factor and ended "approaching a labour shortage." As expanding production in the wars years continued to have its effect, the Governor feared a shortage of port labor so much that he expressed concern that new regulations designed to rationalize the casual labor system might backfire by making the workers "nervous."[56] Governors were not always so solicitous.

No matter how much the size of the labor pool reflected workers' desire to decide when to work or the pressures of competition for jobs, casual labor was highly wasteful of scarce and increasingly expensive urban space. An idle worker slept in the same sized bed as someone on the job. In 1945, during a new attempt to register casual workers, the stevedoring and shorehandling companies were each employing somewhat over eight hundred workers a day; the registered pool was then six thousand men.[57] Casuals, no matter how peaceable they might be, thus contributed to the strains that agitated monthly workers. The wartime disorders reemphasized the point that the 1939 strike had brought home: the state and capital could not avoid paying the social costs of labor.

The problem monthly laborers faced was how expensive it was to work. Wages tended to be sticky. Government policy was the main determinant of wages in the war years. The "large employers"—who absorbed two-thirds of the estimated 24,000 workers in monthly jobs in the city in 1943—were predominantly government departments. Ninety-four percent of the raw unskilled labor of the large employers in Mombasa worked for government departments. Government policy was to treat African workers as so many interchangeable units of labor power, with little dis-

---

56. Mombasa District, AR, 1940; LC, Mombasa, to PLO, 21 February 1940, LAB 9/1049; Governor Moore to Secretary of State, 16 June 1942, LAB 9/1835.

57. Report of the Warren Wright Board of Inquiry, February 1944, copy in EST 13/1/1/1. In a busier time, in August and September of 1944, an average of 1,445 and 1,723 dockers worked each day of the month, 2,187 and 2,498 on the busiest days of the two months. This still was a modest fraction of the pool. LO, Coast, to LC, 2 October 1944, LAB 9/1053.

tinction made for experienced workers and few opportunities for advancement. Thus 80 percent of the Railway's employees in Mombasa—and 77 percent of the workers for "large employers" as a whole—received Shs 40 or less per month. Only 18 percent of railwaymen and 12 percent of all workers for large employers received more than Shs 91.[58] Improving wages for monthly employees was above all a question of inducing Government departments to raise their minimum rates of pay.

The common situation of most workers contributed to the pattern of labor unrest that emerged during the 1940s: the rolling strike. This had happened at the beginning of the 1939 strike, before it became a general strike. A group of workers in a particular workplace would strike briefly, returning when managers promised to consider their demands. This would inspire another group of similarly paid workers to do the same, until the whole issue was thrown into the lap of a commission appointed by the government to reconsider wages throughout the civil service or to revise the legal minimum wage. The rumor of still wider strikes and the memory of 1939—in the atmosphere of wartime—further encouraged the anxious responsiveness of the government. As each commission sat, the Battle of the Budgets was resumed. The question of wages once again became the question of recalculating, with seeming objectivity, how much money it took to keep a single man alive.

The first flurry took place in October 1942. About two thousand railway workers in Mombasa struck for four days beginning on 15 October. The administration agreed to appoint a committee to investigate.[59] Railway workers continued to hold meetings, and officials thought that "the more unruly element" was urging further strikes. The commission, headed by Justice Lucie-Smith, worked fast: "you must be patient for a week or two," said the General Manager to his workers, and he promised that the award would be retroactive to 1 October.[60] But their decision had not yet been made when two hundred Public Works employees struck on 20 October. Although the tribunal chairman and the Acting Governor opposed putting this case before the tribunal as well, the only way officials could get the workers to return was to make a carefully hedged promise that came close to admitting that the Railway award would decide the issue for Public Works as well. Kenya, the Labour Commissioner warned, was teetering on the brink of a general strike of Government laborers.[61]

---

58. Warren Wright Report, 1944.

59. Governor to CO, 15, 18, 21 October 1942 (telegrams), CO 533/526/38091/6.

60. Speech by R. E. Robins, broadcast in English and Swahili on 20 October 1942, copy in LAB 9/1835.

61. Director of Public Works to CS, 20, 21 October 1942, and LC to CS, 22 October 1942, LAB 9/1835.

TABLE 3.2
THE LUCIE-SMITH AWARD, OCTOBER 1942

	Old Rate (Shs)	New Rate (Shs)
Basic Wage	15	15
Rations	4	6
Fuel	1	2
Housing	3	5
	23	28
War Bonus	—	5
Totals	23	33

SOURCE: Tribunal Award, 27 October 1942, LAB 9/1835.

The tribunal reported two weeks after the first strikes, and within a day the Government decided to apply it to Government monthly workers as well, fearing the consequences of not keeping up with the railway. The award reassessed the basic needs of a worker, as table 3.2 shows. The first figures under the new rate were a reassessment of preinflation needs. The tribunal then added Shs 5 as an adjustment for the wartime cost of living, bringing the minimum wage for affected employees to Shs 33. The various increments applied to all workers earning up to Shs 40, while those earning Shs 40–90 received a straight Shs 7/50 cost of living bonus, made retroactive to 1 October and with no penalty for the strike.[62] The form of the award is as interesting as the final figures: it implied that the basic worth of African labor had not changed, but that more pay had to be given; it also implied that the proper way to define wages was by objectively assessing basic needs, but that the 1939 assessment had been inadequate. Future bodies would follow the precedent of conceding wage increases at times of agitation without conceding that a concession on wages had been made.

The strikes kept rolling. At the East African Power and Light Company, 150 workers struck; at the Naval Hospital 60 to 70 workers went out; 550 military construction workers struck, as did others at the Mombasa cold storage plant and the vegetable supply board. At the Shell Oil Company works, 500 men—virtually the whole African staff—left work on 9 November. They demanded a Shs 5 bonus similar to that received by Government workers, but management was willing only to bring the lowest paid workers up to Shs 33, in effect compressing the wage scale. Management argued, however, that all Shell workers got some overtime at time and a half, so that all were above the new official minimum. These

62. Tribunal Award, 27 October 1942, and Circular Letter No. 73 from Chief Secretary, 28 October 1942, LAB 9/1835.

arguments in effect treated the Lucie-Smith minimum as something akin to a scientifically justified poverty datum line, although that term had not yet come to Kenya. The police intervened promptly in the Shell strike, arresting 300 workers on 10 November. The Director of Intelligence and Security of the police visited the strikers in jail and offered to get the charges dropped—none had been convicted yet—if they would return to work. The next day, the strike was over.[63]

Casual laborers at the KL&S Co. demanded an explanation of the wage situation, and officials feared a strike; but it did not materialize.[64] Meanwhile, the police heard rumors that workers were traveling up the railway to various stations to sound out opinions about a possible strike. Some brief strikes, involving 7 to 70 workers, had taken place among railwaymen in Nairobi on 22–23 October; the strikers soon returned to work, completed their month's contract, and signed off. More strikes followed the Mombasa railway award. The General Manager rightly feared that the line of rail would be a line of resistance and that any strike would be system-wide—such was the pattern in, most notably, the French West African railway strike of 1947.[65]

The Government had felt that something like the Mombasa award had to be extended to Nairobi, but it decided that the cost of living award should be in kind—rations—rather than cash. Railwaymen objected, holding large meetings on 11 November, a brief sit-down in front of the engineering offices, and finally a strike. On 16 November 750 railwaymen stopped work, and after being told to go back to work or lose their jobs, 80 of them signed off. At about the same time, 90 percent of the 300 or 400 railwaymen at Eldoret, far to the west, struck against the payment in kind. By the end of the day 92 workers had been discharged in Nairobi, 20 in Eldoret. The rest returned to work, and soon many of those who had signed off asked to be reinstated. They were refused. The strike had fizzled out.[66]

As the lists of discharged workers suggest, the strikers were scattered among different divisions and workshops in Nairobi and Eldoret.[67] The

63. Director of Intelligence and Security to CS, 9, 10, 12, 13, 14 November 1942, LAB 9/59; on the other strikes, see ibid., 3, 6, 7, 9 November 1942.

64. Director of Intelligence and Security to CS, 3 November 1942, LAB 9/59.

65. LO to LC, 22, 23 October 1942, LAB 9/1835; GM, Memorandum on "Wages of Native Labour," 15 October 1942, T/LAB/B1/Vol. 1, Railway Archives; Director of Intelligence and Security to CS, 4 November 1942, LAB 9/59.

66. Director of Intelligence and Security to CS, 11, 15, 16, 17, 18 November 1942, LAB 9/59; CME to GM, 12 November 1942, and LO to LC, 16 November 1942, LAB 9/1812.

67. The fired workers came from eight shops in the Chief Mechanical Engineer's division, eight sections in the NS Engineering District, and two other Engineering Districts. Engineer in Charge, NSD, NWSD, and NESD to District Engineer, 27 November 1942, CME to LC, 23 November 1942, LAB 9/1812.

other side of the diffusion of strike information in the vast railway system could have been this diffuseness of response. Instead of planning a strategy that would cripple vulnerable points in the railway system, small and scattered groups of railwaymen expressed their dislike of the way their grievances were handled. The very size and diversity of the Nairobi rail yards, compared to the simpler division of labor and geographic concentration of the docks of Mombasa, made coherent action more difficult. And the authorities in Nairobi and Eldoret showed none of the diffidence they usually did in Mombasa. A modest show of force and threats of dismissal made the workers back down. Dock-centered Mombasa and railway-centered Nairobi offered quite distinct patterns of interaction and militance among the working classes.

The rolling strikes in Mombasa which had provoked this flurry elsewhere were bracketed by a series of investigations that helped to build up the ideology of a scientific approach to the study of poverty and to wage determination, even if it took unrest to transfer the concern into the workers' pockets.[68] The "Committee to Inquire into and Report Whether the Essentials of Life are Beyond the Economic Capacity of the Officers of the Government and of the Kenya and Uganda Railway and Harbours, European, Asian and African in the Lower Grades" decided on 1 October 1942 that the essentials were beyond the African workers' means. The Committee looked at how many pounds of maize meal, salt, beans, and meat the Railway and the Public Works Department gave their workers; the Government Biochemist said this was not enough, and the "Biochemist's Diet" entered the lexicon of scientific wage determination. This diet cost Shs 12/30, as opposed to the 11/20 of the Public Works Department diet; the European and Asian diets, obviously, were not the same.[69]

Next, the "Cost of Living Relief Committee" was told to consider the above report and decide whether any particular grades of employees were being hard hit and what should be done about it. It decided that markets for food, fuel, and housing were so chaotic that such essentials should be guaranteed to the lower paid Arab and African employees and that relief should be in kind. Then the Stronach Committee was appointed to decide if the recommendations of the above committee were practical. It decided, in December 1942, that they were not. It tinkered with the amount of cash relief that should be given Government employees (railway workers had been dropped from the committee's charge).[70] As

68. The sudden growth of studies of nutrition and social welfare from the late 1930s onward would make a fascinating topic for detailed study.

69. Report in LAB 9/1835.

70. The work of all these committees is summarized in the report of the Philips Committee, p. 15.

the committees added and subtracted a shilling or two from the bio-chemist's diet or the Railway diet or from fuel and soap standards, the only committee that had any effect on workers' standard of living was the Lucie-Smith tribunal, which had deliberated in the midst of the strike wave of October. Those deliberations had been a reflection less of consid-eration of elaborate quasi-scientific requirements than of panicked necessity.[71]

In 1943 and 1944, things were calmer and the issues that riled workers the most had to do with perceived injustices in the previous settlements. Between the award of October 1942 and 1945, the lowest paid railway workers received one shilling increases in the cost of living allowance in February and again in April 1943. But higher grade employees in the same period got four bonus increments—including one given by another commission charged specifically with looking at the higher grades—total-ing between Shs 5 and Shs 11/50.[72] There were reports of agitation in the port, and in October 1943 the pointsmen at Mombasa left work briefly. They were persuaded by the Labour Officer (LO) to go back pending discussion of the bonus issue and backed down when the Railway Admin-istration refused to budge and threatened the strikers with prosecution.[73] But the Government was concerned enough to appoint yet another ad-visory board, and this one decided that "raw" migrant labor was not paid so badly considering what it was.[74] So at the beginning of 1945, the lowest paid railway workers in Mombasa were receiving wages and emoluments of Shs 35, 25 percent above the figure that the experts said represented the minimum requirements at prewar prices; housing and food had, by then, probably doubled in cost.[75]

Despite all this, 1944 was a quiet year. A brief strike of railway firemen at Mombasa over work rules was settled with the promise of an investiga-tion, and a more serious walkout at Nairobi by 130 engine drivers and firemen resulted in the firing of the strikers and the humiliation of work-

71. The Lucie-Smith tribunal saw the Essentials of Life Committee budgets but changed them around a bit. Lucie Smith to Chairman, Essentials of Life Committee, 31 October 1942, LAB 9/1835.

72. Mundy Commission, 1944; GM to Phillips, 17 April 1945, LAB 9/1813; Phillips, pp. 17–18.

73. Sr. LO, Coast, to LC, 2 October 1943; Railway Administration to Sr. LO, Coast, telegram, 2 October 1943; LO, Coast, to PC, Coast, 6 October 1943, EST 13/1/1/1.

74. Record of discussion held at Government House, Nairobi, between the General Man-ager and the Governor, 26 October 1943, EST 13/1/1/1; Meeting of Employers Advisory Committee, 8 October 1943, LAB 9/1835; Phillips, pp. 16–17.

75. During these years there was further agitation over payment in kind, especially in Nairobi, and the Railway did make some compromises, such as issuing maize meal weekly instead of monthly after the workers asked for it daily. Director of Intelligence and Security to CS, 3, 5 May 1943, LAB 9/59; Asst. CME to CME, 12 May 1943, EST 13.

ers who pleaded to get their jobs back. The social isolation of the strikers—who thought that their skill would give them power and did not act as part of an urban community or a larger body of railway employees—contributed to their defeat.[76] As the year ended, the head office of the railway sent a memorandum to all departments urging that the fired strikers not be rehired in any capacity. The officials thought that if firm action were taken, they would have peace for years to come.[77]

A Strike Movement Deflected, March 1945

The peace—and the policy of firmness—did not even last a few months. By 18 January 1945, news of the general strike in Uganda had traveled down the railroad to Nairobi and "spread throughout Kenya like wildfire."[78] Police spies reported rumors, strike notices, and a meeting in railway housing that decided to demand a substantial pay hike and threatened a strike if the demand were not met.[79] By this time, a Railway African Staff Union (RASU) based in Nairobi was coming into existence. Yet, despite the union, the agitation would take off not in Nairobi but in Mombasa.

The Nairobi-based union was largely an organization of clerical workers. The officers asked the General Manager to write the forword to their newspaper, and they hoped he would let them print his picture. Later, the GM, Reginald Robins, was to claim that the union had essentially been his idea. He wrote the Government's Chief Secretary in April 1945 that he had "put trade unionism into an active policy." Three years previously, he claimed, he had taken a "personal interest" in developing a union as a channel for grievances. He tried to get two Europeans with trade-union experience to serve as "mentors and guides."[80] But this was a retrospective view. In 1943 Robins had brushed off suggestions that a union should be organized from above with the typical comment that Africans were not ready for a union, and his response in 1945—three months before his self-congratulatory letter—to a list of grievances presented to him had been to dismiss them. The fledgling union had presented on 29 January a list of demands to the acting Welfare Officer: a raise in basic pay

76. LD, AR, 1944, p. 5; Inspector in Charge of Railway and Harbour Police to PC, Coast, 23 August 1944, PC Archives L&O 16/2; Sr. LO, Nairobi, to LC, 24, 25 August 1944, LAB 9/1812. In November, a notice addressed to employees of the Municipal Board of Mombasa was tacked to a tree, stating, in Swahili, that unless they received a bonus, they should "stop all [their] work." No stoppage occurred. Municipal Engineer to DC, 6 November 1944, LAB 9/1835.

77. Sr. LO to AgLC, 15 December 1944, LAB 9/1812.

78. Makhan Singh, *History of Kenya's Trade Union Movement to 1952* (Nairobi: East African Publishing House, 1969), p. 122.

79. Director of Intelligence and Security to CS, 31 January 1945, EST 13/1.

80. GM to AgCS, 18 April 1945, EST 13/1.

to Shs 20 in the lower grades and Shs 35 for educated workers; better rations and housing; a revised wartime cost of living bonus; and better opportunities for advancement. The strike rumors that police had picked up at this time came to naught on the alleged strike date of 1 February, and a week later, the GM had lectured a meeting of workers. He rejected outright their "petty little grievances" and told them, "I do hope that now that I have explained everything to you you will be more content and work as hard and as loyally as I know you can."[81] Neither the rejection nor the insulting language provoked further response. The railway did not have to put to use its plans to deal severely with any strike.[82]

The workers of Mombasa were not so easily cowed. RASU had come to Mombasa, but it was not the focus of militance there—indeed, it did little to organize strikes for many years. But it did give a name to the meetings of workers that took on increasing importance in Mombasa in late March of 1945. The Welfare Officer reported that a meeting he held on 9 February was supposed to have been with a RASU committee but was really a "general meeting" at which strong demands for higher wages and a bonus were put forward. By 23 March, RASU members were reportedly trying to calm meetings that "became more and more rowdy."[83] On 28 March, RASU held a meeting with the Port Manager and the Labour Officer present. A letter from the General Manager denying all demands and threatening "severe action" was read, and it produced a hostile reaction. A second meeting was held, with no Europeans present, and it led to a call for a strike in ten to twenty-one days. A further meeting was proposed, this time in the native quarter of Mombasa, so that all city workers, not just railwaymen, could be involved. The security officers believed that the casual workers of the KL&S Co. and the Municipality workers were sympathetic to strike action.[84]

The evidence of police and other informers suggests that the best paid railway workers—the running staff and skilled workers—were not sympathetic to the strike, but that nonrailway workers in the city were. Petitions from KL&S monthly workers and customs watchmen came to au-

81. GM to CME, 5 June 1943; GM to CS, 30 January 1945; Draft Statement, 7 February 1945, and Notes for Speeches, in Memorandum to African Workshops Committee, 19 February 1945, EST 13/1; Ag. Welfare Officer to GM, 29 January 1945—all in EST 13/1.

82. The prepared plan was to fire "intimidators," dock the pay of strikers, pay "loyal" workers double, and use European and Asian employees to do the Africans' work. GM, Circular, 29 January 1945, Memorandum to Governor, 31 January 1945, EST 13/1; Director of Intelligence and Security to CS, 2 February 1945, EST 13/1.

83. WO, KUR&H, to Phillips, 24 April 1945, PM to GM, 24 March 1945, EST 13/1/1/2.

84. GM to African Staff Committee, 26 March 1945; Director of Intelligence and Security to CS, 29 March 1945, EST 13/1/1/2. There were also rumors of a "passive strike" by workers of the port companies and the railway. PM to GM, 27 March 1945, ibid.

thorities. The leaders of the strike movement came mainly from Nyanza Province, from the Luo and Luhya ethnic groups. These were the core of the distant migrants who had come to Mombasa. The crucial issues were, as the initial demands and later investigations made clear, basic pay and the meager bonuses extended to the lower paid workers.[85] The Labour Department officials had, by February, become convinced that such demands were largely justified because of the increase in the cost of food, clothing, blankets, pots, and other necessities, not to mention housing. The Labour Commissioner recommended that the Mombasa basic wage for the Railway be increased from Shs 15 to Shs 18. The Railway Administration refused.[86]

But by the end of March, Government officials were near panic. The Labour Commissioner was convinced that strikes and pay increases were inevitable in any case, and that workers would get the idea that striking paid.[87] The Government decided to play a card of its own. It flew two leading chiefs from Nyanza, Paul Agoi and Amoth, to Mombasa. On 31 March they met two thousand railwaymen. They did not receive the respect due to elders. They were verbally abused and accused of being spies and of having hard hearts. The next day they tried again. Chief Amoth met with Luo; Chief Paul Agoi, with Luhya. Their report of the meeting stated that they had persuaded the workers that strikes would blacken the names of the Nyanza tribes, as the Ugandan people had blackened theirs in their recent strike and riots. The two groups then met jointly and voted unanimously not to strike but to lodge formal complaints with the Labour Officer, which the chiefs would support. The Acting Labour Commissioner thought that if the chiefs had arrived twelve hours later, the strike could not have been averted.[88]

What happened to change the tone of the second meeting? Was it merely the appeal to ethnic loyalty that the official report suggested or the concern which Luo migrants are generally known to have had with the reputation of their group? John Lonsdale—based on his studies of chiefly power, land, and labor migration in Nyanza—suggests that the pattern he uncovered for the early 1950s may well have applied earlier: the chiefs could have issued a threat, veiled or otherwise. In the changing system of land allocation, chiefs had great influence on land rights back home, and the long-term migrants who worked on the railway were vulnerable to the

85. Director of Intelligence and Security to CS, 29, 31 March 1945, EST 13/1/1/2; LO, Coast, to LC, 27 March 1945, LAB 9/1812; Phillips, p. 10.

86. Memorandum of meeting of CS, GM, and LC, Nairobi, 10 February 1945, AgLC to CS, 6 February 1945, GM to CS, 9 February 1945, EST 13/1.

87. AgLC to CS, 27 March 1945, EST 13/1.

88. Verbal report made by Chiefs Paul Agoi and Amoth, 5 April 1945, incl. AgLC to GM, 23 April 1945, EST 13/1/1/2; AgLC to Air Officer, Nairobi, 16 April 1945, LAB 9/1835.

possibility that the security and income for which they were working could be jeopardized behind their backs.[89] Perhaps that is why the two private meetings with Luo and Luhya workers had such a dramatic effect.

Be that as it may, the response to the chiefs suggests that the activism of workers must be interpreted in terms of the total configuration—rural and urban—in which their economic lives took place. This multidimensional life is no a priori reason for them to be quiescent or militant, but the forces that might inspire them to act or constrain them from challenging authority need to be understood in relation to the entire social field. In addition to the possibility that migrants from western Kenya had to worry about how their actions in Mombasa might affect their farms back home, the urban milieu of which they became a part also shaped responses to common deprivations. In Nairobi, responses to the strains of urban living in 1945 and to the stimulus of the Uganda strike died abruptly. In Mombasa, workers' responses grew over two months. Mombasa's railwaymen had already seen a general strike spread from small beginnings in government departments to the docks and then throughout the city, and when they began some actions of their own, they saw them roll through the close quarters of the urban working class. Yet, largely because most railwaymen lived in Railway housing, they were more isolated than other workers in Mombasa, and they were vulnerable to threats that applied to them specifically: the usual danger of being fired, the possible loss of housing and therefore of all access to urban jobs, and the sanctions associated with their migrancy. In Nairobi, the vast railway housing estates were more isolating still; the working-class culture of the city was less defined and interconnected; and the railway strikes that had taken place were limited to specific points within the complex railway division of labor.[90] But even in Mombasa, the near strike of 1945 was to be the high point of railway militance for over a decade; the true strength of the working class lay not in the railway quarters but in Majengo.

The separation of the two cities is clearest of all when it comes to the official reaction. There was no hesitancy to the Administration's response

89. John Lonsdale, personal communication. Dr. Lonsdale emphasizes that this is a hypothesis to be tested. In any case, the relationship between labor history in Mombasa and social structures in other parts of Kenya remains a fascinating subject for further investigations.

90. The differences between the working classes of the two towns are clearest if one compares the general strikes in Mombasa in 1947 and Nairobi in 1950: the former was solid and successful; the later, not. The single body of workers with greatest potential impact in the two cities—dockers in Mombasa, railwaymen in Nairobi—showed contrasting tendencies: the dockers were effective strikers; the railwaymen, divided and weak. The extremely militant Nairobi "crowd" of Kikuyu squatters and ex-squatters could in fact be separated from the regular workers.

to the stirrings in Nairobi. But in Mombasa, the Government did not feel so much in control: they called it a "native town."[91] Officials, above all, feared that they would face, not a railway strike alone, but a mass urban movement. Hence the effort to detach the largely Luo and Luhya railwaymen from other workers, especially the coastal dockers. Hence, too, the Labour Department's eagerness to make concessions.

The workers quickly followed up their decision not to strike by submitting their demands, as the chiefs had encouraged them to do: payment of war bonuses that had gone only to Europeans and Asians; cost of living raises to match rising expenses; and higher allowances for housing, fuel, and water.[92] The chiefs had already made good on their promise to state officially their view that "there was a real basis in the complaint of low wages."[93] The Government response was as typical of Mombasa as firing strikers was of Nairobi: on 13 April, the Labour Commissioner appointed a committee under Arthur Phillips, a Crown Counsel. Its mandate was not only to ask whether wages and emoluments were adequate, but to make a broader investigation of the "position of the unskilled staff of the Railway at Mombasa," and to inquire into the "causes of the present African labour unrest in Mombasa." The Committee's work turned out to be a new departure in commissioned thinking, and the Government paid it the honor of suppressing its report.[94]

Even before it had pondered these questions, the Phillips Committee recommended an immediate cash increase of Shs 5 in the minimum gross wage, bringing the railway minimum to Shs 35 exclusive of housing.[95] It added that its findings were equally applicable to other employees in Mombasa. Meanwhile, it began to study the still largely unexamined mass of labor power that the railway had bought. The report reflected the earlier stress on minimum budgets and drew on a growing body of social research in South Africa that put the "poverty datum line" on a seemingly more scientific basis.[96]

But, for the first time, the Committee took note that workers not only

91. Explaining why the 1930 casual labor rules were not being enforced in Nairobi, the District Commissioner noted, "conditions in Mombasa and Nairobi are quite dissimilar. Mombasa is an old Arab and Native town." DC to Chief Registrar of Natives, 17 June 1938, LAB 9/1049. The Labour Commissioner in 1944 again invoked the phrase "native town" to explain why registration did not work there. Labour Review, 15 February 1944, CO 822/117/7.

92. A. A. Kinywa, Secretary to RASU, Mombasa Branch, to Governor, 4 April 1945, EST 13/1/1/2.

93. Phillips Report, p. 9.

94. Ibid., p. 1; AgLC to CS, 22 August 1945, LAB 9/1838.

95. Phillips, pp. 46–48.

96. The leading light on these studies was Edward Batson of the University of Cape Town, and he is much cited in the Phillips Report, especially on pp. 23–27.

had stomachs but lived in societies. The Government had to face, the Committee concluded, the "Emergence of [an] Urbanized Working Class."[97]

The state had not been trying to create such a class, but that class had brought itself to the city. The Committee discovered that over half the workers earning *less* than Shs 43 had been employed for over two years. In the largest department, over 10 percent of all African laborers had worked there for over ten years, 20 percent for over five. Moreover, nearly 80 percent of the lower-paid staff were married, and about two-thirds of them had their wives in Mombasa.[98] All this meant the single-male basis of all the complex budget calculations that had been made had little bearing on reality.

Most important was the Committee's recognition of a direction in the working man's life. The "raw migrant" had assumed exaggerated importance in policymakers' eyes, but even he came to want more than to meet day-to-day needs. The unskilled were experiencing a growing desire for a "civilized standard of living." One worker had told the Committee what lay at the root of the labor problem: "there is no *faida* [profit] in working these days." All a man's earnings went to obtain a bare subsistence. The expression is similar to one used in South Africa—working for *boroko,* for a place to sleep and no more.[99]

Hence, this Committee's focus at last shifted from the level of the minimum—although it went over that yet again—to the fact that most workers were bunched close to that minimum and had few opportunities to go beyond it. As the Labour Commissioner had noted earlier, the railway's policy of not giving increments in basic wages as workers acquired experience "will condemn its unskilled staff to a completely celibate life."[100] On the General Manager's copy of this letter in the railway archives, "Nonsense" is scrawled in the margin at this point. The General Manager, or whoever did the scrawling, had reason to be defensive.

The perspective that the Committee was just beginning to understand, that work had to be examined over the worker's life-cycle, was critical. The long-distance, long-term migrants—frequently Luo or Luhya—who were concentrated in railway work in Mombasa labored to accumulate, be it to marry, to acquire capital for farming, or to set up a household in Mombasa.[101] The crisis of faida that had been described to the Commit-

97. Ibid., p. 49.
98. Ibid., pp. 53, 65.
99. Ibid., pp. 38, 52; Marion Lacey, *Working for Boroko: The Origins of a Coercive Labour System in South Africa* (Johannesburg: Ravan, 1981).
100. Phillips, pp. 52, 53; AgLC to CS, 6 February 1945, EST 13/1.
101. The raw migrant, in the Committee's view, was more likely to be a Kamba. Phillips, p. 52.

tee was not just a subsistence crisis. After six years of inflation, the long-term migrants had little to show for their labors. Perhaps that is why the relatively long-term workers of the railway—as opposed to, say, the Municipality workers—were so crucial in 1945, compared to the 1939 and 1942 crises, when the question of merely getting through the month or even the day was the focal point. But the possible vulnerability of Nyanza workers to threats to land showed that the accumulation process was one that crossed the rural-urban divide: the anger of frustration and the caution of vulnerability were equally parts of the workers' individual and collective struggles. The frustration thus threw the ever-so-slightly better-paid worker in with the worker earning the basic wage, and the Committee recognized that "different classes of African workers" were facing very similar situations. All of them, in turn, compared their long-range and immediate possibilities to Europeans and Asians. The Phillips Committee thus saw in Mombasa "the beginnings of class-consciousness, complicated by race-consciousness."[102]

This added up to a strong indictment of the basis of Kenyan labor policy. What the Committee called "the system of 'cheap' Migrant Labour" was actually not so cheap. Migrant labor, the Committee decided, was linked to inefficiency. Malnutrition—arising from rural as well as urban impoverishment—sapped workers' strength. Meanwhile, with workers moving into and out of jobs, the "'sanction of the Sack' is largely inoperative."[103] For these reasons the Committee thought that productivity was declining, but it had only impressionistic evidence for this, and the productivity issue, raised only briefly in the report, did not then seem central.

What was crucial was the instability of urban society that had led to the Committee's appointment in the first place. Workers were not living like migrants; they were merely being paid like migrants. In the vocabulary of the day, they were defined not by what they were becoming in the city but by their having left mechanisms of control characteristic of traditional Africa—they were the "detribalized natives." But Phillips, at last, saw beyond the laments for rural Africa that this phrase usually evoked: "There seems to be no escaping the fact that the evils which are commonly attributed to 'detribalisation' can only be cured by more complete detribalisation."[104]

If there was to be an alternative to such detribalization, it could only be a more systematic reliance on a migrant labor policy—a "bachelor compound system,"[105] with repatriation of all but those male workers actually

102. Ibid., p. 43.
103. Ibid., pp. 56–57.
104. Ibid., p. 50.
105. Ibid., p. 98.

on the job. In a broad sense, these were the two options that the South African government pondered during the 1940s, opting for the latter after the election of 1948, and turning the pass laws, urban residency rules, and labor recruitment systems that had deliberately been allowed to develop leaks into a basis for draconian regulations of migration.[106] But, as we shall see below, such a choice was beyond the capability of the Kenyan state, especially in the open environment of Mombasa. And repatriation would have placed an enormous burden on rural reserves, which were already strained. The reproduction of an urban work force through migration, as the Phillips Committee recognized, was unlikely to continue to deliver up workers in good enough health to work.[107]

Stabilization of the urban work force had been thrust upon the state and the employers. The workers were in the city, and they were staying there, and more of their families were coming to join them—they had already presented the state with a fait accompli. The Phillips Committee believed that the state should seize the initiative and move toward the payment of wages sufficient to support families, build increments and incentives into the wage structure, and build on the growing and self-propelled socialization of Africans into "civilized" ways. "The more decent and progressive elements" in the work force, it argued, should be given a "reasonable standard of living and opportunity for a civilized life."[108]

Even though the Labour Department's thinking had influenced Phillips, this part of the report was considered too "contentious" to be released.[109] The concrete result of the Committee's efforts was its interim report—a wage increase to Shs 35 (40 with housing) extended to the major government employers and, voluntarily, to the major private employers.[110] In lieu of acting or acknowledging the more far-reaching results of the report, the Government commissioned a report on the report, and this report in turn recommended another report, this one to be written on the basis of a social survey. The report on Phillips came out of the growing South African school of social work and carried even further the tendency to turn class struggle into the scientific determination of nutritional and social norms.[111]

---

106. Stanley Greenberg, *Race and State in Capitalist Development* (New Haven: Yale University Press, 1980).

107. Phillips, pp. 58, 97.

108. Ibid., p. 97.

109. AgLC to CS, 22 August 1945, LAB 9/1838. This file itself is filled with memoranda from the Labour Commissioner to Phillips, suggesting how closely integrated was the thinking of the two.

110. Phillips; Ag LC to CS, 7 July 1945, LAB 9/1838.

111. This serious purpose was carried so far that learned social scientists pondered how much the average African worker should be spending on underwear. See Leo Silberman,

The author, Professor Silberman, insisted on the importance of the social: "Africans do not live by posho [corn meal gruel] alone." He, too, noted that a "consciousness of class is springing up," and he agreed with Phillips that poverty was especially dangerous when it was a general and inescapable condition: "Africans are less and less willing to be lumped pell mell into substandard groups of remuneration and *made to remain there.* Very keen interest is taken in *advancement* possibilities."[112] The most significant aspect of this sequence of reports was the elaboration of the still "contentious" point that social needs had to include change over a lifetime, and that these needs had to become part of state policy and reconciled with the profitability of industry. But the first Mombasa-wide survey on which this assessment of needs depended was only done—unsatisfactorily according to officials—in 1947 and more satisfactorily in 1958, by which time massive strikes and the growth of trade unionism and collective bargaining had diminished the relevance of "scientifically" determined wage structures.

Much of this discussion of families, nutrition, and civilization was far removed from the reactive, ad hoc manner in which Africans were actually given wage adjustments at the time. Silberman, nonetheless, got back to the crucial concern with disorder:

> Often the true seat of trouble is not where it manifests itself most vociferously, and dock labour with all its irregular and violent habits which spring from the instability and irregularity of its employment conditions may still form the "hard core" of the Mombasa problems, or at any rate continue to be a disturbing element, an uneasy substratum, too wretched to take the initiative itself but always there, ready to join in other people's fights, and counted on as an ally in the fray.[113]

The monitors of social order had returned to casual labor, which embodied in extreme form all the dangers of poverty and uncivilized behavior intrinsic to the indictment of all forms of migrant labor. The Phillips and Wright reports had also prodded the Government to think about implementing the Willan Commission recommendations of 1939 on decasualization, but they had not dwelled on the point, and Phillips noted— although without hard data on how often casuals worked—that dockworkers in 1945 could earn fairly decent monthly incomes by working often. But whatever casual workers were doing, they seemed to undermine the reforms that were being contemplated for other workers,

---

Brief Comments on certain sections of the Phillips Report on Labour Unrest in Mombasa (Nairobi, 1946), p. 21.

112. Ibid., pp. 3, 4. Emphasis in original.

113. Ibid., p. 3.

whether in the workplace or in housing, which were intended to create a stable and civilized urban work force. As Phillips put it, some control over nonworkers was essential "for the purpose of assisting and protecting the existing body of African workers who are in process of becoming stabilised."[114]

Reactions: Casual Labor and Urban Expulsions

The Government had already begun to act, although in ways that avoided the opposition of the stevedoring companies and the railway to changing the structure of employment, but which conveyed the illusion, at least, of doing something about the urban rabble. Wartime anxieties, the long-time worry about urban unrest, a belief that too many people were in Nairobi and Mombasa, and concern that conscripts for war services were hiding in the urban morass led in 1944 to the use of the Defense (Limitation of Labour) Regulations to expel unemployed and idle workers. In Nairobi, where the kipande system was used more or less rigorously, this was a clear enough proposition, even if its implementation was arbitrary and far from thorough: between May and December of 1944, 2,968 people were dealt with, half of whom were sent to their rural homes, while most of the rest were conscripted or directed into an approved occupation. But in Mombasa, where the vitally needed casual workers were indistinguishable from the idlers and stiffs, only voluntary repatriations—when someone wanted a ride home—could be carried out.[115] While such measures as restricting travel into Coast Province and requiring Africans who were unemployed for more than forty-eight hours to report to the Labour Office could be proclaimed, they could not be implemented without registering "legitimate" casuals.[116]

This chain of reasoning, based not on a concern with or analysis of conditions of dockwork but on fears of the idle and the uncontrolled urban population, led at last to registration. Under the regulations, it became illegal for a worker to take a casual job or for an employer to offer one without the worker being registered. The registration officer was given the authority to exclude anyone not already domiciled in the District if he determined that the number of casuals already registered exceeded the "needs of the essential services in the Municipality." He could also exclude anyone who did not seem like "a bona fide casual labourer" or who had been convicted of vagrancy or violations of the casual labor regulations. Violators were subject to a fine of £5 or a month in jail.

114. Phillips, pp. 39, 92.
115. LD, AR, 1944, pp. 8–9; Warren Wright Report; LC, Labour Review, 15 February 1944, CO 822/117/7.
116. LO, Coast, to LC, 21 October 1944, LAB 9/1053.

Officials began to register casuals in August 1944, and as the number signed up passed 4,000 in October, orders went out to enforce the rules in November. Employers of casuals had to register and could only hire registered casuals. The unregistered could then be repatriated, and kipandes could be required. By 11 November, 5,276 Africans and 415 Arabs were registered.[117]

Yet even as this large new step was being planned, the Labour Department was anxious about the feelings of the casual workers. The Labour Officer for the Coast asked the District Commissioner of Kilifi to refrain from conscripting people from his district who were living in Mombasa, lest he drive away the dockworkers who came from Kilifi District. Only when registration was complete would the unregistered be fair game.[118] The pool was supposed to reach a maximum of 6,000—the average number of port casuals at work on any day had been 1,445 in August and 1,723 in September, and on the busiest days, 2,187 and 2,498, respectively, had worked, plus perhaps 1,000 casuals elsewhere in the city.[119]

Casual laborers were duly registered without incident, and officials were then able to go after anyone not registered as a casual or permanent worker. Use was made of rules restricting African travel to the coast and requiring new arrivals to report to the Labour Officer within forty-eight hours of arrival. The Labour Department was able to repatriate 1,300 Africans in 1945, compared to 4,390 in Nairobi. The District Commissioner reported in 1945, "Mombasa's reputation as a workers' and loafers' paradise soon lost currency, and a steady exodus was noticeable toward the end of the year, to the benefit of the indigenous inhabitants."[120]

In fact, the procedures were as leaky as a sieve, and they did not change the process of hiring or working processes on the docks, except to limit the pool. Two or three men had to be allowed to stay in Mombasa for every job—let alone those who stayed on their own initiative. Actually, officials allowed the pool to reach 7,200 in July 1945, and, even so, experienced occasional shortages of port labor in the first part of the year. They then cut the pool down to 4,152 at year's end by requiring everyone to reregister. Only in May 1945 did officials begin to record job performance. The data revealed that defining legitimate casual laborers was not the same as getting them to work steadily. In the second half of 1945, only 257 men worked more than twenty days per month; 2,656 worked under

117. The Defence (Casual Labour, Mombasa) Regulations, 1944, *Kenya Government Gazette* 23 (24 July 1944): 196–98; LO, Coast, to LC, 21 October 1944, AgLC to Information Officer, 25 October 1944, LO to LC, 28 October, 6, 17 November 1944, LAB 9/1053.

118. LO, Coast, to PC, 17 May 1944, LAB 9/1053.

119. LO, Coast, to LC, 2 October, 1944, LAB 9/1053. See also Warren Wright report.

120. LD, AR, 1945, p. 15; Mombasa District, AR, 1944, 1945.

fifteen. December's reduced pool was still 2.6 times the average number of workers called on during the month and 1.5 times the number employed on the busiest day.[121]

The companies, however, continued to oppose any measures that affected their control of work. The most they would do would be to hire within a pool large enough to cover peak demands and therefore requiring many idle hands during normal times. The solution to the social problem of the city, the Railway's General Manager suggested, was to provide more housing, and not necessarily at the employers' expense. As before, the port employers did not want to pay for labor time when ships were not being unloaded or for the social costs of a permanent labor force.[122] As the war ended, Labour Department officials held before the employers—as other officials had when the war began—the spectre of disorder created by "this large floating population of casual labour."[123] Only more disorder and more pressure on performance would push the port employers to make more serious efforts to alter patterns of work in the port.

The General Strike of 1947

The workers of Mombasa, the Labour Department thought, were content with the raises they had obtained from the Interim Report of the Phillips Committee. Between the middle of 1945 and the end of 1946 relative calm reigned.[124] Crane drivers—fairly well-paid workers employed by the Railway—threatened a strike over the slow rate at which increments were given, but they were forced to back down by threats of dismissal. Workers in one government department stopped work briefly to demand the dismissal of an overseer, but they too backed down.[125] But by December 1946, rumors of labor trouble in Mombasa were heard anew. The Port Manager and the Director of the KL&S Co. both accorded them considerable legitimacy—as well as fear—arguing that a wage increase

121. Mombasa District, AR, 1945; LO to LC, 27 February 1946, LAB 9/1053.

122. LD, AR, 1944, p. 2; GM to CS, 17 October 1945, LAB 2/128; Labour Department, Memorandum, "Casual Labour—Mombasa Port," n.d., 1945, ibid.

123. LC to CS, 29 September 1945, LAB 2/128; Minute 29/45 of Labour Advisory Board, 1945, ibid.

124. LC to CS, 10 November 1945, LAB 9/1838. The Attorney General told the Legislative Council after the general strike, "At the beginning of January of this year the labour position in Mombasa appeared to be calmer and more satisfactory than had been the case for a considerable time. . . ." Legislative Council Debates, 28 January 1947, c. 807.

125. Petition to GM, 18 September 1946; District Locomotive Superintendent to CME, 10 October 1946, GM to CME, 2 November 1946, EST 9/9/2I; Appendix VII, p. 7, to draft LD, AR, 1946, LAB 5/21.

should be given before a strike so that workers would not get the idea, if they did not have it already, that strikes paid.[126] The workers did not get a raise, and the employers got a strike.

Rumors of labor trouble stepped up in early January, and the promulgation in Nairobi on 9 January of a minimum-wage ordinance for Mombasa, effective on 1 February, was too little too late. The Shs 40 per month minimum, with deductions if the employer paid for housing or rations, did not affect casuals or the large number of workers already bunched near that wage figure.[127] At about the same time, news of a wage increase following a dock strike in Durban, South Africa, had made its way up the coast and, officials thought, inspired workers in Mombasa.[128]

On 7 January, workers from the port, railway, Municipality, and Public Works Department held the first of the many mass meetings that were to be the central organizational focus of the general strike. About three thousand workers attended. The Port Manager believed that employees of the KL&S Co. were taking the lead in urging a strike for 12 January. The still fledgling railway union—RASU—met in the Railway Institute in Shimanzi (in the railway complex), and the crane drivers took a militant stance, as they were to do repeatedly in ensuing years. The Labour Commissioner, attending the meeting, listened to the grievances and pled for calm. "The RASU," wrote the Port Manager, "were undoubtedly talked over to the side of law and order, but I am dubious of their hold on the mass of the employees."[129]

Over the weekend of 11–12 January, the Labour Commissioner addressed six meetings with workers, including one with 150 "representatives" of the workers. He brought with him Mr. Osgathorp, the Staff and Welfare Assistant of KUR&H, an experienced trade unionist from England, and promised that Osgathorp would assist RASU in its organizing and would help the recently formed committee of KL&S Co. staff—largely clerical—to form a legal trade union. At these meetings, the Commissioner tried to stress the progress that had been made toward improv-

126. PM to Baldwin of KURH, 3 December 1946; Director KL&S Co. to GM, 2 December 1946, HBR 12/8/3.
127. The Minimum Wage (Mombasa Island) Order, 1946, *Kenya Government Gazette* 26 (9 January 1946): 12.
128. PM to GM, 7 January 1947, EST 13/1/1/3.
129. PM to GM, 8, 11 January 1947, EST 13/1/1/3. Perhaps typical of the tenor of these meetings was the railway meeting in which an Engineering Department employee, Paul Ouma, spoke, claiming that railwaymen were against a strike but wanted something done about their pay, which was not enough to support a family. The officials present promptly challenged him to produce a family budget and made hay over the fact that he could not. Other employees present, however, supported Ouma's argument. Notes of the Meeting in Railway African Institute between Welfare Officer, LO, and one thousand Africans, 8 January 1947, ibid.

ing labor conditions and steps that would be taken. As far as officials could tell from these meetings, their efforts with workers' "representatives" paid off: the representatives said they would advise against a strike.[130]

But at the critical mass meeting on Sunday, the PC later reported, the workers "decided at instance [sic] of the hooligan element not to support their own representatives, whose advice it had been that the men should not go on strike."[131] The strike began on Monday, 13 January, and quickly "paralyzed work at the docks and on the Railway and practically all hotels, offices, banks and private houses are without African servants." Some 15,000 workers were thought to be involved—out of a total work force in Mombasa estimated at over 20,000.[132] The strikers included monthly employees and casuals and even the most atomized of employees—domestic servants and Africans who performed odd jobs. A participant recalled seeing a European try to get an African to carry his luggage, but even a high tip failed to get any response. He went on, "At Changamwe we saw an African askari [policeman] who was in his uniform. He had gone to buy some meat. When people saw him in uniform, they got so annoyed that he went home and removed his uniform. Even the tembo-tappers joined the strike."[133] Ethnic associations became involved in calling out their members: testimony suggests that the Taita Union and Meru Association struck in some kind of collective way. Taxi drivers drove people around Majengo to spread the word.[134] The mass meetings of groups of regular workers in the port, railway, and government departments thus sent calls for action via a variety of social linkages throughout the city. The strike was not just a phenomenon of the workplace, but of Majengo as well.

The strike was also a regional phenomenon, as the rural connection of many of Mombasa's coastal workers spread the word that important events were taking place. This was particularly true on the coast of Kenya to the south of Mombasa, the home of Digo people, who were numerous among dockworkers. Between 15 and 18 January, a serious strike took

130. See the account of these efforts given by Attorney General Foster Sutton in Legislative Council Debates, 28 January 1947, cc. 808–09. See also EAS, weekly ed., 17 January 1947.

131. Reported in EAS, weekly ed., 17 January 1947.

132. EAS, 14 January 1947; Singh, p. 141.

133. Interview with Bwana Musa Juma, a clerk, cited in Karim Janmohamed, "Labour Protest in Mombasa," staff seminar paper, Department of History, University of Nairobi, 1979, p. 13. Tembo is palm wine, obtained by tapping coconut trees.

134. Testimony of Andrew Kuba, Secretary of Taita Union, Mtwathamia, President of Meru Association, and James Ombugwa Kinanga to deportation hearing of Chege Kibachia, 5 September 1947, CO 537/2109, pp. 71–72, 76, 81; Anthony Clayton and Donald Savage, Government and Labour in Kenya, 1895–1963 (London: Cass, 1974), p. 277.

place at the Kenya Sugar Company, Ltd., plantation at Ramisi. There was violence and twenty-seven arrests. Shorter strikes took place at the Gazi Sisal Estate and among Public Works Department road laborers. North of Mombasa, an important ferry on the coast road was shut down by workers for some days, and a second ferry was shut more briefly. At two sisal estates, workers struck but were persuaded to call off their strikes by the District Commissioner.[135]

The railway union sat out the strike; its President later called it "foolishness."[136] The KL&S Co. staff association, founded two years earlier, was more active, although its membership was largely clerical and its leaders were later fired for their pains.[137] Neither of these organizations was important to the strike: planned at mass meetings in the railway and port area and spread along the dense and interconnected social networks of Mombasa's workers, the focus of the strike shifted back to the mass meeting but away from the port-railway locus.

On the second day of the strike, a crowd of some ten thousand people, in the DC's estimate, assembled in a soccer field next to the Sakina mosque, on the road connecting the center of the city with the causeway to the mainland on the edge of Majengo. The field was renamed Kiwanja cha Maskini—the Field of the Poor—and it became the organizational hub of the strike and its most powerful symbol. That day the DC was allowed to speak to the assembled crowd: he told them that he would not discuss their grievances and that their strike was illegal. His words were received in silence.[138]

Each day, workers assembled in the Kinwanja cha Maskini. Later testimony described an open, democratic atmosphere. A witness said he "never saw anyone telling people what to do." Anyone could speak.[139] People also brought cassava, potatoes, and bananas from their own nearby farms to the Kiwanja. Others, such as Digo or Giriama who lived farther away, sold crops and brought cash to buy maize. People cooked together in the

135. Digo District, AR, 1947; Kilifi District, AR, 1947; Coast Province, AR, 1947. These connections suggest that researchers in various rural parts of the coast might learn much about work, labor organizing, and work culture in Mombasa as part of studies of rural political economy.

136. Simeon Nguru, President of RASU, to 3d Annual Conference, Kampala, 11 June 1947, EST 26/1.

137. See the list of people fired in LO, Coast, to LC, 28 January 1947, LAB 9/1836. The KL&S Co. first claimed that it was firing these strikers for bad work, but gave up this explanation after hard questioning from the Thacker Tribunal. Testimony of Tomwero Tumuyunja and J. Stephens to Thacker, 28 February 1947, LAB 5/29, pp. 5–6.

138. P. F. Foster, DC, Testimony to deportation hearing for Chege Kibachia, transcript in CO 537/2109, pp. 5–6.

139. William Kihege (a Kamba bakery worker) to Kibachia hearing, p. 79; Garrison Mwangi (a Kikuyu Christian), p. 89.

field, while others went to their homes to use their rural resources so that others could hold out for longer in the city.[140] Indeed, in interviews with people who were young workers or students in Mombasa at the time, the Kiwanja cha Maskini is the focus of memory:

> I was very young in those days. I used to go there just to see what people were doing. . . . And the assembly of the people made them contact various groups there, because the railway workers would come, municipal workers would come, those working in separate firms also came, so sort of communication was there. . . . But the fact that people are assembling at a certain place, say today one hundred people; tomorrow everyone went and told his colleagues that we have met. Eventually people came together.[141]

On the third day of the strike, the assembly was addressed by Chege Kibachia, an educated Kikuyu for whom this speech represented the debut of a brief but important career as a labor and political leader. He told the crowd not to attack Europeans or Indians or women and children of any race. When he was later detained and tried, the judge was to make much of the fact that he had not spoken against the intimidation of adult male Africans.[142] Several days later the DC came to the Kiwanja with some policemen and found five to six thousand people sitting in an open circle around twelve African men in two rows. The men's heads were shaven in "fantastic shapes," as two men with razors kept up the job of humiliating accused scabs. The barbers were arrested.[143]

This act of intimidation was carefully orchestrated—an African eyewitness referred to the proceedings as a "tribunal."[144] British officials claimed as well that gangs of twenty to thirty strikers had made the rounds of homes and businesses, removing employees who were at work. In concluding that a "systematic plan of intimidation" existed, the Secretary of

140. Interviews with Hussein Ramadan (a Digo), who worked for Shell at the time of the strike and is now staff officer of Kenya Cargo Handling Service (KCHS), and Mohamed Shallo (a Somali), welfare officer for KCHS. See also Kerstin Leitner, "The First General Strike in Mombasa (January 1947)," paper presented to the meeting of the Historical Association of Kenya, 1972, p. 4. Another important topic for research would be the role of women in the strike, a theme brilliantly developed in Sembene Ousmanne's novel of the French West African railway strike of 1947–48, God's Bits of Wood, trans. Francis Price (London: Heinemann, 1981).

141. Interview, Salim Ferunzi, now Director of Social Services and Housing, Mombasa. These themes are also stressed in the interviews with Hussein Ramadan and Mohamed Shallo.

142. Chege Kibachia, testimony, pp. 49–51; T. D. W. Bartley, Judge, H.M.'s Supreme Court, Coast, to Ag. Governor, 11 September 1947, CO 537/2109.

143. DC, testimony, pp. 5–6.

144. Interview: Mohamed Shallo.

State for the Colonies was perhaps giving the strikers more of a compliment than he intended. No one died during the strike; nor were there serious injuries, a record British police forces in Africa were often unable to equal in the volatile atmosphere of mass unrest.[145] One of the most important African members of the administrative service in Mombasa, Henry Gibson Shadrack Harrison, Assistant Municipal African Affairs Officer, testified that he had witnessed crowds stopping people from working and slapping, punching, and pushing around nonstrikers. He himself had given a speech at the Kiwanja cha Maskini telling the strikers that they should go back to work. The crowd had yelled at him and closed in, but he had been protected by the leaders and taken to his house. Harrison was not too shaken by the event to return regularly to Kiwanja cha Maskini for the Sunday meetings of the African Workers Federation after the strike.[146]

Some unlikely sources were more complimentary. The President of the Chamber of Commerce of Mombasa testified that "the behavior of the strikers [was] exemplary." The South African publicity office in Kenya concluded that "despite all their limitations, and given the necessary leadership, East African Natives are today able to hold a strike in a most efficient and comprehensive way." The District Commissioner thought that the strike was "well-organized and comparatively free from serious unpleasant incidents and it must be admitted that it took the Island by surprise."[147]

Perhaps other Europeans were upset less by the disorderliness of the strike than by the fact that its order emerged outside of established institutions. The Port Manager thought that the entire city during the strike acquired "a very alien look about it. We had a 'New Government,' we had 'People's Courts,' and we had all the town burglars acting as policemen and calling themselves police askaris." But the East African Standard in the midst of the strike revealed most clearly of all how the stereotypic language used to describe the seeming disorder of Outcast Mombasa precluded any serious probing of an alternative order. It was convinced that the strike was being orchestrated from above and noted

> the cautious way in which the leaders keep safely in the background pushing minor figures forward to do their work, surrounding themselves by a gang of idle roughs who call themselves their askaris. These roughs are drawn from the many loafers who are always to be

145. Arthur Creech Jones to Rev. R. W. Sorensen, MP, 7 March 1947, FCB 115/3.
146. Testimony to Kibachia hearing, pp. 14–15.
147. G. Coventry, testimony to Thacker Tribunal, 20 February 1947, LAB 5/28, p. 171; "East African Background," Public Relations, South Africa Office, Nairobi, copy in LAB 9/1836; Mombasa District, AR, 1947.

found in Mombasa and who very rarely do any work, and they are used in an attempt to intimidate the law abiding peaceful African who form the great majority of the population."[148]

But though the newspaper editors knew just who the enforcers must be, they did not have any idea who the leaders were. Some officials defined leadership in ethnic terms: Kikuyu from Nairobi provided the brains of the strike; "Kavirondo," the brawn.[149] Retrospectively, a particular Kikuyu, Chege Kibachia, emerged as the prime candidate for leadership, as a personification of the idea that inchoate masses can act coherently only if led, much the role assigned a few years later to Jomo Kenyatta when an explanation for the Mau Mau Emergency was required. Kibachia had appeared at Kiwanja cha Maskini on the third day of the strike, and, more importantly, he emerged after its conclusion as the prime figure in the African Workers Federation, an organization that came to symbolize to officials the dangers of an organized mass. The DC of Mombasa, after the strike, insisted that the AWF had led the strike and that Kibachia led the AWF, but at Kibachia's deportation hearing he had to admit that neither the AWF nor Kibachia had committed any criminal offense and that "I have no sure knowledge that Chege or the Federation organized the strike." Some scholars, however, have followed the DC in asserting that Kibachia must have provided the leadership that transformed inarticulate grievances into concerted and effective action.[150]

This argument may confuse cause and effect. The evidence suggests that the AWF emerged from the strike, not that it led it. As in 1939, the density of social connection among workers in diverse workplaces in Mombasa—organizing themselves, at the critical time, in daily mass meetings—emerges through the cloud of official incomprehension as the most basic ingredient of planning and coordination. The AWF later became the embodiment of the spirit of Kiwanja cha Maskini. One informant, in fact, called an organization that is clearly the AWF by the name "Chama cha Maskini," the union of the poor.[151]

Kibachia was twenty-eight years old at the time. He had attended the most prestigious African secondary school in Kenya, Alliance High School, and there he had met Eliud Wamba Mathu, who in 1944 became

148. PM, Testimony to Thacker Tribunal, 27 February 1947, LAB 5–29, p. 3; EAS, weekly ed., 24 January 1947.

149. Mombasa District, AR, 1947; Coast Province, AR, 1947.

150. Hearing, pp. 6–8, 9; Clayton and Savage, p. 276. Some years later, Kibachia gave himself a central role in the story of the strike. See the passages based on interviews with Kibachia in Leitner, "General Strike," and John Spencer, *The Kenya African Union* (London: KPI, 1985), p. 169.

151. Interview: Mohamed Shallo.

the first African member of the Legislative Council. Mathu recalled that Kibachia's school career had been "distinguished"—he was a senior prefect and school captain.[152] Although a relatively young man, he owned a farm, goats, and cows, and he paid workers to care for them. He had sold some trees on a farm for Shs 1000, which he used to begin a chicken and egg business and he was involved in this business throughout the time of the Mombasa turmoil. He started another business in Mombasa in December 1945, but in June 1946 the Municipality declared the premises unsuitable and closed it down. Meanwhile, Kibachia had held a job in Nairobi, and since October 1946 he had been employed by the East African Clothing Factory in Mombasa for Shs 80 per month. During the period between the strike and his deportation—the height of the AWF's efforts to organize the workers of Mombasa—he was trying to go to India for further study, but he failed to get the scholarship he sought.[153]

The African Workers Union, as the AWF was first called, was created at the Kiwanja cha Maskini on the first day of the strike, according to Makhan Singh.[154] The officers were Mohamed Kibwana, President, Mwangi Macharia, Secretary, and Mabaruk Kenze, Treasurer: two Muslims and a Kikuyu. Kibachia testified that the leading figures involved in the meetings at the field first used the name African Workers' Union on 15 January, that is, day three of the strike.[155] On that day, Kibachia both spoke to the mass meeting and did his first important service. Because he knew Mathu, he was chosen by the leadership to go to Nairobi to contact him. He was thus away from Mombasa from 15–17 January, but he was unable to contact Mathu. According to his testimony, he then did clerical work for the "strike committee," which included writing a letter to the *East African Standard,* dated the eighteenth and published three days later. This letter gave a succinct statement of the "motives behind the strike": "(1) Indifference toward paying them equally with the other workers of other races who performed identical or same duties. (2) Partiality and disrespect shown to African workers wherever they are employed. (3) Deliberative [*sic*] devices to keep the African poor that he may keep at his work all the time. . . . (4) Not giving wives and children allowances. (5) Taking no notice of the present high cost of living."[156]

Kibachia's contacts with Mathu were considered so important that on

---

152. Testimony to Kibachia hearing, pp. 61–63. For background on Mathu, see Jack R. Roelker, *Mathu of Kenya: A Political Study* (Stanford, Calif.: Hoover Institution Press, 1976).

153. Testimony of Chege Kibachia, pp. 39–40, 46–47.

154. Singh, *History,* p. 141.

155. Testimony, pp. 40–41.

156. EAS, 21 January 1947, quoted in Singh, p. 142. Singh writes that Kibachia was appointed to the Executive Committee of the AWU on 15 January. Kibachia testified that he was appointed President three weeks after the strike. Hearing, pp. 40–41.

21 January he went off to Nairobi to try again to find him. This time, the Government, for its own reasons, had already despatched Mathu to Mombasa. In the midst of his ultimately successful efforts at mediating an end to the strike, Mathu suggested that the organization change its name from African Workers Union to African Workers Federation. Evidently, he was anxious to avoid association with the Kenya African Union, the leading political organization of the time.[157]

By then, the strike had been going on for ten days. From the start, the Government had insisted that the strike was illegal—the port was covered by the Essential Services Act, and in any case few legitimate ways to initiate industrial action yet existed under Kenyan labor law. The Government dropped leaflets from airplanes over Mombasa to remind workers of the illegality of the strike and the Government's intention to investigate grievances once the strike had ended.[158] The Government had sent troops to the city and taken other—fairly mild—measures to repress the strike. But in the port only 124 African workers showed up on 23 January.[159] The strike was holding extremely well. Even the large, amorphous body of work seekers and occasional workers was not acting as scabs to any significant extent.

The workers, meanwhile, had asked Archdeacon Beecher—a missionary thought to be sympathetic and a member of the Legislative Council appointed to represent African interests—to help them. Beecher told the workers that he would fight for their demands if they returned to their jobs. The workers ignored him. Mathu—with better relations to the workers and better ability to talk to them—convinced them that he would, in fact, fight if they returned to work. Mathu met with the strike committee—before Kibachia's return from Nairobi, he later testified—and persuaded them to end the strike. Kibachia, returning the next day, apparently did not agree, but his influence was not great enough to change the move toward a settlement. On the afternoon of 24 January, Mathu addressed a mass meeting and said, "The matter will be settled within three months, and if I am not able to settle it by then, I shall come back to you." He advised the workers to return to work the next day. Unanimously, the meeting agreed.[160] The key to the settlement, as usual, was the appointment of a tribunal, announced by the Government that same evening. By Saturday, 25 January, the workers were returning to their jobs.[161]

157. Kibachia, testimony, pp. 40–41.

158. EAS, weekly ed., 24 January 1947.

159. Port Notes, incl. PM to GM, 27 January 1947, EST 13/1/1/3. Some Arab workers were drifting back by then.

160. Mathu, testimony, pp. 61–63; Singh, p. 143.

161. EAS, 25 January 1947, in Singh, p. 143.

Chege Kibachia does not emerge from this account as the embodiment of the proletarian vanguard. If he had reason to minimize at his deportation hearing the extent of his involvement in planning and organizing the strike, the prosecution was unable to present any evidence—including the testimony of various people who had spent much of the strike period at Kiwanja cha Maskini—to prove that he had directed the strike. Kibachia came to the fore, not because of his deep roots in the working class of Mombasa, but because of his connections to the small world of the Kenyan petty bourgeoisie, through its most prestigious institution, Alliance High School. He himself attributed his rise within the AWF to recognition of his efforts to reach Mathu.[162] This is not to denigrate his credentials as a leader of the working class: only by forging such connections could African workers move their struggle beyond the workplace. By tying together the fortunes of workers and of politicians—whatever stratum they came from—the relationship with Mathu affected not only the resolution of the strike but the evolution of Kenyan politics as well. At the same time, Kibachia's skill as a speaker and writer were important to a movement whose primary organizational basis lay in social networks that linked predominantly illiterate workers.

The central question is not the class from which Kibachia came but the direction in which he sought to move. From the simple and direct solidarity that developed in the course of the 1947 strike, Kibachia and the AWF built a movement that, however brief its heyday, captured the essence of what had gone before and gave it a new form. Kibachia built on the symbolism of the strike: the AWF met each Sunday in the Kiwanja cha Maskini and was addressed by Kibachia and others on basic issues of grievances and tactics. Although the AWF later sought registration as a trade union, it insisted that it would represent all workers and not be divided by craft or industry. This conception of a movement of the working class as a whole came out of a general strike and pointed to further general strikes.

It was this conception, too, that brought on vigorous government repression of the AWF and also gave the state a new impetus to undermine the surprising solidarity of the urban mass and to foster—even at considerable expense—a more differentiated, less easily united Kenyan labor force. The deportation of Chege Kibachia, substantial increases in wages in key sectors of Mombasa's work force, and restructuring of port labor were all to be parts of this transformation.

---

162. Hearing, p. 53; B. E. Kipkorir, "The Education Elite and Local Society: The Basis for Mass Representation," in B. A. Ogot, ed., *Hadith 4: Politics and Nationalism in Colonial Kenya* (Nairobi: East African Publishing House, 1972), pp. 252–69.

AFTERMATH: REFORM AND REPRESSION

Lessons

Even before the end of the strike, the opinion-makers of white Kenya were explaining what it meant. The strike could be fitted, without too much strain, into the familiar categories of the critics of casual labor. The *East African Standard* quickly decided that the uprising of the masses was further proof that a more differentiated, respectable working class had to be made:

> Mombasa has been a too-frequent source of trouble. . . . These disturbances and disputes are no mere accident of circumstances. They are indications of the social change which the African is passing through. In Mombasa, perhaps more than anywhere in Kenya, the migrant labourer has left the land and settled in the town. He is trying, with or without the necessary skill and experience, to make a living and raise his standards on a permanent basis. It is essential to his emergence as a good and self-respecting citizen that he should have social security in his new life.

The first priority, the editorial went on, must be "the organisation of the various groups of African workers into *their proper categories* and the application to them of the best principles of trade unionism suitable for the conditions of Africa."[163]

In his speech to the Legislative Council at the end of the strike, Attorney General Foster Sutton picked up the theme more specifically: "As honourable members are no doubt aware, one of the major causes of unrest on Mombasa Island has been the large number of casual labourers who had little or no security of employment." He emphasized the attention that the Labour Commissioner had given this problem, and saw in the efforts to create permanent labor pools a step in the right direction. This, he pointed out, had been explained to the workers' representatives during the meetings they held with the Labour Commissioner in the weekend before the strike.[164] Apparently, the news of tentative moves toward decasualization had not been greeted with joy by the dockworkers. Nor was it clear from the Attorney General's remarks just what the connection between casualism among dockworkers and a strike that embraced all segments of the working population was.

On reflection, the connection of casual labor and disorder still appeared clear. S. V. Cooke—by Kenyan standards a liberal member of the Legislative Council—wrote in an article in the *East African Standard* in

163. EAS, 17 January 1947. Emphasis added.
164. Legislative Council Debates, 28 January 1947, c. 811.

June, "The attempt to decasualize labour in Mombasa will have important soical effects and will minify the chances of labour trouble in the future for it was from this source that strikes derived in the past." He thought the higher wages workers received from the post-strike tribunal would have a good effect in more ways than one: they would encourage employers to reduce their levels of employment, and "the African must learn sooner rather than later the hard lessons which unemployment teaches. It will inculcate in him the 'fear of the sack,' a fear which does not at present exist."[165]

A second lesson emerged from the frustration of officials in confronting workers who were not organized into clearly structured institutions. This was the point which Arthur Creech Jones, Secretary of State for the Colonies and a good trade unionist himself, emphasized when first questioned about the strike in Parliament. Asked if the unions were behind the strike, he stated: "No, it is a very confused strike. There have been no demands, there is no union involved. It is a suffused feeling of disquiet, and the men simply refuse to work." Questioned further, Creech Jones revealed that it was equally hard to repress and to conciliate this kind of strike. The principal action of the government, he repeated, was to try to find out what the grievances were "in order that they should be examined." Some months later, explaining his actions to a fellow Fabian, he repeated, "The demands put forward by the strikers were confused and contradictory. . . ."[166]

Much of the Attorney General's recital of how his government had tried to cope with the strike focused on the frustration of trying to find "representatives" who would state grievances and listen to official reason, and the further frustration that, when a few representatives were found, the workers ignored them.[167] Even when an official tribunal obtained extensive testimony from workers about the conditions that led up to the strike, its head, Justice Thacker, associated the witnesses' lack of organization with their failure to produce moderate, negotiable demands. He berated African witnesses, saying that they were "impertinent, extravagant and had refused to recognize the authority of their own elected representatives." He complained that he was not investigating a trade dispute alone, but a "political agitation on a large scale with people who were asking for the sun, moon and stars."[168]

165. S. V. Cooke, "Mombasa Award Points Way to New Approach to African Problem," EAS, 27 June 1947.

166. Oral Answers, 22 January 1947, 432 House of Commons Debates, c. 206; Creech Jones to Rita Hinden, 22 May 1947, FCB 25/2, f. 58.

167. Legislative Council Debates, 28 January 1947, esp. cc. 807–08.

168. Minutes of third informal meeting of Tribunal, private session, 24 February 1947, LAB 3–15.

The *East African Standard*'s solution to the problem presumed a re-organization of work: the mass of workers flung together in Mombasa had to be sorted into "their proper categories" and then it would be possible to create "machinery for the proper consideration of disputes as between employer and the employees in the various branches of industry and employment." Implicit in the editorial's advocacy of the "best principles of trade unionism," was the assumption that unions should be organized around the branches of employment.[169] Neither the trade unionist Colonial Secretary, Creech Jones, nor any respectable authority in Kenya had any tolerance for the alternative form of organization presented by the African Workers Federation, and the government was not pleased when that organization tried to legitimize itself by seeking registration under Kenya's trade-union legislation.

Others thought that the need for effective grievance procedures should not go as far as trade unions. Meeting a few days after the strike ended, the employer-dominated Coast Labour Committee agreed that more contact with workers was necessary, but that trade unions would only generate exorbitant demands. The Committee favored Whitley Councils (employer-employee councils within an industry) and resolved that each employer should create councils among his employees and meet with them once a month. The Chairman of the Committee suggested that one object of this resolution was to discredit the AWF and to develop "reasonable conduct" among whatever trade unions there were. The Committee thought an African representative should join it and selected him for the Africans: John Silas, who was also the one African on the Thacker Tribunal.[170] But however limited a vision employers had of African labor organization, most seemed to agree that in January 1947 they had got the worst of all possible worlds: the absence of trade unions had not diminished the effectiveness of a strike, but it had been a serious obstacle to preventing or ending it.

Even though important officials saw the strike as reinforcing their preconceptions about the organization of work and workers, most also saw that the twelve days of disruption in East Africa's leading port was a sound, pragmatic reason why the colonial state should do something to raise urban Africans' standards of living. Officials, from the local level to the Secretary of State, did not question the legitimacy of workers' assertions of material deprivation, but claimed that remedying it was already state policy. In this respect they were focusing on the African as consumer, while insisting—through their focus on previous and future stud-

169. EAS, 17 January 1947.
170. Minutes of the Coast Labour Committee, 30 January 1947, EST 26/20.

ies of budgets and their dismissal of workers' own definition of their needs as extravagant—that African consumption be defined objectively.

The Attorney General's postmortem on the strike asserted that the government had planned more comprehensive minimum wage legislation, fixing a minimum wage of Shs 40 per month in Mombasa even before the strike, although it was only to be effective on 1 February. He acknowledged the shortage of consumer goods in Mombasa but claimed that the government had given a large firm there a "special allocation of piece and other imported goods" and applauded the Railway for making goods available in its shops at controlled prices. He regretted the increased cost of maize but thought other food prices were under control. Housing—officially assigned much of the blame for the general strike of 1939—was still a sore point. The Government's plans, under way since 1945, focused on Government housing: constructing blocks of flats, all planned and built by the state, as "permanent schemes for providing housing accommodation for the workers." The Railway was again praised for housing 95 percent of its staff: the planned housing estate linked directly to the job was the Government's solution to the housing crunch.[171]

About a week later, the Chief Secretary of the Government brought the Legislative Council up to date on "what action has been taken over the week-end to deal with the labour situation on Mombasa Island." He had appointed a tribunal under Mr. Justice Thacker and named H. S. Booker, an economist with experience conducting cost of living inquiries in England and a recommendation from the chairman of the Social Science Research Council in London, to conduct a "sociological and economic survey of conditions on Mombasa Island." But he was at pains to assert that neither investigation had been promised to the workers as a condition for their return to their jobs: "the general return to work on the following morning took place without any such undertaking having been given." The appointed member who was to represent African interests, Archdeacon Beecher, withdrew his earlier motion calling for implementation of previous commission awards (mainly that of the Phillips Committee), and congratulated the Government on its decision to investigate. He carefully made only the most delicate illusions to the fact that the impetus behind yet another pair of investigations had been a general strike, applauding "the expedition with which these steps have been

171. Legislative Council Debates, 28 January 1947, cc. 808–13. The year-end report by the Government on the state of the colony virtually repeated the diagnosis of the general strike eight years previously: "Probably the biggest single factor that has caused African discontent in the urban areas is the lack of accommodation." Kenya, Colonial Report, 1947, p. 17.

taken." The myth of official objectivity toward the conditions of Mombasa's workers was being maintained.[172]

In London the next month, Creech Jones replied to a question about the supposed deterioration of productivity in East Africa by placing stress on

> improving the efficiency of workers in terms of health and sound conditions, by increasing the incentive to work and by making the actual conditions of work more attractive. Greater efficiency should follow from the health, education and social services provided for in the long term programmes now being made. Increased incentive depends not necessarily on wages though these are receiving attention, but also on an increased supply of consumer goods which is only possible to a limited extent in present circumstances. All the East African Governments are taking active steps to secure an improvement in the general conditions of labour and with this object have, since the end of the war, given attention to improved welfare provisions and considerably strengthened the organisation of their Labour Departments.[173]

The Fabian Colonial Bureau, looking toward the same sorts of provisions, remained skeptical of the Government's zeal. Less concerned to retain the facade of scientific detachment, it pointed out that the new minimum wage had only been announced with the strike, that many improvements in living conditions had already been recommended by Phillips but had not been implemented, that housing allowances remained inadequate, and that cost of living adjustments and a social survey had been very slow in coming.[174] Perhaps the concern with African welfare had been developing in Whitehall for some years, but the imperative to act on it seemed to follow directly from the general strike.

A final deduction from the events of January 1947 was to have a long-term, if subtle impact. In his speech to the Legislative Council after the strike, the Attorney General made special mention of "the part played by the honourable member Mr. Mathu, one of the members for African interests in the Council in advising the strike leaders to call off the strike. (Hear, hear.) His intervention undoubtedly accelerated a return to work and I hope has had the effect of preventing bitterness which might otherwise have resulted if the workers had been compelled, through economic

172. Legislative Council Debates, 4 February 1947, cc. 1010–1013.
173. Written Answers, 12 March 1947, 434 House of Commons Debates, c. 182.
174. Draft Letter on Kenya," Fabian Colonial Bureau to Creech Jones, 16 April 1947, FCB 115/3.

reasons, to abandon the strike."[175] Mathu's intervention had come after the failure of a white member for African interests, Archdeacon Beecher, to get workers to pay any attention to him whatsoever. Mathu's promise that grievances would be attended to had been somewhat more specific than Beecher's, but the main difference was who was making them.[176] The uproars of the African masses, it seemed, might at times be handled more effectively by respectable African politicians than by colonial officials.

The twelve-day-long shutdown of East Africa's leading port city was one of a series of events that forced a rethinking of the labor problem on an empire-wide basis. It also gave a powerful argument to those forces within the colonial state who had already been arguing for new approaches and new forms of organization in the labor system. Officials had long been uneasy about the rapid circulation of labor, about maintaining wages and working conditions at minimal levels, and about confronting African workers as a homogeneous mass, but between 1939 and 1947 workers had kept the dangers and costs of the cheap labor system before their eyes.

Investigations

In February 1947, consideration of the labor question in Kenya shifted to a tribunal appointed under the Defence (Trades Disputes Tribunal) Order of 1942. Headed by Mr. Justice Thacker, it included the President of the Nairobi Chamber of Commerce, the Economic and Commercial Advisor to the Government, a white farmer, the President of the Mombasa Indian Association, and a single African—John Silas, a clerical employee of the Railway and Vice-Chairman of the Mombasa branch of RASU.[177] The Tribunal began meeting in February and issued an interim report on 20 March and a final report on 21 June. It called numerous African witnesses, who were browbeaten and frequently accused of misrepresenting the situation, spending all their money on palm wine, or failing to provide specific, verifiable budgets. What the Tribunal wanted was concrete data that it could plug into its budgetary model of labor conflict, and after some weeks a member concluded that "there has been no help from the African at all."[178] But the testimony is a rich record of what workers expected from their working lives and what they got. So,

175. Legislative Council Debates, 28 January 1947, cc. 815–16.

176. Later that year, two African members of the Legislative Council in the Gold Coast had similar success in settling a railway strike. See chapter 6 below.

177. Kenya, Information Handout No. A10, 6 February 1947, LAB 9/1841. Silas did not play a very active role in the tribunal.

178. F. T. Holden, 5 March 1947, Transcript, p. 13, LAB 5/29.

too, is the social survey—whatever its flaws—that also emerged from the Government's acute need to understand the labor situation in Mombasa.

The evidence suggests that the minimal efforts so far taken to alleviate distress and shape a more respectable, controllable working class had had very little effect. About half the city's labor force was receiving the minimum wage of Shs 40, many of the rest only a little more. Two years later, another survey found that only 16 percent of Mombasa's African workers were earning over Shs 80 per month.[179] The 1947 survey found that prices had increased by 100 percent between 1939 and 1947, with housing up from Shs 5 to Shs 10 for a room per month, food up 60 to 100 percent, and clothing up threefold. Only later in 1947 did the supply of cotton cloth improve, marking the end of wartime shortages, but by then postwar development spending was pushing prices upward. Equipment imports, an indication of new capital spending, were 70 percent higher in 1948 over the previous year, seven to eight times the prewar rate. The Mombasa African Retail price index, with its base of 100 in 1939, hit 192 in October 1947, 206 at the end of 1948.[180]

Wages for railwaymen and monthly shorehandlers had risen by 77 percent and 36 percent between 1939 and 1947. Daily wages for casuals had gone up 33 percent for shorehandlers and 25 percent for stevedores, so that even increased availability of daily work would not necessarily keep up with the inflation that had been so high throughout the war. But neither the increased tempo of work in the port nor the fledgling registration schemes of 1944 had produced a major breakthrough in the patterns of port labor. Perhaps the frequency of working rose somewhat between 1945 and 1947, but still 80 percent worked less than twenty days, and although registration rules required that workers put in ten days per month to keep their registration, many did not meet this none-too-exacting standard.[181]

Workers' testimonies suggest that making ends meet, day by day, for the single worker was far from the only consideration that motivated strikers. A casual worker, Hussein bin Said, had worked for twenty-one years as a stevedore; he had gone on strike in January because he was getting the same inadequate pay as every other casual stevedore and no

179. The railway had a more differentiated African work force. About 42 percent were at the minimum wage in 1947, down from 52 percent in 1939. Booker and Deverell Report, p. 7; East Africa Statistical Department, Earnings of African Labour in November 1948 (Nairobi, 1949), p. 10.

180. Colonial Office, Inflation in the Colonies, 1949, CO 852/1052/1; idem, Digest of Colonial Statistics 24 (1956): 81; Coast Province, AR, 1947, 1948.

181. Casual Labour, Mombasa, incl. LO, Coast, to LC, 27 February 1946, LAB 9/1053; Booker Report, pp. 10–11, 18. For detailed evidence on working patterns see below, table 4.2.

sick pay or other benefits. Other casual workers complained of getting the usual Shs 2/50 even when they handled dangerous cargo. Others complained of the arbitrary authority of company officials and the lack of provident funds to provide for a day when they could no longer work.[182]

The most stabilized and urbanized workers complained that they had little to show for their long periods of service. A sixteen-year veteran of the Railway was still sharing a small room in railway housing with another worker and getting the minimum wage. His basic wage had been increased only once, by Shs 2, and the wartime raises had been designated war bonuses, so they would not affect the gratuity he would receive on retirement (six months basic pay, after twelve years service). Workers from the KL&S Co. similarly complained about the lack of opportunities for long-term workers.[183] A skilled worker testified that he had to pay for his own tools, and an unusually well paid employee—earning Shs 188/33—stressed the cost of school for his three children.[184]

The Tribunal was being told that working, even for the better paid, provided little toward the accomplishment of basic goals over a lifetime: housing sufficient for a long-term worker to live with his family,[185] a lump sum on retirement, savings to make rural investments, or money for school fees. With a job structure clustered near the minimum wage and a lack of increments to provide returns for long service, workers were indeed being pushed into a mass.

The casual stevedore who put in fifteen days of work a month earned Shs 37/50, roughly the same as a monthly railway worker (including the cost of housing) who might have worked for a decade. The casual worker, in turn, got no more for each day than his Shs 2/50. He could not build a career, and so had every incentive to maintain rural ties in nearby areas, as many did, and take whatever gains the urban economy had to offer for what they were worth. But with daily wages up only 25 to 33 percent since before the war—and prices up perhaps 100 percent—casuals were getting less for each day's work.

Yet casual labor was still an option that many coastal workers thought desirable, even if they struggled to improve their daily wages. To be sure, nearly six thousand coastal people had accepted monthly work in Mombasa by 1947, about a third of the regular work force in the city. Still, coastal people remained reluctant to take wage-labor jobs in agriculture,

182. Testimony of employees of stevedoring companies, 4 March, pp. 9–10, LAB 5/29.

183. Testimony of Irungu Muragee and Murao s/o Mutoe, 24 February 1947, and Tomweru Tumuyanga and others from the KL&S Co., 28 February 1947, Transcript, vol. 2, pp. 1–4, LAB 5/29. See also the testimony of the Port Manager, 26 February, p. 12.

184. Gamaliel and Juma Hamisi, 24 February 1947, pp. 2–3.

185. According to the Railway's figures, its 2,641 African employees on Mombasa Island had 1,063 wives and 2,035 children. Port Manager, 27 February 1947, p. 5.

even near their homes. In the plantations south of Mombasa there were substantial labor shortages, although workers were paid Shs 40 per month, plus housing and food, while numerous Digo workers from that region sought casual labor jobs in the city. Labor seemed to be flowing from a region of shortage to a region of surplus even when the net earnings of the most successful in obtaining daily work were below the earnings of monthly agricultural laborers, although such wages could have been supplemented by petty trade or some other urban activity that full-time wage labor would have made difficult.[186] Even after the casual dockworkers were accounted for, there were another five thousand African men in Mombasa who were "engaged in various independent pursuits or unemployed" out of an estimated total African population of 56,574.[187] The choices make most sense when one remembers that plantation labor both required a total commitment of time for the duration of a contract and offered no long-term prospects. Casual workers—moving between their own fields and daily jobs—were seeking to preserve an overall pattern in their economic lives, shifting their time between jobs that gave them cash and farms that provided food and long-term security. Yet the casuals' active part in the strikes of 1934, 1939, and 1947 suggests that their incomplete involvement in the urban economy was no reason for them not to face the question of improving wages and conditions of work: the individual struggle through migration and the collective struggle in the city itself went on simultaneously.

The fluidity of relations between country and city for a portion of Mombasa's population went along with substantial urbanization for another. The 1947 survey disclosed that nearly 60 percent of the 56,000 Africans resident in Mombasa had been there over six years, and, most important, of these longer-term inhabitants, there were 10,300 women and 10,200 children to the 12,400 men. Among Africans with less than six year's residence the man-woman ratio was over 4:1. The survey concluded that a single man could live on the current wages, but a family could not.[188] The issues of housing a family, providing sufficient wages for a family, and for wage increments as family obligations rose, were thus quite relevant to a large portion of the urban population. The most stable workers—such as the railwaymen who had put in ten or fifteen years of service—were distinguished from the least stable not so much by what

---

186. Testimony of C. W. Howard, 11 March 1947, vol. 3, p. 103, LAB 3/16; LC, Testimony, 14 February 1947, vol. 1, pp. 25–26, LAB 5/28; African Labour Census, 1947, tables 13, 15.

187. These figures are based on registration efforts for a rationing scheme that existed at the time. Municipal Affairs Office, AR, 1946, in CP 106/53.

188. Booker-Deverell Report, pp. 2, 72.

they had to show for their years of work but by the way in which wage labor was integrated into a wider pattern of economic life.

The testimony to the Thacker Tribunal and the social survey showed that the most footloose workers of Mombasa faced declining real daily wages, while the most steady received few increments over the years and the wages of the large majority clustered around a figure not far removed from either the minimum monthly wage or what a fairly consistent casual worker might expect to earn in a month. There was nothing new about these patterns in 1947, and the unrest which erupted in January also fit into a longer pattern of unrest that began in 1934 and remained at a high pitch throughout the war years. The pattern was shared, too, in other African cities in these same years, and if the news of the Durban strike had provided some inspiration to the workers of Mombasa, and if the Mombasa strike in turn influenced the dock and general strike in Dar-es-Salaam in September 1947 or the Zanzibar general strike in 1948, labor strife was endemic as well in cities outside of the Indian Ocean sea-based communications system.[189]

Although the casual workers had gained somewhat from a Sh /50 rise in 1942 and from greater activity in the port during the war, their gains were eaten up by the accumulated inflation between 1939 and 1947, while the structure of work had not changed in any basic way. If monthly workers had been pinched especially hard before 1945, the gains they had received from the agitation of the war years were modest and did not even touch the larger issues affecting their overall working and family lives. For all the complexity and differentiation in the ways Africans lived and worked in Mombasa, the patterns overlapped and the spectrum of rewards clustered near the bottom. People who aspired to a higher wage for a day's work and those who sought a wage sufficient to support a family after ten years of labor often lived side-by-side in Majengo housing and interacted with each other outside of work, as much as on the job: only 20 percent of the workers of European firms in Mombasa in 1947 lived in company housing, compared to 56 percent in Nairobi.[190] The general strike of 1947 was a movement of Outcast Mombasa, only there was no respectable working class to separate it from the class of property owners, employers, and businessmen.

189. David Hemson, "Dock Workers, Labour Circulation and Class Struggles in Durban, 1940–59," *Journal of Southern African Studies* 4 (1977): 88–124; Iliffe, "The Creation of Group Consciousness"; Anthony Clayton, "The General Strike in Zanzibar, 1948," *Journal of African History* 17 (1976): 417–34. On the African context more generally, see chapter 6 below.

190. Only 5 percent of such workers received rations in Mombasa, compared to 35 percent in Nairobi. East Africa Statistical Department, Earnings of African Labourers in November 1948 (Nairobi, 1949), p. 12.

The Rise and Fall of the African Workers Federation

In the midst of the strike, Outcast Mombasa had achieved a coherent focus in its daily meetings in the Kiwanja cha Maskini. The strike had been a truly mass movement, involving a spectrum from the skilled worker to urban riffraff, and the mass had held together, distributed food to strikers, maintained order and discipline, and gone back to work in as orderly a fashion as it had gone out. Most important, the formation of the African Workers Federation—with officers and an executive commiitee—during the strike gave organizational content to this mass identity. In the aftermath of the strike, this organization was to clash directly with the efforts of the Government, and particularly the Thacker Tribunal, to objectify the labor question and to solve it with measures sent down from on high to ameliorate scientifically determined needs. In the months after the strike, the initiative in labor conflict was very much at stake. The testimony taken during February had shown the unity of frustration across the Mombasa work force, and from then on, the AWF and the Tribunal came to epitomize opposed ways of transforming the conditions of labor.

After the strike, the AWF began to build on the traditions and symbols developed during the strike itself. It held meetings every Sunday in the Kiwaja cha Maskini, attended by up to two thousand people. "Very important words [were] spoken," said an African teacher who attended.[191] Kibachia claimed that the AWF had two thousand members, and that its tiny staff was supported by "spontaneous donations."[192]

For a time, the AWF expanded into other parts of Coast Province, just as the strike had spread. Again, the most serious developments took place south of Mombasa, where a branch office was opened and recruiting among Digo had some success. Also echoing experience during the strike, the union apparently held some trials (of what offenses is not stated), and the local branch secretary and chairman were eventually prosecuted for illegally holding court proceedings. Representatives of the AWF also visited Tana River, Lamu, and Malindi Districts during 1947. There are reports of meetings being held in a branch office at Malindi in June and July of 1947. But these efforts declined during 1947 and virtually disappeared in 1948. Nonetheless, an indication of how seriously the state took this abortive process was that every annual report on Digo District until 1952 mentioned the AWF, although after 1948 all they had to say was that it was moribund.[193]

---

191. Obede Matue, testimony to deportation hearing for Kibachia, p. 80, CO 537/2109. Crowd estimates are from K. J. M. Holmes, Police Supt., Coast, ibid., p. 31.

192. Ibid., pp. 42, 55–56.

193. Digo District, AR, 1947–52, Kilifi District, AR, 1947, Tana River District, AR, 1947, Coast Province, AR, 1947.

The AWF's first critical test came when the Thacker Tribunal announced its interim award on 20 March: an increase of Shs 6/75 in basic wages for workers earning under Shs 54/50, plus an increase of Shs 3/25 in housing allowance. The award only applied to a specified list of employers, accounting for about five thousand workers: the railway, the port, the Municipality, the oil companies, and the Public Works Department. Most important, the award applied only to monthly employees of those concerns. This went directly against the way the AWF conceived of its relationship to the Mombasa working class: the Tribunal divided a working class that the AWF was trying to unite.

Chege Kibachia called a meeting to discuss the award, and officials estimated that three to five thousand people came to the Kiwanja to hear it discussed. The District Commissioner explained the award, and his remarks were translated into Swahili. Kibachia spoke vehemently against it, emphasizing that it applied to only a fraction of the workers.[194] The meeting passed a resolution condemning the award as "confined to certain classes and sections of workers" and originating in a tribunal with only minority African representation. It called for a boycott of the award—which had to be accepted by the workers concerned—as well as a boycott of the shops which the Government had designated in an effort to control prices, plus a boycott of "demoralizing" Government-run palm wine canteens. The meeting also condemned Government efforts to remove the unemployed from Mombasa as "a serious betrayal of the principles of freedom and democracy," directed only at blacks. And the meeting urged that a Parliamentary delegation from England look into labor problems in Kenya.[195]

The Administration was sure that the AWF was instrumental in mobilizing resistance to the interim award.[196] In April, over 80 percent of the monthly workers rejected the award. In May, 1,359 Municipality and 402 Shell Oil Company workers gave in, but that still left 40 percent of the work force rejecting it, including most railwaymen and KL&S Co. employees. Undoubtedly the immediate need for the Shs 10 increase in wages and housing allowance was becoming harder to refuse: it was, after all, nearly a 20 percent raise for workers earning under Shs 54/50. While casual labor was not covered by the Tribunal award, the major companies offered a Sh /50 per day raise, and workers split over the question of accepting it. At the KL&S Co., daily paid casuals accepted, but many piece

194. Director of Intelligence and Security to Member for Law and Order, 24 March 1947, LAB 3/17; Municipal Native Affairs Officer, Monthly Report, March 1947, PC's Archives, Mombasa, PUB 3/13.

195. EAS, 1 April 1947, in Singh, pp. 144–45.

196. Municipal Native Affairs Report, April 1947, PC's Archives, Mombasa, PUB 3/13.

workers joined monthly employees in refusing. The stevedores of the African Wharfage Company and the Tanganyika Boat Company refused, but the workers of the East African Lighterage Company gradually gave their assent to it. Meanwhile, the shop boycott advocated by the AWF held for only two days.[197]

The final award in June contained no provision for acceptance or rejection—a wise move on the Government's part. The only possible countermove would have been another strike. The award and the inability of the AWF to respond to it were to restore the initiative to the Kenyan state.

The final Thacker Tribunal award added slightly to the cost of living adjustment given monthly workers and significantly to the wages of casual workers. Shorehandlers were to get Shs 2/75 per day, up from Shs 2 before the strike; stevedores' wages went from Shs 2/50 to Shs 3/25. The wages of pieceworkers and specialty workers were adjusted as well. Monthly workers were guaranteed leave, holidays, and paid overtime according to a specified formula. The Tribunal made no binding order about retirement compensation, but recommended that provident funds be established and gratuities paid for retiring employees with twenty-five years of service.

Most important, the award began to come to grips with the fact that the existing structures of wages in the lower scales did "not provide sufficiently for the normal development of a man's life." For six months, the cost of living increments of the final award would be withheld from new workers. Then, they would receive a cost of living bonus on a scale from Shs 7/50 to Shs 19. The Tribunal wanted to do something as well for long-time workers "to make marriage financially possible." Yet it did not want to become involved with the problems of verification necessary for marriage or children's allowances or to pay different rates for the same job, as long as it was Africans who were doing the job. So it provided that a man with five years continuous service with one employer must be paid at least Shs 7/50 over the minimum wage. For higher-scale workers, it insisted that raises could only be given for increased output, but recommended (and only recommended) that Government and Railway scales offer more opportunities for rapid promotion.[198]

Incremental wage scales had been vehemently opposed by the General Manager of the Railway, even though he admitted that the unskilled worker was not at present receiving enough increments "to reach a wage

197. Senior LO, Coast, to LC, 3 April 1947; same to same, 4 June 1947, LAB 9/1843; Manager, KL&S Co. to PM, 9 April 1947, EST 13/1/1/3; Municipal Native Affairs Report, March 1947, PC's Archives, Mombasa, PUB 3/13.

198. Final Award, 20 June 1947, LAB 9/1844.

level comparable to the needs of a married man with an urban standard of living." He felt that paying experienced workers more than new ones was pointless because of the African's tendency "to do as little as possible." By making a special minimum wage for five-year veterans compulsory, the Tribunal rejected this conclusion, but not its basis. The Tribunal itself rejected the principle of equal pay for equal work on the grounds that true equality of work was not simply a matter of quantifiable output, but of "the sense of responsibility of the worker."[199] And responsibility—judging by the wage scales for Europeans, Indians, and Africans in Kenya—was a racial characteristic. The Tribunal's step toward a structure of wages that would move upward over the course of a working life was a cautious one; the issue of just how salary scales would reflect experience, productivity, and race would become a central issue of industrial relations in the 1950s.[200]

The Thacker Tribunal also added its voice to the previous calls for the decasualization of port labor. It suggested that a pool of six to eight hundred stevedores be set up and paid Shs 40 per month if they appeared for work every day. If they actually worked, they would receive Shs 3/75 per day. The port employers waited for only one day before jumping on this proposal. The permanent pool would require amenities; the wage was too high. The Coast Labour Committee—after strong statements by officials of the stevedoring comparies and the Port Manager (of the Railway)—decided that the pool should not have the aura of permanency that the Tribunal implied but should be a pool of registered workers who could be hired by the day, and that the stevedoring companies would decide about attendance money as they saw fit.[201] This was essentially the status quo, and it would be a decade before they saw fit to pay dockworkers for their attendance. They would move instead to compel regular attendance by pool members before they would provide new forms of incentives for it.

Finally, in the midst of a series of recommendations designed to prevent another surge of urban anger—rent control, government-controlled shops, and so on—the Tribunal unanimously recommended that the "surplus population" of Mombasa be removed and prevented from returning. It suggested new legislation on this subject.[202] All in all, the

199. GM, Memo to Thacker Tribunal, 5 May 1947, LAB 9/1841; Thacker Tribunal, Final Award, LAB 9/1844.

200. The next year, a study of wages in the civil service also rejected equal pay for equal work on the ground that "the African is at the present time markedly inferior to the Asian of the same educational qualifications in such matters as sense of responsibility, judgement, application to duty and output of work." Report of the Commission on the Civil Services of Kenya, Tanganyika, Uganda, and Zanzibar, 1947–48 (London: HMSO, 1948), pp. 24–25.

201. Minutes of Coast Labour Committee, meeting of 21 June 1947, LAB 9/1844.

202. Final Award, LAB 9/1844.

Tribunal's award reflected the kind of thinking that had been going on within the Labour Department for some time, but its binding wage adjustments and its suggestions for further measures gave this thinking a more concrete form. The dangerous urban mass would be split by awarding wage increases, leave privileges, and other benefits selectively. The distinct minimum wage for workers with five years of continued service to one employer would separate out a body of workers who might one day hope to marry and live off their wages. The Tribunal hoped to bind port workers into steadier work rhythms through pools and attendance payments. And it wanted to throw everyone else out of the city.

The AWF seems to have been taken aback by the complex award, and when the award was announced on 20 June it at first tried to "sidestep" the question of what to do.[203] The Sunday meetings in July began to take on an increasingly strident tone. On 13 July, people were told that the award was not acceptable, and that they should wait for a strike call. The next Sunday, there was talk of setting a date for a colony-wide strike. And on 27 July, a strike date three months hence was declared. Meanwhile, the AWF planned a procession in Mombasa for 3 August. Kibachia addressed this meeting, telling the people that the strike would be not only to obtain better wages but to protest bad treatment of African workers. He remained true to his stress on unity, pointing out that the final award did not cover all of Mombasa's workers, but only those who had struck or filed notice of a dispute. As Kibachia told his audience, clerks and houseboys who had remained faithful to their "masters" during the general strike received nothing from the Tribunal. The next strike, he said, must not cause a disturbance, but anyone who went to work would have his ears cut off.[204] But as the rhetoric escalated, attendance at Kiwanja cha Maskini dwindled down to a thousand in the July meetings, as low as five hundred in one estimate for Kibachia's speech on 27 July.[205]

The most basic mistake the AWF made was to underestimate the workers' success. Movements are built out of accomplishments and growing self-confidence; their development is not directly proportional to the magnitude of their grievances or the inadequacy of official responses to them. The workers of Mombasa had made concrete progress toward improving the harsh living conditions against which they had struck. Their success was measured not only in the wage increases granted by the

203. Municipal Native Affairs Report, June 1947.

204. Municipal Native Affairs Report, July 1947, PC's Archives, Mombasa, PUB 3/13; Report of Asst. Inspector Rafinus Joseph, Kenya Police, on a meeting of the AWF, 27 July 1947, EST 13/1/1/3; Testimony of Asst. Inspector Joseph, Deportation Hearing, pp. 11–12, CO 537/2109.

205. Municipal Native Affairs Report, July 1947; Police Asst. Inspector Joseph and Sergeant Ongango Mjoho, Testimony, Deportation Hearing, pp. 11–12, 32.

Tribunal, but in the dynamics of the strike situation itself. The Government had proved unable to use the repressive labor laws of Kenya, which made violations of labor contracts, including absence from work, criminal offenses; and it had even pressured the one employer who wanted to bring an action against strikers to drop the case.[206] Troops had been brought to Mombasa, but they had not attempted to disperse the crowds that congregated daily in the highly visible center of the strike, the Kiwanja cha Maskini. Despite the usual fulminations that the strike was illegal and "a definite attempt to coerce Government and the country as a whole," the Government had handled the working class of Mombasa with kid gloves, as it had in 1939.[207] Even during the tense moments before the strike and while it was under way, the Administration had taken actions that had long been stalled in the bureaucracy: a minimum wage was gazetted, a Coast Labour Committee with African representation (however token) was appointed, and amenities were placed in the port.[208] In the end, the casual and monthly workers who had struck or declared a dispute received substantial wage increases, and the most serious—if still cautious—steps yet taken to alter the wage structure were applied, not to the workers of Kenya generally, but to their most activist component, the strikers of Mombasa. The changes cut two ways: they were attempts to give workers more of a stake in retaining their jobs and to cement their interests to a single employer rather than to collective struggles for advancement, even as they made concrete the welfarist notions implicit in earlier investigations.

The Thacker award was both a victory for those who had struck six months previously and a fundamental challenge to the AWF's conception of the working class. The Federation had consistently fought to unite the urban masses, from the domestic servant to the railwayman, and to press for changes in the character of relations between employer and employee as well as for universally shared economic gains. It had led workers to maintain the symbols of unity created during the strike and to remain steadfast enough to compromise the interim award that did not address the needs of all categories of workers. The final award was somewhat broader in scope—applying to casual as well as monthly workers in the largest occupational categories though not to workers as a whole—and the gains the two awards together offered to the segments of the working class to which they did apply were considerable indeed. In the Labour

206. Attorney General to LC, 28 February 1947; LO, Coast, to LC, 12 February 1947; same to same, 3 April 1947, LAB 9/1836. The KL&S fired some clerical employees who had attempted to organize a staff association, but received considerable heat from the Thacker Tribunal for doing so. Transcript, vol. 2, pp. 5–6, 12–13, 20, LAB 5/29.

207. Attorney General, Legislative Council Debates, 28 January 1947, c. 815.

208. Clayton and Savage, p. 279.

Commissioner's estimate, 30 percent of the city's workers were not covered, although he was bringing pressure on their employers to use the award as a guideline.[209]

According to Kibachia, the final award applied to less than fifty percent of the island's workers.[210] Kibachia told his audiences at Kiwanja cha Maskini that the award did not benefit workers as a whole, but beyond that he failed to develop a critique of the award or an appreciation of how much both its benefits and the sense of victory it entailed meant to the workers. The meetings in July foundered, and the Acting Provincial Commissioner wrote in mid-month that the award was being "quietly accepted" by those to whom it applied, although the "general attitude, however, seems to be one of acquiescence rather than of acceptance." Significantly, he felt that it was the better-paid workers who were least captivated by the size of the award and thought a higher cost of living adjustment and higher increments should be given them. But that was a problem for a segment of the workers; the majority, he felt, were not aroused, and their leaders were not pushing a strike. By the end of the month, the population seemed at least overtly content.[211]

The Government at last felt secure enough with the muted response to the AWF's agitation in July to reverse its diffidence toward the militant workers of Mombasa. The day after Kibachia's call of 27 July for a strike and his threat to cut off the ears of scabs, the Port Manager wrote to the General Manager of the Railway that it was time for "firm action." The General Manager spoke to the Labour Commissioner about Kibachia's threats. The latter did not think that the AWF was dangerous, but the General Manager contended that it should be suppressed.[212]

The Mombasa authorities began to clamp down. The AWF was refused permission to hold its proposed procession on 3 August, and one of its officers, James Mwangi, was arrested for entering Coast Province without a permit. The AWF discussed holding a sit-down strike in protest against the arrest, but nothing happened. The August meetings proved even less stirring than the July ones, and the Municipal African Affairs Officer felt the tension in the city relax.[213]

On 12 August Kibachia sent a letter to the Colonial Office in London, enclosing a memorandum from the AWF that—two months after the award—at last provided a coherent critique of it.[214] His letter attacked

209. LC, Statement of Coast Labour Committee, 19 September 1947, EST 26/20.

210. Kibachia to Creech Jones, 12 August 1947, CO 537/2109.

211. Ag. PC, Coast, to Member for Law and Order, 12 July 1947, LAB 3/14. See also Municipal Native Affairs Report, July 1947, PC's Archives, PUB 3/13.

212. PM to GM, 28 July 1947; GM to PM, 29 July 1947, EST 13/1/1/3.

213. Municipal African Affairs Report, August 1947, PC's Archives, PUB 3/13.

214. Kibachia to Creech Jones, 12 August 1947, CO 537/2109.

the lack of African representation on the Tribunal, the application of the award to less than half the city's workers, and the inadequacy of the cost of living adjustments. He called for a Parliamentary delegation to "study the labour question afresh and effect a square deal to all," and threatened that the AWF was "preparing to launch another strike which will be a Colony-wide one." It protested, too, that the AWF had not received recognition under the trade-union legislation four months after its application.

The memorandum contained a comprehensive attack on the "cheap labour policy" of the Government, arguing that the state was deliberately taking a "precaution against African rapid economic progress" in order to cheapen labor; meanwhile, it alienated land and exterminated cattle in rural areas, bringing "an urbanised generation into this world." This was having lasting effects, for "should the parents feel any desire to leave the Towns and go home their town-born-and-brought-up children refuse to do so. They are at once sucked by the ways of the towns. This creates another big problem . . . economic as well as social." In towns, "giving of low wages is purposeful," and "giving of low pay has resulted in an irrelevant blame that an African worker is lazy and irresponsible. One thing we would like to clarify is that they work empty-stomached. . . . This low pay policy is also responsible for many of the vices that prevail such as moral and culture decline, crime and destructivity of the African economic machinery, pauperism, mental and physical deterioration due to malnutrition." The low-wage system was racially based—Europeans and Indians received better pay for the same work. At best, the African worker could "barely exist and no more," although "workers have it in mind that one day it shall be necessary to give their children some education and in one way or other pave the way for their future."

Kibachia wrote of the "desperation" of the workers that lay behind the January strike, and criticized the inadequacy of the Government response. Both the award and the process by which it was made were "inconsistent with democratic principles as voiced by the British Government" and a "betrayal of responsibility and lack of courage." The Tribunal had only a sngle African, and two of its members were "first class capitalist." Although the "Tribunal made a thorough investigation," and "there were facts and data enough to show that the Africans were all under intolerable high cost of living conditions," the "recommendations confine itself more to those workers of all concerns that contribute more to the economic machinery of the Colony. This is a sad sort of affairs for all citizens who pay tax are equal in the eyes of His Majesty."

The AWF memorandum demanded a Parliamentary Delegation; the "establishment of the principle of equal pay for equal work . . . this is essential"; equal treatment for workers of all races; a minimum wage of at least Shs 100 (presumably per month) and Shs 10 per day (15 per night) for casuals; allowances for wives and children; better sanitary, traveling, and educational provisions; sick pay and workers' compensation; warnings before dismissal; recognition of trade unions, including the AWF; the end of pass regulations for Africans; and the closing of beer canteens, a Government enterprise which "is deleterious and ruins culture and character of the African worker."

Kibachia's memorandum is remarkable, not only for its comprehensive and astute critique of Kenya's labor system, but for the way it developed, in vastly different terms, an agenda that paralleled what was slowly emerging from official bodies like the Phillips Commission and the Thacker Tribunal. The Government had begun to think about the problems of poverty, the social consequences of migrancy, family formation, and the woeful inadequacy of welfare provisions. Such demands as equal pay for equal work, workers' compensation, and family wages were not yet on the official agenda, but they would be under discussion by the 1950s. Nonetheless, Kibachia's cynical reference to the "appointment of commissions one after another" made clear the gap between official thought and action.

Most important, the state and the AWF saw welfare issues in opposite contexts. The AWF perceived them in terms of human entitlement, reflecting the needs of African workers as a body. Officials viewed reform as part of an exercise in differentiation and separation, an attempt to isolate from the rest of Kenyan society a compact working class for whom services and opportunities for urban life could be provided. The AWF and the Labour Department seemed to be working along similar lines and toward opposed ends; perhaps that explains the venom with which officials regarded the fledgling labor organization.

The most important misanalysis in this perceptive document is found in its final words on the Thacker Tribunal: "It has left things as they were before." This was above all a political error, a misreading of the importance of success in the course of a struggle. Had the AWF argued clearly in its educational and political forum at Kiwanja cha Maskini that partial success was all the more reason for workers to unite behind its leadership, it is by no means sure that it could have overcome the very concrete differentials that the Thacker award had placed within the work force. The segmentation of a working class was expressed in shillings and working conditions, although in July 1947, the process was still in its infancy. But the AWF's inability to address this issue no doubt contributed to the rapidity of its decline. In August, the Administration was ready for a crackdown on the workers' organization the likes of which it had not attempted during the strike or in the six months of effective political organizing by the AWF.

By the time Kibachia's letter arrived in London on 18 August, the decision to deport him from Mombasa had already been made; the letter itself received a reply (of the we-are-taking-care-of-these-matters variety) only in April 1948.[215] In early August, the AWF was discussed at the highest levels of state: the Acting Governor and his Council decided that no criminal charges could be brought against Kibachia, but that he should be deported from the coast. The Labour Commissioner, Wyn Harris, discussed the issue with the Secretary of State for the Colonies in London, and Creech Jones cabled the Acting Governor, "I am satisfied, in view of the full explanation of the trend of events given by Wyn Harris, that Government must maintain its authority." He agreed to the use of the deportation ordinance, but went on, "Wyn Harris assures me that action will not be taken under this Ordinance unless you are satisfied that the evidence available will ensure that proceedings will be successful."[216] The Kenya Government began its legal proceedings fully satisfied of their outcome.

Kibachia was arrested on 22 August. He had been trying to establish an AWF presence upcountry and had just presided over a ceremony naming a spot under a tree in Nairobi "Ofisi ya Maskini," the Office of the Poor, bringing the symbolism of the Mombasa strike to Kenya's capital. Mwangi Macharia, Secretary of the AWF, had been actively meeting with trade unionists and other activitists in Nairobi. The AWF was then cooperating with the Kenya African Union, then the leading political force among Kenyan Africans, and officials interpreted its upcountry efforts both as a drive to build a colony-wide union and to undertake political action. A number of strikes seemed to accompany Kibachia's upcountry tour.[217]

But when the arrest occurred, neither Kibachia's followers in Mombasa nor his friends in Nairobi were able to organize an effective protest. Although some reports suggested that Nairobi was seething, the KAU pulled back from the brink: Jomo Kenyatta went before a meeting on 11 September to denounce illegal strikes and meetings and to counsel workers to bring grievances to their individual employers. The event symbolized a parting of the ways in Kenyan nationalism, as Kenyatta and the

215. The Government of Kenya proposed in March a reply that the Secretary of State was "satisfied that this Government is doing its utmost to improve the condition of the worker by every possible means and to give the workers themselves the opportunity of further improving their conditions and their relations with their employers through the medium of trade unions." Creech Jones authorized the government to reply "in the sense proposed." Governor's Deputy to Creech Jones, 6 March 1948, and Creech Jones to Governor Mitchell, 6 April 1948, CO 537/3587.

216. Creech Jones to Ag. Governor, 15 August 1947 (telegram), CO 537/2109.

217. Municipal Native Affairs Reports, August, September 1947, PC's Archive, PUB 3/13; Singh, *History of Trade Unions*, pp. 156–58; Spencer, *Kenya African Union*, pp. 171–72.

constitutionalist wing of KAU became increasingly isolated from the militant labor leaders of Nairobi and the Kikuyu youth gangs.[218]

As Nairobi's poor agitated, attendance at the AWF's Sunday meetings in Mombasa continued to dwindle. The working classes of the two cities had developed their own esprits and ways of communicating: Nairobi had not joined the general strike in Mombasa, and Mombasa did not join the Nairobi general strike of 1950.[219] Mombasa's coastal workers, like Nairobi's Kikuyu, had their links to the hinterland, but Mombasa's hinterland was not an angry one riven by acute agrarian conflict between vigorous accumulators, white and black, and those who were excluded from rapid economic growth. A sufficient proportion of Mombasa's masses could, eventually, be pacified, so long as the state and employers were willing to pay the price.

They had begun to do so in 1947, and in September Chege Kibachia was in court. Public and press were excluded from the hearing to determine whether he could be deported from Mombasa, although its transcript provides historians with a rich record of the atmosphere at Kiwanja cha Maskini during and after the strike (used extensively in the above account), though not a shred of evidence that Kibachia or the AWF planned or directed it. The judge decided that the AWF had organized intimidation during the strike, had compromised the integrity of the Thacker Tribunal while it was still sitting by accusing it of bias, and had incited people to take the law into their own hands by Kibachia's threat, in his speech of 27 July, to cut off scabs' ears. He found Kibachia "dangerous to peace and good order," and that was all he needed to find under the Deportation Ordinance. Kibachia was duly deported to a remote part of Rift Valley Province—far from any working classes—where he was to be "received and detained until further notice." The Colonial Office wanted the word *detained* dropped from the deportation order but was glad to have him received—he stayed for ten years. Other AWF leaders were arrested as well.[220]

At first, some of Creech Jones's former associates in the Fabian Colonial Bureau asked in Parliament whether Kibachia was to be "detained indefinitely without a charge being made?" The Parliamentary Under-Secretary of State assured them that the order would be reviewed every six months, but that "This man is rather a dangerous individual. In July,

218. D. W. Throup, "The Origins of Mau Mau," *African Affairs* 84 (1985): 419–20; Spencer, pp. 172–73.

219. Municipal Native Affairs Reports, August–November 1947, PC's Archive, PUB 3/13; Mombasa District, AR, 1950.

220. Hearing Transcript, Judge Bartley to Ag. Governor, 11 September 1947, incl. Foster Sutton to CO, and CO to Foster Sutton, 8 December 1947—all in CO 537/2109; Singh, p. 157; Clayton and Savage, p. 282.

1947, he threatened that any person failing to come out on a strike which he proposed to call should have his ears cut off. His Majesty's Government do not feel that this constitutes good trade union practice, and until he learns to behave himself he will be detained."[221] Later, the question was repeated and the threat to workers' ears again invoked, with the comment that "he is making good progress in rehabilitation." "Progress in what?" asked the questioning MP. "In coming to a right state of mind," was the official reply.[222]

Proper trade-union practices and right states of mind were more than Parliamentary witticisms. The opposition between trade unionism, as conceived of and promoted by the Colonial Office, and the vision of working-class organization embodied in the AWF was a deadly serious issue. Trade unions had emerged as an important component of the state's plan for restructuring the labor problem in the aftermath of the strike. Thacker himself had argued that tribunals such as his would function better if trade unions were organized, for in their absence there was no way to accredit the representatives of workers who appeared before tribunals.[223]

But the AWF had been trying to register itself as a trade union since January, and Eliud Mathu had tried to help it. The application had met with various blocking tactics: Kibachia was told that the application was incomplete, then received no further replies.[224] The AWF was not what officials had in mind for trade unionism. As James Patrick, sent out in 1947 by the Colonial Office to assist Kenyan unions in organizing themselves and meeting registration requirements, told a meeting of the Coast Labour Committee in September, "The Federation were incompetent of industrial negotiation. and moreover attempted to represent all classes of labour as opposed to the Trade Union principle of separate trade unions for separate trades." Others at the meeting opposed registering the AWF on the grounds that it would hurt the "orthodox trade union movement."[225] In October, the AWF wrote Creech Jones to complain about its nonregistration, as well as the absence of replies to other communica-

---

221. Caught up by an MP in his use of the word "detained," Under-Secretary Rees-Williams replied "that he is now not exactly in detention but excluded from the area in which he was misbehaving himself." Oral Answers, 25 February 1948, 447 House of Commons Debates, cc. 1940–41. The questioner was Mr. Sorensen.

222. Sorensen and Rees-Williams, Oral Answers, 5 May 1948, 450 House of Commons Debates, c. 1240.

223. Memorandum by Mr. Justice Thacker, 2 September 1947, LAB 9/61.

224. Mathu, testimony to deportation hearing, pp. 61–63, CO 537/2109; Kibachia, ibid., pp. 40–41.

225. Minutes of the meeting of the Coast Labour Committee, 19 September 1947, EST 26/20. These issues are discussed further in the following two chapters.

tions, including one about Kibachia's deportation. The Colonial Office decided not to reply.[226]

For the state, channeling specific groups of workers within a differentiated labor force into organizations and regularized forums for raising problems was consistent with its overall effort to disengage a working class from an inarticulate and chaotic mass. The AWF wished to give that unitary mass coherent and effective form. Patrick put the case clearly and emotionally in 1949 while summing up his first two years as the government's principal gesture on behalf of trade unionism:

> When I arrived in Kenya two years ago an organization calling itself the African Workers' Federation was very much to the fore. The Leader became such a danger to the maintenance of law and order he had to be deported. I personally had to discourage the growth of this Federation because I believed it would be completely impracticable to administer. There was not restriction, limitation or qualification on membership. You could be a baker, a tailor or a candle-stick maker, it didn't matter what your occupation was, if you wanted to join, the African Workers' Federation would only be too pleased to accept you. . . . I am firmly convinced that at the present moment workers in Kenya must confine themselves to separate Unions for different occupations.[227]

In some ways, the initiatives of Kibachia and the AWF passed to other radical labor leaders, like Fred Kubai and Makhan Singh, and influenced the radical wing of the Kenya African Union. That is another story.[228] In Mombasa, the initiative had passed to the state by the summer of 1947. The assault on the AWF and the Thacker award proved to be the twin thrusts of this initiative, to be continued in the form of a slower but thoroughgoing restructuring of the nature of work and of its place in the lives of workers.

Toward the poorest workers, minimum-wage legislation became a key ingredient of the approach. From the Shs 40 minimum (including housing allowance) that had been proclaimed in the midst of the strike, minimum wages rose to Shs 45/25 in May 1948, Shs 47 in August 1950, and Shs 50 in October 1951. Rising by varying increments, they passed Shs 80

226. H. Muchondu, Secretary of the AWF, to Creech Jones, 30 October 1947, and Minutes of 16 December 1947 and 13 January 1948, CO 537/2109.

227. James Patrick, "Memorandum on Trade Unions—Development and Policy—Kenya," n.d. [1949], FCB 118/1, p. 5.

228. Sharon Stichter, "Trade Unionism in Kenya, 1947–1952: The Militant Phase," in Peter C. W. Gutkind et al., eds., *African Labor History* (Beverly Hills, Calif.: Sage, 1978), pp. 155–74.

before the next major strike in Mombasa, in 1955.[229] Meanwhile, the binding awards to different categories of workers under the Thacker Tribunal were replaced by 1949 with negotiated agreements—approved by the Labour Department—between individual firms and their workers (organized or not). In the view of officials these agreements were as good or better than the terms of the Thacker award, and they were a step toward establishing distinct patterns of negotiation and rewards within each branch of industry.[230]

The AWF, meanwhile, never recovered from its failure to react decisively to the Thacker final award or to the arrest of its leader. A strike rumor surfaced in December 1947, apparently because of anger within the AWF over the absence of replies to its missives to the Colonial Office, but thirteen more AWF members were imprisoned on 22 December, and the Government issued stern warnings that strikers would be dismissed. Nothing happened.[231] In July 1948, the Ismaili community, which owned Kiwanja cha Maskini, decided that they wanted their football field back, and the movement lost its best symbol. It tried to arouse interest over a number of labor issues in late 1948 and early 1949 but failed.[232]

The Workers' Challenge and the Transformation of Work
The state—from the Coast Labour Committee to England's Labour Government itself—had gone after the AWF with a vengeance as soon as the Federation's grip on the workers of Mombasa had begun to loosen. Yet the period of turmoil between the general strikes of 1939 and 1947 had redefined the labor problem in fundamental ways. Not least of them was that it strengthened the hand of the Labour Department in establishing its own initiative over that of the leading employers in Mombasa to transform work. If the stevedoring companies, in particular, were concerned above all with their own labor costs and profits, the colonial state could not forget that Mombasa was the only major port serving Kenya and Uganda, and that its functioning in a smooth and predictable manner affected the profits of capital throughout the colony and the interests of the state itself. Then, too, whatever the social and political consequnces of employers'

229. Memorandum from Port Employers Association to Tribunal, 15 March 1955, Strike File, 1955, Railway Archives.

230. Minute from Coast Labour Committee, 20 July 1949, and from Labour Advisory Board, 28 November 1949, LAB 9/1844.

231. The arrested AWF members were convicted of exercising the judicial powers of a tribunal, presumably for judging violations of union discipline, and sentenced to four months in prison. Municipal Native Affairs Report, December 1947, January, February 1948, PC's Archives, PUB 3/13.

232. Ibid., July, October, December 1948, January, February 1949. Similarly, the branch offices throughout the coast ceased to show signs of life. Coast Province, AR, 1948, 1950.

relations with their employees were, the state would have to face them. The tensions between state and capital in Kenya had emerged periodically throughout the colonial era, and in Mombasa the issue of casual labor was at their center.[233] The state's concern with the short-sightedness of capital was best expressed in a private memorandum of Justice Thacker to the Labour Department, in which he claimed to be "appalled" at the "meager wages" paid to dockworkers, who were the "hardest worked Africans in the Colony." The port companies, Thacker insisted (although without figures) made "very large profits" yet were not "in any way generous with their men."[234] The state, and the Tribunal in particular, had been shackled with the consequences of this situation.

Especially since the strike of 1939, the state—through the Labour Department and various commissions—had been warning companies that their stubborn insistence on hiring dockworkers by the day and avoiding the payment of the full social costs of their labor might bring down the urban social order. As unrest continued and culminated in another general strike, this argument acquired added immediacy. In 1947, the stevedoring companies were still resisting the payment of minimum monthly wages for their casual workers or providing amenities and improved conditions of service for long-term day laborers. The General Manager of the Railway still looked at his workers as a mass of reluctant labor power undeserving of incremental wage scales. The dangers of such policies had emerged in the strike and been made clear in the testimony which state officials had heard since then. Africans were likely to act not just in response to the inadequacy of food and shelter, but to the inadequacy of wages to cover their needs over their life cycle. The attitudes of the employers of both monthly and casual labor had led to the convergence of two crises of social reproduction: the difficulty of workers, day by day, to renew themselves for the next day's work, and the inability of increasingly long-term, increasingly urbanized workers to sustain the family unit over the course of their lives.

At the same time, the ad hoc responses of numerous tribunals and commissions to the wave of strikes and near strikes since the 1930s—the repeated wage hikes—had made it doubtful that cheap labor could be kept cheap, or that the capital itself could determine the wage rate. But when amenities and social services were needed to preserve urban order, and wages were being continuously forced up, productivity became a

233. See especially John Lonsdale and Bruce Berman, "Coping with the Contradictions: The Development of the Colonial State in Kenya," *Journal of African History* 20 (1979): 487–506, and Bruce Berman and John Lonsdale, "Crises of Accumulation, Coercion and the Colonial State: The Development of the Labor Control System in Kenya, 1919–1929," *Canadian Journal of African Studies* 14 (1980): 37–54.

234. Memorandum, 2 September 1947, LAB 9/61.

growing concern. Barely had the January strike ended when the General Manager of the Railway wrote the Port Manager that output must be increased as a consequence of the wage increase. Otherwise the cost of living in East Africa would rise. He immediately suggested a new target— 600 tons per day—for discharging coal.[235]

The issue of productivity was made all the more acute by the issue of order. Adding another worker might once have made up for the sluggishness of current employees, but if that worker contributed to the dangers of urban overcrowding and unrest as well as to the wage bill, then the entire system that circulated masses of anonymous labor power through the port could be threatened. Officials' deeply felt prejudices against casual labor and casual laborers had rapidly been transformed into calls for reform once casual labor began to act up in 1934 and 1939. By the 1940s, new upheavals and the continuing atmosphere of tension in Mombasa had revealed a still more threatening prospect: a working class that would act together, begin to organize itself as a single collectivity, and challenge reforms of the labor system which divided that class without remedying the fundamental basis of its common exploitation. The actions of the laborers had put the initiative into the hands of the state, an initiative it was to use in earnest. And the strike of January 1947 was to be the last general strike—the last action of a fluid but essentially united working class—in Mombasa's history.

235. GM to PM, 27, 28 January 1947, EST 13/1/1/3.

4 The Reorganization of Dockwork

In the years of recovery from the Great Depression and through the wartime emphasis on production and the commodities boom of the post-war era, colonial powers were confronted with the difficult and dangerous social consequences of economic expansion. In the early days of colonialism, the imperial powers had worried that Africa provided potential workers with too many attractive alternatives to a life of wage labor. By and large, colonial states learned to live with and profit from a great variety of ways of getting workers to work for part of their lives, and these systems proved adaptable to the uneven pattern of economic growth that characterized colonial Africa. But the challenge of expansion was far tougher than the challenge of depression, and meeting it led to changes in imperial attitudes toward African labor and African society far more radical than anything that had occurred since the sharp escalation of European penetration in Africa in the late nineteenth century.

Had the imperial powers been able to plug along, soaking up larger quantities of labor without changing the labor system, doubtlessly they would have tried. Such an option often had powerful support. But from the 1930s through the 1940s the imperial powers faced time and again the social consequences of expansion without structural change. The tensions in Mombasa were echoed from Dakar to Durban, from Lagos to Zanzibar—indeed, from Jamaica to Malaya and Indochina. The crises transcended the strikes, riots, or rebellions that actually took place. They raised an even more serious question in an era of economic growth: would the Africans do the work? To the old concern about the shortage of African manpower was added a new one about its quality, a point that became more acute as key points—like the docks of Mombasa—emerged as potential bottlenecks for the economic potential of entire regions. If enough bad workers could not safely be packed into these critical places, the question of how to create good workers became inescapable.

These were empire-wide questions, and I shall be considering them in future studies in that context. The point here is to explore the relationship of the rethinking of the labor question and the remaking of time, authority, and space in the specific and complex situation of the dockyards of Mombasa. The critique of casual labor had for some years been a way of articulating a wider dissatisfaction with the system of migrant labor.[1] The daily hiring and discarding of labor power carried to an extreme the wastefulness and dangers of other forms of migrancy and provided a stark contrast to the most obvious alternative: developing a stable urban working class. In Mombasa, casual labor—and a way of urban life built around it—was blamed for much more than it had caused, and its termination promised much more than could be delivered, but the argument for this change became a leading wedge for a wider transformation of work in East Africa.

In Kenya, the debates during the 1940s and 1950s over the reorganization of work were quite explicit. The case for a low-wage economy, with little attention to stabilization or welfare, came from the settlers and was powerful enough to protect agriculture from too much reform for many years. The argument for restructuring—moving toward a stable work force with relatively high wages and expecting it to produce a high level of output—came most strongly from within the state, especially from Labour Commissioners like Hyde-Clarke, Carpenter, and Luyt; it was taken up, in a different political context, by the African trade unionist Tom Mboya. The leading sector for this new emphasis was transportation, above all the port and the Railway. Not only did the state exercise direct control over the Railway and considerable leverage, through the Railway, over the port companies, but even the most reactionary capitalists in Kenya had much to gain from stability in transport. Profit rates were not all that mattered: with a single line of rail and a single port connecting the producing zones of Kenya and Uganda to world markets, a small group of workers could shut down the entire economy.

THE LABOR PROBLEM IN THE POSTWAR ERA

The debates over what kind of capitalism postwar Kenya was to have are the subject of important ongoing research by John Lonsdale, Bruce Berman, Michael Cowen, and others. Before plunging into the details of what restructuring meant in one area of work, I wish only to sketch the main tenets of the transformers' argument in the critical years for change in the port, from the war to roughly 1955. Elements of these arguments had already been rehearsed in the critique of casual labor and in the immediate response of officials in Nairobi and London to the disorders between 1939 and 1947. But in the postwar era it became clear that these questions did not only concern day laborers in a port. The question was not just the remaking of a working class but finding a new conception of capitalism for postwar Africa.[2]

1. For an overview of the history of migrant labor in Kenya, see Sharon Stichter, *Migrant Labour in Kenya: Capitalism and African Response 1895–1975* (London: Longman, 1982).
2. The efforts of some Kenyan capitalists to create a new look for themselves and to

Traditional Workers and Modern Work

Postwar reconsideration of the labor question began with an old belief very much in mind: shortage of labor was a major obstacle to recovery and progress. The Colonial Office's Labour Advisor, Orde Browne, had written during the Depression, "Unlike the rest of the world with its long-standing unemployment problem, tropical Africa suffers in normal times from a constant shortage of labour to a degree that renders it a perpetual brake on the wheels of progress." He predicted that as soon as the Depression ended, the brake would become an immediate problem, and stressed that the problem lay not only in the unwillingness of Africans to tear themselves from their tribal economies, but from the wasteful use of the manpower that was forthcoming, owing to lack of training and the need for close European supervision.[3] Right after the war, in his important study of "Labour Conditions in East Africa," Orde Browne repeated his contention that European-centered development in Africa was proceeding faster than the transformation of African society, and that a fundamental consequences of this disjuncture was the lack of economic compulsion on Africans to work.

> To a greater degree, therefore, the African is independent of paid work for his subsistence. . . . He is thus largely a target worker. . . . Consequently, the offer of more money seldom has much attraction for him; increased wages enable him to leave earlier, but do not persuade him to remain longer. In this way, the tribesman gradually builds up a household for himself on the modest native scale until, after a limited number of absences at work, he is established in what are, for him, comfortable conditions. . . . All told, therefore, he probably does not work for wages for more than five or six years of his life, and the idea of continuous employment as his main support is entirely strange, and in fact repellent, to his mentality."[4]

Long a problem, the ability of Africans to stand somewhat aloof from the enticements of the labor market was critical to the anticipated boom in

---

articulate new ideas through the Association of Commercial and Industrial Employers, founded in 1956, and later the Kenya Federation of Employers, are discussed in Alice H. Amsden, *International Firms and Labour in Kenya, 1945–70* (London: Cass, 1971), and Colin Leys, *Underdevelopment in Kenya* (Berkeley: University of California Press, 1975).

3. "Labour and the Economic Development of Tropical Africa," typescript, n.d., but evidently written during the Depression, Orde Browne Papers, Rhodes House, 2/1, pp. 5, 17–18. He dismissed the then standard ways of recruitment, such as additional taxation, as "crudities" that produced only "fictitious and ephemeral results." Ibid., p. 28.

4. Major G. St. J. Orde Browne, "Labour Conditions in East Africa," Colonial No. 193, 1946, pp. 5–6.

tropical commodities that might help pull Britain out of its war-induced crisis. Wages had risen during the war, and if this meant that Africans would be working less when their time was needed more, the colonial economy could be caught in a vicious circle. At the Colonial Office, the Africa specialists of the Colonial Labour Advisory Committee agreed with Orde Browne's report on East Africa, and one member commented that East Africans now could dispose of "large stocks of money" accumulated during the war.[5]

The implications, then, of Africans' entry into wage labor was not that it was a step toward fuller involvement in capitalist agriculture and industry, but that they used wages to sustain their own, very different, forms of agrarian production. To be sure, Orde Browne and his compatriots appreciated the savings which migration brought employers—they did not have to pay for social security and other essential elements of social reproduction—but cost minimization was no longer the most critical issue.[6]

Some scholars have argued that this subsidy which precapitalist economies give to capitalists has led to structural tendencies and policies to conserve African economies at a level of output high enough to pay for reproduction but low enough to make labor migration essential.[7] But for Orde Browne and other policymakers, the problem in the postwar years was quite the reverse. Instead of African economies reproducing a labor force for European employers, wage labor for Europeans was helping to capitalize African agriculture. The structuralist argument is seriously flawed by being unable to distinguish between the two interpretations: it presumes what it sets out to show, the dominance of capitalism in a situation where it has not remade the countryside in its own image. Such an assumption was precisely what officials could not make.

The implications in an era of expansion were as serious in the long run as in the immediate postwar situation: as Africans used their earnings to develop their own farms, capital might have access to less labor rather

5. Meeting of African Subcommittee, Colonial Labour Advisory Committee, 5 June 1946, CO 888/4.

6. Orde Browne, "East Africa," p. 7. Economists resurrected this issue some years later in a discussion of "backward-sloping labor supply functions" and "target workers." This version did not do justice to the relationship of work to different economic and social systems or to the nature of conflict between them. See Elliot J. Berg, "Backward-Sloping Labor Supply Functions in Dual Economies—the Africa Case," *Quarterly Journal of Economics* 75 (1961): 468–92, and Marvin Miracle and Bruce Fetter, "Backward Sloping Labor-Supply Functions and African Economic Behavior," *Economic Development and Cultural Change* 18 (1970): 240–51.

7. Harold Wolpe, "Capitalism and Cheap Labour Power: From Segregation to Apartheid," *Economy and Society* 1 (1972): 425–56; Claude Meillassoux, "From Reproduction to Production," ibid., pp. 93–105.

than more. Moreover, Africans could use the power of their access to land to resist discipline within the workplace and to thwart the vital effort of capital to raise productivity: as Orde Browne put it, "any increase in efficiency will prove unpopular, since an attempt to raise the normal very moderate standard of performance may lead to a general exodus of workpeople."[8]

This concern with workers' ability to resist discipline was consistent with the perception Orde Browne and others had that the productivity of African labor had in general fallen during the war and was not picking up.[9] Although undocumented, this widely held assumption in a period when productivity was more imperative than ever stimulated a search for a breakthrough in the control of African labor. Asked in Parliament about Orde Browne's contention that "the general native working output has deteriorated as a result of their being able to achieve their target more easily than before the war," the Secretary of State, Creech Jones, agreed that this was a problem. The way out was "improving the efficiency of the worker in terms of health and sound conditions, by increasing the incentive to work and by making the actual conditions of work more attractive." The remedy amounted to the demolition of the cheap labor system.[10]

The urgency of the task was heightened by the increasing ambition of British development projects under the Colonial Development and Welfare Act of 1940, refunded at a higher level after the war.[11] Not only did the capital projects under the act require considerable labor, but they were intended to unleash forces of agricultural and industrial expansion throughout the economy. Officials worried that all such plans would be held back not only by the long-lamented scarcity of African labor, but by its ineffectiveness and lack of skill.[12]

Five years after the war, when the Colonial Office pondered its experi-

---

8. Orde Browne, "East Africa," p. 6. Responding to the publication of Orde Browne's report, the *Tanganyika Standard* (28 February 1946) also noted migrant workers' option of quitting their jobs, which resulted in "great difficulty of introducing innovations which clash with established native customs and therefore meet opposition from the very people they are intended to assist." Clipping in CO 822/130/2.

9. Orde Browne, "East Africa," p. 15; Mombasa Port Enquiry, 1953, p. 15.

10. Creech Jones, written answers, 434 House of Commons Debates, 12 March 1947, c. 182.

11. J. M. Lee and Martin Petter, *The Colonial Office, War, and Development Policy: Organisation and the Planning of a Metropolitan Initiative, 1939–1945*, Commonwealth Papers, no. 22 (London: Maurice Temple Smith, 1982).

12. Sir William McLean, "The Position of Colonies in the Production Drive," CO Memorandum No. 19, October 1947, copy in ACJ 44/2; Memorandum by the Secretary of State for the Colonies on the Memorandum by the Chief of the Imperial General Staff on his Visit to Africa, 6 January 1948, PREM 8/923 (Public Record Office, London); Colonial Office Memorandum, "Inflation in the Colonies, 1948–49," CO 852/1052/1.

ence with "Reconstruction and Development," officials still saw the problem in much the same way as Orde Browne had. "The difficulty has been to find an incentive that appeals to the African." Wages had indeed been increased, but especially given the inability of war-damaged Britain to supply more consumer goods (and its unwillingness to allow hard-currency imports), they were not the answer. Higher wages were translated into shorter periods of work. Laborers also resisted working for set hours, preferring task work, and "post-war competition for labour has unfortunately resulted in the setting of smaller and smaller tasks."[13] The bind that capital faced, then, was that its incomplete hold over the working lives of its laborers meant that it could not control what workers did in the workplace, let alone the process of getting them there. Top officials feared that they could improve neither the quantity nor the quality of labor when they needed to do both.

Officials could see the dilemma more easily than its solution. Lord Hailey, the imperial establishment's reformer, chronicled some new perceptions but had only an old vision for an answer. In his vast study of Africa—redone during the war and published in 1945—he argued that the old way of looking at Africans as "crude manpower" was fading, and with it various coercive forms of recruitment. But "deficiency in the labour supply still gives rise to problems." He worried, as British officials long had, that wage labor was "disruptive of those intimate personal bonds, which are the ultimate source of moral restraint" in African tribal society, and he was not convinced that hesitant moves toward stabilization in mining towns in the Copperbelt had created alternative forms of social security and social control. In the end, he rested his hopes on the vague paternalist ethos that had long helped a portion of the colonial establishment to evade tough problems: "Industries depend on the existence of a supply of relatively low-priced native labour; the contribution which the workers made to industry, and through it to the financial prosperity of the country, carries an equivalent obligation for a recognition by the community of its social responsibilities towards them."[14]

A clearer vision of how to seize the initiative was coming from a part of the Kenyan Administration. The arguments put foward by the commissions headed by Willan in 1939 and Phillips in 1945 were taken up after the war by E. M. Hyde-Clarke, Kenya's Labour Commissioner. In 1949, he told the Legislative Council that "in order to increase production we

13. "The British Territories of East and Central Africa," Parliamentary Papers, 1950, VIII, 1, pp. 48, 139. For a similar argument within the Colonial Office about wages and leisure, see W. L. Gorrell Barnes, Minute, 25 January 1949, CO 859/150/12284/1946–48.

14. Lord Hailey, *An African Survey* 2d ed. (London: Oxford University Press, 1945), pp. 603, 605, 696, 711.

have got to have either more labour or better labour, and I have a very firm conviction that the answer lies in the second." And there was only one way to achieve better labor. "We have got to achieve a stable and contented labour force, because without stability and contentment we shall never do anything to increase our output." This was particularly difficult to achieve in urban areas, where employer-employee relationships were impersonal, and the answer lay in the development of institutions that dealt with urban workers as collective units. For Hyde-Clarke, a more contented labor force did not at all mean a more loosely controlled one—quite the contrary, "very much better supervision" was part of the package, and stability was an implicit part of making that supervision effective, allowing for cumulative effects on "a fairly primitive people." He cited the railway as an example of how better supervision had substantially improved output.[15]

Hyde-Clarke drew out the implications of his stabilization program for urban life.

> By far the most important factor in contented labor in the urban areas, and therefore the most important factor in output is, to my mind, the question of housing, and of housing on a family basis. The question, as I see it is this. Until the African industrial worker is assured of as great a degree of social security at his place of employment as he gets in his own native reserves, he cannot be expected to be a stable and contented worker.[16]

From the anxiety of Orde Browne to the clarity of Hyde-Clarke, one sees the emerging concern that the question of how a labor force reproduced itself could not be separated from its role in production. The ways in which workers were housed, how they combined farming and wage labor, how they accumulated the resources they needed for marriage payments, investment, or social security, and how they associated with one another shaped the ability of managers and state officials to control production and maintain order.

That the railway administration in Kenya commissioned a study entitled "African Labour Efficiency Survey" in 1947 was itself a sign of a concern with something more than acquiring a larger quantity of labor power. The General Manager made clear that he saw the problem of productivity in the context of the problem of social reproduction, asking the head of the survey team, C. H. Northcott, a labor expert from a

15. Legislative Council Debates, 35 (21 December 1949), cc. 638, 642–43. The relationship of more stable labor forces and better supervision was also stressed by the East Africa Royal Commission, Report, 1954–55, p. 158.

16. Legislative Council Debates, c. 646.

progressive English firm, to "study the efficiency of African labour in relation to feeding, housing, social environment and incentives."[17] The survey looked specifically at the implications of lifetime nutrition, education, and incentives as determinants of the output of African workers. Childhood malnutrition, the surveyors thought, left permanent mental and physical handicaps that reduced efficiency once the child became a worker; the legacy of traditional attitudes toward work and supervision was equally deleterious. Stability was thus a central concern: what the surveyors saw as the backwardness and ignorance of traditional African society were critical obstacles to running a railway. Northcott's survey amounted to a powerful argument that capitalist enterprise required severing the African worker from African society: "He is ineffective in many industrial techniques by the very nature of his birth, his upbringing, and his native culture. To enable him to become efficient in this modern age the resources of the environing industrial civilization must be placed in his hands and he must be taught to use them."[18]

The argument had been faced earlier by the Phillips Committee in the context of wartime Mombasa on the brink of civil disorder. Phillips had stressed that African workers were becoming far more urbanized than anyone had realized, and that this fact posed an immense social danger which had to be faced squarely. Forcible repatriation was neither feasible at this stage nor desirable for industrial or urban development. After the war, officials like Hyde-Clarke were arguing that the inevitable was not coming about fast enough—that the state had to make urban workers more urban in order to make them better workers. But the two vantage points produced a similar conclusion: in Phillips's trenchant phrase, "the evils which are commonly attributed to 'detribalization' can only be cured by more complete detribalization."[19]

The contention that the backwardness of rural Africa was holding back the advancement of urban society took into the realm of culture an argument that had been made specifically about food. Both Phillips and the Efficiency Survey had argued that malnutrition was a major cause of inefficiency, drawing on an official study published in 1939. The Committee on Nutrition in the Colonial Empire had been commended by the Secretary of State for the Colonies for being the first to study this problem. It argued that malnutrition was an empire-wide problem, rooted

17. C. H. Northcott, ed., *African Labour Efficiency Survey,* Colonial Research Publications No. 3 (London, 1949), preface, p. 4. Northcott was the former Labour Manager of Rowntree & Co. and a fellow and past president of the Institute of Labour Management.

18. Ibid., pp. 12–13.

19. Report of the Committee of Inquiry into Labour Unrest at Mombasa (Nairobi, 1945) (Phillips Report), p. 50.

above all in ignorance and in a low standard of living, what today would be called a lack of economic development.[20] But though the rural empire ate badly, the creation of an urban proletariat was "nutritionally disastrous." The shortage of foods and ignorance about proper foods was compounded by the absence of women to cook them; the male-centered pattern of colonial urbanization led to malnutrition and consequently to inefficiency. The result was a vicious circle: the development that might raise the standard of living and therefore nutritional levels instead compounded the problem. The Committee thought that employers and the state should feed the workers; they, at least, knew how to do it properly.[21]

By the time of Phillips, officials thought they were observing the "ill-effects of a generation or two of poor feeding." But the solution, by that time, was not to bring the men their food, but to let them bring their women to the city. Phillips realized that "the African is just as averse as anyone else to having his life outside working hours organized for him by those who know better." Proper feeding meant proper families, located permanently in cities where they could learn how to do it right. The argument about nutrition became an argument that the working class had to be reproduced within the city itself.[22] All other solutions were temporary expedients; no other addressed simultaneously the problems of childhood and adult malnutrition; no other recognized that the resentments of a working class, as well as its caloric intake, affected performance; none would contribute to the complex process of building at-

20. Related to this study was the creation of a group by the International Institute of African Languages and Culture to study nutrition in African tribes, one of whose results was an influential book by the anthropologist Audrey I. Richards, *Land, Labour and Diet in Northern Rhodesia: An Economic Study of the Bemba Tribe* (London: Oxford University Press, 1939). Richards argued that dietary deficiencies were rooted in a cultural complex: methods of growing and storing food, incentives to work, and attitudes toward food were intrinsic parts of a complex and integrated tribal system. These systems were now strained by the increased physical effort required by the "new industrial and agricultural conditions" and the state's desire "to allow the African to advance" (pp. viii, 3–4). Richards's argument was based on the organic conception of tribal society that was part of the anthropology of the time, as well as rooted in considerable sympathy towards Africans. The argument, however, could be used by those more interested in managing African laborers to explain why improving efficiency and welfare required breaking out of the unity of African society.

21. First Report of the Committee on Nutrition in the Colonial Empire, Parliamentary Papers, 1938–39, X, 55, pp. 42–43, 92, 98. Orde Browne also was highly critical of how Africans fed themselves with their wages and looked more favorably upon systems where companies rationed their men. "Labour Conditions in West Africa," ibid., 1940–41, IV, 1, p. 11.

22. Phillips, pp. 56, 71. The Efficiency Survey (esp. pp. 86–92, 113) also stressed the consequences of the bad cooking of single men, as well as those of childhood malnutrition.

titudes and knowledge that would slowly bring the African into the role of laborer in a modern economy.[23]

The desired changes were incompatible with the system of cheap migratory labor, and advocates of restructuring it did not shy away from its costs. At the Colonial Office, Pedler had predicted immediately after the 1939 strike that wages and output would have to change very quickly "to something much nearer the standard of European manual labour and the European labourer's wage." The Acting Labour Commissioner in 1945 put it this way: "We have got to break into the vicious circle of low wages and low output at some point."[24] After the experience of strikes and tribunals, officials faced rising wages as an inevitability that—in the absence of structural change—made cheap labor no longer cheap.[25] In his 1949 speech, Hyde-Clarke reminded the Legislative Council that the cost of migrant labor was paid not only in rising wages for inefficient workers, but in devoting to "large, uneconomic labour forces . . . a very great deal more in housing, supervision, accommodation, and feeding than is really necessary, and until we can reduce the amount of uneconomic labor, we shall not have found any answer to this problem of output."[26] By 1952, the Railway's Chief Engineer thought that "African labour at its present level of output is by no means cheap." And the next influential government commission to address the overall labor problem blamed the failure to attack it on the belief that labor "*appeared* cheap."[27]

This, not surprisingly, was where the argument became thorny. As Hyde-Clarke put it over twenty-five years after he resigned in the midst of many frustrations with Kenya's politics, "everyone was in favour of a stabilised African work force but no one wanted to pay for it."[28] The settler counterargument—that such radical changes were too expensive for Kenya's whites and too ambitious for its blacks—carried much weight in local politics. But the views of Willan, Phillips, and Hyde-Clarke had emerged in the first place because of crises in Mombasa in 1939, 1945,

23. For a related argument, see George Chauncey, Jr., "The Locus of Reproduction: Women's Labour in the Zambian Copperbelt, 1927–1953," *Journal of Southern African Studies* 7 (1981): 135–64.

24. Frederick Pedler, Minute, 18 August 1939, to Brooke-Popham to MacDonald, 31 July 1939, CO 533/513/38397/2; Acting LC to CS, 6 February 1945, EST 13/1.

25. The Government accepted the Salary Commission Report in 1948 and saw the inevitability of rises in the general wage level. Kenya, Colonial Report, 1948, p. 1. See also Governor Mitchell to Creech Jones, 21 January 1947, CO 822/130/46787/1.

26. Legislative Council Debates, 35 (21 December 1949), c. 648.

27. Chief Engineering Office, Minute for GM, 25 October 1952, EST 6/1 II; *Report of the Committee on African Wages* (Nairobi, 1954) (Carpenter Report), p. 15. Emphasis in original.

28. Interview, 1966, by Alice Amsden, quoted in her *International Firms and Labour*, p. 49.

and 1947, and their successors would gain more leverage when the state had to put forth an enormous military effort to save the colony from the social and political consequences of its postwar economic breakthroughs.

The Case against Casual and Migrant Labor

At bottom, the critique of the cheap labor system in Kenya as a whole was an extension of arguments made against casual labor, and the implementation of these ideas in the dockyards of Mombasa thus represented a serious test of their relevance to actual encounters with African workers. The rethinking of the labor problem could not proceed far without rethinking the nature of time and discipline. The argument took officials from concern with what Africans accomplished during the working day to a concern with the working life, and from a focus on individual incentives to consideration of society-wide structures that would shape what kind of working class Africans would become. The focus on the working life and class structure had three critical dimensions: imparting fear of the sack, socializing a body of workers into its collective place in the labor process, and creating institutions to regulate conflict.

The first dimension was implicit in nearly two centuries of liberal economic thought: the ultimate basis of production in a free labor economy was the "sanction of the sack." Casual workers—and even monthly workers who did not expect to be wage laborers for long periods—were immune from this basic sanction, for all that was at stake when they contemplated an hour's loafing on the job or joining a strike was a day's pay, not a job. "Discharge is no hardship," worried Orde Browne. A coastal representative on the Legislative Council wrote in 1947, "The African must learn sooner rather than later the hard lessons which unemployment teaches. It will inculcate in him the 'fear of the sack,' a fear which does not at present exist." He specifically argued that this implied decasualizing labor in Mombasa, raising wages, and reducing the size of the labor force.[29]

Hyde-Clarke used much the same language: employers and the state still had to strive to create "a 'fear of the sack' since we know that it is only because of such fear, generally speaking, that the European and even Asian races have a fundamentally different outlook toward work from the African." The autonomy of the rural economy sapped this fear, but with a work force committed to urban life and the job, "the sanction of the 'sack' will apply and it is then that a really marked improvement in output must take place." The Kenya Labour Department's *Bulletin* expounded

29. Orde Browne, "Notes on the Proposed Programme of Work for the Committee of Experts on Native Labour," n.d., Orde Browne Papers, Rhodes House, 2/1, p. 4; S. V. Cooke, EAS, 27 June 1947.

on this theme, citing as its first reason for the "low productivity" of the African worker the face that "he is very rarely worried about getting the 'sack,'" and then listing other causes that also focused on the question of tying a specific class into wage labor: the migrant worker lost contact with his family; housing and consumer goods were in too short supply to make a life of work attractive; workers were not educated enough to appreciate the gains that hard work would bring them; diet was inadequate; and proper supervision was lacking.[30]

Officials were quite explicit that the kinds of changes they were talking about were tantamount to creating "a permanently urbanized working class," and they recognized the consequences. Phillips noted that, one day, the state would have to face the questions of old-age pensions, unemployment compensation, and disability benefits.[31] As early as 1946, the Colonial Annual Report on Kenya stated, "Long-term policy is now directed toward the stabilisation of urban workers, with a consequent need for increased social services and higher wages."[32] It would be some time before the state had faced all the costs of a more efficient and disciplined labor force, but officials had realized what they were.

Second, the difference between short- and long-term workers was more than a matter of disciplining individuals, but required molding a collectivity with habits and values distinct from other Africans. The African Labour Efficiency Survey had again defined the goal: "building up a body of efficient workmen."[33] By concentrating on a smaller body of good workers, employers and the state could bring these workers the benefits of good housing, knowledge of nutrition, education, knowledge of English, and socialization into the work process and transform these benefits into higher producticity. Selecting that body of workers was the starting point, and casual labor—even migration—was immediately an obstacle. Even after some progress had been made in restricting the pool of registered casual dockers, the Mombasa Port Enquiry of 1953 complained, "selection of labour is difficult, if not impossible," and saw this as a major cause of the perceived decline in productivity.[34]

A select body of men would still have to be made into the efficient body. The African Labour Efficiency Survey saw this process as a transforma-

---

30. LC to CS, 6 September 1948, 25 August 1949, LAB 9/776; LD, *Bulletin* 3, no. 1 (1949): 2. The Commissioner thought that rural decay would eventually bring about fear of the sack, but that before this happened measures should be taken to raise both wages and output. For more comments on fear of the sack, see Phillips Report, p. 56, and Carpenter Report, p. 81.

31. Phillips Report, p. 51.

32. Kenya, Colonial Annual Report, 1946, p. 24.

33. Northcott, *Labour Efficiency Survey*, p. 12.

34. Mombasa Port Enquiry, 1953, p. 15.

tion of workers' lives, from the way they ate to the culture they transmitted to their children. This conception implied that workers not only had to be selected but isolated from the backward forces of Africa that could not be overturned in one instant. The Efficiency Survey actually did very little surveying of efficiency: it is more important as an ideological statement on the relationship of industrialism and African culture.[35] Instead of going around with stop watches performing time-motion studies, the team contented itself with rather casual observations in the railway shops of Nairobi, and decided that Africans, after all, could be efficient workers. Most workers surveyed were ordinary laborers—they were as concerned with making the unskilled and semiskilled efficient as they were with skill—but even for them, the basic question was cultural:

> The East African has not been bent under the discipline of organized work. In his primitive economy, the steady, continuous labour is carried out by women. . . . Though the tasks he performed were prescribed by tribal law and custom, he could do them in his own way and at his own speed, for to him time had no economic value. . . . To work steadily and continuously at the will and direction of another was one of the hard lessons he had to learn when he began to work for Europeans.[36]

To redefine attitudes and values toward regularity and discipline, managers and officials had to face a problem—as their predecessors in Europe had had to in previous centuries—far broader than the workplace itself, "how to influence the conduct and effort of men in respect of their life-at-work."[37] This would entail a structure of incentives and increments that would reward performance, increasing knowledge, and loyalty over the years; it involved providing urban workers with housing, education, and other facilities to keep them and their families—the next generation of workers—within the environment that fostered new attitudes toward work; and, above all, it meant paying wages high enough to make stabilization feasible and desirable to African workers.[38] The sur-

---

35. In other contexts as well, the literature on scientific management was less important for its concrete impact than for its attempt to take discussion of the labor process out of the realm of class conflict and into a discourse defined by technology and the universal principles of industrial organization. See Charles Maier, "Between Taylorism and Technocracy: European Ideologies and the Vision of Industrial Production in the 1920s," *Journal of Contemporary History* 5 (1970): 27–61, and Michael Burawoy, "Toward a Marxist Theory of the Labor Process: Braverman and Beyond," *Politics and Society* 8 (1978): 247–312.

36. *Labour Efficiency Survey*, p. 7.

37. Ibid., p. 15. The magnitude of the task of transforming work culture is discussed brilliantly in E. P. Thompson, "Time, Work-Discipline and Industrial Capitalism," *Past and Present* 38 (1967): 56–97.

38. The survey reserved its harshest criticism for the high rate of labor turnover. *Labour Efficiency Survey*, pp. 66, 71, 74, 117–23. The report went far enough for the General

vey report, published in 1949, clearly implied that transforming the working day of the African laborer was necessary but not enough: the working life had to be transformed.

Richard Luyt, then an official in Northern Rhodesia and a future Labour Commissioner in Kenya, was thinking about similar problems in 1949:

> The answer probably lies in greater stabilization of labour forces at the place of work and less migrancy. Stabilized labour will break from tribal ties and restrictions, be less wasteful; be more responsive to normal incentives and more readily subject to the advantages of education, health and housing improvements. A worker, domiciled at his place of work, will become a "careerist" and presumably develop normal ambitions and wants.[39]

The word *normal* is the most revealing of all. It was the antonym of *tribal;* it was defined by the presumed behavior of European workers; and it was now considered a realistic aspiration for Africans. But Luyt thought that normalizing the African was no easy task. He noted that the meanings of family, mutual aid, and leadership in urban society would have to be fundamentally altered and he concluded, "Stabilization of labour will be nothing short of a social revolution in Africa."[40]

The argument had gone beyond the worries of the early boom years that labor would be insufficient in quantity. By the time of the important investigatory commission that London sent to Kenya in 1953, the East Africa Royal Commission, the argument about shortage had become one about the efficiency of a body of workers. In its report two years later, it insisted that stabilized labor and higher wage rates "will make that labour more amenable to improved methods of labour management." Not only would such workers be better nourished and less subject to the "social evils" of migration, but they would have more stake in their jobs. As Africans responded in a better way to discipline, some of them could even begin to enforce it at the lowest level: the Commission looked forward to the creation of an African "foreman class."[41]

Manager to suggest that he had got more than he had originally bargained for. He thought the report insufficiently appreciative of what the Railway had already accomplished and over optimistic about what could be expected of Africans, owing to Northcott's "lack of real experience of African labour conditions." The Government, however, saw the value of having its own predilections for change confirmed by "independent authority," GM to CS, 6 October 1949, and CS to Administrator of East Africa High Commission, 12 January 1949, LAB 9/776.

39. Richard E. Luyt, *Trade Unionism in African Colonies.* New Africa Pamphlet No. 119 (Johannesburg: Institute of Race Relations, 1949), p. 32.

40. Ibid., p. 35.

41. East Africa Royal Commission, Report, pp. 153, 154, 158. The Carpenter Report (p.

By 1954, the efficiency argument for stabilization had been blessed not only by commissions and committees, but by the Secretary of State in the Conservative Government, Oliver Lyttleton. He circularized officials in Africa with a pronouncement that paying workers only enough for a single man was no longer acceptable, even if workers could be found at such a wage level: "to maintain the bachelor system is to perpetuate an artificial and unjustifiable criterion in the processes of wage determination; and even where the 'bachelor wage' still represents the supply price of labor, it may be below the level of wages necessary to secure efficient production."[42] His predecessor in the Labour Government had similarly insisted that workers must be paid "reasonable wages" even if their skills at collective bargaining were inadequate to win them from their employers. In their characteristic ways, then, Labour and Conservative governments saw adequate living standards as objectively determinable and as a goal that overrode both the free market and free collective bargaining.[43]

The problem of urban stabilization acquired a particular urgency in Kenya when the Mau Mau Emergency shattered any remaining illusions that rural tranquility might be preferable to urban ferment. The revolt, which gathered steam in 1950 and became an official Emergency in 1952, seemed to represent all that was backward about Africa: official explanations termed it an atavistic uprising.[44] The imagery in which Mau Mau was discussed was heavily psychopathological: it was a disease of rural life faced with the traumas of the modern world. One of the tragedies of the period was the extent to which officials took this imagery as a basis of action, devising elaborate and heavy-handed programs to "rehabilitate" the disease's victims. But the rural focus of the discourse on Mau Mau

---

115) had also concluded: "The ultimate solution to the problem of supervision in this country lies, in our opinion, in the emergence of a foreman class from among the African workers themselves. Stabilization of labour will undoubtedly assist in this development." Apparently, the ultimate solution could be reached without Africans moving *beyond* the status of foreman.

42. Oliver Lyttleton, Circular Letter, 2 June 1954, EST 26/26/1. In London, there was no clear difference between the parties after the war over colonial labor policy, and colonial policy in general in the 1940s and early 1950s was most often bipartisan, a point Lyttleton took pains to assert on assuming office in 1951. Draft reply to a Parliamentary Question, 14 November 1951, CO 537/6696. ·

43. James Griffiths, Circular Despatch, 26 July 1951, CO 859/183/12254.

44. Carl Rosberg and John Nottingham, *The Myth of Mau Mau: Nationalism in Kenya* (Stanford, Calif, 1967). For a perceptive discussion of the relationship of Mau Mau to urban policy, see Richard Stren, *Housing the Urban Poor in Africa: Policy, Politics, and Bureaucracy in Mombasa* (Berkeley, 1978), pp. 205–12, and for the latest foray into the forests of Mau Mau historiography, see D. W. Throup, "The Origins of Mau Mau," *African Affairs* 84 (1985): 399–433.

provided a vivid contrast for the imagery being used to discuss the urban working class: stable jobs, stable housing estates, stable family life—in short a "civilized life."[45]

The Emergency gave a new immediacy to the question of order that was the legacy of the strike wave of the 1940s, and it raised in a new and deadly serious way the old anxiety about the way migrant and casual laborers contaminated the city with their rural infection. Governor Mitchell, writing his memoirs in 1954 having recently passed a deteriorating situation to his successor, admitted that his government had erred in not making a bold leap out of the cheap labor system. Instead, it had taken "wrong decisions, which amounted to a prolonged—and fruitless—struggle to hold prices and rents down to what was in fact an excessively low wage level." In cities, this policy contributed to a lost opportunity and a current danger. He contrasted the existence of a "steady, reasonably well paid, self-respecting urban African population" that had adopted a "largely European way of living" with "a sort of casual proletariat only too ready for any mischief that may be going." The latter "are all poor and ignorant, lacking in social stability and easily induced to join to form a mob and take part in disturbances at the bidding of the sort of bosses and rabble rousers whom bad social conditions always throw up."[46]

Such an analysis of urban labor, combined with the indictment of traditional Africa, implied that both rural and urban Africa had to be remade, and the report of the East Africa Royal Commission during the Emergency was in effect an argument for that. The Commission hoped to replace the "static security" of "African tribal society," which brought all members down to a low common denominator, with a more dynamic system of property relations that would allow efficient producers to accumulate land and to constitute themselves into a solid, progressive farming class, just as those detached from the soil would be made into a respectable working class. Officials, however, shrank from the prospect of unleashing a rural class struggle more divisive than that which they already faced, and hoped to create a class of yeoman farmers rather than of nonworking exploiters of labor.[47] But this balanced vision of urban and rural stability and progress was a difficult and distant goal.

45. There was an urban component to both the rebellion and its repression. The state's assault on urban suspects, Operation Anvil, was ethnically defined—a roundup of Kikuyu, Embu, and Meru in Nairobi—and it most frequently resulted in repatriation to rural homes or condemnation on the basis of evidence of dangerous rural connections. The operation was, in a sense, aimed at preventing the ruralization of the city.

46. Sir Phillip Mitchell, *African Afterthoughts* (London: Hutchinson, 1954), pp. 233, 236–37.

47. East Africa Royal Commission, 1953–55, esp. pp. 48–53; David Gordon, *Decolonization and the State in Kenya* (Boulder, Col.: Westview, 1986), chap. 6; Michael Cowen, "The British State and Agrarian Accumulation in Kenya after 1945," in Martin Fransman, *Industry and Accumulation in Africa* (London, 1981), pp. 142–69.

The problem of urban labor was immediate, and cities at least were smaller. The enormity of the overall problem brought the experts on labor back to a position that echoed the concerns of Victorian reformers in England with protecting a respectable working class from the contamination of the residuum, only here the residuum was much the larger part of society. Even as the East Africa Royal Commission slowly examined East African society, the Committee on African Wages under Labour Commissioner Carpenter put forth in 1954 a clear policy toward urban labor: "We cannot *hope* to produce an effective African labour force until we have first removed the African from the enervating and retarding influence of his economic and cultural background." The state should take the lead to provide "such conditions, both social and economic, as will induce the African to sever his ties with tribal life and virtually start afresh in a new environment."[48]

Severing Africans from African society meant "the payment of a wage sufficient to provide for the essential needs of the worker and his family; regular employment; a house in which the worker and his family can live; and security for the worker's old age." With that would come not only the end to dangerous frustrations but the "self-respect" and "responsibility" that were essential to transforming the organization of work.[49]

The Carpenter Report at last translated the long concern with stabilization into specific government policies. As the Minister for Education, Labour and Lands made clear in presenting it to the Legislative Council, the Government's main concern in the document was "to increase labour efficiency and productivity."[50] It was this goal that required the separation of the worker from his origins and the creation of a new environment. For all its focus on the family as the key to creating a true working class, the report could only indirectly address it. Despite concern that promoting stabilization simply by paying urban workers higher wages might backfire—producing inflation or even encouraging target workers to leave the city sooner—officials had trouble devising a program of planned social change.[51] Colonial Office experts had already rejected paying family allowances as a policy, for fear of encouraging polygymy, out of concern with paying different wages for the same job, and proba-

48. Carpenter Report, pp. 11, 16. Emphasis in original. Amsden (*International Firms and Labour*, p. 17) sees the Carpenter Report as a response to the Emergency.

49. Ibid., pp. 14, 16.

50. Legislative Council 63 (16 December 1954), c. 1208.

51. The Deputy Chief Secretary of the Kenya Government noted that stabilization "is a matter of changing the habits and thoughts of the African, through such things as housing, property ownership, and old age security schemes," and a wage increase alone would only send additional money into the reserves. Notes on Wages Policy by C. H. Hartwell, 11 November 1952, CO 822/657.

bly, above all, because African families seemed too complex to fathom.[52] While resources like schools could be concentrated where it was "desired to stabilise the labour force," the core of the stabilization policy came down to raising urban wages to a level that could support a family.[53]

The Carpenter Report proposed renaming the old minimum wage as "bachelor" rate, and applying a "family" rate 2.5 times that to adult males over twenty-one with thirty-six months continuous employment outside a reserve, a goal that would be attained by gradual rate revisions over ten years. The Government changed the ratio to 1.67 to save money and renamed the two rates "youth" and "adult." Recommendations for tackling the implications of the new policy for social security were sent on to other committees, which slowly pushed forward pensions, insurance, and other social security measures. The Government's compromise version— almost as much as the report itself—had been honored with strong settler opposition, largely on the grounds of cost, and agriculture largely protected itself from reform.[54] The debate signaled that the *logical* consequences of officials' new understanding of the issues of social reproduction and African culture would not be pursued to their end. The question of precisely where the labor system would be transformed was of central concern, and unevenness would be a leading feature of change. Nevertheless, the Carpenter Committee had made into official policy the argument that the families of urban workers should be weaned, during the course of a decade, from their rural connections, splitting the country into a stable, self-reproducing working class and a distinct rural population. And it had decided to press forward in a highly simplified way, by raising urban wages.

Shortly after the Carpenter Report appeared, a second committee, under Sir David Lidbury, reviewed the salary scales on the Railway and in government service and came up with a new principle to be applied to the labor problem in Kenya, nonracial scales. The old grading systems that had specifically categorized workers by race were replaced by a complex

52. See the long discussion of this question in the Minutes of the 55th meeting of the Colonial Labour Advisory Committee, 18 June 1953, and Minutes of the Subcommittee on Wage-Fixing and Family Responsibilities, meeting of 28 July 1953, in CO 859/257. In Kenya, officials of the Railway had earlier insisted that family allowances would be too expensive and "will inevitably be dissipated in further polygyny." PM, Memorandum on Labour Unrest in Mombasa, 21 April 1945, EST 13/1/1/2. See the Carpenter Report (pp. 70–85) for its effort to calculate objectively a family minimum wage.

53. CO Memorandum, "Labour Productivity in Africa," January 1953, CO 859/304; CLAC, meeting of 18 June 1953, and Subcommittee on Wage-Fixing and Family Responsibilities, meeting of 28 July 1953, CO 859/257.

54. Legislative Council Debates 63 (16–17 December 1954), cc. 1207–1355. See also the discussion in Clayton and Savage, pp. 372–75. The next generation of committees included the Report of the Social Security Committee (Nairobi, 1957), and other such.

system based on functions. In practice, the occupational categories over-lapped to a very high degree the racial divisions, and the Railway African Union, among others, carried out long disputes with the Administration over the details of grading; only as independence loomed did the Railway get serious about Africanization in the higher grades, and by then it had to proceed at a headlong pace.[55] The Lidbury Report, nonetheless, gave wage increases to many workers and articulated very clearly the principle that the African worker was entering a career line, not just a category of "laborer."

The issue of pay and stability received the clearest treatment of all from Tom Mboya when he emerged onto the political scene in the late 1950s. Mboya liked migratory labor no better than had his patron, Richard Luyt. His explanation for the causes of migration centered directly on low wages: "the lack of security at the place of employment and the terribly low wages, poor housing arrangements and inefficient social services." The cure for that was simple enough, and by the time he became Minister of Labour in the Government that preceded formal independence, he called it the "high-wage economy." At a meeting in 1962, Mboya per-suaded his fellow ministers of Uganda and Tanganyika to agree that it was better to have a "smaller but satisfied and efficient labour force than a large, badly paid and frustrated labour force." He argued as well that social security for the aged—a logical consequence of stabilization that had been both recognized and largely avoided since the Phillips Report—was "a necessity."[56] Mboya did not use euphemisms like family wage or adult wage, and behind his directness was his familiarity with workers' own demands for a better standard of living. But there was nothing incompatible between the black trade unionist's vision of raising the gen-eral wage level and the goals of a compact and efficient labor force pushed by the white officials of the colonial Labour Department.

The third aspect of the critique of labor circulation also reflected the efforts of capital to come to grips with workers as a collective entity. In transforming the inchoate mass of rapidly circulating workers into a dif-ferentiated and defined working class, they could establish predictable procedures for regulating class relations.

The postwar concern with productivity never got very far from the

55. Report of the Commission on the Civil Services of the East African Territories, 1953–54 (Nairobi, 1954); R. D. Grillo, *Race, Class, and Militancy: An African Trade Union, 1939–1965* (New York: Chandler, 1974).

56. Tom Mboya, "Trade Unionism in Kenya," *Africa South* 1 no. 2 (1957): 82; Labour Department, AR, 1962, cited in David Goldsworthy, *Tom Mboya: The Man Kenya Wanted to Forget* (London: Heinemann, 1982), p. 204; Kenya Legislative Council Debates 89 (19 July 1962), c. 1014.

anxieties over order that had become so immediate during the 1940s. Stability and discipline were the keys to both productivity and tranquility. "The more remote the control," wrote the Labour Commissioner in 1949, "the greater the likelihood there is of unrest."[57] Day by day, this took the form of concern with the chain of command in the workplace. Once again, the Labour Efficiency Survey epitomized the critique of older methods of supervision and the argument for rationalizing authority and coordination.[58] In the docks, as will be discussed below, the obsession with control took the form of a shift from a gang-based work organization and payment by results, to a top-down chain of command and payment by time.

But if authority had to be strengthened within the work process itself, the vast challenges to industrial order required other sorts of mechanisms to ensure predictable patterns of conflict resolution. The Government became a promotor of trade unions. Earlier, officials had complained that Africans were unable to articulate their grievances and present reasonable demands, a situation that became serious when Africans were vociferously presenting their inarticulate grievances and unreasonable demands. The argument for trade unionism emerged from this experience with strikes without unions and was sharpened during the era of anticolonial uprisings and the cold war by fear of fundamental challenges to empire and to capitalism. Luyt's influential pamphlet on trade unionism in the colonies made the connection, arguing that the choice was not whether or not labor was to organize, but "between an unrecognized, hence unfriendly and perhaps irresponsible union and a recognized, assisted and thus (we hope) reasonably behaved union. There is no other choice in the long run bar shooting down the workers." Unrecognized unions, he argued, tended to be led by "men more revolutionary and more irresponsible and less reasonable than the accepted and recognized trade union leader would have been." A few pages later, he predicted dire consequences unless colonial governments supported unionization: "Lack of sympathy and unreasonable, obstructive opposition will create conditions ideal for the wholesale adoption of Communism by the workers and for the success of foreign propaganda."[59] The best way of preventing the strikes and disturbances such as the British had faced in Mombasa in 1947 or in the West Indies in the 1930s from becoming the revolutionary struggle they faced during the late 1940s in Malaya was to develop institutions to contain class conflict.

Organized revolt was only one of the fears that colonial officials had

57. LC to CS, 25 August 1949, LAB 9/776.
58. *Labour Efficiency Survey*, p. 12.
59. Luyt, pp. 16, 18.

about urban labor. They also were anxious about the apparent anomie of the city, the social evils, crime, and social disorganization that developed where traditional institutions of social control were ineffective. Luyt again saw stabilization and unionization as the solution. He argued that workers in cities would begin to form communities and these communities would begin to generate leaders. Trade unions, he thought, were naturals to replace the "traditional African system of family or tribal mutual aid," and their leaders would play vital roles in community formation, eventually becoming the first leaders in local government, which the Colonial Office was then promoting.[60] Two years later, the Secretary of State for the Colonies was also arguing for a social role for trade unions: "An alternative society must be created for men no longer bound by tribal and village affiliations or else we should be faced with a people without roots, a 'lumpen' proletariat. It was essential that a social structure should be created for these newcomers to industry and urban life in which they would have a 'sense of belonging.'"[61]

If unions and union leaders were to take up the social functions of complex "tribal" institutions, as well as play their role in industrial relations, the quality of union leadership was of vital concern to the state. In Kenya in the late 1940s the Labour Department was more adept at rejecting leaders—Chege Kibachia and Makhan Singh—who were inappropriate to the task than in finding suitable trade unionists who could do it. Luyt himself would eventually point the way out of this bind in the mid-1950s through his cultivation of Tom Mboya. Meanwhile, however, the colonial state spruced up its legislation covering trade-union organizing and industrial relations, sent a trade-union organizer to Kenya in 1947 to help the colony's fledgling unions, and resolutely fought unions it deemed to be of the wrong sort (see chapter 5).

The most important point for the present argument is that the cautious promotion of respectable trade unionism was part and parcel of the effort to build a stable and differentiated working class.[62] Officials from the District Commissioner to the Secretary of State for the Colonies had gone after the AWF with a vengeance precisely because it sought to organize workers as an undifferentiated mass. The union tied to a specific trade, which would negotiate for a unique body of workers in respect to the particular conditions of a single industry, was the alternative.[63] Officials

---

60. Ibid, pp. 36, 38.
61. James Griffiths, remarks to 48th meeting, CLAC, 5 October 1951, CO 888/8.
62. Luyt, p. 32.
63. For a defense of unions representing "sectional" interests within a framework of "responsible" trade unionism on British models, see the Colonial Office memorandum on "Trade Unionism in the Colonies" (1951), CLAC(51)11, as well as the application of this argument to Kenya discussed in chapter 5.

were optimistic that developing these particularistic lines of communication and bargaining would contain the kind of spreading disorder that
had engulfed Mombasa in 1947. After the much less successful general
strike in Nairobi in 1950, the Acting Labour Commissioner noted that in
firms where some form of collective agreement between workers (usually
not in a union as such) and management existed, workers generally had
not joined the city-wide strike.[64]

Industry-specific collective bargaining presumed a relatively stable
body of workers to do the bargaining; unionization would eventually
create within the working class structures and individuals with vested
interests in such stable, dues-paying bodies of workers. Mboya put it
succinctly: "One cannot expect a regular dues-paying membership until
there is stability in the labor force."[65] Although it was the state and the
port employers who took the initiative in decasualizing port labor, the
fledgling dockworkers' union eventually came to share an interest in the
process. The rank and file, and especially the old-line leaders of the work
gangs, would be in a more ambivalent position.

When officials thought about how the process of transforming work
was going, they sometimes used the language of class. In 1951, Governor
Mitchell applauded, albeit prematurely, the changeover of dockworkers
from "what I may call the 'coolie standard'—rags and tatters and semi-
starvation with a hall in which to sleep—into a reasonably paid working
class."[66]

These ideas were not new in the 1940s and early 1950s. The quest for a
stable, disciplined, properly socialized work force had been implicit in the
attack on slavery in Africa and on casual labor in London in the 1890s.
The stress on the role of the state in planning for the needs of workers
over the course of their life-cycle, the emphasis on managerial control in
the workplace, the belief that industrial relations could be rationalized if
the proper institutions were created, and the notion that all these dimensions of planning and control could be analyzed in terms of the technical
demands of modern production and objectively determined human
needs had been part of European and American thinking about industry
and the welfare state for much of the twentieth century.[67] What was new

64. Legislative Council Debates, 39 (21 November 1950), c. 250.

65. Tom Mboya, *Freedom and After* (Boston: Little, Brown, 1963), p. 191. In his 1957
article ("Trade Unionism in Kenya," p. 82), Mboya had called migratory labor the major
obstacle, after the Mau Mau Emergency, facing trade-union development.

66. Mitchell to Sir Hilton Poynton, CO, 18 August 1951, CO 537/7583. In a similar vein,
the Phillips Committee in 1945 called one of its chapters "Emergence of Urbanized Working
Class" (p. 49).

67. The *Labour Efficiency Survey* (p. 123) invoked these parallels, arguing that the "chief
recommendation" of its proposals was the fact that they were standard practice elsewhere in

in the late 1940s was that such ideas were applied to Africa. They were, indeed, applied with an urgency that suddenly transcended the vague uneasiness officials had long had in regard to an organization of labor that did not take account of the European lessons of containing class conflict. Years of strife in leading ports, commercial centers, and mines in Africa, and in the context of labor unrest throughout the empire, had given these old concerns with undisciplined workers and unruly masses a new immediacy. That the problem of urban labor in Africa existed in the context of vast and backward countryside was all the more reason, not less, for the state to push ahead with its urban transformation. If city workers were to cease to be disorderly and inefficient, the advancing forms of labor organization in the city had to be nurtured and protected from contamination.

The Mombasa Problem

In Mombasa, the pressures to promote order and efficiency among urban laborers were particularly acute for two reasons. One was the vulnerability of the East African economy to anything that happened in its leading port and second was the reputation for truculence that its workers had acquired between 1939 and 1947. The very narrow pathways of African communications put a tremendous burden on the port during the period of postwar expansion, a burden it was barely able to shoulder. The dockers of Mombasa were handling nearly twice as many tons of cargo in 1948 as in 1938, and port activity was rising (figure 4.1). The figures reflect not only the export boom, but the increasing diversification of imports for development projects, including varied items that were the most difficult to handle.[68]

Port congestion and delays in getting ships to the berths became a minor problem in late 1947 and 1948 and a serious one in 1952. Ships had to wait for up to fifty-one days until a system of phasing arrivals was introduced. Officials called the congestion "disastrous" and feared the transport bottleneck was "a brake on other forms of development in East Africa." The crisis provoked Parliamentary Questions and further capital expenditures piled on the already extensive capital development program since the war.[69]

---

the world. See also Maier, "Between Taylorism and Technocracy"; Richard Edwards, *Contested Terrain: The Transformation of the Workplace in the Twentieth Century* (New York: Vintage, 1979); Burawoy, "Marxist Theory of the Labor Process."

68. EAR&H, AR, 1949, p. 7, 1950, p. 9; Kenya, Colonial Reports, 1946–55; Irene S. van Dongen, *The British East African Transport Complex.* University of Chicago Research Paper No. 38 (Chicago, 1954), p. 82.

69. Kenya, Colonial Report, 1947, p. 69, 1948, p. 77, 1952, p. 114; C. J. J. T. Barton (CO) to J. D. Rankine, 27 August 1948, CO 852/871/3; EAR&H, AR, 1952, pp. 4–5, 10; Report

FIGURE 4:1

IMPORTS AND EXPORTS AT MOMBASA, MONTHLY AVERAGES (Long Tons)

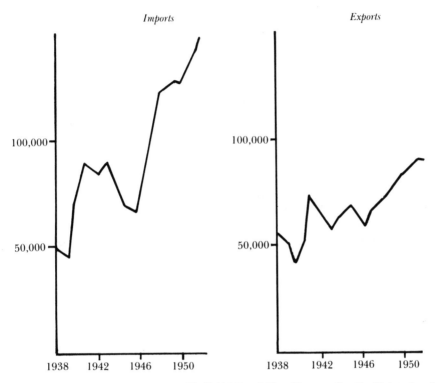

SOURCE: After Irene S. van Dongen, *The British East African Transport Complex*, University of Chicago Department of Geography Research Paper No. 38 (Chicago, 1954), p. 84.

Capital investment in the port had meant above all building more deep-water berths and adding more (or higher capacity) cranes. Two new berths came into use in 1946, and by 1949 a decision had been made to build two more.[70] These improvements meant more goods piling up for stevedores to move on ship and shorehandlers to move among berth, warehouse, and railway.[71] During the 1952 crisis, officials began to contemplate the difficult task of mechanizing cargo handling, but even the

---

on Port of Mombasa Import Cargo Phasing Scheme, incl. Minister of Transport to CO, 26 February 1952, and Notes of meeting at CO, 19 February 1952, on the Port of Mombasa, CO 822/176; General Manager's Comments on the Mombasa Committee of Enquiry (Nairobi, 1953), p. 5; van Dongen, pp. 75–77.

70. EAR&H, AR, 1950; van Dongen, pp. 121–22, 140.

71. Thacker, Memorandum, 2 September 1947, CO 533/544/30891/6, and *East African Railways and Harbours Magazine* 1, no. 5 (June 1953): 19–20.

use of pallets and forklifts later in the 1950s would add new kinds of operations rather than end the centrality of the semiskilled stevedores and shorehandlers, as well as the skilled crane drivers, to the labor process (see below). There was no technical solution to the port labor problem, no substitute for the smooth and efficient organization of dock labor.

While the port was in danger of becoming a vulnerable spot in times of disorder and a bottleneck in times of boom, officials believed that the productivity of Mombasa's workers was falling, as it supposedly was throughout East Africa.[72] During the war, the Labour Commissioner called Mombasa "more wasteful of labour than elsewhere in the colony." In 1946, the District Commissioner of Mombasa claimed that "The output of Port labour has deteriorated since the war and plans are being drawn up for mechanizing the port if the output of work does not improve," although relatively little was done about that for another six or seven years. The report by Booker on his survey of Mombasa in 1947 argued that the port was bedeviled by inefficiency, perhaps related to the workers' discontent.[73] The committee that investigated the port after the congestion crisis of 1952 stated, "it seems generally agreed that labour has deteriorated since pre-war days." It was particularly concerned with the companies' inability to choose some workers and reject others, as well as with the quality of supervision, as causes of the decline.[74] All these arguments were distinguished by lack of evidence and lack of any serious consideration of how to look for evidence on productivity if one wanted it. But that was no obstacle to the officials who wished to transform the nature of work.

Meanwhile, dock workers were being paid more, propelled by the momentum of their effective strikes even during the period of relative labor peace between 1947 and 1955. The railway noted that the cost of handling cargo had gone from Shs 3.36 per ton in 1939 to Shs 7.61 in 1949. On an index of 100 in 1939, the cost had hit 180 in 1945 and 226 in 1949. The corresponding index for the Railway's port earnings had only reached 123 in 1945 and 182 in 1949.[75]

Throughout 1947, as noted in the last chapter, officials were anxious lest the events of January be repeated. The rather unimpressive efforts of the AWF to organize a strike in December 1947 and January-February 1948 were taken very seriously. In January 1949, officials thought that

72. Orde Browne, 1946, pp. 15–17; Native Affairs Department, Report 1939–45, p. 4.

73. Labour Review, by LC Wyn-Harries, 15 February 1944, CO 822/117/7; Mombasa District, AR, 1946; H. S. Booker and N. M. Deverell, "Report on the Economic and Social Background of Mombasa Labour Dispute," April 1947, pp. 12–13.

74. Mombasa Port Enquiry, 1953, p. 15.

75. There was, nonetheless, a substantial margin between labor costs per ton and earnings per ton, which were Shs 8.18 in 1939 and Shs 14.93 in 1949. EAR&H, AR, 1949, p. 61.

discontent with the growing differentials in pay among workers in Mombasa had led to a "near conflagration," and the next month police prepared for a strike that never happened.[76] Later that year, Labour Department officials were so worried that Mombasa port workers would be "bothered" by wage increases in Dar-es-Salaam and Tanga that they recommended raises. At year's end, no strike had occurred, but officials thought there was "sufficient general unrest to make it possible that failure to adjust a serious grievance might have caused a strike affecting many types of workers." Once again, it was the threat of a strike spreading throughout the city that loomed the largest.[77]

In 1950, the Central Minimum Wage Board of Mombasa proceeded with the thought on their minds that "very little provocation would bring on a strike." The next year, the absence of unrest "may be attributed to timely announcement, on three separate occasions during the year, of increases in the basic minimum wage and of cost of living allowances." In 1952, the general strike was five years in the past, but officials congratulated themselves on "forestalling any threats to law and order" through more increases in the minimum wage and cost of living allowance.[78] Mombasa's workers were being handled gently, as they had been in the midst of the strikes.

Actually, the work stoppages that occurred in Mombasa between 1947 and 1955 were minor affairs. For example, 34 workers at the Shell Oil Co. refinery struck on 12 August 1948 over excessive tasks; some of the tasks were revised. Two groups of railwaymen in Mombasa struck in 1949 for a few hours over complaints about promotions and an abusive foreman, but went back to work when the officials agreed to investigate. In October 1950, 43 workers of the KL&S Co.—all Teita—struck for an hour over a dispute about pay records. The supervisor tried to dismiss four of them, but they were reinstated and the Labour Officer settled the dispute.[79]

The power of Mombasa's workers was as much myth as reality, but worries about their sensitivity were, as officials admitted, behind the continual upward revision in the minimum wage proclaimed by the Government and the wages paid to port workers by the companies. As table 4.1 reveals, basic wages, cost of living allowances, and housing allowances for monthly workers were regularly being revised upward, as were daily wages for casuals. The rate of increase, not counting the major gains of the 1947 strike, was somewhat behind the furious pace of inflation in the

76. Native Affairs Reports, January, February 1949, PC's Archives, PUB 3/13.

77. LO, Coast, to LC, 18 July 1949, PLO to LC, 23 August 1949, LAB 9/420; Mombasa District, AR, 1949.

78. Proceedings of Central Minimum Wage Board, Mombasa, 25–27 July 1950, PC's Archive, LAB 10/1 II; Mombasa District, AR, 1951, 1952.

79. List of strikes, 1947–1950, in Labour Department Reports, PC's Archive, L&O 16/2.

TABLE 4.1

RATES OF PAY AT MOMBASA, 1946–1955

	Daily Wages		Minimum Wage (per mo.)			L&S Co. Monthly Labor				Colony COL	Mombasa COL
	Shore	Ship	Basic	Housing	Total	Basic	COLA	Housing	Total	Index	Index
											(1939 = 100)
1946	2.00	2.50	35.00	5.00	40.00	40.00			40.00		
Feb. 1947	2.75	3.25					14.50		54.50		
July 1947						(1)40.00	14.50	3.25	57.75		
						(2)40.00	30.50	3.25	73.75		
Dec. 1947	3.05	3.55									
May 1948	3.10	3.60	37.00	8.25	45.25	(1)40.00	16.50	3.25	59.75		
						(2)40.00	32.50	3.25	75.75		
July 1949						(3)54.00		8.25	62.75		
						(4)66.00		8.25	74.25		
Aug. 1950			38.75	8.25	47.00	(3)54.00	10.00	8.25	72.25		
Jan. 1951						(4)66.00	10.00	8.25	84.25		
Mar. 1951	3.50	4.00	39.25	8.25	47.50					216	
Aug. 1951						(3)54.00	15.00	8.25	77.25		
Sept. 1951						(4)66.00	15.00	8.25	89.25		258

Date	(1)	(2)	Wage	+8.25	Total	Grade	Wage	Allow.	Allow.	Total	Colony COL	Mombasa COL
Oct. 1951	3.70	4.20	41.75	8.25	50.00						218	283
Dec. 1951	4.00	4.50	45.75	8.25	54.00						225	289
Jan. 1952						(3)	60.00	15.00	8.25	83.25		
						(4)	72.00	15.00	8.25	95.25		
Feb. 1952											228	289
June 1952			49.75	8.25	58.00						235	303
Aug. 1952	4.25	4.75	52.25	8.25	60.50	(3)	60.00	20.00	8.25	88.25	237	311
						(4)	72.00	20.00	8.25	100.25		
Oct. 1952											239	323
May 1953	4.35	4.85	54.75	8.25	63.00	(3)	63.00	20.00	8.25	91.25	244	326
						(4)	75.00	20.00	8.25	103.25		
Nov. 1953						(3)	101 to 111, by increments of 2				244	324
						(4)	113 to 119, by increments of 2					
Mar. 1954	5.00	5.50	64.75	12.00	76.75						250	
Oct. 1954											257	
Jan. 1955			68.50	12.00	80.75							

SOURCE: Port Employers Association, submission to the Windham Tribunal, March 1955, in Strike File, 1955, Railway Archives.

NOTES: The Colony COL Index is the Colony-wide Cost of Living Index; the Mombasa COL Index was intended to measure changes in the cost of items consumed by Africans in Mombasa. It was discontinued at the end of 1953.

(1) Wage for workers with under six months service
(2) Wage for workers with over six months service
(3) Wage for a Labourer II (lower of the two grades)
(4) Wage for a Labourer I (upper grade)

late 1940s, but when that cooled off after 1950 and money wages kept
rising, Mombasa's workers made real gains. Between the end of 1951 and
1953, the Mombasa African retail price index rose by 12 percent, the
minimum wage (including housing) in Mombasa by 26 percent, and
wages for monthly KL&S Co. employees by around 32 percent. Daily
wages stayed even with this inflation index.[80]

Most important, in this period the minimum wages for monthly workers were beginning to be less indicative of the wages of the working
population as a whole (see below, pp. 158–61), so that this was an era of
concrete gains for those workers who could get a job in the port. With the
next great strike in Mombasa, in March 1955, and with the subsequent
growth of the Dockworkers Union, the direct action of dockers would
again come to the fore in the wage-setting process and dockers would be
at the front of the upward trend in wages for organized workers.

The upward trend in wages suggested that the one asset of a cheap
labor system—low wages—was a precarious one. The indirect costs of
cheap labor, and above all the threats the system of rapid turnover and
the growing concentration of part-time workers posed to urban order,
were an even more powerful consideration. The vulnerability of the city
had been an issue for the state for some years; the productivity of urban
labor was becoming a growing concern. By the late 1940s, order and
efficiency were parallel objectives, both inextricably linked to the social
nature of work. The African Labour Efficiency Survey—superficial as its
investigations of the workplace were—at least emphasized that workers
were not simply a mass of labor power: they were social beings who could
be efficient and orderly or dangerous and unproductive. Which they
were to be depended on how workers were brought to the workplace, how
they were supervised on the job, and what they did when they went home.
The following pages will examine the long process of transforming the
labor process on the docks: the restructuring of time, authority, and
space.

THE REMAKING OF TIME

Decasualization

The Labour Department's first venture into the working patterns of
casual workers had been put forward as a defense measure in 1944 (chapter 3). It intervened in the hiring process only to require employers to
engage registered workers, and it displayed a similar degree of deference
to the wishes of the workers, imposing few obligations on them. Although

---

80. The Mombasa index was specifically based on goods consumed by Africans. It ran
ahead of the colony-wide cost of living index. The Mombasa index was discontinued in 1953.

the goal of registration—in the context of wartime fears of the dangerous masses—was to rid the city of all but a pool of fairly regular workers, the Labour Officer stated in 1945 that only workers who put in less than seven days of work per month would lose their registration. Even then, he wanted to be more lenient with Coast Province natives. The next year, officials insisted that strict enforcement of the rules was necessary to keep out the "unemployed and undesirables," for whom casual labor was "just one more method of earning a few shillings now and again."[81] But they decided that anyone who worked over ten days each month was doing enough, and that coast natives (or upcountry natives with a good excuse) who put in five to nine days of labor per month would be reregistered as well. A provision that any African convicted of an offense connected with work would lose his registration was intended to combat the disorderly tendencies of casual workers, but the failure to prosecute strikers the next January suggested that this was not a very meaningful sanction.[82]

After the strike, officials still made occasional references to the importance of keeping "spivs and drones" out of Mombasa, but they maintained the labor requirement at ten days. Later, reregistration was required every six months instead of every year, but even so, only thirty days work was demanded in each six-month period.[83] Coastal people were thought to be especially likely to abuse regulations, using certifications of registration to avoid labor obligations in home districts and selling or sharing certificates with nonregistered workers in Mombasa.[84] And it was these gently treated and devious coastal workers who constituted the bulk of port labor: 58 percent of the 4,000 registered casuals in 1947, 69 percent of a somewhat altered pool in 1953.[85]

Officials felt that they were up against the casual laborers' refusal to let anyone tamper with "their right to work when they liked." The Labour Officer complained in 1950 of the "stubborn resistance" to the registration scheme by port workers "who have decided that it was an infringement on their rights to work when they felt like it."[86] Their concern

81. LO, Coast, to Acting LC, 2 July 1945, LAB 9/1053; LO to LC, 27 February 1946, LAB 9/1053.

82. LO to Registrar of Natives, 19 July 1946, LAB 9/1053.

83. Chief Native Commissioner to LC, 6 December 1947, and Senior LO, Coast, to LC, 4 November 1947, LAB 9/1053; Supt. of Port and Lights to GM, 3 February 1949, HBR 12/8/3.

84. LO to LC, 17 May 1945, PC's Archives, LAB 8/5; Capt. Burgess, in Minutes of Special Meeting of Management Committee of Port Casual Labour Scheme, 23 March 1954, LAB 9/220.

85. Progress Report No. 2 on Phillips Report, n.d., c. January 1947, LAB 9/1838; Senior LO, Coast, to LC, 8 June 1953, PC's Archives, LAB 8/5.

86. Progress Report No. 3 on Phillips Report, incl. LO to LC, 23 August 1948, LAB 9/1838; Senior LO, Coast, to LC, 26 October 1950, LAB 9/221.

translated into diffidence: officials feared that if employers demanded too much work on too rigid a schedule, they would not get any workers at all.[87] In Dar-es-Salaam, a somewhat different approach to regularizing port labor also met with resistance from workers, and in both ports, workers' dislike of—or at least ambivalence about—such efforts to control their time while increasing their income endured for some time.[88]

Steady work had never been a demand of the dockworkers; better pay for daily labor, the end of arbitrary discipline, and more recognition for long and diligent service within the framework of flexible work routines were the goals apparent in dockers' testimony at tribunals and from their behavior in labor markets. The initiative—cautious at first—for reorganizing work came from the state, and then capital.

The Labour Department had leapt to the conclusion that casual labor had to go immediately after the general strike of 1939. The KL&S Co. had moved soon after the strike toward employing more monthly workers and viewing their terms of service in a long-term context. Unlike the stevedoring companies—private concerns that made their own arrangements with shipping companies—the KL&S Co. was jointly owned by the three major stevedoring companies and the Railway and had a cost-plus contract with the Railway. It thus stood to be able to pass along its added labor costs to the Railway, while the Railway itself—earning revenue on its entire operations—had more to lose from disruption and less to gain by minimizing costs at Mombasa. The Director of the Company seemed to anticipate some of the testimony to the post-strike tribunal by long-term workers who had gained little from their steadiness: labor, he said in 1946, had "little to look forward to; and probably judging by the example of the past, reasons that the only way to obtain increased remuneration is to strike." If he saw that incentives structures had to take into account the entire life-cycle, discipline in sheds and yards themselves required decasualization, since it was only possible "to obtain increased efficiency by increasing the power of dismissal."[89]

In May 1946, the KL&S Co. had nine hundred monthly employees; its daily workers put in an average of 5,370 shifts per month, or 176 per day, while pieceworkers averaged 10,360 shifts per month or 340 per day. Of the monthlies, 250 to 300 were guaranteed a minimum wage of Shs 40 per

87. LC to Port Representative, Ministry of Transport, 21 November 1950, LAB 9/343; Capt. Williams of L&S Co., in Minutes of Coast Labour Committee, 20 July 1949, EST 26/20.

88. L&S Co., AR, 1957, p. 77, HBR 12/21/3; LD, AR, 1957, p. 11; John Iliffe, "The Creation of Group Consciousness: A History of the Dockworkers of Dar es Salaam," in Richard Sandbrook and Robin Cohen, eds., The Development of an African Working Class (London: Longman, 1975), pp. 64–66.

89. Director, KL&S Co., to GM, 2 December 1946; PM to Baldwin, 3 December 1946, HBR 12/8/3.

month and were paid piece rates and cost of living bonuses on top of that; the rest received at least the minimum monthly wage specified in the Phillips Report. Under the Thacker Tribunal decision, the company's monthly workers with over six months' experience received a cost of living allowance that sent total wages in 1947 to Shs 73/75; new workers got Shs 57/75. The monthly work force rose to 970 in January 1947 and to 1,212 in September. By 1954, about two thousand shorehandlers were on permanent terms.[90]

The stevedoring companies did not follow suit. Indeed, the Railway's Port Manager cited the KL&S Co.'s progress toward decasualization as a reason not to create a common pool of stevedoring and shorehandling labor, arguing that the shorehandlers had less need of such a pool and that its labor might be contaminated by the "meaner" stevedoring laborers.[91] There was some discussion among employers and officials in the late 1940s about forming a proper stevedoring pool with guaranteed minimum wages and high expectations of regular attendance. But the stevedoring companies did not act on the basis of these discussions, and officials blamed the workers for the irregularity of work.[92] The registered port workers, instead of shrinking into a compact, intensively worked pool, expanded from four thousand men in 1947 to five thousand in 1950.[93]

Work in the port thus remained a very irregular affair. Only a fraction of the registered workers were putting in something like a working month: between 13 and 25 percent throughout 1946 and 1947 (table 4.2). A much higher number of the registered workers spent less than five days a month on the job, 35 to 40 percent of the pool throughout 1947. Although these workers were subject to deregistration, the diffidence of the Labour Department toward them—and the fact that they would be replaced by equally irregular laborers as officials tried to maintain a pool of over four thousand men—slowed down the vigor of enforcement and the movement toward a tight labor force. Officials blamed the coastal people—above all, their tendency to move between casual work and farm-

90. PM to GM, 29 May 1946, 4 September 1947, HBR 12/8/3; Labour Department, "Memorandum on Casual Labour Scheme, Mombasa," 1954, LAB 9/217; "Mombasa Rates of Pay," enclosed in Memorandum of Port Employers Association to Tribunal, 15 March 1955, Strike File, 1955, Railway Archives.

91. PM to GM, 29 May 1946, HBR 12/8/3.

92. Memorandum from African Wharfage Co., East African Lighterage Co., and Tanganyika Boat Co. to LC, 23 December 1946, HBR 12/8/3; Minutes of Coast Labour Committee, 21 June 1947, EST 26/10; Ag LC to Commissioner for Labour, Malaya, 31 October 1950, LAB 9/221.

93. Supt. of Port and Lights to GM, 3 February 1949, HBR 12/8/3; "Casual Labour Scheme," incl. Senior LO, Coast, to LC, 26 October 1950, LAB 9/221.

TABLE 4.2
WORKING PATTERNS OF CASUAL WORKERS, 1946–1947
Days worked per month, by percent

Date	Pool size	under 5	5–14	15–19	over 20
Mar. 1946	3,638	34	34	14	18
Apr. 1946	4,000	31	34	16	20
May 1946	4,096	36	35	15	14
June 1946	4,629	29	38	15	18
July 1946	4,557	31	38	14	17
Aug. 1946	4,254	37	39	10	14
Sept. 1946	4,369	24	34	17	25
Oct. 1946	4,414	34	34	14	18
Nov. 1946	4,180	33	41	13	13
Jan. 1947*	4,273	39	48	9	4
Feb. 1947	4,624	36	37	14	13
Mar. 1947	5,059	38	31	14	17
Apr. 1947	4,307	36	37	14	13
May 1947	4,646	35	30	13	22
June 1947	4,214	40	35	12	13
July 1947	4,771	40	35	12	13
Aug. 1947	5,723	40	27	13	20
Sept. 1947	4,990	40	27	13	20
Oct. 1947	4,685	38	36	13	13
Nov. 1947	4,536	40	32	13	15
Dec. 1947	4,470	36	33	13	18

SOURCES: "Casual Labour, Mombasa," incl. LO to LC, 27 Feb. 1946, LAB 9/1053; Progress Report No. 2 on Phillips Report, c. Jan. 1947, and Progress Report No. 3 on Phillips Report, incl. LO to LC 23 Aug. 1948, LAB 9/1838.
*This period includes the twelve-day strike.

ing—for the "alarmingly large" number of very irregular workers.[94] But a switch to monthly labor would be opposed, the Acting Labor Commissioner concluded, by the "casual worker himself."[95] Thus, as the pressure of increased ship movements rose in the late 1940s and early 1950s, so did the pool—to over 5,500 between July 1952 and June 1953.[96] Port labor was not being restructured.

In the midst of the port congestion crisis of 1952, the Labour Department slowly tightened the screws on irregular workers. In the first six

94. LC, in Progress Report No. 2 on Phillips Report, c. January 1947, LAB 9/1838.
95. Acting LC to Commissioner for Labour, Malaya, 31 October 1950, LAB 9/221.
96. Labour Department, "Casual Labour Scheme," 1954, LAB 9/217. The increase dated to 1948, when the numbers registered went from around 4,000 to 5,800. Meeting of Coast Labour Subcommittee, 19 October 1948, LAB 9/1053.

months of 1952, 5,145 casuals had worked an average of 13.64 shifts per man per month—that is, once the 373 "bad workers" who appeared less than thirty times in six months are excluded from the calculations. The average for the not-so-bad workers was down from 14.94 in the final six months of 1951. The Senior Labour Officer told the *Mombasa Times* that this performance would not do: the Department was about to raise the requirement for reregistration to 15 shifts per month, then to 20, while reducing the pool from 5,000 to 3,600. This would enable the more compact group of dockworkers to improve their standard of living.[97]

Between 1952 and 1954, the Labour Officers deregistered workers in some earnest, increasing the standard from 15 to 20 shifts per month in June 1953. Each renewal period produced a "spate of protests" from workers, but no collective action.[98] African representatives—now included on the committee that made recommendations about port labor—pointed out to a meeting in late 1953 that many long-time port workers were losing their jobs and that applying the work requirement each month was especially difficult for Mijikenda workers who went home at harvest time.[99]

But this symbiosis of work and farming was exactly what management and the Labour Department wanted to break. The committee made note of the fact that some workers might have valid reasons for their absences, but insisted that any worker who put in less than twenty days in each of the last two months was out. In December 1953, for example, three hundred casuals were deregistered.[100]

With that, the pool began to shrink, from 5,518 in June 1952 to 5,123 by the end of the year, to around 4,500 throughout 1953. At that time, the pool that served both port and town employers (who had a much smaller demand) was divided into separate sections and somewhat enlarged. A "dormant list" of workers who had failed to meet the quotas rose from 373 in June 1952 to 1,347 by year's end.[101]

At last, the working patterns of Mombasa's dockworkers began to

97. Interview in MT, 29 December 1952, clipping in HBR 12/8/3.

98. Minutes of Meeting of Management Committee of Port Casual Labour Scheme, 25 January 1954, LAB 9/220.

99. There was an exodus of workers, mainly Mijikenda, from Mombasa for the cotton harvest each December, according to Kadenge Mulewa. That would probably hurt attendance in January, a busy month in the port. Minutes of Meeting of Management Committee, 31 December 1953, LAB 9/220. The interplay between seasonal farming tasks and the urban job market is an example of the topics that could be illuminated by the kind of rural field work suggested in the preface.

100. Minutes of Meeting of Management Committee, 31 December 1953, 25 January 1954, LAB 9/220.

101. Casual Labour Scheme, 1954, LAB 9/217.

change. From a low point of 13.6 shifts in early 1952, the average monthly performance rose to 16.16 in the second half of the year. In 1953, the average hovered around 20, and by the summer of 1954, it held between 21.2 and 21.8 excluding the dormant list, and 18.4 to 19.2 even if the dormant list is included.[102]

Perhaps the protests over more rigidly enforced standards were muted by the fact that stevedores' wages rose 38 percent between March 1951 and March 1954, while those of shorehandlers went up by 43 percent, compared to about a 16 percent rise in the colony-wide cost of living index.[103] Higher daily wages might, from some points of view, be an incentive to work more days per month; from another point of view, they are an incentive to work less. But the choice was not left to workers: the working month was being redefined through the cooperation of the state and the port companies. The difference between a port worker and a fired worker was becoming unambiguous, and it was finally having an impact on the way dockers worked.

There were abuses and evasions. Workers sold registration certificates, and companies sometimes misfiled them. Some companies were slow to cooperate in getting rid of bad workers. The African Wharfage Company had to be warned about hiring fifty unregistered workers, while the KL&S Co. worried that the pool was becoming too small and that its labor supply might fall short on busy days. In March of 1954, it in fact had shortages of 4 to 355 workers on all but nine days and claimed that too low a percentage of the pool was turning up each day, so that its daily call-on figures reflected the supply of labor more than the demand.[104] Meanwhile, port officials were kept busy hearing appeals from workers who had been dismissed by error or through failure to consider a legitimate reason for absence, and they had to register new workers and dismiss others. The casual labor scheme was "in rather a muddle at the moment," said the managing committee in February 1954.[105]

The Labour Department wished to resolve the muddle, and it had begun to think about a further step—paying a guaranteed minimum wage to all workers.[106] In proposing a new casual labor scheme as a step in this direction, the Department reviewed what had been accomplished so far and revealed the extent of the changes in the ten years since registration began, as a comparison of table 4.3 with table 4.2 would suggest.

102. Ibid.

103. See table 4.1.

104. Minutes of Meeting of Management Committee, 4 December 1953, 22 February 1954, 23 March 1954, LAB 9/220; Senior LO, Coast, to LC, 24 April 1954, Acting LC to Senior LO, 26 April 1954, Senior LO to LC, 6 May 1954, LAB 9/222I.

105. Minutes of Management Committee, 22 February 1954, LAB 9/220.

106. Ibid., 4 December 1953.

TABLE 4.3

WORKING PATTERNS OF PORT WORKERS IN SEPTEMBER 1954

Shifts Worked in Month	No. of Workers	Percentage	Earnings (Shs.)*
0	644	17	
1–14	379	10	6/55–92
15–19	114	3	98–124
20–24	1,069	28	131–157
25–29	930	24	164–190
30–45	674	18	196–295

SOURCE: Labour Department, Memorandum on Casual Labour Scheme, Mombasa, October 1954, LAB 9/217.
*Based on 6/55 per shift, the average for all categories.

After various excuses were accepted, 615 of these workers were classified as dormant and eventually dropped from the list. The rest had averaged 21.62 shifts in the month (21.77 in the previous month). Most important, 70 percent of the port laborers were working over twenty days per month, compared to under 20 percent in most of 1947. Those steady workers were earning from 1.7 to 3.8 times the Government minimum wage, which itself had nearly doubled since 1947. The earlier characteristics of the labor force—a mass of highly irregular workers with earnings clustered near the minimum—had already been substantially changed.

But officials were not satisfied. On the average day, their statistics showed, 63 percent of the pool turned up, and the companies had to take on 96 percent of them to meet their needs: it did, indeed, seem as if the workers' decisions, more than managements', determined the size of the labor force each day.[107]

Much to the delight of officials, however, restricting registration had produced a waiting list of people trying to get into the pool. Coastal people were to be favored under the new scheme, but as the names were called, a worker who failed to answer in three days was dropped from the waiting list—work discipline began before work.[108]

The casual workers, as before, were predominantly of coastal origin, as table 4.4 indicates. Mijikenda, Swahili-speakers, and Arabs—the people with the oldest and closest connections to Mombasa—accounted for 54 percent of the workers. The composition of the registered casuals thus seems not to have changed in the postwar years: coastal predominance

107. Casual Labour Scheme, 1954, LAB 9/217; Meeting of Port Casual Labour Committee, 5 November 1954, LAB 9/220.
108. Casual Labour Scheme, 1954, LAB 9/217.

TABLE 4.4
ETHNIC ORIGINS OF REGISTERED CASUAL LABORERS, PORT POOL, 1954

	Port Pool		Total African Work Force in Mombasa, 1952 (Percentage)
	Number	Percentage	
Coastal African (Total)	2,532	66	38
Giriama	903		
Digo	158		
Other Mijikenda	357		
Meriakani Kamba	303		
Taita	768		
Swahili speakers	31		
Other Coastal	12		
Arabs (may include Mombasa Swahili)	259	7	
Upcountry Kenya (Total)	830	22	58
Luo	251		
Manyala	230		
Kamba	222		
Kikuyu, Embu, Meru	29		
Luhya	67		
Other	31		
Tanganyika tribes	161	4	} 6
Uganda tribes	20	1	
Other	8		
Totals	3,810	100	102

SOURCE: Labour Department, Casual Labour Scheme, 1954, LAB 9/217. The figures for the total African work force in Mombasa are from evidence presented to the Royal Commission, reprinted in Mombasa Social Survey (1958), p. 265. They refer to a total of 30,755 people.

was clear, and the ethnic distribution of casual workers quite distinct from that of the African working population of Mombasa as a whole.

The casual labor scheme set forth in October 1954 was explicitly intended to pave the way for guaranteed minimum wage payments made in accordance with the type of job for which the worker was registered.[109] Already in November 1953 the casual labor pool from which all Mombasa employers eligible to use daily labor could draw had been divided into two: one for the port, the other for town employers, such as warehouses.

109. Ibid.

The port pool had been set at just over 3,000 workers before the 1954 scheme went into effect: it rose to 3,810 and was trimmed to 3,195 by the removal of bad workers in September. The town pool started at 700 and was in the range of 879 to 1,164 by the end of 1954. It stayed in the 1,100 to 1,200 range for most of the 1950s, and the average man in it worked between 15.7 (1959) and 21.8 (1957) days per month.[110]

In accordance with the new scheme, the port pool was further divided into stevedoring and shorehandling pools in January 1955. The two pools worked for different companies, the shorehandling pool for the KL&S Co., the stevedores for the three major and one minor private companies. Stevedores had for some years been paid about Sh /50 more than shorehandlers per shift for the more difficult and dangerous shipboard work, but their employment was more erratic. The increasing divisions of the pool thus represented a step toward linking men to specific jobs rather than the interchangeable tasks of the generalized casual worker. Tying specific jobs to specific and predictable rates of pay would be the next step in the transformation of work.

Each pool had its own men. A new Labour Compound was to be built, planned for June 1955, with separate calling on points and assembly areas for each pool. Every morning, a card would be filled out for each worker taken on, including his registration number. If a worker reported but was not called, a Proved Attendance Card was made out instead and counted toward the twenty working days required per month. He also received a priority chit that put him in front of the queue for afternoon call-on. The cards were sorted by the workers' numbers and each month the attendance record of each worker could be calculated. Absence for sickness or for annual leave (two months) had to be reported as for monthly workers. Cancellations were to take place monthly, based on the previous month's record, and a deregistered worker could only join the waiting list for registration after two months. At the same time, good workers were protected—they could not be denied registration if they met their working quotas.[111]

The Mombasa Port Casual Labour Committee—empowered to make decisions about the size of the pool and the rules—included African representation, although the minutes of the meetings suggest that Africans took a passive role and, if they spoke up, were put down by sug-

110. Casual Labour, Town Pool, 1953–54, LAB 9/225; Labour Department, AR, 1958, p. 11, 1959, p. 12.

111. Casual Labour Scheme, 1954, LAB 9/217. These issues were also discussed at the Management Committee of Port Casual Labour Scheme, meetings of 29 March and 11 June 1954, and of the Mombasa Port Casual Labour Committee, 28 July 1954, LAB 9/220. On security of registration, see LC to Senior LO, Coast, 21 November 1958, LAB 9/221.

gestions that the speaker "acquaint himself with the Casual Labour Rules."[112] The plans for dock work to be done by a class of dockworkers, a subject of anxiety since the 1890s and of serious concern since the strike of 1939, had at last become reality.

The pool system worked, if not always smoothly. In 1955, efforts to keep the pools tight and eliminate workers who did not meet the quotas led to temporary shortages—up to 330 shorehandlers and 93 stevedores in the first week of February.[113] In 1956 the Suez crisis interrupted shipping and caused larger than normal fluctuations in the port—in August attendance averaged only 54 percent of the pool and only 76 percent of those who came were given jobs.[114] Perhaps the uncertainties were connected with the stevedores' boycott for the next four months of the nonworking attendance card system, in which they were joined for four days in October by shorehandlers, whose own call-on in September had dropped to 40 percent of an already low turnout (46 percent) of a compact pool.[115] These bad periods and the workers' willingness to make clear their displeasure may have helped both sides to agree on the question of attendance money, a mere promise between 1954 and 1956.[116]

After "protracted negotiations" with the Dockworkers Union, which was beginning to be a presence on the scene (chapter 5), attendance money was introduced in January 1957. Each casual worker who attended both morning and afternoon call-on without getting a job received Shs 3. That year, the older committees that oversaw the system were replaced by the Port Labour Utilization Board (PLUB) with representatives of the stevedoring companies, the KL&S Co., and the Railway. PLUB took over all hiring and paying, allotting workers to particular companies and keeping track of how much each should refund PLUB for what its workers were paid. The laborers were queued up in the Labour Compound, chosen in order, sent off to a company in accordance with the numbers it wanted, and given a ticket at the end of the day either for the daily wage or attendance money. The ticket could be cashed on the spot or within three days.[117] Thanks to PLUB's coordinating capacity and the strong incentive which attendance money gave to keeping pools at optimum sizes, the port companies made sure that the pools were steadily

112. Comment made to Kombo Mohamed, meeting of Mombasa Port Casual Labour Committee, 30 November 1954, LAB 9/220.

113. The Committee had to deregister 438 workers under its own rules even during the shortages. Mombasa Port Casual Labour Committee, 10 February 1955, LAB 9/220.

114. The attendance and call-on figures are in LAB 9/223 II.

115. Senior LO, Coast, to LC, 11 October, 21 November, 21 December 1956, 21 January 1957, LAB 9/223 II.

116. Clayton and Savage, *Government and Labour*, p. 398.

117. Mombasa Social Survey, pp. 343–45.

reduced.[118] PLUB was the final step in allowing centralized hiring and payment of attendance money for casual workers without requiring the amalgamation of stevedoring companies that had been an opposing factor to the initial proposals for decasualization in 1939.

Ideologically, however, PLUB's importance had ironic implications. The one aspect of business that capitalists could not handle directly was labor. The firms had to create—with a heavy directing hand from the Labour Department—a collective institution to supervise their workers' time. Almost literally, committees of the bourgeoisie had been entrusted with critical tasks in the work process.[119] Moreover, labor discipline was defined as time discipline, showing up punctually. Capital, in its collective wisdom, was so anxious to secure workers' presence that it in effect gave up its greatest power to insure that they did something with their time—PLUB workers could be deregistered for nonattendance only.

As casual labor became more regular, the companies also increased their hiring of monthly workers: wage costs for the two categories were comparable (see below), while signing-on procedures for monthlies were predictable, and their time even more predictable. Table 4.5 shows the trend. In reducing the casual labor pools, the companies were making good use of the rules they had gradually developed, and by the 1950s, violations of time discipline were being used not only to get rid of unreliable workers but to effect a net reduction in the size of the casual labor pool, as table 4.6 reveals.

The shorehandling company had in fact started to build its monthly contingent in the 1940s. By the end of the 1950s, it had reduced the casual labor pool to nothing more than a reserve. The stevedoring firms were still using a work force that was two-thirds casual, even though the pool from which it was drawn had been reduced by over half between 1955 and 1959. Table 4.7 shows the composition of the work force at the end of the decade.

The way dockers—even within the casual labor pools—worked continued to change under the 1954 scheme and the vigorous enforcement of time discipline and the payment of attendance money.[120] Table 4.8

118. Minutes, Port Casual Labour Committee, 1 August 1957, LAB 9/220.

119. The Government, for its part, insisted that it was not making the decisions. Were the Labour Department to decide "who may and who may not take up casual employment," eyebrows might be raised. Earl Barltrop, Report of the Labour Advisor on his visit to Kenya, incl. Barltrop to Governor, 3 December 1952, CO 822/657. The committees running PLUB had worker as well as employer representatives, but the available transcripts of their meetings in LAB 9/220 suggest that the workers were largely overawed and were told to remedy their ignorance on the few occasions when they did intervene.

120. During the period of high fluctuation in port usage in 1956, officials were less strict with the rules. Wilson, Interim Report on Port Labour, November 1956, EST 30/12/3/1.

TABLE 4.5

NUMBER OF DOCKWORKERS, AS OF 31 DECEMBER

	1953	1955	1957	1958	1959
Monthly	1,683	2,614	3,079	3,077	4,432
Casual	4,800	4,254	2,268	1,783	1,030
	6,483	6,868	5,347	4,860	5,462

SOURCE: Labour Department, Annual Report, 1959, p. 11.

reveals that a daily turnout of under two-thirds of the pools in 1955, averaged over the whole year, became a four-fifths turnout in 1959, for both ship and shore workers. This gave a certain margin to the companies in the percentage of attending workers they actually had to take on. By 1959, however, and most strikingly with shorehandlers, the size of the pool had been reduced so much in favor of monthlies that utilization factors over the year dropped, and the pool became more a reserve for seasonal peaks than a source of steady labor. In busy months like October 1958 or January 1959, the KL&S Co. called on all its reporting casual shorehandlers throughout the month, while in the low season, July and August 1959, it employed less than half. The stevedoring companies kept larger margins, and the increasing discipline of the casual labor force was reflected in decreasing fluctuations of turnout throughout the year: attendance went from a range of 52 to 79 percent in 1955 to 78 to 89 percent (averaged monthly) in 1959. Both in ship and shore work the trend was clear: attendance became more reliable from 1955 to 1959, and

TABLE 4.6

OUTFLOW AND INTAKE IN CASUAL LABOR POOLS, 1958

Cause	Number of Men Affected		
	Stevedores	Shorehandlers	Total
Outflow			
Worked less than 20 shifts	248	133	381
Overstayed leave	69	39	108
Overstayed sick leave	50	21	71
Other disciplinary action	54	18	72
Transferred to monthly terms	136	65	201
Totals	557	276	833
Intake (including reinstatements)	55	265	320
Net outflow	502	11	513

SOURCE: Report of a Board of Inquiry Appointed to Inquire into Employment in the Port of Mombasa (Parkin Report), Nairobi, 1959, p. 24.

TABLE 4.7

THE PORT LABOR FORCE, 1959

	Stevedores	Shorehandlers	Total
Monthly	567	2,644	3,211
Casual	1,180	359	1,539
Totals	1,747	3,003	4,750

SOURCE: Parkin Report, p. 11.

the companies' needs became more decisive determinants of the fluctuation of the labor force than were the shifting or cyclical desires of the workers.

The trend is even more apparent if one looks at the individual performances of casual laborers (table 4.9) before and after the introduction of PLUB, although the available comparison takes a particularly bad month for the earlier date and a mediocre one for the later one. The bad workers had all but been eliminated by July 1958. Even so, workers still had ways of adjusting their rhythms to give themselves a chance to go home. A worker could carefully attend during the first three weeks of one month and the last three weeks of the next, giving himself two weeks in between.[121] The importance of this kind of option was one reason why many dockworkers did not want to be shifted to monthly terms, despite the supposed advantages of job security, and the carrot of increased casual wages that went with the stick of time discipline meant that an adequate money income and some control of time were still compatible goals, even though wage packages during the late 1950s were intended to discriminate in favor of monthly workers.[122] This was precisely why the companies—both shore and ship—kept up the process of shifting workers onto monthly terms even when the nature of casual labor was no longer what its name implied.

Coastal workers continued to show a strong preference for the type of work that had been the least decasualized, stevedoring. The percentage of coastal workers in that category of work was well ahead of their place in the Mombasa work force as a whole, as table 4.10 shows. The difference applied to actual patterns of working. In 1956, when the minimum attendance rules were being enforced relatively laxly during the shipping slowdown of the Suez crisis, analysis of attendance patterns revealed that only 38 percent of coastal stevedores put in twenty shifts per month throughout the year. The most consistent stevedores were those from

121. Interview: Bruce Minnis, former Labour Manager for KL&S Co.
122. See chapter 5 and LD, AR, 1957, p. 11.

TABLE 4.8

ATTENDANCE AND UTILIZATION OF PORT WORKERS, 1954–1959

Year	Pool Size	Attendance Factor	Net Utilization Factor
		COMBINED POOL	
1954	3,960	66	92
		STEVEDORES	
1955	2,351	65	92
1956	2,429	63	89
1957	1,657	74	77
1958	1,550	71	83
1959	1,070	81	73
		SHOREHANDLERS	
1955	1,683	64	83
1956	1,398	57	68
1957	895	76	78
1958	585	79	83
1959	339	85	67

SOURCE: "Casual Labour, Port, Mombasa: Attendance and Utilization Factors," LAB 9/222–226.

DEFINITIONS: Attendance Factor = average no. attending/average no. in pool × 100; Net Utilization Factor = average no. called on /average no. attending × 100.

note: Data were unavailable for January–March 1954, September–December 1956 (stevedores) and October 1956 (shorehandlers).

TABLE 4.9

WORKING PATTERNS OF CASUAL PORT LABOR, BY PERCENTAGE

No. of shifts worked in month	July 1956		July 1958	
	Stevedores	Shorehandlers	Stevedores	Shorehandlers
35 or more	4	3	9	0
30–34	11	10	31	35
25–29	25	23	39	53
20–24	23	24	19	14
under 20	39	33	1	1
Attendance Factor	55	47	72	80
Net Utilization Factor	78	60	90	68

SOURCE: Mombasa Social Survey, p. 269.

TABLE 4.10
REGIONAL ORIGINS OF WORKERS, 1958, BY PERCENTAGE

| African Workers in Mombasa | Casual Workers | | All PLUB Workers* | |
	Ship	Shore	Ship	Shore
Coastal	33	76	59	68	46
Upcountry	67	17	41	28	51
Arab	—	7	.3	4	4

SOURCE: Mombasa Social Survey, p. 351; Parkin Report, p. 25.
*These figures are for 1959

farthest away—70 percent of Ugandans, 62 percent of Tanganyikans, 57 percent of Luo, and 62 percent of Arab stevedores did their twenty days. Casual shorehandlers in general came less consistently, perhaps because the monthly work force did the bulk of the regular labor, but only 13 percent of coastal shorehandlers made the twenty-shift mark.[123]

But all workers were getting less and less choice about their pattern of working. That coastal workers remained on the docks indicates that they could adapt to regular work when they had to. The Welfare Officer of the cargo-handling service told me that it had once been the upcountry people who sought permanent jobs in the port. But "this sort of thing has changed. It's changed completely. There is big competition now. Everybody wants to retain his job, nobody wants to leave his job."[124]

The data on work patterns that the Labour Department collected pertain to the part of life over which employers had a direct say: the job. How workers countered the controlling thrust of management with their own strategies—over the course of a lifetime and with the cooperation of their kin—is a question that they did not pursue. Even the Mombasa Social Survey of 1958, for all its concern with restructuring dock labor, did not follow through. A detailed social survey of lifetime employment and other economic activities, both inside and outside Mombasa, would be

123. Mombasa Social Survey, p. 352.
124. Interview: Mohamed Shallo. David Parkin's recent research among Giriama suggests that Giriama men associate security and control over one's destiny with having a permanent job ("kazi ya mwezi"), whereas fishing or casual and informal sector work appears insecure. He notes that "this folk distinction between preferences completely reverses the notion of many social scientists who see permanent monthly wage employment as leading to irreversible dependency and less control by the wage earner over his labour. . . ." He fails to ask, however, whether these folk concepts might be of quite recent origin. "The Categorization of Work: Cases from Coastal Kenya," in Sandra Waldman, ed., *The Social Anthropology of Work* ASA Monographs No. 19 (London: Academic Press, 1979), p. 324.

necessary to understand the overall impact of the transformation of work. But the trend to which workers had to respond in the 1940s and 1950s is clear enough: the casual labor rules and the shift to monthly wages increasingly presented dockers with a stark choice between working on management's terms or not working at all.

Wages: Toward a Differentiated Labor Force in Mombasa
If the Labour Department, followed by the port companies, had aimed to create a more compact and reliable dock labor force, they had also intended to give that work force a better standard of living, high enough to detach them from the "enervating" connection to tribal Africa and to separate them from the dangerous classes of the city. On the docks, that objective was to a large extent met. In the city as a whole, however, the Carpenter Commission's vision of a working class paid enough to support family life remained far from reality. The wage reforms since the general strike of 1947 did not knock out the bottom of the wage-earning spectrum, but they did add a top, among whom the dockworkers figured prominently.

Their relative improvement, compared even to other transport and Government workers, can be seen in table 4.11. Casual dockworkers— based on working patterns that are, if anything, optimistic—moved from the middle of a fairly narrow range of earnings in 1938 and 1947 to a position well ahead of other workers in 1958. The minimum shift requirements had forced dockers to earn more, and the 40 percent of stevedores who worked over thirty shifts in July 1958 would have earned over Shs 228. According to the Labour Department, the increased utilization rates in the port pushed average monthly earnings for all dockworkers to over Shs 200 in 1958. When Kenya became independent in 1963, the *minimum* wage for dockworkers had reached Shs 254/13, and the average was Shs 350, about three times the official minimum adult wage for Mombasa. They had become, and were to remain, among the best paid manual workers in the country.[125]

Benefit packages still fell far short of the social security system of advanced capitalist societies, but they had at last come into being. Workers earning over Shs 180 per month paid 7.5 percent of their wages to the Staff Provident Fund, and the company matched their contributions; lower paid workers who had been with the company fifteen years or more received a retirement "gratuity" of a half month's pay for each year of service, plus an extra day's pay for each year over fifteen up to a maximum gratuity of a month's pay per year of service. There were some provisions for overtime, sick pay, leave, and set procedures for termina-

125. LD, AR, 1958, pp. 6–7, 1963, pp. 4–5.

TABLE 4.11
COMPARISON OF LOWEST WAGE RATES (SHILLINGS)

	1938	1947	1958
Government and municipality— monthly	16	40	87*
Railway—monthly	20	35/50	87*
Shorehandlers— monthly	40	54/50	152/25
Shorehandlers—daily	1/50	2/75	7/20
Stevedores—daily	2	3/25	7/60
Monthly earnings— casual shorehandler	18 (12 shifts)	38/50 (14 shifts)	156/20 (22 shifts)
Monthly earnings— casual stevedores	24 (12 shifts)	45/50 (14 shifts)	167/20 (22 shifts)

SOURCE: Mombasa Social Survey, p. 274, except that the wages for casuals in 1947 are revised, since the survey table used pre-Tribunal figures.
*Plus free housing of Shs. 21/, so that Shs. 108 should be used for comparison with casual workers, who were not housed.

tion or suspension. These provisions were gradually improved, and medical and other facilities were made available specifically to dockworkers.[126]

Dockwork has never been known for the opportunities it offered for advancement; the way forward has been to work longer and to improve base pay, a pattern that has contributed to dockers' reputation for collective action in many ports. Experienced monthly workers in Mombasa began to get annual increments, within the limits of their category as long as they had satisfactory records, but these increments were only Shs 2 for ordinary workers and Shs 6 for serangs.[127] As the next section will show, the efforts of the port companies to assert authority within the workplace in fact limited the importance of the positions to which ordinary dockers could aspire, while vesting more authority in a hierarchy of supervisors who had to be literate—most before 1960 were white or Asian. In 1957, the 243 tindals, the lowest level of gang leader, received over Shs 180 per month, compared to Shs 175 for the most experienced

126. Terms and Conditions of Employment of African Staff of Landing and Shipping Co. of East Africa, Ltd., Mombasa, included in Memorandum by Port Employers Association to Tribunal, 15 March 1955, Strike File, 1955, Railway Archives; Report of a Board of Inquiry appointed to Inquire into Employment in the Port of Mombasa (Nairobi, 1959). (Parkin Report), pp. 16–19.
127. Terms and Conditions, 1955.

ordinary monthly stevedores. There were only fifty-five monthly serangs on the shore, and fifty on the ships—paid less than 50 percent more than ordinary dockers—although casual serangs received a modest premium to ordinary daily wages.[128] As table 4.12 suggests, the wage hierarchy within dockwork was modest. For monthly workers overtime was valuable—stevedores averaged Shs 49 and shorehandlers Shs 48 in monthly overtime earnings in 1958—while casuals could work more shifts.[129] But for the large majority of dockers, raising wages for the work force as a whole was a more relevant aspiration during the 1950s than moving upward through the hierarchy as an individual.

But outside of the docks, the fate of Mombasa's workers was mixed. The Mombasa Social Survey of 1958 went over the data on subsistence budgets that had figured so prominently in the dreary discussions of wage increases in the 1940s and concluded that the official minimum basic wage had gone up 177 percent since 1947, while the cost of basic foods had risen 147 percent. By putting together various combinations of food, housing, clothing, and other costs, the Survey suggested that workers at the statutory minimum wage were moderately better off than they had been in 1939 or 1947. But the median wage in Mombasa, the Survey found, was now 50 percent over the minimum. The next year, the Labour Department reported that one African in four employed in Mombasa was paid the minimum wage.[130]

In Kenya as a whole, 85 percent of male nonagricultural workers in 1947 had been earning under Shs 50 per month. In 1963, when Shs 100 would have been worth a roughly equivalent amount, 24 percent of workers in private industry and commerce, 15 percent of public sector workers, and 79 percent of agricultural workers earned less than that figure. No longer were all African workers bunched near the bottom; but the bottom was still large, and it still represented as miserable a standard of living as it had in 1947.[131]

The point to be stressed is the growing differentiation of the African work force, not that dockers were privileged by any other standard. A comparison with white wage earners is salutary. In 1960, 99 percent of wage-earning whites earned more than the average docker; half the whites earned at least ten times as much.[132]

128. Senior LO, Coast, to LC, 19 December 1957, LAB 9/1883.

129. Parkin Report, p. 24.

130. Mombasa Social Survey, pp. 276–88, LD, AR, 1959.

131. *East African Statistical Bulletin* 7 (1950), table E5; *Quarterly Economic and Statistical Bulletin* 46 (1959): 45; *Economic and Statistical Review* 4 (1962): 69; Statistical Division, Ministry of Finance and Economic Planning, Employment and Earnings, 1963–1967 (Nairobi, 1971), p. 33.

132. East African Statistical Department, Kenya Unit, *Reported Employment and Wages in Kenya, 1948–1960* (Nairobi, 1961), p. 17.

TABLE 4.12

THE WAGE HIERARCHY, 1954-1957

	1954	1957
	Monthly Workers (Shs per month)	
Shorehandlers	101–19	145–65
Stevedores		145–75
Tindals—shore	122–30	180 and up
Serangs—shore	144–214	195–315
Serangs—ship		205–235
Senior serangs—shore	258–412	
	Daily Workers (Shs)	
Shorehandlers—per shift	5/00	6/75
Stevedores—per shift	5/50	7/25
Monthly earnings—minimum permissable shifts (20)	100–10	135–45
Monthly earnings—30 shifts	150–65	203–18

SOURCE: Terms and Conditions of Employment of African Staff of Landing and Shipping Co. of East Africa LTD, Mombasa, in Memorandum by Port Employers Association to Tribunal, 15 March 1955, Strike File, 1955, Railway Archives; Senior LO, Coast, to LC, 19 December 1957, LAB 9/1883.

The structure of earnings had, nonetheless, changed; so too had ways of thinking about it. In the 1940s, visiting experts on minimum standards had done their budget surveys and decided what was needed to keep a man—eventually a family—alive. Officials had insisted that the procedures to set and adjust minimum wages follow objective criteria and respond to measured increases in the cost of living, even as anxious officials made hasty and ad hoc wage revisions when faced with urban disorder. By the mid-1950s, the Poverty Datum Line was still an all too relevant—if crude—approximation of an income threshold for a barely tolerable life that many urban Africans had not yet attained. But for workers like the stevedores and shorehandlers of Mombasa, the universal minimum was no longer the issue.

The Mombasa Social Survey of 1958 is replete with efforts to calculate different minima for different categories of workers. Like the commissions and investigators who had sought a general minimum for individual workers, the Government Sociologist in charge of the survey was still trying to find ways of objectively defining how Africans should live. But just as widespread urban disorder had done more than the numerous committees of the 1940s to bring about wage increases, so a new form of pressure was beginning to be felt during the 1950s, that of the trade union. The powerful argument of the Carpenter Commission in favor of fostering African family life in the cities had not, after all, been translated into direct support to families, but mainly into increases in the adult minimum wage. If dockworkers were by the 1950s able to support a family with their wages, the arguments of the Carpenter Commission only explain part of the reason why companies were willing to pay such wages. The workers had been demanding them, through the inchoate struggle of the general strike and eventually through cogent memoranda and planned industrial action. The ongoing pattern of disputation and negotiation will be discussed in chapter 5. But in transforming the meaning of the job and the place of dockworkers within Mombasa, the state and capital had taken a major step toward redefining the terrain of struggle.

The End of an Era
The decade ended with one more step in the transformation of work. The port employers decided, this time after consultation with the Dockworkers Union, to eliminate daily labor altogether. They turned to workers hired by the week to be their buffer against seasonal and other fluctuations. On 1 January 1960, the first weekly workers were hired and guaranteed a minimum of Shs 33 per week, regardless of how often they worked in that period. Intended as an experiment, weekly labor became a permanent feature of the port, and by December of the first year, 4,731 monthly workers and 763 weeklies constituted the port labor force.[133] The weeklies received no benefits other than their earned wage or weekly minimum, but officials reported that people eagerly sought this work, "since regular attendance and good conduct guaranteed admittance for a proportion of the employees to the permanent labor force to replace normal wastage."[134]

That suggests just how full the transformation of work had been. For the companies, weekly labor was a reserve, not the basis of the labor force that casual labor had once been. For the workers, casual labor was no longer a pattern of working that, combined with farming or other economic activities, was in itself desirable. The initiative in decasualization had come from the state and eventually capital, not from the workers, and by January of 1960, casual labor in the port was no longer a viable alternative in itself. The choice was between a job and no job, and weekly labor was essentially a waiting list. The eagerness with which workers sought to get on it clearly revealed how profoundly their working lives had been altered.

133. LD, AR, 1959, p. 12, 1960, p. 11. The weekly work force was later allowed to expand. Ibid., 1963, pp. 3–4.
134. LD, AR, 1961, pp. 5, 11.

THE REMAKING OF AUTHORITY

The increasing complexity of industrial work in the twentieth century, some would argue, has made a stable work force increasingly necessary to cope with the skill requirements of modern work. Others would insist that the more important trend of the twentieth century has been capital's ability to fragment tasks, to separate the conception of a job from its execution, and thus to "deskill" the work force. The Federated Chamber of Industries in South Africa explicitly argued that the deskilling of the modern labor process made the expansion of industry in Africa feasible: "Natives possess a natural aptitude for the performance of repetitive tasks which are the basis of mass production manufacture."[135] But if industry has been able to break up the complex sequences of tasks performed by the skilled worker into minute and repetitive jobs, it has also created great demands for supervisors, engineers, and service workers to maintain the human and technological continuity of the labor process. The question is not one of inherent tendencies in capitalism or industrialism to demand higher or lower levels of skill. Machinery and organizational techniques are, on the one hand, the cause of new power relations within industry, altering the ability of specific groups to bargain and to influence the production process itself; and, on the other hand, decisions to develop or to use particular technologies or management techniques themselves reflect struggles within the workplace.

The Marxist conception of deskilling as a strategy of industrial capital, put forward by Harry Braverman, has been answered by a Marxist criticism of this argument's assumption that capital, in its choice of technology as much as anything else, always has its way.[136] Capital's desire to remake the workplace most often arose in the context of resistance to work discipline, including the effectiveness of skilled workers in deflecting assaults on their craft traditions and power on the shop floor; and even capital's successes have often led to new kinds of struggle, as in the case of assembly lines that forced workers to conform to a set pace of work but could be shut down completely by workers at a single point. David Gordon, Richard Edwards, and Michael Reich argue that in the United States the ability of workers to counteract the foreman-based discipline in large industries in the nineteenth century led to reliance on technological control—machine-paced work—and layers of bureaucratic authority

135. Federated Chamber of Industries memorandum to Tomlinson Commission, 1953, quoted in Stanley Greenberg, *Race and State in Capitalist Development* (New Haven: Yale University Press, 1980), p. 192.

136. Harry Braverman, *Labor and Monopoly Capitalism: The Degradation of Work in the Twentieth Century* (New York: Monthly Review, 1974); Burawoy, "Toward a Marxist Theory of the Labor Process."

within monopolized industry. But that process, in turn, was met by the growth of industrial unions, eventually leading to a more segmented structure of work: in monopolized industries, capital was willing to pay high wages and incorporate unions into an established structure of wage determination and discipline in order to ensure its long-term control of the work process itself. In other industries, especially where profit margins were lower and where more vulnerable groups of workers—immigrants, blacks, women—could be drawn upon, harsher forms of discipline prevailed. The process of obtaining consent in the workplace extended into society as a whole, as capital tolerated (and often promoted) changes in government policy toward education, social security, and access to property that integrated workers into a world defined by work and commodities.[137] The repeated transformations of the workplace cannot be understood as a linear process intrinsic to capitalist or industrial development; the process is far more uneven and far more closely related to struggles, within and outside the workplace, over the nature of work as much as its remuneration.

On the docks of Mombasa, the restructuring of the labor process reflected in large measure the belief of the cargo-handling companies that they had to rebuild their authority after the challenges of collective actions from 1939 to 1947. The changes had something to do with technology but affected areas of dock work where technical change had little impact as much as, if not more than, areas where mechanization mattered. And if altering the nature of supervision on the docks was seen as a way of improving productivity, the decisions were made in the absence of concrete data on labor efficiency and the results assessed without systematic collection of new data. The issue was authority, and closer supervision itself was a goal as much as a means.

The African Labour Efficiency Survey had as clear an idea of the nature of management as it had of the nature of workers' lives: "It is characteristic of efficient organizations that they plan before a job is begun; they provide sufficient equipment and tools, give explicit instructions to their foremen, and keep careful watch upon the progress of the job."[138] Centralized control and assuring performance by monitoring were axiomatic to this conception of modern management. Such a notion, however, was quite distinct from the nature of authority and motivation that had long existed in the docks of Mombasa.

The overwhelming number of the dockers who have been the focus of

---

137. David Gordon, Richard Edwards, and Michael Reich, *Segmented Work, Divided Workers: The Historical Transformation of Labor in the United States* (New York: Cambridge University Press, 1982); Edwards, *Contested Terrain;* Ira Katznelson, "Community, Capitalist Development and the Emergence of Class," *Politics and Society* 9 (1979): 203–37.

138. *African Labour Efficiency Survey*, 1947, p. 12.

the previous chapters were semiskilled workers. They had to learn how to handle the cargo that was being moved on and off cranes and railway cars, and into and out of warehouses, but they did not themselves operate machinery. The skill differentials in dockwork were much less critical than in, say, railway work. The port's crane drivers were the closest equivalent to the self-conscious vanguard of skilled labor on the railway. In Mombasa, they worked for the East African Railways and Harbours Administration, not for the shorehandling or stevedoring companies. As crane driving became an increasingly Africanized job after World War II, the Railway made sure that it was kept as a distinct job category, with a relatively high pay scale. The drivers' scale in 1946 had unusually large increments for experience for the time, ranging from Shs 60 per month to Shs 150 for a fifteen-year veteran. By 1962, the top of the scale ranged from Shs 212 per month to Shs 495, plus housing allowance.[139]

As is so often the case with a small body of quite skilled men who have the potential power to shut down entire operations or to influence daily labor in a variety of subtle ways, crane drivers soon acquired a reputation as a feisty group of workers. Their issues, however, were their own, and had much to do with tensions over multiracial pay scales, comparisons with other railway workers, and numerous disputes over crane operations.[140] Their relationship with port workers was potentially conflicting: by determining the pace at which cargo was moved, crane drivers could make life miserable for a time worker or unprofitably slow for a piece worker.[141] By and large, the crane drivers and the cargo handlers seem to have worked out a modus vivendi, and they went their separate ways in wage struggles.[142] As active members of the Railway African Staff Union at least as early as 1948, crane drivers were not involved in the Dockworkers Union once it was founded and the separation remained institutionalized.[143]

139. There were about a hundred crane drivers in 1947, about two hundred in 1960. Acting CME, Memorandum on Refusal of Certain Drivers to Work Overtime, 10 November 1947, EST 9/9/2/6; CME to GM, 2 September 1960, EST 9/9/13/13/3; CME to GM, 23 October 1946, EST 9/9/2I; Inquiry into Crane Drivers, 24 August 1962, Railway Archives.

140. Such issues included overtime, whether cranes could be operated while seated, and complaints about supervisors. Staff and Welfare Assistant, Note, 1 March 1948, EST 9/9/2/6; Acting PM to GM, 16 February 1944; Asst. Inspector in Charge of Port Police to District Locomotive Superintendent, 15 April 1947, EST 9/9/2/6; Acting CME, memorandum on refusal of certain drivers to work overtime, 10 November 1947, EST 9/9/2/6; Acting GM, Note on Crane Drivers' Case, 1 September 1947, EST 9/9/2/6; Inquiry into Crane Drivers, 1962.

141. Apparently, piecework gangs occasionally manhandled a crane driver they thought was acting deliberately slowly. Interview: Bruce Minnis.

142. Ibid.

143. The crane drivers were described as a section of RASU in 1948. Staff and Welfare Assistant, Note, 1 March 1948, EST 9/9/2/6.

For the bulk of the dockworkers, any increased output in the operation of cranes meant not so much a change in how they worked as more of the same. Whatever crane drivers wanted to do to control the pace of work, the Railway preempted them to some extent by installing increasingly high-capacity cranes during the recapitalization effort in the port beginning in the late 1940s. On the ships, larger loads were a potential strain: how laborers and supervisors settled on new work rhythms was a question of give and take within the labor process.[144] Only when the container revolution came to East Africa in the 1970s would technology offer another way of controlling shipboard work. On the shore, higher capacity cranes made work harder during the early 1950s, but by 1953 the introduction of pallets, forklifts, and Scammel mechanical horses began to change the manner of working. It was during and after the port congestion crisis of 1952 that the port authorities began to advocate the "intensive mechanization of cargo handling." This meant, above all, palletization. Bags or boxes of "suitable commodities" could be stacked on pallets as soon as they came off the ship or the railway and moved on the pallets using forklifts among dockside, warehouse, and railway yard.[145] This was especially useful with the bags of coffee and other export commodities that Kenya produced, but was less useful with imports, since they were so varied.[146] By 1956, the port had 41 forklift trucks, 42 one-ton platform trucks, 5 electric fixed platform trucks, 35 Scammell trailers, and 15 Scammell horses.[147] In the case of coal (although of diminishing importance as the railway converted to oil as its main fuel), mechanized offloading eased one of the most unpleasant tasks, but with the loading of caustic soda from Lake Magadi, dust damaged the machines and left the large sacks of the material literally on the backs of manual workers. The KL&S Co. in fact reported in 1953 that the possibilities for mechanizing cargo handling in East Africa were limited.[148] While crane drivers and forklift operators joined the ranks of specialized workers, the work of over five thousand dockers remained what it had long been, arduous manual labor. What changed most of all was the nature of supervision and the nature of ties within the workplace.

144. For a stimulating analysis of this problem in an American factory, see Michael Burawoy, *Manufacturing Consent: Changes in the Labor Process under Monopoly Capitalism* (Chicago: University of Chicago Press, 1980). He shows that management's quest for tighter control and faster procedures was often compromised by shop-floor foremen, who were in closer touch with the men and understood the dangers of conflict should management push the pace too hard or stop the various dodges that workers developed.

145. EAR&H, AR, 1953, p. 57; Mombasa Port Enquiry, 1953, p. 10.

146. Interview: Bruce Minnis; Port Manager's Office, "Port of Mombasa, November 1956," Rhodes House, MSS. Afr. s912.

147. "Port of Mombasa."

148. Interview: Bruce Minnis; L&S Co, AR, in EAR&H, AR, 1953, p. 128.

The transformation of work time embodied in the registration schemes and the shift to monthly labor were paralleled by a transformation of the mechanisms by which workers were induced to put in a good day's labor once they were on the job. As with hiring, the restructuring of authority in the workplace cut into the web of social affiliation and individual decision making that characterized the gang system and casual labor, replacing it with a top-down system of supervision. These changes were most clearly described to me in a long interview with Bruce Minnis, the labor supervisor of the Kenya Landing and Shipping Co. during the late 1950s, the man on the front lines of the company's encounter with labor.[149] The old system of piecework and payment by the gang was very much in question in 1954 and 1955, and Minnis described the changes in a part of dockwork where technological change was of little help, for example, in handling imports like ironwork (pipes, rails, angle iron, and so on) that could not be bulked readily and was handled all along by cranes and human labor. The task of sorting and stacking these items in the sheds was as difficult as loading them off ships. The gangs of shorehandlers who moved such items had been paid by the tonnage moved. The serang brought a list of men, each of whom had an identity number, and presented it to the clerk after the shift. He was then paid the total amount due for the tonnage moved. In Minnis's retrospective view, the old system of discipline enforced within the gang had its merits:

> If one man was lazy, they just didn't pay him, they gave him a little, and he wasn't engaged the next day. He was chucked out of the gang. Once he became freelance, the chances of getting employment were very low. . . . Some of the gangs were all related to each other, in the African system of relationships, and the gang leader was the senior man, i.e. it was a small tribe and he was the chief. Hence, discipline, work discipline, was good; if they didn't work they didn't get paid.

This discipline would be enforced not just by the serang but by "the other members of the gang," who stood to lose if a sluggard caused the total tonnage moved to be lower. As a result, "there was a third as many supervisors as there are now. Because they supervised themselves." The gangs had other kinds of informal sanctions: when taking bags of caustic soda from railway cars to the sheds, "two men stood in a railway wagon and loaded a sack on another man's back. If they didn't like him, they let it scrape a wee bit on his back. Now when you do that all morning, you haven't got a back left." The piecework gangs could also act together to make sure that others did their bit: sometimes, according to Minnis, they beat up clerks or crane drivers who slowed them down.

149. Interviewed at his home in Mombasa on 30 May 1979.

The system got the job done. But the workers grew to know "the dodges." When checks were run, management found that wages had been paid on 25 percent more tons than had actually been moved; the clerks, in addition to their monthly wages paid a bonus on work that the gangs they monitored performed, had slightly inflated each tally, raising the gangs' wages and their own bonuses. The gist of Minnis's memory is confirmed by the comments on piecework in the KL&S Co. annual report for 1954: "owing to the many irregularities and abuses by the labour of this type of employment, every endeavor will be made to discontinue their employment, except in certain isolated sections where machines cannot be employed."[150] But machines could only be part of the answer to work gangs' manipulative abilities.

Learning the dodges was part of gangs' ability to work their way into particular phases of dockwork. Such job differentiation was frequently reinforced by ethnic lines: Luo concentrating in the soda sheds, along with some Giriama; Digo providing the mainstay of coaling labor; coastal people in general working as stevedores.

The changes in hiring practices were a critical blow to this system. After 1954, workers were no longer hired as gangs. They queued up, with separate lines only for stevedores and shorehandlers, at a central labor compound. As the KL&S moved toward monthly labor, it balanced its commitment to employ workers every day by insisting on being able to send them wherever they were most useful in the day's operations. Both registered casuals and monthlies could be sent individually to particular sheds without the company having to go to the trouble of signing people on to do specific tasks. Similarly, the fact that piecework and payment-by-gang were less effective in some areas than in others, where for instance delicate cargo was being handled or mechanical devices set the pace of work, meant that any port-wide system of hiring and paying would be difficult to combine with the system of gangs as it had long existed in Mombasa. The Casual Labour Scheme of 1954, added to the longer process of decasualizing shorehandling, was a blow to the gang system. Cut off from their specific connections to hiring and to work, gangs lost their collective identity and role in the labor process. But with the loss of gangs as an instrument of collective self-discipline, a distinct class of foremen had to direct the work.

Supervision from above was in any case the byword of the era in the Railway and Harbours Administration, and more generally in Kenya. The General Manager of the Railway had written in a memorandum in 1947 that "the general tendency in recent years has been for the mass of the African employees to do as little as possible, thus requiring intensive

---

150. L&S Co., AR, printed in EAR&H, AR, 1954, p. 130.

supervision at very high cost." Twelve years later, another General Manager made much the same complaint about the low output of the African labor force, and his Chief Mechanical Engineer added that the situation had become worse since 1955: "He felt that apart from Time and Motion Studies, increased productivity could be achieved only by increased supervision, generally European supervision." In 1960, the GM and Commissioner of Transport of East Africa, Arthur Kirby, defined the problem of management in East Africa as supervising "employees who are so near the primitive that they have not yet developed industrial esprit de corps or civic pride." The workers were "people who have no pride of property and whose native way of life has for generations been the perfection of idleness."[151] Such remarks bracket a period in which the structure of work on the railway underwent substantial change, and in which the KL&S Co., partly owned by the railway, transformed the nature of discipline in an even more clear-cut manner.

But if direct supervision, above all European supervision, as an answer to African work habits was an article of faith even on the eve of decolonization, the transition from gang-centered to foreman-centered discipline engendered problems of its own. In 1955, after the discovery of how clerks padded the books in the ironwork yards, the piecework system there was changed into work by time. There was resistance. Casual workers did not return to work there, but Minnis replaced them by monthlies. About 250 workers, in his recollection, were involved in what Minnis considered an unreported strike, lost from the records because for casual workers it could be treated as nonattendance.[152]

Shifting to work by time was to put great reliance on supervisors and ultimately on a single means of enforcing obedience: the sanction of the sack. Yet a large stack of KL&S Co. employment records from 1953 to 1959 found strewn around a shed of the Kenya Cargo Handling Service (successor to the KL&S and the stevedoring companies) suggests that workers were very rarely fired for working badly. These cards for monthly workers contain comments about workers as well as records of disciplinary action: they are too disorganized to make quantitative analysis worthwhile, except for the observation that firing for bad *quality* of work is rarely mentioned. The overwhelming majority of workers who were in fact sacked were punished for not showing up at all: the records state that they were fired for absenteeism or overstaying leave. One worker, taken

151. Memorandum No. 294 for Railway Advisory Council, 3 February 1947, EST 13/6; Extract from Minutes of Chief Officers' Meeting, 16 April 1959, EST 13/11. Arthur Kirby, reprint of an article from "Railway Steel Topics," in *EAR&H Magazine* 4, no. 8 (April 1960): 250–51.
152. Interview.

on in 1955, was described in 1956 as "extremely lazy and very indolent," but he was only fired in 1958 for theft. Another, hired in 1953, was suspended in 1954 for "inefficient and slack work," labeled "indolent" and a "bad worker" in 1956, then transferred to the casual pool, but only fired in 1957 when he overstayed his leave. A sweeper hired in 1942 was cited in 1954 for being a "shirker," but he continued shirking for another two years, when he resigned. A laborer was suspended briefly in 1953 for refusing to work on the cement wharf, was cited in 1954 for "slack and idle work," but hung on until 1957, when he was fired for a long absence. But on several hundred cards examined, even such observations were rare—workers who showed up elicited few comments.[153]

The quality of work in this system was no higher than the quality of supervision. As Minnis put it, "When piecework was taken away, you wanted very good supervision." He emphasized the importance of personal qualities—how good supervisors were at intimidation and cajolery. That had its negative side, too: when in 1958 Minnis called the workers in one shed "wanawake" (women), they walked off the job in a wildcat strike. The Dockworkers Union called, unsuccessfully, for his removal.[154] Especially when the union took root in the port, discipline became bureaucratized: charge sheets had to be written up and meetings held, all with the possibility of a work stoppage lurking in the background.[155] As the next chapter will show, wildcat strikes over issues of discipline in the daily running of the port were rather common in the late 1950s. Several years after the shift to time work, the KL&S Co.—which had no African supervisors prior to 1961—began to Africanize its supervisory staff, a progressive move in some ways, but one that removed the advantage which Kenya's racist society had given to white supervisors, the expectation that whites would command. Out of an establishment of 106 supervisors, the company had thirteen Africans in training in Mombasa in 1961. Its policy was to recruit the new African supervisors from clerical positions, and manual workers had little respect for them.[156]

Most company officials apparently thought that shorehandlers worked more slowly under the new time discipline than under the old piecework system. Minnis thought so himself, but believed that this might have been offset by the fact that the men worked more effectively, for example, sorting iron as it was offloaded instead of rushing to move it as quickly as possible. None of this can be confirmed statistically: the data are lacking,

153. Employment records of L&S Co., 1953–59.
154. Deputy LC, Notes of 2d and 3d meetings with Dock Workers Union, 23 December 1958, LAB 10/345. See also pp. 232–33 below.
155. Interview: Mohamed Shallo.
156. Minnis; L&S Co., AR, 1960, 1961.

and it would be nearly impossible to isolate the effect of changing forms of management from other variables, even if better measures of output were available.[157]

Whether the actual effect of the changes was to raise productivity or to lower it, the transformation of supervision reflected concern with issues of authority that transcended the question of efficiency. The port companies distrusted the people who occupied the middle ground between management and the workers, fearing both the autonomy of these people and their close ties to laborers. The serangs came from the Swahili milieu of Mombasa, and their history included Beni as well as the strikes of the 1930s and 1940s. Many had spent years, if not decades, in the docks, and it was this intimacy with their work gangs that made the system function. The official Government Sociologist, Gordon Wilson, looked into port labor for the Mombasa Social Survey of 1958 and came down on both sides of the question of serangs. On the one hand, they "did an effective job"; on the other hand, "This group of workers, sociologically and psychologically, must be divorced from the ordinary labourers if the port is to run smoothly in the future."[158]

The companies had earlier begun to refocus the loyalty of serangs from their gangs to the firms by putting some of them on retainer. In 1944, the stevedoring companies started to pay some—but not all—of their serangs and tindals retainer fees of Shs 12–20 per month, besides the extra shilling they got for each shift worked. But in other respects, they were treated like ordinary casual workers.[159] The Casual Labour Rules of 1954 had of course broken the power of serangs to recruit their own gangs and present them as a unit to the companies, but as the companies organized their own gangs, it was up to them to alter the role of serangs within the work process itself. The KL&S Co.'s shift to monthly labor and its reduction of piecework—where gangs had been paid as a unit—made serangs into a kind of foremen. The Company's official hierarchy, divided into nine segments, lists tindals, two classes of serangs, plus assistant head serangs, the head serangs, and senior serangs, each with a specified monthly salary range and annual increments.[160]

---

157. The data on "port working" published in the railway annual reports include measures like tons moved per quai foot or per gang hour. These do measure net effectiveness, but are strongly influenced by the pace at which ships arrive, the weather, crane usage, railway arrivals, and so on—all of which varied greatly from year to year.

158. Mombasa Social Survey, pp. 337, 365.

159. Warren Wright Report, pp. 36–37; LO, Coast, to LC, 15 January 1946, LAB 9/1053; Interview: David Amimo.

160. Terms and Conditions of African Staff of Landing & Shipping Co., incl. Memorandum by Port Employers Association to Tribunal, 15 March 1955, Strike File, Railway Archives.

The Government Sociologist compared this reformed structure as of 1956 to that of the stevedoring companies, where the serangs still formed gangs from the workers hired daily and did so on the basis of "friendship and nepotism." These serangs, he thought, were opposed to the use of monthly labor by the stevedoring companies, and they weakened the gradually developing Dockworkers Union. They had a "vested interest" in the structure of authority as it was and did not like union shop stewards or a hierarchy of company officials acquiring more power in the workplace.[161]

Although in 1957 and 1958 most of the stevedoring labor was still casual, the PLUB decided to remove the serangs from the casual list. At the time, the stevedoring companies had forty-three monthly serangs and twenty-six casual serangs. PLUB made eleven of the latter into monthly workers, mostly as specialists, and demoted the rest to ordinary casuals. The DWU opposed this move, and the dispute dragged on for nearly a year, with the companies insisting successfully that they get their way.[162] Meanwhile, the staff of supervisors above the level of serang was beefed up, and in 1959 the Parkin Board, after its study of port labor, recommended a new grade of "junior foreman" between the serang and the foreman, until then the lowest level of management. These supervisors would have to hold a school certificate and would be sent to the Labour Department's school at Kabete. This plan built upon the KL&S Co.'s recent initiative to recruit African supervisors largely from the ranks of clerical employees, and it already had a training scheme for supervisors of all races.[163] By elaborating the supervisory hierarchy among Western-educated employees, the companies could hardly have made a bigger break with the Swahili milieu and the gang structure that had played such a big role in recruitment, work discipline, and payment in an earlier era of dockwork.

By 1964, the port labor force included 467 supervisors (not including serangs) and 844 clerks, out of a total establishment (including weekly and monthly workers) of 8,290.[164] Did all these changes improve productivity? There were too many changes in capital equipment in the port, as well as too many fluctuations in the pace of ship arrivals and the delivery of agricultural goods to the port to make an accurate evaluation of such

161. Interim Report on Port Labour, November 1956, EST 30/12/3/1. Similar points were made in interviews by Minnis and Hussein Ramadan.

162. Acting General Secretary, DWU, to LC, 23 January 1958, Notes on Conciliation Meeting, 28 January 1958, LAB 10/326; Manager, PLUB, memorandum, 15 October 1958, Industrial Relations Officer to Deputy LC, 6 November 1958, and SrLO, Coast, to LC, 3 December 1958, LAB 9/221.

163. Parkin Report, 1959, pp. 19, 20; Minnis.

164. LD, AR, 1964, p. 5.

variables possible. What is more surprising is management's willingness to discuss how to make labor more productive without showing much interest in measuring productivity. The one, quite crude, measure used in such discussions was the average tonnage of general cargo per ship working day. This is a measure of how quickly the workers could unload ships, not taking into account how much labor was expended in the process. This figure rose by 32 percent between 1955 and 1957. Then the rate held roughly steady until 1961 and fell 14 percent over the next two years. The decline was blamed on port congestion, problems with the railway, changing composition of cargo, but also on the declining productivity of dockworkers.[165]

The lament over falling productivity was heard again in yet another commission that studied the port in 1962. The Railway's annual report in 1963 referred to a "marked general decline in labour productivity" at Mombasa. Yet more precise measures of productivity were not devised.[166] This study, in the context of Kenyan independence, resulted in a restructuring of the management of the port—as a parastatal corporation, the East African Cargo Handling Service absorbed the KL&S Co. and the stevedoring companies, an amalgamation first suggested in 1939. But although the reorganization did not fundamentally alter the labor system, officials blamed ill feelings on the part of workers for yet another drop in productivity—27 percent over the period 1962 to 1964.[167] A Productivity Council had been proposed to bring workers and management together to discuss the problem, but the workers boycotted it, claiming that they—and particularly the union—were being blamed unfairly for the supposed fall in productivity.[168]

Other indices suggest that the overall transformation of the docks in the 1950s—new berths, cranes, and equipment, as well as the reorganization of labor—had a significant effect on port working. From 1954 to 1962, the time that ships had to wait to get to a berth declined from an average of 2.87 days to .43 days, and the average time ships spent in port went from 5.39 days to 2.90. The total cost of handling general cargo,

165. EAR&H, AR, 1955–63.

166. Amos Landmann, "Report on the Port of Dar es Salaam" (Nairobi: GM's office, 1962); EAR&H, AR, 1963, p. 25. Landmann also visited Mombasa, and his findings had considerable influence there. Nonetheless, his report was criticized for its lack of concrete data on the supposed inefficiency of port working. East African Common Services Organization, Proceedings of the Central Legislative Assembly, 2, 1 (9 May 1963), esp. the remarks of Sheikh Alamoody and Mr. Alexander, cc. 482–84, 486.

167. LD, AR, 1964, p. 5.

168. Ibid., 1965, p. 3. Some years earlier, Colonial Office officials had noticed that despite all the talk about productivity, no one had much knowledge of the subject. Minutes by E. Barltrop and N. D. Watson, 8, 13 October 1953, CO 554/202.

which had doubled between 1952 and 1957, declined from Shs 22.72 per harbor ton to Shs 20.51 over the next four years.[169] But the contribution of the new ways of supervising labor remains impossible to isolate. Officials were concerned to rationalize authority without taking the seemingly rational step of measuring its effect on the bottom line.

The earlier structure of gangs had evolved out of convenience: buying units of anonymous labor power by the day, the port companies were in fact hiring workers who were developing relations among themselves that organized the hiring and the work process, presenting management in effect with a fait accompli. This process was not unlike what went on in early factories in Europe and the United States; it was a form of subcontracting. In early industry, capitalists often hired skilled craftsmen and paid them by what they produced, allowing the craftsmen to hire their own helpers. Braverman argues that, from the late nineteenth century, American industry began to destroy this kind of structure. The assault was occasioned as much by craft solidarity and the authority over other workers that emerged within this structure as by direct concern with output and cost.[170] Piecework, too, was a common feature of an earlier era of capitalist development, and capital eventually came to question it. As Richard Edwards notes, piecework often led workers to work more slowly or to falsify output in order to create low standard rates and a chance to earn bonuses for modestly exceeding easily met quotas.[171] In the docks of London, as well as in Mombasa, the minute details of rates, quotas, and work rules were a key cause of conflict between labor and management, and managers attempted to dismantle parts of the piecework system during their efforts to rationalize port labor after World War II.[172]

In the Mombasa dockyards, the discovery of how work gangs and clerks fiddled the books on iron weights is an example of how the combination of worker solidarity and autonomy in the work process could be used against the interests of management. More generally, the opportunity of gangs to work hard for a time, then to take it easy—like the possibility of casual workers even under the 1954 rules to take two weeks off every two months—illustrates the dangers of the old autonomy. The quest for steady, predictable output came by the mid-1950s to outweigh the uneven

169. EAR&H, AR, 1949/62. Both turnaround and cost figures took a bad wobble at the time of Kenya's independence.

170. Braverman, *Labor and Monopoly Capitalism*.

171. Edwards, *Contested Terrain*, p. 99. See also Eric Hobsbawm, *Labouring Men* (London: Weidenfeld and Nicolson, 1964), pp. 361–62.

172. Peter Weiler, "British Labor and the Cold War: The London Dock Strike of 1949," in James Cronin and Jonathan Schneer, eds., *Social Conflict and the Political Order in Modern Britain* (New Brunswick, N.J.: Rutgers University Press, 1982), p. 165.

energy of gang-centered labor. But control based on the direct authority of the foreman can be an illusion: the supervisor must be both willing and able to command obedience. Whether the port companies attained the substance of steady output or the illusion of discipline was a question that had not been answered by the early 1960s.

In 1934, officials had blamed the first dock strike in Mombasa's history on the serangs, who had led their gangs out of the docks just as they usually led them in. The social basis of both forms of discipline lay in the bonds formed by workers themselves and in the culture of the city. By the 1950s, the state and capital were not seriously worried that serangs would become the vanguard of a working class about to seize the docks. But the companies' once blissful ignorance of the complexity of the human labor power they had bought had been sharply reversed after 1939, and the growing concern with labor as a social phenomenon, as well as the daily experience of dockwork, had led the stevedoring companies, the KL&S Co., the Railway, the Government Sociologist, and Labour Department officials to think very seriously about the nature of authority in dock labor. The semiautonomous gang leaders, with their complex ties to gang members, had come to stand for a structure of work that was no longer acceptable. No longer was management satisfied with the fact that a job had been done. The new need for top-down authority had something to do with a sense that central control was needed to introduce innovations and to adjust labor distribution to changing requirements in the port. But even more important, transforming the nature of supervision itself constituted an integral part of establishing predictable, orderly relationships between management and labor. In fact, rather than let the social relationships of Mombasa shape the organization of work on the docks, the state and capital now hoped that by seizing control of the docks they could begin to assert control over the dangerously independent city of Mombasa.

THE REMAKING OF SPACE

If limiting the working population to those who would labor steadily promised to improve productivity and social order, the question of where to put them and what to do with everyone else still had to be faced. The colonial state after the war had little faith that a free, colony-wide labor market would redistribute the population in a suitable manner. Indeed, mounting land pressure, the rationalization and mechanization of estate agriculture, and more intense—and more conflictual—land accumulation in several African areas were pushing more and more people out of rural areas. Although in the early years of the postwar economic expansion British officials thought of the entire African empire as a region of labor shortage, it soon became clear that expansion and rising unemployment were perfectly compatible. The idea of the streamlined, efficient urban working class and of an orderly city, uncluttered with idlers, entailed a new sort of contradiction: if in the older form of urban labor, casual workers embodied a bit of the serious worker and a bit of the idler, decasualization threatened to bring into relation with each other two now distinct sorts of people, and risked undoing by contamination the social progress gained by making laborers work more steadily.

The Kenya Government's solution to the problem in the immediate postwar years was coercive—the use of force to expel nonworkers from the city and restrict entry. In these terms, the state was trying to redefine space on a colony-wide scale: to regulate, through law and the police, who could be where. In the longer term, the state also sought to redefine space within the city, arguing that the kind of working class it sought to create could not be housed any old way, but that neighborhoods and housing types had to be shaped by state authority to build a milieu suitable for workers and their families.[173]

When two leading officials in Nairobi wrote in 1941, "Indeed, we should look to the creation of a Nairobi urban working class," they were in fact writing about housing. The classness of the working class was rooted in the stability of its attachment to the city, and residence was as important as workplace in creating that attachment. The authors also were responding to the events of 1939 in Mombasa, for they accepted Willan's diagnosis that a housing crisis had been a central cause of a work stoppage. Solving the problem meant the creation of a "permanent Nairobi urban native community with its own institutions and its own sense of responsibility and communal pride."[174] To bring this about required state intervention in the location and quality of housing.

Spivs and the State

The impetus for this complex of changes lay in the conflicts that arose inside the city, not in a dynamic originating in agricultural change or a colony-wide process of economic transformation. It was for this reason that the state's concern with purging the city—South African style—of its unwanted population was such an important aspect of a wider range of reforms. This solution was not a solution at all, but an attempt to

173. For a theoretical approach to issues discussed in this section, see my "Urban Space, Industrial Time, and Wage Labor in Africa," in Frederick Cooper, ed., *Struggle for the City: Migrant Labor, Capital, and the State in Urban Africa* (Beverly Hills, Calif.: Sage, 1983), pp. 7–50.

174. Report on the Housing of Africans in Nairobi by Senior Medical Officer of Health and Municipal Native Affairs Officer to Nairobi City Council, 30 April 1941, CO 533/528/38397/2.

banish the problem from the dangerous city into the countryside, where—for all too brief a time—it appeared to be less menacing. When Orde Browne cited Nakuru as a model for a solution to the housing problem, he described state-sponsored housing estates, but equally critical to this model were "Township regulations [that] prevent the influx of people who have no definite occupation." Nakuru was distinguished by a "lack of the loafer and semi-criminal element which is so often a feature of African towns."[175] But the failure of influx control in Mombasa illustrates another aspect of the state's efforts to reshape the city: its vision of control was difficult to impose.

Since 1944, officials in Mombasa had had authority under the Defense (Limitation of African Travel to the Coast) Regulations to repatriate Africans. In the first half of 1946, 1,562 Africans were ejected from the city. But officials thought the law was being abused and began to repatriate only if they had a court order—against destitute people, vagrants, and so on—and only 131 of them were sent out in the next six months. After the strike, the Thacker Tribunal was told that repatriation had been a failure: Africans who had been put on a train heading upcountry got off it as soon as it left the island and walked back.[176] But Judge Thacker was emphatic that "the benefit of the Awards made by it would be very largely nullified unless steps are taken to remove this surplus population and prevent further immigration into the island."[177] Indeed, as a local official had warned, measures to stabilize the urban work force and improve its standard of living might produce higher output from fewer workers but might also attract more work-seekers, requiring "greater control over shifting loafers."[178]

The obstacles to cleansing Mombasa of the idle and the itinerant were considerable: short of South African pass laws, with all the administrative apparatus they required, Africans were hard to trace. The Kenyan kipande (passbook) was a less stringent form of control than the South African pass, had always been enforced very laxly in the fluid environment of Mombasa, and was coming under fire (ultimately successfully) as a humiliating and counterproductive way of supervising a working class from which employers were beginning to expect higher standards of performance and consent.[179] The repatriations only affected upcountry people. Those from coastal regions had legitimate reasons—even within the state's premises—to come to Mombasa; the island could hardly be

175. Orde Browne, "Labour Conditions in East Africa," p. 74.

176. C. W. Howard, Testimony, vol. 3, p. 106, LAB 3/16.

177. Thacker, memorandum, 2 September 1947, CO 533/544/30891/6.

178. Municipal Native Affairs Officer, Review of African Housing, March 1945 to March 1946, incl. DC to LC, 10 April 1946, LAB 9/1775.

179. Clayton and Savage, Government and Labour, pp. 295–96.

quaranteened from its hinterland. But it was the coastal people, officials thought, who had the worst work habits.

Nonetheless, officials were eager to retain authority to throw people out of the city, even if they could not keep them from coming back in. When the wartime travel regulations expired four years after the end of the war, they were replaced by the Voluntary Unemployed Persons (Provision of Employment) Ordinance of 1949, which made it an offense for anyone "voluntarily" out of work (that is, who had not been laid off) not to register with an administrative committee, which was to direct them to a job or send them away. The Provincial Commissioner had warned before the new legislation was passed that "there are large numbers of 'spivs' on the Island who continued to live on their wits, and who are an incipient source of labour trouble." The new law, the DO of Majengo wrote, was aimed at the local "spivs"—unemployed seamen, illegal hawkers, and coast Africans who claimed to be barbers, water carriers, or casual workers but who really "live by their wits in Mwembe Tayari." There were also Hadrami "spivs" who came to town during the dry season when they had little to do on their farms and could pick up a bit of money somehow or other in the city, not necessarily by legal means. The District Commissioner thought it necessary to deter the "would-be spivs" before they became actual spivs and thought a "spiv camp" should be opened into which to dump those who came anyway.[180]

The language in which the supposedly idle or dangerous classes of the city were being discussed reveals a conception of urban life with a quaintly preindustrial air to it. When the ordinance was up for renewal in 1950, the member of the Legislative Council from the Coast, Cooke, thought the act's title rather pompous and suggested that " 'in the tongue which Shakespeare spoke and Milton wrote,' this might have been more the 'Rogues and Vagabonds' Bill, or in more common parlance the 'Spivs' Bill." He was, to some extent, serious:

> I think we are apt to forget that the African in these days is living, I mean the mass of Africans—there are exceptions like my hon. friends on this side of the Council [the African members of the Legislative Council]—who are living rather the life that was lived by the mass of people in England two hundred years ago when the

180. Coast Province, AR, 1948; DO, Majengo, to PC, 4 April 1951, PC's Archives, LAB 8/9 II; DC, Mombasa, to Supt. of Police, Coast, 31 October 1951, ibid., LAB 8/9. The term *spiv* originated in England in the 1890s, and its meaning was a "petty crook who will turn his hand to anything so long as it does not involve honest work" or "a man who gets a good living by his wits without working"; Eric Partridge, *Dictionary of the Underworld,* 3d ed. (London, 1968), p. 668. I am grateful to David Sacks for the reference. The resurgence of gangs of idle youth in postwar England may have provided a link for readers of the English press to this kind of social concept.

sanctions then were very much severer than they are to-day. . . . So
that we are really dealing rather mildly with these spivs in our towns
to-day, and . . . if we tolerate this situation, we will get in this country
gangs of juveniles as they do in Europe, who will start beating up
decent people and using coshes and all sorts of things. Now is the
time to nip such a potential menace in the bud.[181]

The African member whom Cooke had magnanimously exempted
from his generalization, Eliud Mathu, was equally concerned with the
threat to urban order, but his remarks made a good deal more sense. He
pointed out that "as a result of the operation of it [the proposed bill] the
spivs leave the island, and go to the mainland. . . . Put them in jail, Sir, if
you like. I do not object to dealing with these people and putting them in
jail, all I object to is removing them from one part of Kenya and moving
them to another part of Kenya." But a settler Councilor had an answer to
that:

> These people with whom this Ordinance deals are people, who put,
> shall we say, an excessive value upon leisure! But they must eat and if
> they are in Mombasa, they have got to get food somehow and they
> tend to do it by theft and by indulging in dubious professions. If they
> go on to the mainland they can indulge their love of leisure, they have
> only to lie under a tree and a mango will drop into their mouths. I
> think they are better there.[182]

Based on arguments like this, the renewal of the ordinance was carried.
    But the anti-spiv campaign never got off the ground. In its first year or
so, over 1,000 people passed through the Voluntary Unemployed Persons Committee, and 300 were released, 260 repatriated, 8 prosecuted,
215 directed to jobs (most deserted or were fired), and 315 permitted to
choose a job. The repatriated Africans were expected to return to Mombasa sooner or later. The District Officer of Majengo thought this exercise
did little good and recommended that the ordinance be allowed to become dormant. It did, between May and October of 1951, and was then
revived briefly, only to lapse into disuse in 1953. The whole business
seemed pointless, wrote the DC in 1952, since there were no longer jobs to
which to direct the voluntarily unemployed; in fact, he estimated that
there were 2,000 involuntarily unemployed persons in Mombasa.[183] The
state was trying to solve the wrong problem.
    The episode is best summed up in the copy of some minutes in the files

181. Kenya Legislative Council Debates, 39 (21 November 1950), cc. 269–70.
182. Mathu and Usher, ibid., cc. 268, 271.
183. DO, Majengo, to DC, Mombasa, 4 April 1951, DC to CS, 3 October 1953, DC to PC, 8
October 1952, 27 September 1954, all in PC's Archives, LAB 8/9 II.

of the General Manager of the Railway. The Coast Labour Committee had resolved in its meeting of 29 July 1954 that "this committee feels strongly that men proved unsuitable for employment in urban areas by virtue of their inefficiency in output should not be allowed to remain in urban areas." Someone—whether or not it was the GM himself is unclear—underlined the words *feels strongly* and wrote in the margin "and that's about all they can do about it."[184]

By 1956, an estimated 4,000 Africans were entering Mombasa district annually, and employers' organizations were complaining.[185] The growing advantages accruing to workers in the port and railway were drawing more workers to Mombasa at the same time that decasualization and stabilization made such jobs less likely to turn over. Kenya was beginning to develop a segmented labor market: the better paid segment was becoming more or less self-contained in regard to promotion and job changes, while new workers were likely to come from sectors of the population with privileged access to education or personal connections to job holders. It was becoming increasingly difficult for someone holding other kinds of jobs or no job at all to break into this market.[186] In Kenya as a whole in the decade after 1955, production rose substantially, African wages doubled, prices rose only slightly, but employment actually fell off slightly.[187]

When A. G. Dalgleish undertook a survey of unemployment for the Kenya Government in 1960, he was in effect giving official blessing to the definition of a new social problem. The contradictions of comparatively high urban wages and high urban unemployment central to the African city of the 1960s and 1970s emerged in large part from the contradictions of underemployment in the 1940s and 1950s, in the quest to isolate and develop a respectable working class. As Dalgleish noted, "The drift is encouraged by the minimum cash wage payable in towns, which is based on calculations designed, very properly, to encourage the development of the family unit as an integral feature of stabilized African labour in urban areas, and which is appreciably higher than wages offering in the rural

184. Minutes of Coast Labour Committee, 29 July 1954, EST 26/20.
185. MT, 7 August 1957.
186. An argument that such a job structure exists in Kenya is made by William House and Henry Rempel, "Labour Market Segmentation in Kenya," *East African Economic Review* 8 (1976): 35–54. On the theory of labor market segmentation, see Gordon et al., *Segmented Work, Divided Workers*. The segmentation of urban employment is an important complication to models describing the relationship of employment and wages based on an urban-rural dichotomy, although the relatively slow pace of rural development and the lag in agricultural earnings that such models stress remain critical. The pioneering study is John R. Harris and Michael P. Todaro, "Migration, Unemployment and Development: A Two-Sector Analysis," *American Economic Review* 60 (1970): 126–42.
187. Gavin Kitching, *Class and Economic Change in Kenya: The Making of an African Petite Bourgeoisie, 1905–1970* (New Haven, Yale University Press, 1980), pp. 379–98.

areas." Mombasa was his prime example: wages in the port had then reached Shs 165 per month, compared to Shs 70–80 on coastal sisal plantations, so that the plantations faced a labor shortage and the port a surplus. Mombasa, he estimated, had 34,000 workers and 6,000 unemployed; the country as a whole, he guessed, had 120,000 unemployed out of an adult male population of around one and a half million. Outcast Mombasa was still alive.[188]

The dangerous classes had appeared in the city in a new guise. The state's desire to preserve the infant urban working class from the contagions of the idle, the criminal, and the rural had in fact resulted in a more segmented work force, but not in a purified city. Urban migration is a gamble, and segmentation has raised the stakes, but the city is inhabited by those still waiting to win as well as those who have won. Yet the ability of the state and capital to create a stark dichotomy between job and no job has not led to an equally stark division between job-holder, job-seeker, and the person using a variety of strategies to survive. As numerous studies have shown, an individual is likely to be in all such categories at one time or another and to retain ties with people in others. Nor has the urban-rural divide become as sharp as policymakers in the 1950s hoped to make it.[189]

Scholars and bureaucrats have recently relabeled what the British used to call "living on one's wits" as the "informal sector." It is neither informal nor a sector, but its designation as such represents the urgent desire of social engineers to separate an economic arena where legal regulations and official categories prevail and an arena where they do not. The discovery that life goes on where the labor inspector or the tax collector does not penetrate should not be astonishing, but recognition of this fact is fraught with ambivalence for insecure states. People can survive without jobs that show up on state records, and in surviving they provide cheap services for others. But they simultaneously challenge the state's notions of its own hegemony, create alternatives to the discipline of the narrowly defined job hierarchy of capitalist firms, and develop social networks and relationships outside of the principles of commoditization and bureaucratization. The so-called informal sector represents a negation of the

188. A. G. Dalgleish, "Survey of Unemployment," Nairobi, 1960, pp. 6–8, 20–22. The Deputy Chief Secretary of the Government, C. H. Hartwell, had correctly predicted seven years previously that the casual labor scheme "might land us in difficulties by the creation of an unemployment problem in Mombasa." He hoped that the unemployed who were generated by decasualization would find work in other jobs, such as on plantations, "provided they are willing." But apparently many workers in Mombasa thought that trying to get a good job was preferable to settling for a bad one. Hartwell to P. Rogers, 29 January 1953, CO 822/657.

189. See, for example, Janet Bujra, "Proletarianization and the 'Informal Economy': A Case Study from Nairobi," *African Urban Studies* 3 (1978–79): 47–66.

kind of well-ordered, hard-working city that capital and the state in Kenya have been trying to build since the late 1930s. The existence of such a complex of economic relationships—and the interplay between the respectable working class and undisciplined, uncontrollable nonworkers—raises the old threats of contamination and popular alliances of the respectable and unrespectable poor. Such processes cannot, yet, be stopped, and the best most states have been able to do has been to label them.[190]

Housing a Working Class
Ideologically, the housing problem and the work problem were of a piece. Access to housing could be defined by a variety of complex relationships involving social affiliation and property, or it could be neatly linked to a single job, or at least to a steady wage income. The low-cost housing market of Mombasa before World War II supplied housing in much the same way as the gang system supplied workers: African entrepreneurs, mainly Swahili, rented land, built houses using local techniques and materials, and jammed people into them. The relationship of landlord and tenant could be exploitative and hostile, but it also had a personal element to it. Landlords could accommodate to the uncertain time schedules and unsteady incomes of their tenants, and long-term indebtedness to a landlord could allow a certain autonomy from the tyranny of the monthly wage packet. Coastal people in particular, with the multiple linkages between them and the Majengo landlords, frequently saw distinct advantages of Majengo housing to the kind of job-linked, bureaucratized housing system the state was promoting in the early 1950s.[191]

The colonial state was just as ambivalent about Majengo housing as it was about the gangs that Swahili serangs provided to the cargo handling companies: African-supplied housing was cheap and, for officials, effort-free, but it was also dangerous. What Maynard Swanson calls the "sanitation syndrome" in early-twentieth-century South Africa had more than a germ of truth to it, but it had to do with far more than the real risks of the spread of disease. The report on "Sanitary Matters in the East Africa Protectorate, Uganda and Zanzibar," commissioned from an expert in 1913, was in fact a blueprint for urban segregation. Europeans would be protected from contagion and African laborers housed through government acquisition of land, while cities would be regulated through building and sanitary codes.[192]

But the Government's enthusiasm was tempered by the cost of any such

190. Some of these ideas are elaborated in Frederick Cooper, "The Guerrilla Army of the Underemployed: The Labor Process and Class Struggle in Post-War Africa," paper for a conference on the "Urban Informal Sector" at Johns Hopkins University, June 1984.
191. Wilson, in Mombasa Social Survey, pp. 535–37, 440–41.
192. Maynard Swanson, "The Sanitation Syndrome: Bubonic Plague and Urban Native

plan, while the belief that Mombasa could never be a truly European town—as Nairobi was, in officials' eyes—tempered the urgency for segregation.[193] But a more modest program of street widening, plot consolidation, and building regulation attempted to keep the areas of uncontrolled housing to a minimum and to spruce up the rest of the city. In Nairobi, however, officials destroyed the neighborhood where African entrepreneurs had done the most to develop housing in 1938, pushing urban workers into housing provided by employers or the Government or into settlement schemes (notably Shauri Moyo) where they could be more readily watched.[194] In fact, many of the victims of such urban improvement were being sent to accommodations that did not yet exist.

The more pragmatic attitude in Mombasa led to government approval in 1927 of "village layout" plans: a large private plot could be subdivided into rectangular subplots, and buildings of an approved design, size, and quality could be put up. With the upcountry migration of the 1920s, areas such as that between Makupa Road and the railway developed rapidly as "native quarters," housing workers and what officials still called, as they had in the 1890s, the "floating population" of the city. By 1941, fifty-seven such schemes had been put into effect on the island on land owned by Europeans, Arabs, and Asians, who allowed Arabs, Swahili, or other Africans to put up houses and rent out rooms to lodgers. Yet the scheme did not allow the house builders to use permanent materials or to hold title; the administration retained the right to clear the village layout plots if it so chose. And in 1935, the Municipal Board of Mombasa banned further layouts on the ground that they were "degenerating into slums," a pattern to which its own rules about construction materials had no doubt contributed.[195]

Up to World War II, houses in Mombasa were mostly provided by Africans and Arabs on land owned by Arabs, Asians, or Europeans, and the Government's concern with sanitary and social dangers had only made this system work less well. When economic growth resumed in the mid-1930s, overcrowding and high rents quickly became serious concerns.[196] Distress and anger did soon lead to an urban crisis: housing was one of the main roots of labor unrest from 1939 onward.

Policy in the Cape Colony, 1900–1909," *Journal of African History* 18 (1977): 387–410; W. J. Simpson, Report on Sanitary Matters in the East Africa Protectorate, Uganda and Zanzibar (Nairobi, 1914).

193. Stren, *Housing the Urban Poor,* p. 120.

194. Ibid., 189–92; Luise White, "A Colonial State and an African Petty Bourgeoisie: Prostitution, Property, and Class Struggle in Nairobi, 1936–1940," in Cooper, *Struggle for the City,* pp. 167–94.

195. Mombasa District, AR, 1927, 1929; Stren, pp. 132–33.

196. In 1934, as this process was beginning, the DC declared that housing was now adequate. Mombasa District, AR, 1934.

The Willan Commission's investigation of the causes of the 1939 general strike put housing at the center of official concern. It was worried not only about cost and availability but about the kind of milieu Swahili housing was creating. "The real solution is to get the labourers away from those huts at Majengo and other places which are unsuitable for human habitation." Its dislike of African-owned housing echoed statements expressed elsewhere at the time and lay behind plans labeled "slum clearance" that were intended to replace unregulated houses with "real little houses" meeting government standards, if not with capital-intensive projects built by the state itself.[197] The Commission had an alternative model in mind: Kenyan labor law required that employers provide housing for their workers, but the Railway in Mombasa was one of few that did. Its willingness to house 80 percent of its employees was "an admirable example" of what should be done. One of the strongest arguments the Commission had for abolishing casual labor was that having a work force limited to those who actually worked would make possible the solving of the housing crisis: the port companies could then be made to house their workers in the manner of the railway. Others should be made to do likewise, and the Municipality should build a Municipal Native Housing scheme modeled on Nairobi for the laborers of small employers.[198]

The net effect of such measures would have been to link housing directly to the job: to lose a job would be to lose a home. If a family was living in that home, a double tie would restrain the footloose African worker, saving him from his supposed tendency to work irregularly, desert employers, switch jobs, and alternate wage labor with periods of self-employment or subsistence farming.[199]

Nonetheless, the only immediate result of these radical proposals to solve the housing crisis in Mombasa was the Government's decision to increase the housing allowance of monthly workers, and this was promptly eaten up by inflation. The Willan Commission had itself admitted ruefully that the fact that most of Mombasa Island was privately owned made any significant development of Nairobi-style locations impossible.

197. Major G. St. J. Orde Browne, "Labour Conditions in West Africa," Parliamentary Papers, 1940–41, IV, 1, pp. 88–90. For an important study of the way such slum clearance ideology was used to reshape urban space—breaking up a vibrant city neighborhood and displacing its inhabitants to planned suburbs—see Peter Marris, *Family and Social Change in an African City: A Study of Rehousing in Lagos* (Evanston, Ill.: Northwestern University Press, 1962).

198. Report of the Commission of Inquiry appointed to Examine the Labour Conditions in Mombasa (Nairobi, 1939) (Willan Report), pp. 16, 21.

199. By the mid- or late 1930s, similar concerns were surfacing in Nairobi. I am indebted to Luise White for discussing with me her analysis of housing in Nairobi, which will be a critical dimension of her important forthcoming publications.

After six more years of tension in Mombasa, the Phillips Committee found only more house seekers and still higher rents. It, too, saw casual labor as a principal cause of overcrowding, but did not think through the implications that its stress on a stabilized labor force implied the growth of a different, and potentially more demanding, category of migrant—the wives and children of workers. It worried instead that critics might deem its proposed standard of housing for married men—one room, 10 × 10 feet—"grandiose," although it might soon prove inadequate.[200]

Meanwhile, decasualization and influx control, combined with increased efforts by the Municipality and others to provide new housing units, would be the major steps forward. The report noted that South African legislation on influx control was intended to "prevent the growth of a stabilized native urban population." But in Mombasa, the same laws were "required for the purpose of assisting and protecting the existing body of African workers who are in process of becoming stabilized."[201] A major task for the postwar state would thus be to nurture this infant working class, in its 10 × 10 rooms.

Five years later, the state had in fact made urban housing a priority for spending under the Colonial Development and Welfare Act, and had some new housing estates in Mombasa to show for its concern. Still, the Provincial Commissioner wrote in 1950, "the most urgent and pressing problem in Mombasa continues to be the lack of housing, particularly for Asians and Africans, and it remains a mystery where many of them live."[202]

Postwar thinking about housing evolved in a curiously contradictory way. On the one hand, officials' quest for a more "modern" society demanded planning and regulation of urban neighborhoods and architecture. Hyde-Clarke echoed the Willan Commission's contrast of the well-organized housing scheme with the way Africans housed themselves in "all sorts of shanty towns" that bred "social evils and crime."[203] The rising tide of rural revolt in central Kenya, especially after 1952, accentuated the state's quest for a rational vision of urban society protected from the atavistic rural society that threatened to penetrate it. The rural struggle in central Kenya, in fact, had its urban dimension, above all in the apparent

200. Willan Report, p. 63; Phillips Report, p. 93. Governor Mitchell grasped the problem, pointing out that the standard of housing envisioned in development plans right after the war would quickly become obsolete as families came to the city, demanding better houses. Mitchell to Creech Jones, 5 December 1947, CO 822/130/2.

201. Phillips, p. 92.

202. Coast Province, AR, 1950. The Deputy Chief Secretary also told the Colonial Office that housing was "one of our worst headaches." Hartwell to Rogers, 29 January 1953, CO 822/657.

203. Legislative Council Debates, 35 (21 December 1949), c. 647.

riff-raff who hung around the tea houses of Nairobi's least controlled neighborhoods and who fomented various acts of banditry and political assassination.[204] The existence of well-controlled housing schemes in Nairobi facilitated Government efforts to clear out the rest and to sift through the housing estates in a thorough and brutal fashion, looking for Kikuyu and screening them for supposedly subversive activities. Thorough control of urban space was the only way to keep the rural contagion from the city.[205] As Richard Stren points out, the language of the reports on the Mau Mau Emergency juxtaposed the notion of "social unrest" as embodied in a mass, tribalistic, backward-looking movement against "stability," which entailed a stable family life, a stable home, and a stable job.[206]

The language in which rural unrest was discussed was thus the mirror-image of the language used to discuss urban labor in the mid-1950s. Anything that encouraged an African to become more "modern" or "civilized" was a step toward solving that crisis of order which had enveloped Kenya as much as it was a step toward increasing productivity within the workplace. The East Africa Royal Commission drew a clear conclusion: "The first step in the formation of a healthy urban society is the growth of a settled urban population whose loyalties are directed towards their town rather than to their areas of origin." Africans not only had to "abandon the security of their holdings in the countryside," but they had to build communities in the city based on "a common level of education or wealth, irrespective of divisions of tribe or race."[207]

If Mombasa was one step removed from the turmoil of the Emergency, it was close enough so that officials proclaimed a policy of "Closer Administration" in the city in 1955. Mombasa was divided into locations and wards, each with a chief specially trained by district officials.[208] Two years later, the District Commissioner concluded:

> Closer Administration has now become part of the existence of every African in the District, which has resulted in much closer scrutiny of ordinary African life; petty law breakers and tax evaders have been given shorter shrift than ever before; trends in African political and social thought have come to note much more promptly and chiefs are now well up to the mark with currents of African opinion and activity generally; each chief has his own well-established sources of informa-

204. Frank Furedi, "The African Crowd in Nairobi," *Journal of African History* 14 (1973): 275–90.
205. The Railway Archives have revealing files on this sifting operation (Operation Anvil) in its housing estates.
206. Stren, pp. 207–08.
207. East Africa Royal Commission, p. 214.
208. DC, Progress Report on Closer Adminstration, 6 August 1955, HOU 10/4/2; Mombasa District, AR, 1955, 1956.

tion and is in a position to give a reasonably accurate report on any individual in his ward.[209]

The plan's accomplishments no doubt fell short of the degree of repressive surveillance of which this British official boasted, but the thrust of the policy was clear enough. Just as the new style of management subjected Africans to closer supervision where they worked, this idea of closer administration built around the urban locations and their chiefs subjected the same people to closer scrutiny where they lived.

On the other hand, the state began to take a new attitude toward those Africans who had made some progress in desirable directions. In reality, colonial regimes had always needed African collaborators, although they had often insisted on thinking of them as rather quaint if useful figures— the chiefs. But in thinking about urban Africa, officials had thought of the African landlords of Majengo as being afloat in the same cesspit as their tenants. The sanitation syndrome had condemned both, as the Willan Commission had made particularly clear. The very fact that Africans might become permanent city residents at first made officials even more worried about the credentials of their landlords. In 1938, Nairobi officials had destroyed Pangani at a time when the idea of stabilizing the work force was being bandied about. Much of the property there was built in stone; it met the housing needs of many workers. But prominent among the property owners were prostitutes, not the most visible or potentially disorderly members of that profession, but the most circumspect. As Luise White argues, such an unrespectable petty bourgeoisie was intolerable in close relationship to a working class just beginning to be pushed into respectability. The prostitutes the state cracked down on, the house-owners of Pangani, were precisely those with the most stable relationships to other classes.[210]

But if the state was concerned with redefining African class structure, it had to think about the kind of petty bourgeoisie it would support. Edward Vasey, in his famous report on Nairobi housing in 1950, was, as usual, a few years ahead of his fellow officials, but he saw the promotion of home ownership among Africans as essential to "open the door to a stable urban population." The home owner would be "more likely to let go of his hold upon the native reserve." African housing would have to be carefully zoned and planned, and complemented by employer-owned and public housing "as a measure of social control and to prevent the spread of unsatisfactory conditions," but at least small plots and low-cost construction (under supervision) should, in Vasey's view, be encouraged.[211]

209. Mombasa District, AR, 1957.
210. White, "A Colonial State and a Petty Bourgeoisie."
211. E. A. Vasey, Report on African Housing in Townships and Trading Centers (Nairobi, 1950), pp. 9–10, 15–27.

By the time of the East Africa Royal Commission report of 1955, offi-cials' line on the class structure of African society was quite different from that of Willan: African investment in urban real estate would create a "responsible African middle class," with an interest in order and in long-term urban development. Indeed, the Commission thought that the frus-trations of people aspiring "by their own efforts [to] raise themselves above the squalid conditions in which they live" and "denied the rights and advantages which members of other races enjoy" was the "major cause of the crime, immorality and drunkenness which are rife in many East African towns." Frustrated capitalists were as dangerous to civic order as frustrated workers, and the key to taming the frustrations of both was to bring about greater differentiation and social mobility in the African population.

In these terms, the Government-planned housing estate was the wrong approach, and the "densely populated African areas, although un-hygienic and uncontrolled, are in many respects suited to African needs." The African entrepreneurs of Majengo now seemed like the solution to the provision of accommodation and the easing of the unrest for which they were once, in part, blamed. Tenant purchase of their own houses was encouraged. Current African landlords were mildly criticized for the squalid condition of their homes, but they were seen as the nucleus of urban respectability.[212]

The result was a revised attitude toward Majengo housing. The trans-formation was less a change of policy than of language. Majengo—most often the same Swahili-style houses—was where workers, especially coast-al people, had lived in 1939, and it was still where they lived in 1955. But though the state did not solve the housing problem, at least it convinced itself that it had the problem under control. A spruced-up, regulated version of Majengo—supplemented by other, more "modern" kinds of schemes—could continue to provide much of Mombasa's housing. It was no longer the source of a dangerous social contagion that might spread to all workers; instead, property in Majengo could be the source of stability within a differentiated urban population. Similarly, the Mombasa Social Survey of 1958 concluded that African-owned housing in village layout schemes just off Mombasa island—if "properly supervised and con-trolled"—not only housed workers in a less alienating environment than a housing estate, but were a means of "building a class of urban Africans which has a stake in the urban community and which because of its vested

212. East Africa Royal Commission, 1955, pp. 209, 213, 214, 228–32. The change in policy did not go unnoticed. The Parliamentary Labour Party's Commonwealth and Coloni-al Group studied the commission report and criticized its housing section for the abandon-ment of "high" standards. Report on East Africa Royal Commission Report, 9 April 1957, Creech Jones Papers, Rhodes House, 21/3, ff. 154–55.

interests accepts the normal obligations of urban citizenship of paying taxes, participating in Local Government, Ward Councils and the like." The private Swahili-style house—the symbol of all that was wrong with Mombasa in the 1930s and 1940s—became the basis of a practical solution to the provision of housing and the stability of urban life in the 1950s.[213]

But more than an ideological sleight of hand was going on. The state had between 1940 and the mid-1950s made a determined effort to bring a new kind of housing to Mombasa. The revised attitude toward Majengo housing represents both frustration with the practicalities of keeping up with the housing crunch and a rethinking of the meanings of class and social stability in African society. Beginning in 1943, Kenyan authorities worked out plans to use funds from the Colonial Development and Welfare Act of 1940 to pay for housing projects. Mombasa was at the center of their concern, and was to get £50,000. It in fact got £78,000, and the Kenya Government and the Municipality chimed in with funds of their own. The Secretary of State for the Colonies commended Kenya for its good "example."[214] By the end of 1946, the Government, the Municipality, and the Railway had added 2,859 housing units, while Swahili-style houses had grown by 1,824. Temporary housing had been put up to ease the immediate crunch, while a "model satellite town" on the adjacent mainland was begun at Changamwe. Despite these efforts, housing was still tight at decade's end and, most important, the Majengo area remained "over-crowded."[215]

These programs focused on a small number of large, high density, modern housing estates. They were not built with the poorest of Mombasa's population in mind. Quite the contrary, they were aimed at the most stable of its workers, the railwaymen, the Municipality employees, Government workers, and—although port employers did not directly provide housing to their own staffs—at the stable, relatively well paid worker in all major lines of work. The aim of housing estates was not to alleviate poverty but to contribute to the stabilization of the working class.[216]

Another round of spending was directed toward housing in Mombasa in the 1950s, including £534,000 between 1951 and 1954.[217] But as early

213. Mombasa Social Survey, cited in Stren, p. 142 and pp. 36–37.

214. Governor Moore to Secretary of State, 1 July 1943, CO 533/530/38545; Governor Mitchell to Secretary of State, 21 January 1947, and Secretary of State to Governor, 21 June 1947, CO 822/130/46787/1.

215. Progress Report No. 2 on Phillips Report, by LC, n.d., c. January 1947, LAB 9/1838; Mombasa District, AR, 1945, 1949.

216. See Stren for a fuller discussion of estate housing.

217. Mombasa District, AR, 1954.

as 1955 it was becoming clear that the vast expansion of housing was not keeping pace with the demand. The District Commissioner noted the high influx of Africans to Mombasa, as much as 10 percent a year over the last five years. The only solution, he wrote, was to set aside areas on the outskirts of the city and allow Africans to build their own homes, subject to health regulations.[218] The recommendation was an important admission of inadequacy: policy centered on closely controlled, capital-intensive estates had to give way to recognition that Africans not only could, but must house themselves. By 1957, the tone of reports was even more far removed from the ambitious notion that the state could remake urban space, or even from the East Africa Royal Commission's recent advocacy of the respectable African landlord: "The slum position in Mombasa remains bad and there is little reason at present to hope for any notable improvement."[219]

For all the progress in stabilizing dock labor and in providing better amenities and greater security for the dockworkers, housing them remained a problem. Indeed, when a Board of Investigation under Ian Parkin studied the docks in 1959, it applauded the progress, but cited the scarcity, low quality, and high price of housing as the main obstacle to weaning dockers from the "African's tribal way of life." It did not accept the approach of the East Africa Royal Commission and harked back to the idea of planned and controlled urban space: "The African worker must have a place where he can keep his wife and children. . . . Attempts to meet these needs are being made by the creation of housing estates, with shops, community halls, playing fields, churches, etc." In the long-run, it wanted to develop "neighbourhood units" where dockworkers could live near the port at reasonable rents.[220]

The argument had come full circle. The difference between the Board's approach and that of the Royal Commission was that the latter was thinking about urban life generally, while the former was interested in consolidating the great gains made in tying dockworkers to their life of labor. When decasualization was just an aim, controlling workers' time and controlling their space had seemed, to the Willan Commission, as two dimensions of the same problem. Now that decasualization had largely been accomplished, the inability of the state to build a stable urban society in the city as a whole was all the more reason to isolate, protect, and nourish the segment of the working class where some goals had been achieved.

218. Ibid., 1955.

219. Ibid., 1957. The chief architect and planning officer in 1958 called the layout system "possibly the easiest solution to the African housing problem." Quoted in Stren, p. 143.

220. Parkin Report, p. 19.

The Parkin Board, however, found it easier to tinker with the reformed workplace than to make another foray into remaking living space. The state had made progress in providing new forms of housing to the more stabilized workers—although it was not always clear that they preferred this style of housing. The more intractable problem was the urban influx. Officials were worried that new arrivals were doing something that had provoked so much concern in the past: strain the housing resources available to the more established but lower-paid workers of the city.[221] The efforts of state and capital to restructure residence had produced concrete results, but they had not remade the city.

Demographically, the relationship of different forms of housing to urban growth underscores the social complexity of Mombasa. Between 1948 and 1962, according to the always questionable census figures, the African population of Mombasa District grew from 55,000 to 112,000, and the ratio of males to females went down from 1.88:1 to 1.51:1. The starting point for this ratio was much lower than in Nairobi, where it was 3.52:1 in 1948, and the shift less dramatic—Nairobi's sex ratio fell to 1.87:1 in 1962 and continued to drop. Mombasa, unlike Nairobi, had long been a city where Africans lived as well as worked, and it was only becoming somewhat more so during the period of Government stabilization policy.[222] But for all the changes, 66 percent of the population of Mombasa—and probably 80 percent of Swahili and other Africans—lived in Swahili-style houses on the island or adjacent mainland in 1968.[223] Only 12 percent of the population lived in public housing estates. A substantial number of Africans owned their own homes—28 percent, compared to 2.3 percent in Nairobi in 1962.[224] The rental market in Majengo was still largely supplied by African houseowners.

Most interesting of all is the character of the inhabitants of Majengo housing compared to those of the government-run estates. In 1958, coastal people made up 43 percent of the inhabitants of Majengo and 67 percent of the temporary villages in Kisauni, north of Mombasa island. A survey of casual dockworkers suggested that over 90 percent of those of coastal origin lived on the island and that 90 percent of these resided in Majengo, a ten minute walk from the port labor compound. Of the smaller number of Luo in casual labor, slightly over half found housing on the island: Majengo retained, but in a nonexclusive way, its coastal orientation. In contrast, coastal people made up between 11 and 20 percent of the three housing estates surveyed, while Luo, Luhya, Kikuyu, and Kam-

221. Mombasa District, AR, 1957.
222. Figures are from Stren, p. 215.
223. The total population then was 235,000. Ibid., p. 37.
224. Ibid., p. 36.

ba made up most of the estate population.[225] A more detailed survey done by Stren in 1968 revealed that Majengo housing had more diverse populations and that social interaction across ethnic lines was more intense. The housing estate surveyed, by contrast, was overwhelmingly filled by members of the upcountry ethnic groups, and 93 percent of people claiming religious affiliation were Christian. Majengo was 41 percent Christian, 59 percent Muslim. Majengo's population included more older people, and while the large majority of people in both Majengo and estate samples lived with their wives, Majengo housing—allowing for more flexible arrangements of space—contained wider extended families. 24 percent of Majengo respondents were born in Mombasa, and 52 percent considered it their home, as compared to 3 percent and 26 percent respectively in the Tudor Estate. But the committed Mombasa residents claimed that they had not severed rural ties.[226]

Majengo had a much greater mixture of the self-employed and the unemployed among the wage workers, although 62 percent of the Majengo sample and 81 percent of the Tudor Estate sample were unskilled, skilled, sales, or clerical workers. In Majengo, 15 percent of the people surveyed were small traders and self-employed, and 15 percent were unemployed. But in Tudor, 7 percent were self-employed and only a single person in the sample was unemployed.[227] The estate did very much reflect the state's vision of tying house to job, and Majengo was to a significant (but hardly dominant) extent the kind of urban space that the planners had long feared, where wage laborers lived cheek-by-jowl with people who lived on their wits. Majengo society hardly fits the image of the "marginal" settlement often found in discussions of such neighborhoods: its population was stable, family structure was well developed, the majority of its people were integrated into wage labor or service jobs. But marginality has always been more of a political concept than an accurate tool of sociological analysis, and officials had long thought of Majengo as the locus of Mombasa's dangerous classes.[228]

By the end of the 1950s, the state and capital had reshaped the working world of Mombasa, but not quite as they might have wished. The homogeneous urban mass—never truly homogeneous, but sharing the basic circumstances of life—had been divided into more complex occupational categories, each of whose fate seemed detached from that of the others.

225. Mombasa Social Survey, pp. 352–53, 440.
226. Stren, pp. 259, 262–68.
227. Ibid., p. 270.
228. Ibid., pp. 253–75; Janice Perlman, *The Myth of Marginality: Urban Poverty and Politics in Rio de Janeiro* (Berkeley: University of California Press, 1976).

But the city had not been purged of its dangerous classes, the unemployed or those who drifted into and out of various economic activities, and the respectable workers had not been isolated from them. Despite the impact of state policy after the war, the respectable and the dangerous classes frequently lived in the same neighborhoods, paid their rent to the same landlords, and perhaps attended the same mosque.

5 Toward Trade Unionism

If work is the most neglected aspect of labor history, trade unionism is the most studied. As African colonies moved toward independence, Western scholars saw in the growing trade-union movement a sign that familiar institutions were being replicated in new surroundings. To social scientists who conceived of the political arena as a meeting place of interest groups, the idea that the issues facing a specific group of people were being represented by a particular institution had considerable appeal. Africans were entering the modern world.

Such views of trade unions—and the overarching theories of modernization that lie beneath them—have since been criticized heavily. Some scholars have argued that trade unions represent very little of Africa's population and do so ineffectively. And while some more radical scholars conceive of the role of trade unions not so much as leading workers into the modern world as out of their subordination to capital, still others insist that the unions have become a bastion of privilege, winning gains for narrowly defined groups of workers—above all, for the leadership itself—and failing to extend progress any further.[1]

As soon as one gets away from the notion of trade unionism as a preordained path, be it as an interest group or as the vanguard of revolution, the question of why unions took certain paths and not others becomes more complex. Why did trade unions bring together certain categories of workers and leave out others? Why did they take on some issues and ignore others? Did the restructuring of work undertaken at the initiative of capital and the state shape the role of unions, and did the development of unions affect the restructuring of the labor process?

This chapter will focus on such questions, more so than on the institutional history of unions or the history of the trade-union movement in Kenya per se, subjects which have received substantial, although not exhaustive, attention elsewhere.[2] Like the problem of restructuring work,

1. The various arguments are reviewed thoughtfully in Bill Freund, "Labor and Labor History in Africa," *African Studies Review* 27, no. 2 (1984): 1–58. See also William Friedland, "African Trade Union Studies: Analysis of Two Decades," *Cahiers d'Etudes Africaines* 14 (1974): 575–89.
    2. Anthony Clayton and Donald Savage, *Government and Labour in Kenya, 1895–1963* (London: Cass, 1974); Makhan Singh, *History of Kenya's Trade Union Movement to 1952* (Nai-

the question of whether or how to develop African trade unions came to the attention of imperial policymakers during the wave of urban disorder leading up to the strike of 1947.

The managerial and welfarist ideology of the time was in some ways hostile to trade unionism: trying to use scientific and objective methods to improve standards of living, some officials thought that they had all the answers and that trade unions would only interfere with African workers in their stage of development. But others saw no inconsistency between a scientific vision of rationalizing work and the need to rationalize industrial relations. Both points of view emerged during the long discussion of this problem held by the Colonial Labour Advisory Committee during 1951. The consensus that emerged from the meetings was that there was no substitute for the development of trade unions but that it was a long process, and in the meantime the large majority of unorganized workers had to be helped and protected by government wage-fixing machinery.[3] The most important question of all was what kind of unions should be allowed to exist.

DOCKWORKERS/AFRICAN WORKERS

In the seven years after the general strike of 1947, no trade union arose to represent the dockworkers of Mombasa. Despite the theoretical acceptance by the state of the idea of African trade unionism, the situation in Mombasa was not atypical of Kenya in those years; only a few trade unions were successful, and the state seemed far more interested in stopping the growth of what it considered the wrong kind of unions than in fostering the right variety. In the aftermath of the general strike, the workers of Mombasa demonstrated an interest in one form of labor organization, epitomized by the African Workers Federation. The weekly meetings in the Field of the Poor attracted thousands, kept alive the symbols of unity from the strike, and through the political education and the planning that took place at these meetings promised a more organized approach to future disputes.

robi: East African Publishing House, 1969); Makhan Singh, *1952–56, Crucial Years of Kenya Trade Unions* (Nairobi: Uzima, 1980); Alice A. Amsden, *International Firms and Labour in Kenya, 1945–1970* (London: Cass, 1971); Kerstin Leitner, *Workers, Trade Unions and Peripheral Capitalism in Kenya after Independence* (Frankfurt, Ger.: Peter Lang, 1977); Richard Sandbrook, *Proletarians and African Capitalism: The Kenyan Case, 1960–1972* (Cambridge: Cambridge University Press, 1975).

3. See the various drafts of a paper on "Industrial Relations in the Colonies" CLAC(51), 11, 18, 31, and the transcripts of the 43d, 44th, 46th, and 48th meetings of CLAC, January–October 1951, all in CO 888/8. More papers on this question are in CO859/183/12254/1951.

This was an important step. The success of the unionless strikers of 1947 in gaining significant wage increases and in focusing attention on their grievances is no reason to romanticize spontaneity. Demands were posed in a chaotic fashion, and the initiative to formulate specific responses to generalized grievances passed to the state. But Chege Kibachia and the AWF were seeking to combine the unity of 1947 with the force of organization. The choice was not just between the spontaneity of the African masses and British-style trade unionism. Other options were being explored.

And they were repressed with a vigor absent in the Kenya Government's handling of the strike itself, and with approval from the Labour Government then in power in England and little murmur from British trade unionists or the Fabian Colonial Bureau, long the conscience of empire.[4] The idea of a union of all workers was far removed from British trade unionism in the 1940s—although general workers' unions had had a place in English labor history—and such a union was certainly not what even the most progressive colonial officials thought trade unionism was all about.[5] As argued in chapter 4, the concept of trade unionism went along with the notion of a differentiated work force, divided according to occupations and industries. A railway union or a dockworkers union could play a useful role in a developing system of industrial relations; an organization of the African masses could not.

Such thinking lay behind the assault on the AWF that began in mid-1947. After that, officials continued to honor the AWF—and to betray their own obsession with what leadership could forge out of the discontent of the masses—by keeping a close eye on it even when there was nothing to see. In 1950, the Provincial Commissioner of the Coast wrote, "The African Workers Federation as a body has virtually ceased to exist though there is little doubt that it could easily become a source of trouble again should another fanatical and unscrupulous leader arise."[6]

The AWF was in fact gone for good. But workers in Kenya continued to show an interest in similar forms of organization, and the Government took their threat equally seriously. The Indian labor leader, Makhan Singh, made some moves in late 1947 and 1948 toward reviving an older general workers' union, the Labour Trade Union of East Africa, and the

---

4. Some questions were asked in Parliament, but they were about the civil liberties issue in Kibachia's detention—about Kibachia as victim rather than as a person standing for a viable strategy in labor organizing. See House of Commons Debates, 447 (25 February 1948), cc. 1040–41, and 450 (5 May 1948), c. 1240.

5. On general workers unions in England, see Eric Hobsbawm, *Labouring Men* (London: Weidenfeld and Nicolson, 1964), pp. 179–203.

6. Coast Province, AR, 1950.

Government first had him arrested (but could not get a conviction) and then pushed a new law through the Legislative Council requiring all trade unions to reregister and submit to some rather vaguely specified standards.[7] In 1949, the East African Trade Union Congress was formed, with Fred Kubai as President and Singh as General Secretary. Organizationally a federation of trade unions, its ideology and its plans reflected a similar outlook to its suppressed predecessors: the idea of bringing together the African working class as a whole, with unity and mass militance taking precedence over occupational and sectional interests. Once again, the state used trade-union registration ordinances to prevent the organization from growing, and later assisted a less centralized and less militant alternative organization.[8]

For Kenya's trade-union advisor, James Patrick, such organizations threatened to extend their militance far beyond the workplace. As he wrote in 1949: "it is not difficult to anticipate the intention and plan of people like Makhan Singh. Their object is to bring about a similar situation here to what was experienced in places like Malaya, Gold Coast and Trinidad." And by now the Cold War had extended this train of thought: "It is common knowledge that Africa is a target of Communism. The Federation [AWF], the Amalgamation, the General Unions are all part of this approach." The Labour Commissioner, Hyde-Clarke, took a similar line: "Makhan Singh is the leading light behind all agitation in the Colony. He is without a doubt pursuing the communist line. . . . He wants numbers and he wants to be the leader, and so we have the formation of this Trade Union Congress in East Africa, before we have even one decent proper and influential registered trade union. If we are not careful we are going to have a Malaya all over again in Kenya."[9] Hyde-Clarke and Patrick supported the legislation which allowed the Government to deregister unions that did not conform to official standards and which was used against the Labour Trade Union and the East Africa Trade Union Congress, the heirs to the AWF. By 1950, the campaign against general unions had succeeded, although at the cost of helping to provoke through the arrest of Kubai and Singh the Nairobi general strike of 1950. That strike, although it ended without clear gains for the strikers, was powerful

7. For more on Singh and the organizations with which he was associated, see his partly autobiographical, partly historical book, *History of Kenya's Trade Union Movement.*

8. Ibid., pp. 202–69; Clayton and Savage, *Government and Labour in Kenya,* pp. 325–28; Sharon Stichter, "Trade Unionism in Kenya: The Militant Phase," in Peter C. W. Gutkind, Robin Cohen, and Jean Copans, eds., *African Labor History* (Beverly Hills, Calif.: Sage, 1978), pp. 155–74.

9. James Patrick, "Memorandum on Trade Unions—Development and Policy—Kenya," n.d. [1949], FCB 118/1, p. 7; Hyde-Clarke to E. W. Barltrop, 25 June 1949, FCB 115/3.

enough—with over six thousand participants at its peak—to suggest that there indeed had been something to suppress.[10]

What did the colonial state have to offer as an alternative to the AWF and its heirs? Patrick's best moment came at a meeting in 1949 with settlers who were skeptical of the value of his work and who strongly opposed African trade unions of any sort. After a time, one of them grudgingly admitted, "Maybe it would be better to have employees controlled by Mr. Patrick than by Mr. Stalin."[11] "Control" was the right word to use. The Colonial Office had for some time insisted that trade unions be registered. It had made legislation permitting the registration of trade unions a condition for any colony receiving assistance under the Colonial Development and Welfare Act of 1940, the Colonial Office's pride and joy. In 1943, Kenya had revamped its legislation accordingly, and in 1947 the CO had sent Patrick to assist unions in organizing themselves.

But the government-sanctioned approach, by officials' own reckoning, quickly proved inadequate. Noting that Patrick had spent some time in Mombasa during 1947, the District Commissioner wrote, "there was nothing to show for his efforts."[12] In his own retrospective memorandum on his first two years in Kenya, Patrick railed about the illiteracy of the workers and the personal ambitions of the literate. He took pride in not registering unions:

> Today ten unions are registered in Kenya. Before the end of this year the number could be increased to ten times that amount, if I were to encourage such a policy. I will not agree to mass registration until the people concerned know and understand the meaning of what they do. I consider it would be criminal to the workers and a danger to the good government of the colony not to arrest any such tendency.

Of Patrick's ten unions in 1949, one was Singh's General Union, which he was aiming to destroy, five "can be ignored completely at the present moment as they do not understand what it is all about," and two were inactive. Only one, the Transport and Allied Workers' Union, met with his approval, although it too was about to become too radical for officials'

---

10. Stichter, "Militant Phase"; Clayton and Savage, pp. 328–37. That Singh, Kubai, and the legacy of Kibachia were at the center of the Kenya Government's anxiety about "political" or "irresponsible" trade unionism is clear in Mitchell to CO, 28 December 1949, CO 859/203/12267/2/1950–51. The Colonial Office thought that the trade-union legislation which Kenya wanted was too restrictive, but for the moment it was willing to defer to it on a matter of what it considered security. Creech Jones, Minute, 4 January 1950, and telegram to Mitchell, 5 January 1950, in ibid.

11. Remarks of W. B. Havelock to a meeting at the Thika Club, 10 January 1949, reported in EAS 14 January 1949 and quoted in Singh, History, p. 194.

12. Mombasa District, AR, 1947.

tastes. Most of the ten registered unions had been registered before Patrick's time, and he boasted, "otherwise they might not have been registered." Among the unions that were at least specific to an industry, an occupation, or a category of workers, any organization of dockworkers—already veterans of successful struggles—was conspicuously absent. "And what is the net result?" Patrick asked, after detailing his two years of educational work and organizational assistance given to Kenyans interested in founding trade unions. "They have little or no organisation worth talking about. . . . After all the effort and work which has been put in one would naturally have expected better results, and so I now view the general situation in the light of this experience."[13]

Patrick was what the British trade-union movement and a Labour Government in London had to offer Kenya. His condescension and his failures were not only his own: the organizational problems of African trade unions were real enough, and Patrick's dislike of the unions he knew still left him well short of the blanket hostility to trade unionism of most of the Kenya Administration. His boss, Hyde-Clarke, wrote to his friend Hilda Selwyn Clarke at the Fabian Colonial Bureau: "I'm afraid I'm far from happy with the trade union movement here. We are not really ready for it and I think we must legislate for a sort of probationary stage of pre-union status."[14]

The pressure from union sympathizers in England to take a more positive stance was tempered by some of the same fears of the wrong kind of trade-union activity that worried Kenyan officials. To be sure, the British TUC was critical of Patrick for failing to win the confidence of African workers, and it lobbied with some success to modify registration regulations that it thought discouraged legitimate unions.[15] The Fabians, for their part, were saddened by the failures of unionization in the late 1940s and early 1950s, mildly skeptical of the charges that the few able

13. Patrick, Memorandum, FCB 118/1, p. 9. During his valiant effort to convince settlers at a meeting in 1949 that organizing African trade unions was not folly, Patrick was asked, "Has Mr. Patrick met one African capable of being a real Trade Union official in this country?" He replied, "Honestly—no." EAS, 14 January 1949, quoted in Singh, *History*, p. 195.

14. Hyde-Clarke to Hilda Selwyn Clarke, 14 September 1949, FCB 115/3.

15. Walter Hood of the TUC thought that Patrick's "outlook on trade union development in this country is such that he does not appear to serve a very useful purpose in the present situation." Notes on Kenya, incl. Hood to Nicholson, 10 September 1953, FCB 119/1, item 3. On the TUC's successful lobbying to make Kenya's trade-union legislation less restrictive, see Secretary of State Lennox-Boyd to Governor Mitchell, 7 April 1952, and minutes by N. D. Watson, 4 March 1952, on a meeting with TUC officials, and by E. Parry, 19 February 1952, and by E. Barltrop, 23 February 1952, in CO 859/268. See also Peter Weiler, "Forming Responsible Trade Unions: The Colonial Office, Colonial Labor, and the Trades Union Congress," *Radical History Review* 28–30 (1984): 367–92.

trade unionists who came forth were communists, and critical of government's unwillingness to pursue a more forward policy. But even they were fearful of "disaffected elements who have attempted to use trade unions for political and other purposes," and they made it quite clear that certain kinds of trade unionism were acceptable while others were not.[16] In a letter to a Fabian protégé, Rita Hinden (the Bureau's leading light) pointed out that the British trade unionists had earlier faced three choices: a "revolutionary course"; narrow pursuit of "sectional interests"; and realizing "that they themselves could only benefit in the long run if their country was prosperous and to fight for full representation in industry, proper status, and a share in running the show." Of course, British workers had chosen the third, and so should the Kenyans, although "the colonial trade unions are still so young." She rhetorically asked her protégé, "Surely it is the function of people like you to make all this clearly understood?"[17]

The Bureau nonetheless realized that something had to be done and that the Kenya Government was not doing it. Marjorie Nicholson noted that the Government's most progressive document of the mid-1950s, the Carpenter Report, scarcely mentioned trade unions, but assumed that the workers' standard of living was best raised by "reliance on a benevolent government." The East Africa Royal Commission had been more explicit about excluding trade unions from its plans: it argued that wage councils within industries were more useful, and that East Africans were little interested in trade unions.[18]

By then, Government policy was slowly shifting. In the early 1950s, the labor advisors in London argued that government wage-fixing had gone too far and risked encouraging the kind of mass action—aimed at influencing the Government—which was precisely what they wished to avoid. The alternative was to encourage collective bargaining.[19] "Both workers and employers needed careful nursing before they could enter into joint

16. Marjorie Nicholson to F. K. Eady, ICFTU, 12 September 1951, FCB 61/2, ff. 10–11; Hilda Selwyn Clarke to Hyde-Clarke, 24 August 1949, FCB 115/3, f. 134; Memorandum from FCB to Royal Commission on Land and Population in East Africa, July 1953, ACJ 21/3, ff. 10–12.

17. Rita Hinden to Meschak Ndisi, 5 April 1950, FCB 115/3, f. 147. Ndisi had come to Fabian attention while studying trade unionism at Ruskin College, Oxford. On his return, he had been muscled out of a position of influence in the Transport and Allied Workers Union by the more militant Fred Kubai and ended up as a Labour Department official, working with Patrick.

18. Marjorie Nicholson, "Kenya—Report of the Carpenter Committee on African Wages," 13 June 1954, ACJ 21/4, ff. 8–9; East Africa Royal Commission, p. 161.

19. Memorandum by CLAC on "Trade Unionism in the Colonies," 24 May 1951, and discussions with heads of Labour Departments, 24 September–5 October 1951, CLAC(52)4, CO 888/8.

relations in the right spirit," but "the pressure of new ideas was too strong for action to wait on events and we could not afford to allow people to learn by the slow process of trial and error." The nursing image struck a chord in Kenya, where the Member of the Legislative Council for Education, Labour and Lands put it this way: "Mothering them and teaching them improved internal administration and attention to sound bookkeeping—that is the sort of thing I feel is what they really require."[20] Trade union development was going to be slow.

Kenyan trade unionists in 1952 organized what promised to be a more respectable coordinating body, appropriately named the Kenya Federation of Registered Trade Unions. The Government covertly gave it assistance. In October 1953, Tom Mboya, who already had good contacts in the Labour Department and was serving on the Labour Advisory Board, took over its leadership. He was twenty-three years old at the time. Mboya was particularly close to Richard Luyt, who became Labour Commissioner in 1954 and who shared visions of stable labor and higher wages with his predecessors Hyde-Clarke and Carpenter but took a much more positive view of trade unionism.[21] Mboya was to prove to both Government officials and African workers that responsible trade unions had much to offer them.

But that was in the future. The pace of unionization was slow until the mid-1950s, when it soared. Between the two great Mombasa strikes of 1947 and 1955 and except for the Nairobi general strike of 1950, strikes were not numerous, and during the days of repression during the Mau Mau Emergency from 1952 onward, the pace of strike activity slowed, as table 5.1 suggests. Many work stoppages lasted only a matter of hours, while the largest percentage of man-hours lost is accounted for by the Nairobi strike of 1950 and the Mombasa strike of 1955. The pattern, indeed, suggests that periodic urban conflagration, not routine industrial action, was the major feature of labor disputes in Kenya, a situation that must have confirmed some of the unease of officials.[22]

The state was facing one of the classic dilemmas of authority. Officials had learned that peaceful industrial relations required that workers be able to articulate their grievances; the workers needed leaders whom they could trust. But the authorities already had a very clear idea of what labor organizations and labor leaders should and should not do. They wanted the men to be free to organize exactly the kind of unions that officials

20. Notes on discussion with heads of Labour Departments, 1951, CLAC(51)31, CO 888/3; Legislative Council Debates, 69 (5 June 1950), c. 991.

21. David Goldsworthy, *Tom Mboya: The Man Kenya Wanted to Forget* (London: Heinemann, 1982), pp. 17–18, 21–23, 30.

22. See the list of strikes, none earthshaking, between 1948 and 1950 in PC's Archives, L&O 16/2.

TABLE 5.1

STRIKES IN KENYA 1948–1955

	Number	Workers Involved	Man-days Lost
1948			10,885
1949			24,575
1950			34,224 (30,000)
1951	57	6,610	10,708
1952	84	5,957	5,718
1953	39	3,221	2,674
1954	33	1,518	2,026
1955	35	17,852 (14,400)	81,870 (78,000)

SOURCE: Kenya, Colonial Reports, 1949–55.

NOTE: figures in parentheses are those of the Nairobi general strike (1950) and the Mombasa dock strike (1955).

thought they should. In fact, no trade union could effectively channel workers' energy and frustrations into acceptable directions unless it was taken seriously by the men, but the leaders who emerged from the organizing and confrontations of the 1940s were not acceptable to the state. So officials talked of nursing and went on repressing.[23] The attempts of the state, then, to develop institutions where employers and employees could bargain—councils in various industries—foundered on the fact that the African representatives on these councils lacked legitimacy with the rank and file.[24] The old tendency for workers to provoke a grand confrontation and hope for an anxious government and an anxious tribunal to settle it in their favor remained. The Government, willing only to give unions the illusion of autonomy, was to learn painfully that at least some of its substance was necessary to bring workers into an orderly system of industrial relations.

In Mombasa, a dockworkers' union appeared only in May 1954, and most of its early members were clerical workers. The industrial relations machinery of the early 1950s was essentially what Labour Department officials liked: a Joint Industrial Council (JIC) founded in 1952, with employer and employee representatives. In 1954, the employers thought the JIC was operating well, and they claimed to be encouraging the Dock-

23. With the Mau Mau Emergency, the rationale for repression shifted. The state went after unions that deserted their basically "economic" mission for "political" objectives. As Tom Mboya cogently pointed out, the dichotomy was false. "Trade Unionism in Kenya," *Africa South* 1, no. 2 (1956): 77–86.

24. This dilemma was at least recognized in London, where officials noted that such institutions should follow the growth of trade unions rather than precede that process. Minutes of 56th meeting of CLAC, 22 October 1953, CO 859/257.

workers Union, which was "developing slowly."[25] All was peaceful in the East African ports.

These were critical years for the restructuring of port labor, when the nature of dock work was being transformed by the initiatives of state and capital and when the wages of dockworkers were edging ahead of those of the rest of the city's working class. And precisely in these years, neither dockworkers nor the workers of Mombasa as a whole had an organized voice. Their one attempt to institutionalize the unity and the power they had for a time held had been suppressed before it had a chance to evolve or to fail on its own. The momentum of the continued agitation from 1939 to 1947 was broken as much by the significant—but highly differential—gains achieved by some workers in the aftermath of the 1947 strike and by the cooling of inflation a couple of years after the strike as by the repression. And most important of all, the increasingly permanent character of dock work—first because of the registration schemes of the 1940s and then by the new initiatives of 1952 and 1954—was separating dockworkers from the rest of the population. A dockworkers' union could, perhaps, have been a logical follow-up to the strike of 1947; in Dar es Salaam, for example, a union built on earlier strikes and made great strides during this period.[26] But that would have been a drastic change in direction for Mombasa's workers, from a system of communication and solidarity rooted in the city's working class as a whole to an organization based solely on dock work itself. Such a transformation was to occur, but only after the decisive changes brought about by the state and the port companies had taken hold, and only after the traditions of city-wide protest were stirred once more.

THE TRANSITION: THE STRIKE OF 1955

As of early March 1955, no significant labor stoppages or disturbances had affected the docks since the great strike of January 1947. Officials congratulated themselves that the labor situation in Mombasa was "most satisfactory."[27] When trouble came, it appeared, as it had in 1947, unexpectedly, without apparent leadership, and with the same direct and simple demand emerging from the confusion—more money. As in 1947, the strike was not limited to the docks, but enveloped the oil refinery workers and others concentrated in the port area. As the strike pro-

25. EAS, 17 November 1952; KL&S Co., AR, 1954, HBR 12/21/3, pp. 15–16.

26. John Iliffe, "The Creation of Group Consciousness: A History of the Dockworkers of Dar es Salaam," in Richard Sandbrook and Robin Cohen, eds., *The Development of an African Working Class* (London: Longman, 1975), pp. 49–72.

27. EAR&H, AR, 1954, p. 49; KL&S Co., AR, 1954, pp. 15–16, HBR 12/21/3.

gressed, the principal form of organization and decision-making was once again the mass meeting. The working class of Mombasa was still communicating and cooperating. But if the strike that broke out looked as if it was becoming a general strike, the strike that was eventually settled was a dock strike. The strike of 1955 was a watershed, containing within its short duration a transition from the generalized economic discontent of an urban work force to the particular demands of an occupation. This complex pattern reflected the segmentation of the Mombasa working class that had taken place since 1947, and—ultimately—it contributed still more to the segmentation process.

"We Are the Labourers"

The first hint of serious discontent came slightly over a month before the work stoppage, at a meeting on 26 January 1955 of the Joint Industrial Council of the dock industry. Founded in 1952, the structure of the JIC epitomized the Labour Department's concern with occupationally specific industrial relations machinery and with its preference for various kinds of councils over direct collective bargaining between union and management. Its tone reflected the arrogance of capital in using industrial relations machinery as yet another mechanism of control. The JIC was charged with ensuring "that no stoppage of work, lock-out or unauthorized action shall take place until such time as the machinery of the Council and the procedures agreed in this constitution has been exhausted."[28] It had five employer representatives selected by the Port Employers Association, two representatives of monthly employees and three of the casuals—all elected at dockside elections supervised by the African welfare officer and tribal headmen—and a nonvoting chairman, deputy chairman, and secretary nominated by the Labour Commissioner.[29] For a resolution to pass, a majority of each side was needed.

The employee representatives on the JIC had no official connection with the Dockworkers Union that had been founded in May 1954. Largely composed of clerical workers, the union was deemed, correctly, as not being representative of the workers. But the union had a constitution, officers, entrance fees of Shs 2, monthly dues of Sh 1, and the intention of enrolling all dockworkers, except for employees of the Railway as well as staff eligible to join the ethnically defined Asian and European staff associations. The union in 1955 was, as the Labour Department put it, "still in its infancy."[30]

---

28. Memorandum on Casual Labour Scheme, Mombasa, 1954, Appendix 12, LAB 9/217.

29. Ibid.; Clayton and Savage, *Government and Labour in Kenya*, p. 394.

30. Casual Labour scheme memorandum, Appendix 13; LD, AR, 1955, p. 15.

At the JIC meeting of 26 January, the employee representatives brought up the dissatisfaction of the workers. Two African representatives, Israel Jacob Okoth (a Luo) and Sammy Umari (from the Rabai subgroup of the Mijikenda), both thought it was above all the casual workers who were unhappy, and their main concern was the cost of living. Captain Williams of the KL&S Co. said that the issue could not be discussed at the JIC until the employee representatives came up with a memorandum on the subject. He was dubious about the casual workers' hardship because the figures for attendance at the pool call-ons during the past week had been low and his company was experiencing a "grave shortage" of casual labor.[31]

Williams did not dwell on two equally significant facts. The Casual Labour Scheme had just gone into effect, subjecting workers to stricter attendance requirements and eliminating some of the loopholes by which casuals had avoided time discipline. And workers in Tanga had just received an increase in daily pay to Shs 7/50, compared to the Mombasa rate of Shs 5. Later, the employers would complain that these figures were not comparable, since Tanga casuals worked less frequently each month.[32] But Tanga and Mombasa were part of a cultural milieu linked by ethnic and linguistic ties as well as by the effective sea-borne communications systems along the coast. Mombasa's day laborers may well have felt that they had to put up with the rigid rules of a pool system without getting a full measure of the benefits.

No sense of urgency troubled the employers. The workers' report on the cost of living would not be ready in the next month, so the monthly meeting scheduled for 24 February was canceled for want of an agenda.[33] On 22 February, the second warning appeared, notices being tacked around the sheds in the port and on the KL&S Co. notice board:

22.2.55. To all Africans working in Kilindini Msa. Even those who are working in the port on 3.3.55, everybody will go on strike. Clerks, askari, drivers, casual labourers, new and old employees, if you go on work this is your shauri [business] if you die. We are all will stay at home, At Kisauni, Magongo, Changamwe, Mtongwe, and Likoni. We are all must stand in one hand. Nobody can be allowed to leave his home. We are the labourers.[34]

---

31. Minutes of meeting of the JIC, 26 January 1955, in file on the strike of 1955, Railway Archives.

32. Port Employers Association, Memorandum to Windham Tribunal, 15 March 1955, Strike file.

33. JIC Minutes, 26 January 1955.

34. Strike file.

The contents of the notice are revealing. Along with its simple and powerful assertion of the dockworkers' position in the workplace—"We are the labourers"—was a reference to home. The places mentioned were not the island locations of low-cost housing, but the peri-urban zone— some of it recently farmland, some of it moderate-density planned settlement, much of it places where a family could live in a Swahili-style house, with room for a few goats, chickens, a couple of coconut trees, and a small garden. Parts of this zone—for example, Likoni—were traditional dwelling places for Digo, a Mijikenda subgroup (largely Muslim) prominently represented among dockers. Kisauni had a mixture of Mijikenda and Swahili-speakers. This kind of peri-urban settlement reflected the way in which many of the most established casual workers in Mombasa could integrate themselves into urban life—preserving a measure of control over style of life and work rhythms even when intensely involved in wage labor. The expansion of the Mombasa work force had meant that in addition to the Majengo-based dockers—both established Mombasans and room-renters from more distant coastal regions—this kind of peri-urban settlement had acquired new long-term residents and was beginning to share with Majengo a place of prominence in the networks among laborers. A few days after the notice appeared, in the midst of the strike, the administration would be requesting chiefs, mudirs, and headmen in the more distant hinterland of Coast Province—where Digo, Giriama, and other Mijikenda subgroups lived—to put pressure on their people to return to work.[35] Home was as important as the workplace in shaping the strike.

The JIC met on 24 February after all, on an emergency basis. The employers wanted to be assured that the notice did not reflect the views of the employee representatives on the JIC. Sammy Umari, also an official of the DWU, said that this was the first he had heard of it.[36]

At this meeting, the employers' attempt to use the JIC to impose their own stamp on labor relations came out clearly. They insisted that the employee representatives go around and talk to the workers over the coming weekend to find out what the strike notice was about and report back to a special meeting on Monday. The employee representatives, for their part, revealed how out of touch they were with the rank and file. Umari told the meeting that casual laborers often were not prepared to discuss things with the representatives. The strike threat, he felt, probably came from people who would not talk to him.[37]

---

35. Provincial Information Office, Official Statement No. 2, 4 March 1955, PC's Archives, LAB 8/2/D.

36. Minutes of JIC meeting, 24 February 1955, Strike file.

37. Ibid.

On 1 March the employee representatives duly reported back. They had circulated a message over the weekend saying that any complaints the workers had should be brought to their representatives on the JIC, and that "If you do not go to work on 3rd March 1955, without sufficient reason, your employer is at liberty to discharge you." They told their Council colleagues that they had attempted to talk to the men but had been "unable to discover the reason behind the threat to strike." A reply appeared instead tacked on to the gate of the Labour Compound: the laborers wanted a reply to their grievances by 3 March or they would stop work.

The employee representatives had meanwhile come up with a budget for a worker with a family, as shown in table 5.2. The bottom line came to around three times what monthly employees of the KL&S Co. were earning. The employers insisted on waiting for the more orthodox figures likely to come from the next Government report on the cost of living, due on 16 March. The Council adjourned until that date, its desire to contest the Battle of the Budgets on its own terms exceeding its anxiety about the threatened strike.

On 3 March, the strike began as the notice had stated. On the previous day, 2,823 casual workers had turned up for work, according to the routine reports of statistics. On the first day of the strike, ten casuals appeared. Strike breakers among the casuals would never number more than forty-one, about 1 percent of the pool.[38]

Contrary to the expectations of the worker representatives on the JIC, monthly workers were as involved as casuals. The Labour Department later acknowledged that essentially the entire work force of over 6,000 had struck. The strike spread as well to the oil refineries, East African Breweries, some East African Power and Light Co. facilities, and other firms. The next day, the *Mombasa Times* reported that 10,000 workers were out. The Municipality workers, Public Works Department employees, and workers in cement factories, construction firms, and various small businesses struck. The Labour Department claimed that at the peak of the strike, over 14,000 workers participated. Although many workers from Mombasa apparently went home to their rural bases, there was no significant strike action in plantations or other places of employment in Coast Province, as there had been in 1947.[39]

On the fifth day of the strike, the *Mombasa Times* referred to it as "The mysterious Mombasa strike—mysterious because no leaders can be

38. Attendance and Utilization Factors, Mombasa Port, March 1955, LAB 9/222 I; MT, 10 March 1955.

39. LD, AR, 1955, p. 15; Digo District, AR, 1955; MT, 4 March 1955; Report of Disputes and Strikes, 4 July 1955, LAB 9/1852.

TABLE 5.2
THE DOCKWORKERS' BUDGET, 1955

Rent	Shs	40
Food		250/45
Clothing		27/75 plus 25 for wife and children
Water		7
Miscellaneous		20/75
Total	Shs	345/95

SOURCE: Strike File, 1955, Railway Archives.

found, and no official grievance has been aired." Later, the newspaper commented that the strike had been too well organized to be spontaneous, and asked, "Who were the guilty men?" who led it.[40] One reason leaders were not forthcoming was that the strike was illegal. Under the Essential Services Act, port workers were not supposed to strike until they had exhausted an established procedure for mediation and arbitration. Another reason was the paralysis of the employee representatives, who had been coopted onto the existing Council and who were under heavy pressure within the Council to devote more energy to keeping workers on the job than to pressing workers' grievances. Two days into the strike, Sammy Umari added to his earlier laments, telling the JIC that it was pointless for him to come to meetings as a representative of the employees when "it was apparent that the men had other leaders." He had told the men that their strike was illegal, but to no effect. He said that he now wished to resign from the JIC, although he did not in fact do so. In his guise as a DWU leader, Umari was no more effectual, and in one angry meeting he and another JIC representative, Israel Jacob Okoth, were slightly roughed up.[41]

The mystery of how a disciplined strike was conducted without disciplinarians very much interested the Labour Department, police, and employers. This time they could not even come up with a Chege Kibachia on whom to pin the blame. In fact, the mass meeting emerged, as in 1947, as the central decision-making institution.

Just as important as the participation of casual and monthly dockers and other workers in port and town in the strike, was the absence of certain categories of workers. Railwaymen, as in 1947, were not involved in any significant way. Nor were employees of the Kenya Government, except in some isolated departments, although employees of the Municipality were.

40. MT, 7, 10 March 1955.
41. Minutes, JIC meeting, 5 March 1955; MT, 7 March 1955.

Monthly dockworkers, most of whom were employed by the KL&S Co., had not received a wage increase since November 1953. Casual stevedores had been given a raise in March 1954 from Shs 4/85 per shift to 5/50, while shorehandlers' pay rose from Shs 4/35 to 5/00.[42] But they compared their daily earnings to those of their brethren in Tanga and came out short.

Both monthlies and casuals complained considerably about the cost of living. Since the Government had stopped keeping a special index for Mombasa—oriented toward the commodities Africans consumed—in November of 1953, the participants (and the historian) lacked adequate information on the subject. The colony-wide index suggests that inflation was a factor in the mid-1950s, but not the overwhelming one it had been in the immediate postwar years. The cost of living rose around 6 percent in the sixteen months between the last wage increases for monthly workers and the strike.[43]

Dockworkers had more to be concerned about than incremental changes in their real wages. The Kenya Government's movement toward a new wage policy directed from above had penetrated working-class life in a major way. After the recommendations of the Carpenter Committee for a large hike in the minimum wage and of the Lidbury Commission for regrading civil service and railway staffs on a nonracial basis, the pay of Government and Railway workers had taken a decisive step upward. In January of 1955, the Railway had given employees a lump sum of Shs 250 as a retroactive raise in line with the Lidbury Report. Civil servants were now getting higher pay, and some industries were revising their wage scales. But the port employers were stalling, claiming that yet another report had to be produced before they would even consider wage revisions. When Tom Mboya arrived in Mombasa on the second day of the strike, workers immediately told him about the disparities between their wages and the post-Lidbury rates that other monthly workers were receiving as well as raises awarded to daily paid workers in Tanga. This "played a great part in rousing the feelings of the dockworkers. This was aggravated especially by the attitude and utterances of Company officials, who made no effort to hide the fact that they had no intention of improving the wages of their employees."[44]

Mboya realized another danger of falling behind in a period when salary differentiation was critical to the restructuring of the work force. The KFRTU—now dominated by Mboya—had earlier welcomed the

42. PEA memorandum to Windham Tribunal, 14 March 1955, Strike file.

43. Calculated from the Nairobi index in Colonial Office, *Digest of Colonial Statistics* 24 (January–February 1956): 81.

44. Tom Mboya, report to KFRTU on the 1955 strike, quoted in Singh, *1952–56, Crucial Years of Kenya Trade Unions*, p. 157.

new Government reports, and in particular the idea that higher salaries would break workers' dependence on rural sources of income for sustenance during the course of their lives. But the KFRTU pointed out that the way the Government went about implementing these complex reforms—a sudden, sharp wage increase—put more money into workers' hands immediately, tempting landlords to raise rents and merchants to hike the prices of tea, bread, and biscuits.[45] For workers not covered by the raises, such price increases, or even anticipation of them, were both devastating and galling.

In the 1940s, groups of workers in Mombasa had been sensitive to raises others were receiving and put pressure on slow-moving employers to catch up. In those years, when most workers were bunched near the bottom, the pay-raise vanguard tended to bring up the general pay level. The solidarity of the strike of 1947, even as some employers reacted more quickly than others, suggests that in this circumstance, pay differentials could be a dynamic factor rather than a divisive force. But by 1955, the eye that workers cast on each others' wages was becoming a jealous one. The increasing emphasis on stabilizing work forces within particular industries, and the growing difference between having one of the Lidbury-covered jobs and the uncertainties facing those not in the designated categories, posed a serious problem that came to a head in the months after the salary revisions went into effect. The striking workers in 1955, on and off the docks, were those who had not received raises earlier in the year, and they were *not* joined at the barricades by those who had. When the port employers eventually made concessions to the dockworkers, the dockers did not wait around to see how the oil company employees made out. The strike of 1955, like that of 1947, had spread beyond a single industry; but in a much more differentiated labor market, it had not spread as far, and its settlement spread even less. So whereas dockworkers struck in 1947 partly because they had so much in common with the rest of the Mombasa working class, the dock strike of 1955 had much to do with the parting of the ways among the workers of Mombasa.

Such a parting had been a deliberate aim of Government policy. But other aspects of that policy unraveled in the strike—notably, the belief held by the most apparently progressive of Labour Department officials that a weakly organized working class was desirable for the strengthening of managerial control. The strike of 1955 destroyed the industrial relations machinery of the port, based on negotiations without organized negotiators on the labor side. The old complaint of officials from 1939 to

45. Press conference by Mboya, 20 January 1955, cited in Singh, *1952–56*, p. 140.

1947, that it was impossible to find people with whom to negotiate or issues about which to negotiate given a disorganized African working class, surfaced again. The underground strike could still paralyze Kenya's only port without suggesting in the process of the dispute itself how the conflict could be resolved. The African representatives on the JIC, lacking their own organizational base, proved to be utterly useless as agents capable of communicating grievances to management and edicts to workers.

The failure of the old system of industrial relations had become clear by the time the JIC met again on the third day of the strike. The usual attempt of company and state officials to bully employee representatives took place. Williams noted that the representatives of the monthly employees—consistent with their stated opposition to the strike—had reported to work, but that the representatives of the casuals had not. The Labour Officer, putting direct pressure on these three men in the role of workers, warned of the consequences of their not reporting at least twenty times during the month. Kombo Mohamed, a casual representative, replied by asking, "How could we go on duty alone?" Stiffening a bit, the employee representatives rejected the division between casuals and monthlies and expressed the impatience of the workers with the delays in the JIC. Juma Mohamed said that the workers were not prepared to resume work only to be faced with further delays. Kombo Mohamed asked for a token wage increase pending negotiations and the cost of living report due on 16 March.

At the same time, Sammy Umari insisted that the representatives had done their best to stop the workers from striking. They had toured Majengo, Mtongwe, Kisauni, and other places in mobile vans and had tried to talk to the men. But the next day, he said, fewer men than ever had reported to work.[46]

The employers counterattacked, telling the employee representatives that the JIC had agreed to discuss the cost of living question on 16 March and the worker representatives should have explained that to the men. With Williams in the lead, the employer representatives berated their fellow Council members for not convincing the workers to leave the problem in the hands of the JIC. The Dockworkers Union, the employers said, had also been useless. George Usher, current chairman of the JIC, "stated that it would be the biggest set back to the Trade Union movement in the colony that could possibly happen if the representatives failed to get the men back to work." He insisted that "to suggest that the employers do

46. JIC meeting, 4 March 1955.

something *now* was ridiculous. It was not only un-principled, but morally bad."[47]

By their insistence that employee representatives do the bidding of the employers to get the men back to work and their refusal to negotiate, the port employers had demonstrated their own contempt for any real collective bargaining during the first challenge to the new industrial relations machinery. The next forums for negotiation would be mass gatherings, backroom discussions, and ad hoc meetings.

The Dispute Transformed

Tom Mboya had already arrived in town. He had been scheduled, along with Jim Bury of the International Confederation of Free Trade Unions, to run a weekend school on trade unionism at the coast. He was already seen as the Great Black Hope by the *Mombasa Times,* which reported his departure for Mombasa and his advice to dockworkers to call off their strike and put their grievances before the JIC.[48]

Mboya did not approve of the strike. He opposed it because it was illegal; because it was "not supported by the Dock Workers Union and had no direction from any organized workers' body"; and because "we wanted to emphasize the necessity for trade unions to adhere to the principle of putting forward their demands through properly constituted negotiation machinery."[49] For Mboya, the trade-union movement in Kenya required that strikes follow specific forms. He was to learn during his few days in Mombasa that this lesson could not be taught by preaching it, but only by winning for dockworkers concrete gains that could be associated directly with Mboya's kind of trade unionism.

The strike turned out to give Mboya's career a tremendous boost. It is important to stress, however, on what his success was based. Mboya's words and reputation at first had little influence on the workers: they handled him harshly. What counted with them and eventually won him their respect was that he was able to bring them a very favorable settlement from the state and the employers. The people over whom he had influence in March of 1955 were whites. His impact on them during the strike came, above all, from his skill in waving the spectre of disorder before their eyes, a spectre he feared almost as much as they did.

Mboya later termed his first appearance before a mass meeting of strikers on 4 March "one of the ugliest scenes I have ever faced in my life."[50] He had earlier toured Mombasa in a van—as had the African JIC

47. Ibid.
48. MT, 4 March 1955.
49. Report to KFRTU quoted in Singh, *1952–56,* pp. 156–57.
50. Tom Mboya, *Freedom and After* (Boston: Little, Brown), p. 33.

representatives earlier—to urge people to attend the meeting. According to Mboya's report after the strike, five thousand strikers appeared at the Tononoka football field, although by the time he wrote his autobiography, the number had swelled to ten thousand. Mboya reported that he listened to strikers outline their grievances: the rising cost of living, insufficient leave, insulting behavior by supervisors, lack of extra payment for dirty work, and lack of parity with railway and civil service workers under the Lidbury Report or with Tanga workers under their recent arbitration award. Mboya told the strikers that they should go back to work while he carried out negotiations on their behalf.[51]

As Mboya spoke, the crowd shouted, "We want more money!" During the meeting, Okoth of the JIC was roughed up and Umari, who served on both the JIC and the DWU, was threatened. Okoth told Mboya to stop speaking and was himself kicked and struck with a knobbed stick. A crowd of Luo surrounded Mboya to protect him. Mboya also said that the chance appearance of a white reporter almost caused a nasty incident.[52]

Mboya claimed he was having some success in "reasoning" with the strikers when representatives of the Coast Employers Association began distributing a leaflet with an ultimatum stating that if the monthly dockworkers did not appear at work the next day, 5 March, they would be dismissed. "This completely changed the course of events."[53] The meeting broke up in chaos.

The workers did not listen to either the Coast Employers Association or Mboya. Of the 1,700 monthly employees of the port, 40 went to work the next day. Even fewer casual workers showed up on the fifth than had appeared on the previous day—19 instead of 38.[54] The monthlies—even though they were more immediately vulnerable than casuals, who could legally take eleven days off in the month—stuck to their position.

Another mass meeting was held on the fifth, attended by some seven thousand strikers. Mboya had been scheduled to speak, but this was canceled. The workers were told about the acrimonious JIC meeting that had been held and decided to continue their strike.[55]

Having failed in a public meeting to persuade strikers to return to work and faced with the intransigence of the employers, Mboya went to work behind the scenes with Government officials. Through a European friend, he arranged a meeting with the District Commissioner, the Senior Labour Officer, and two strike leaders (whom he discreetly does not name

51. Report to KFRTU, quoted in Singh, *1952–56*, p. 157; *Freedom and After*, p. 33; MT, 5 March 1955.
52. MT, 7 March 1955; Mboya, p. 33.
53. Report in Singh, *1952–56*, pp. 157–58.
54. MT, 5 March 1955; Attendance and Utilization Factors, March 1955, LAB 9/222 I.
55. MT, 7 March 1955; Singh, *1952–56*, p. 158.

in his account) on Sunday evening, 6 March. They agreed to try to arrange a meeting between employers and representatives of the employees on Monday evening.

So another mass meeting took place, announced by another tour in a loudspeaker van. With Mboya in the chair, the meeting elected nine representatives to attend the Monday meeting, including Kombo Mohamed and Juma Mohamed—who had talked decisively to the employers in the previous JIC meeting—but not including the hapless Sammy Umari.[56]

In the Monday meeting of officials, employers, and employee representatives, Mboya at last began to acquire a grip on the situation. He very clearly outlined the grievances of the dockworkers, from the cost of living to the lack of parity in wage increases to their anger over the intractability of the employers. This time—after three more days in which workers had refused to be intimidated—the employers admitted that the workers had a case for consideration, but they were unwilling to consider it at the time. Instead, they suggested that, since any settlement would have wide consequences for the colony, an arbitrator should be appointed under the Trade Disputes Ordinance, and any award he might make should be made retroactive to 1 March. They also agreed not to carry out their threat to punish the monthly workers who had not returned to work.

Mboya did not give way. He wanted direct negotiations. The employers then withdrew from the meeting and caucused. They returned with an offer: a "token advance" of an extra Sh /50 per day to casual workers to show good faith, while turning the dispute over to the arbitrator. The employees then withdrew and returned to say that it would be difficult to get the men to accept Sh /50: They wanted Shs 2. The representatives suggested that the meeting should compromise at Shs 1/50 and leave the remaining Sh /50 to the arbitrator. The Senior Labour Officer warned them that if the offer were not accepted, a deadlock would remain to be arbitrated, but that the concession of Sh /50 and amnesty for the strikers would be withdrawn. Kombo Mohamed replied that the last words of the men at the meeting that morning had been, "Do not come back with an increase of a mere 50 cents."

The meeting nonetheless decided to try this out on the workers, but not without a last threat from the District Commissioner, who warned that if the strike went on, law and order were likely to be endangered. He would then have to call out more police and take firmer action. Mboya then played his best card. He agreed that without a bargain law and order would break down, and the Council would be responsible. He reminded the meeting of the "hooliganism" that had taken place earlier that day. He warned the officials that they should avoid any decision that would make further negotiation impossible. He agreed that the employee representa-

56. Minutes of ad hoc meeting, 7 March 1955, Strike file.

tives should report to the men on the employers' offer and the workers should decide. This was done.[57]

There had been violence, particularly on that day. Roaming crowds had thrown stones at cars, lorries, and buses, and authorities had stopped bus service to reduce the number of targets. Mboya accused "spivs and hooligans" of having caused trouble during his address at the earlier meeting. On the eighth, RAF bombers flew over the city and troops marched through the streets with fixed bayonets.[58]

But the workers were not yet ready to accept a modest award applied to one section of the work force. That evening, they voted down the offer, indicating that they would be willing to settle for Sh 1.[59] This the employers refused to concede, but they asked the workers to be sure to think of the Sh /50 as an interim award only, pending the arbitrator's award that would be retroactive to 1 March. Mboya warned them that the award still might not go over. At this point, Mboya, Jim Bury, and the nine striker representatives decided to push for acceptance of the employers' offer. It remained to convince the workers that they stood to gain significantly from arbitration. Meeting from twelve to two on Tuesday, 8 March, the workers listened to Mboya explain that refusing the interim award and the proposal for a tribunal would "greatly weaken their case and also lose for them public sympathy." The workers voted unanimously to return to work the next morning.[60]

The next morning, 2,301 casual workers went to work; only 29 had turned up the previous day. As workers who had gone to more rural locations returned, attendance reached a near normal 2,995 two days later. The strike had ended in as disciplined a manner as it had begun. Only somewhere along the way—in the course of all the meetings—the docks had become the only issue. What seemed like a general strike had become a dock strike. The oil company workers and others were no longer being discussed at meetings and were not included in the arbitration. Whatever raises they were to get, they would have to get for themselves.

The strike had been costly, and not just on the docks. The man-hours lost are summarized in table 5.3. After a few years of coasting along in the repressive atmosphere of the Emergency, Kenya suddenly was confronted with the consequences of a massive strike in its most vulnerable economic point. Of all the man-days lost to strikes in Kenya in 1955, the Mombasa strike accounted for 95 percent. According to the *Mombasa Times*, shipowners lost £60,000 during the strike plus £35,000 for subse-

57. Ibid., 7 March 1955.

58. MT, 8, 9 March 1955.

59. Minutes, special meeting of the JIC, 8 March 1955, Strike file.

60. Minutes, JIC meeting, 8 March 1955; Mboya's report to KFRTU, in Singh, *1952–56*, p. 159.

TABLE 5.3
MANHOURS LOST IN THE MOMBASA STRIKE OF 1955

	Man-hours
Town Casual Labour Pool	19,000
Municipality and various firms	180,000
Harbor and railway development	96,000
Stevedoring companies (casual)	96,000
KL&S Co. (casual)	76,000
KL&S Co. (monthly)	134,400
Oil Companies	20,400
Total	622,000

Source: Labour Officer, Mombasa, Report of Disputes and Strikes, 4 July 1955, LAB 9/1852

quent delays caused by the backlog and £50,000 from demurage and cargo charges. The railway lost £75,000, for a £220,000 total in the railway-harbor area alone. The economy of the entire colony, and of Uganda as well, had been placed at risk.[61]

All this was very much in mind when the tribunal convened only a few days later, a lightening pace compared to 1947. Mboya had taken over the organization of the dockworkers' case, and he prepared it meticulously, winning congratulations for his conduct from the arbitrator, Justice Ralph Windham. Although rumors of more unrest abounded, Mboya warned the dockworkers that another strike would be "unreasonable" and would harm their cause.[62] The award was announced on 4 April, and it gave dockworkers an impressive 30 percent pay rise. Pay for casual workers on the shore went from Shs 5 before the strike to Shs 6/50; stevedores preserved their Sh /50 differential and were awarded Shs 7. On the basis of a 22-shift month—only two above the minimum required—shorehandlers would receive Shs 143 and stevedores 154, compared to Shs 110 and 121 previously. The minimum wage for monthly workers went from Shs 101 to 130. All dockworkers thus moved even more decisively ahead of the Government minimum wage of Shs 80/50 per month. Other demands were also addressed: workers handling cement, clinker, and coal were awarded dirty money of 25 cents per shift, and monthly workers got another four days of annual leave, bringing their total to fourteen. Mboya's memorandum had asked for concessions along these lines, but for substantially more money; the Port Employers

61. Kenya, Colonial Report, 1955; MT, 15 March 1955. As the Arbitrator was pondering his award, a delegation of the Nairobi Chamber of Commerce came to Mombasa and expressed concern that the port "cannot cope." Their criticisms concerned port management more than labor, but still showed how high Nairobi's stake in Mombasa was. Ibid.

62. Goldsworthy, *Tom Mboya*, p. 43; MT, 16, 17 March 1955.

Association had wanted to pay less. The scope of the award and its contents looked like a classic instance of the settlement of a labor dispute in any industrial society.

The pattern of the dispute had been anything but classic. In its immediate aftermath, Mboya seemed to personify the new day in industrial relations in Mombasa; he was the savior of management as much as of the workers. The District Commissioner put in his annual report that "Mr. Tom Mboya was of considerable assistance in settling the strike."[63] The port employers asked Mboya to suggest how they might restructure the discredited JIC and were willing to allow union representation on it. Mboya presented a draft proposal on 20 May 1955 and it was accepted.[64] Meanwhile, he insisted that the DWU be reorganized so that it would be capable of negotiating through the JIC. After discussion with the executive committee of the DWU, Jim Bury, and the KFRTU, Mboya decided that "building up the Dockworkers Union" would be one of his new priorities.[65]

Making the DWU into a viable trade union after it had failed so badly in the first dispute on the docks since its foundation would be no mean feat. But it had been of central importance to Mboya even as he arrived for the tense mass meeting of 4 March. As his report to the KFRTU made clear, he had at that time opposed the strike largely because it was not being conducted by a trade union and was taking place outside the context of a regular system of presenting grievances and bargaining. Mboya had told the meeting of dockworkers, in effect, that the manner of proceeding took precedence over their demands, and he had counseled them to return to work even before the momentum of two days of work stoppage had been translated into any visible gains or change of attitude on the part of employers. The workers had, however, taught him a lesson that he had learned very quickly. The strikers must first gain the initiative.

At that point, Mboya played on the employers' fear of disorder and their exasperation with the chaotic manner in which the strike took place to focus the dispute on the specific issues at stake. In the process he challenged the employers' arrogant dominance of the existing industrial relations machinery. Only then could Mboya being to exert influence on the workers. And only after the strike was over and a highly satisfactory wage settlement accepted could he begin to push workers toward cooperating with the kind of trade unionism and collective bargaining he advo-

63. Mombasa District, AR, 1955. Back in England, the Fabians were also impressed by the work of one of the few Kenyans with whom they had contact: "Tom did a really good job in that strike." Marjorie Nicholson to Jim Bury, 22 March 1955, FCB 116/1, f. 191.

64. Clayton and Savage, *Government and Labour in Kenya*, p. 398.

65. KFRTU, Newsletter, No. 6, 16 March 1955, copy in FCB 119/1; MT, 25 March 1955.

cated. Having learned much from his overseas trade unionist mentors, Mboya learned a critical lesson from the dockers of Mombasa, bloodied veterans of three major and largely successful strikes over the past sixteen years, all conducted without the benefits of trade-union organization.

For Mboya, the fear of disorder was more than a card to play. He had been shaken by his experience on 4 March, and his remarks about "spivs and hooligans" suggest that his appeal at meetings with employers was to sentiments he also felt. He would later write of the "rioting" that had accompanied the strike, and saw this as a continuation of the pattern of 1947, which—like any good labor leader—he had assimilated as the key moment in the start of the Kenya labor movement.[66] His use of the word "riot"—a large exaggeration of the violence that occurred in both 1947 and 1955—suggests his fear of the chaos that lay outside of the well-ordered realm of orthodox trade unionism.

If Mboya had to grasp, on the spot, the sense of collective purpose among the unorganized workers of Mombasa, these workers could observe in his actions the importance of personal connections with officials, of being able to function in their memorandum-filled world, and of the gains that could be had from working within state institutions. They had won a great deal of money from the Windham decision, and the process of getting it proved to be an excellent advertisement for union organizing.

Employers also learned some lessons. Only recently, the Carpenter and Lidbury reports had seemed to cement the triumph of wage-setting from above, done in the name of complex arguments for social engineering and scientific objectivity. The Mombasa employers shared with the Labour Commissioner a belief that such decisions were best made by those with the proper objectivity, and that industrial relations machinery could remain rudimentary, while employee representatives could be coopted to help management handle problems as long as they had no autonomous organizational base. The strike showed that keeping African worker organization weak did not guarantee labor peace. A new era of give-and-take, union organizing, collective bargaining, the posing of demands, and the making of threats was about to begin.

More clearly than in 1947, the strike showed that it was not enough to have just any form of worker representation in some kind of grievance machinery. Worker representation had to be effective, and it had to be taken seriously by the workers themselves if a predictable pattern of industrial relations was to be developed. After the Windham award, employers soon realized that Mboya's strategy of presenting substantial demands and getting them referred to a tribunal could be expensive. Their experience may well have resulted in an increased willingness to face

66. Mboya, "Trade Unionism in Kenya," p. 79; Mboya, *Freedom and After*, p. 32.

young African trade unions rather than to face Tom Mboya and a judge.[67]

With the announcement of the Windham award, the situation in Mombasa had changed radically from the early days of the strike a month before and from patterns of protest of the last sixteen years. The 1947 strike had been a victory for the working class of Mombasa. The 1955 strike was a victory for the dockworkers.

WORK, WAGES, AND THE UNION, 1955–1963

Over the next several years, disputes arose in the port over issues of work and money. During these years, the climax of decasualization and the growth of an authoritarian style of management led to tensions and occasional work stoppages. They generally began as unofficial actions by the rank and file, the DWU joining the fray with varying degrees of forcefulness. Out of the ups and downs of organizing and bargaining in the post-1955 era developed a structure of labor relations in which the union bargained effectively over money issues but could not fully grasp or articulate the complex tensions over the transformation of work. Organized labor posed no serious threat to the ongoing efforts of the companies to decasualize hiring and restructure supervision on the docks.

By the end of 1955, the Government reported that the Dockworkers Union had a nominal membership of 3,420. In February 1957, according to the *Mombasa Times*, the DWU was claiming to have 4,800 members out of the 6,000 dockworkers and was resolving to work for a closed shop. The Union argued that such a step would end the unofficial stoppages which had occasionally been taking place, allegedly through the actions of nonmembers. At its annual meeting in July, the Union again claimed around 5,000 members, although only about half had paid their dues. According to a former union officer, the payment of attendance money, after discussions with the union in 1957, convinced many casual workers that they should join the Union.[68]

The union was beginning to make itself heard in a modest sort of way. Following the 1955 strike and Mboya's subsequent initiatives, the DWU had acquired a place on the reconstituted JIC. In June and July 1957, possible trouble loomed because of a slowdown in activity in the port resulting from disruptions in shipping following the Suez crisis. As the attendance bonus scheme had just begun, the companies had to pay £8,000 in those months to workers who did not work, and the workers

---

67. Amsden, *International Firms and Labour*, p. 56; Clayton and Savage, p. 391.

68. Kenya, Colonial Report, 1955, p. 16; MT, 20 February, 17 July 1957; Interview: Alex Nyakoko, Industrial Relations Officer for the Kenya Cargo Handling Service and a former DWU official, 1979.

were not happy with the situation either. The companies proposed reducing the size of the pool. But firing an employee who had fulfilled his twenty-day monthly obligations was illegal under the scheme. The DWU made a constructive suggestion for facing the downturn in business: share the losses by laying casuals off in rotation, one day per week, during the crisis. This was accepted. By 1958, traffic was up and the pool had been reduced by attrition and the transfer of more workers to monthly jobs. An official end to the rotating layoffs was agreed upon in 1959.[69] The DWU had successfully proposed a compromise with the companies on issues of job security and work rules.

The Union Intervenes: The Dock Strike of 1957
Despite the Union's growth and its official status in the JIC, the first strike situation that it faced originated from outside the DWU. The difference between November 1957 and March 1955 was that this time the Union was able to gain control over the conduct of the strike as it developed. In the process, a change in the thrust of the demands took place.

When casual stevedores arrived for the afternoon shift on 8 November 1957, they stopped at the barriers where they were signed on to discuss an issue that had arisen the previous night, and they decided not to go through. Monthly workers and casual shorehandlers worked as usual. The next day, a Saturday, most monthly workers reported, but casual workers again refused to pass the barrier, assembling instead outside it. Gangs of dockworkers were seen allegedly intimidating other workers in several locations of the city.[70] The police and the Provincial Commissioner declared a precautionary alert at 9 A.M. At 9:30, casuals entered the port to try to persuade monthly laborers not to work. By 10:30, all monthly workers—stevedores and shorehandlers—had stopped working. As in 1955, the stoppage spread to some other companies in the port area, including the brewery, the power station, and some factories. The oil companies, fearing damage to their installations, sent their men home until Monday.[71]

The issue that set off the strike involved management's control over the allocation of duties, a key element in the ongoing restructuring of the labor process. The companies had served notice two months previously that they intended to change the way winchmen were employed. Winchmen—who operated shipboard winches used in moving cargo—had all along been associated with particular work gangs. But now, with the weakening of the gang system and the centralization of call-on, manage-

69. LD, AR, 1957.
70. MT, 11 November 1957.
71. Provincial Emergency Committee, Report No. 1, 9 November 1957, LAB 9/63.

ment wished to allocate winchmen as needed rather than by a set ratio of winchmen to laborers or by older patterns of association. On the night of 7 November, company officials invoked this rule for the first time. During the third (night) shift, employers wanted laborers but not winchmen. They did not take on the winchmen, and the workers were angry. The President of the DWU, in a later speech to a meeting of strikers, particularly blamed Bruce Minnis, the labor supervisor of PLUB, for failing to consult the union about the change in policy. The strike broke out the afternoon following the turning away of the winchmen from jobs they had expected. Its spread was accelerated by the very centralization that had provoked it: signed on at a single point for the entire port, workers could talk to each other at the beginning of every shift.[72]

The DWU, at least as far as the JIC and the public were told, did not support the strike. As in 1955, the JIC insisted that the Union's duty was to get the men back to work.[73] It must be remembered, however, that until the end of 1958, strikes were illegal in the port under the Essential Services Ordinance, although the strikes of 1947 and 1955 had been far too successful for the act to be used punitively. Even if the Union had been involved behind the scenes in preparing for the strike, public discretion would have been well advised.

Somewhere along the line, the demand for an additional Shs 4 per shift appeared, it was reported in newspapers on 10 November 1957. The Union's first foray into public strike activity was tentative. On the Saturday the ninth, Francis Thiongo, General Secretary of the DWU, and Leonard Stanislaus, President, spoke to a meeting just outside the port. They told the crowd that action was taking place. Minnis had been suspended (this was incorrect: he had been placed on local leave during the dispute to get him out of the way without losing face), and the JIC was meeting to try to reach an agreement. But the leaders were too wary of the temper of the strikers to press—as the JIC had told them to do—for a return to work pending negotiations. The audience was in no mood to return. People insisted that the strike was not just a matter for the dockworkers, but for all labor in Mombasa.[74]

Mombasa's strike history seemed to be repeating itself. The next day Tom Mboya arrived. He had been flown to Mombasa by the Government in the company of Ronald Ngala, the leading Mijikenda politician. Lifting the ban on political meetings it had imposed for the duration of the Mau Mau Emergency, the Government first allowed Ngala to speak briefly to a crowd of five thousand people at Tononoka Hall on that Sunday morn-

72. Ibid., No. 1, 9 November, and No. 2, 10 November 1957.
73. *Sunday Post,* 10 November 1957.
74. Provincial Emergency Committee, Report No. 2, 10 November 1957, LAB 9/63.

ing, the tenth. The crowd then moved to the larger Municipal Stadium to hear Mboya. The audience grew from three to seven or eight thousand as Mboya spoke.[75]

Mboya said that he spoke as General Secretary of the Kenya Federation of Labour. He reminded the audience of his help in 1955. He asked to hear what their grievances were. The audience replied, "wages." Mboya condemned the violence and intimidation during the strike, and told the workers that they should go back to work on Monday on the understanding that there would be no loss of continuity of service in regard to the (increasingly important) benefits they received, and that negotiations would start promptly on Monday. He added, "But while your complaints are being discussed you must return to work and you must behave properly." He reminded them as well—recalling his successful strategy in 1955—that if negotiations failed, the case would still go to an arbitrator.

The response, according to reports, was initially unfavorable, although Mboya faced nothing like the hostility of his first encounter with Mombasa's workers. His strategy had, after all, worked before. Mboya insisted that a strike would not help, and that the Union lacked strike funds. He repeated that the workers should go back to work, and he deplored violence. The crowd finally agreed and applauded Mboya. On Monday morning, the strikers returned to work.[76]

There had been some violence, and fifty-one people were arrested during the strike for disturbing the peace. Six were later convicted of throwing stones. Troops had been called in but not used. Crowds of up to five hundred had also blocked access to the docks and stoned vehicles attempting to pass.[77]

The role of the Union up to this point remains unclear, either because its leaders feared prosecution or because they in fact lagged behind the workers. But in the next phase, the Union departed from the old script. After the promised Monday meeting of the JIC got nowhere, the DWU submitted a notice of deadlock, a legally correct way of proceeding that gave the union a right to strike after a twenty-one-day period. The Union then formulated a list of demands. The items in contention included both wage demands—a raise of Shs 4 per shift for casuals and Shs 20 per month for monthlies—and a series of demands related to terms of hire.[78]

75. Ibid., No. 3, 10 November. The *Mombasa Times*, 11 November 1957, estimated the crowd at ten thousand.

76. Provincial Emergency Committee, Report No. 3, LAB 9/63; MT, 11, 12 November 1957.

77. MT, 12, 27 November 1957.

78. The demands are listed in the Port Employers Association official report of the trade dispute, to which the union agreed. Williams to LC, 21 November 1957, LAB 9/63.

Two days later, when the Union and employers presented their views to the Labour Commissioner acting as a conciliator in the dispute, the issues had boiled down to eight coherently presented and tightly argued points. The form of the dispute is as revealing as its contents, for it shows how well-prepared union officials—working within industrial relations mechanisms that both parties were only beginning to take seriously—sorted out and redefined issues. As the dispute became formalized, the workers' anger with the way management was exercising authority was lost; a series of complex issues regarding time and money came to the fore.

The issues were as follows: (1) The DWU demanded that casuals be paid for an entire shift even if they were only taken on to work part of it, while the Port Employers Association insisted on controlling times of hire and paying for what it got. (2) The Union wanted casual workers injured on the job to be paid each week the full wages equivalent to six days of work, rather than the current half rate. The employers conceded full rates, but only on the basis of the individual's average working pattern. (3) The DWU wanted monthly workers who had to be laid off to be given longer notice of termination and better gratuities, while the PEA insisted that the current policy of "last in first out" was adequate protection for long-term workers and that laid-off monthlies could have priority to enter the casual pool. (4) The Union asked for twenty-four days annual leave for monthly workers, compared to the current fourteen, contending that many came from distant parts of Kenya. The PEA insisted that the dockworkers' home was now Mombasa, and they were unsympathetic to employees' travel plans. (5) The DWU raised anew the problem of expensive and often distant housing and asked employers to provide free housing for monthly workers in lieu of the 15 percent "housing element" included in their wages. The port firms considered this demand "unrealistic." (6) The Union asked for raises of Shs 4 per day for casuals and Shs 20 per month for monthly workers, presenting not only the familiar budgets and figures on the rising cost of living, but the argument that workers now needed to save money to educate their children, care for relatives, and other expenses. The PEA did not want to take on this implication of its stabilization policies, but insisted that the relevant criterion for wage adjustment was the cost of living, and recent changes—compared to recent wage increases—did not justify any such increase. Instead, it emphasized the difference between the keen and the lax worker and that the new labor system offered opportunities for extra earning that workers were not fully using. (7) The Union wanted the size of work gangs to be standardized, fearing that company-directed reduction in the size of gangs meant, in effect, a speed-up. The PEA insisted on control. (8) The Union wanted all categories of workers to receive overtime pay on

Sundays, while the firms argued that since casuals chose when to work (and monthlies were rotated so everyone had equal rest) Sunday overtime was not justified.[79]

The only issue that addressed the question of *how* dockers worked in the era of managerial initiative was the seventh, and the union raised the issue of the pace of work indirectly, focusing on the size of work gangs. The winchmen's grievances that had provoked the wildcat strike got lost in the shuffle. The other issues all concerned time and money. For monthly workers, the DWU was demanding more leave and higher pay, better housing, and improved job security. Its demand for company-supplied housing suggests a remarkable reversal of past habits among dockworkers: having accepted the discipline of monthly labor, many dockers probably felt that at least they might get an apartment for it. The flexibility of work and living arrangements that dockworkers had long seemed to defend was now—at least from the Union's perspective—less critical than other material concerns.

For casual workers, the Union was accepting the basic framework of the casual labor scheme and arguing within this structure for more secure, predictable, and lucrative employment. Its attempts to redefine how injured workers be paid and how shifts and overtime be calculated, as well as its calculations about wages, implied a desire to regularize employment even more, to narrow the difference between daily and monthly work. The Union clearly was trying to address the problems of casual workers and saw a need to assure balance between its casual and monthly members. But in a subtle way, the specific demands that it presented revealed that the issue was not the right of casual workers to maintain their own control over their time, but the attempt to make the casual laborer closer to a full-time worker.

The PEA pressed its argument at the conciliation hearings that casual workers were "not really making the best of their advantages to earn higher wages." Casual workers were still being deregistered for failing to meet their quotas, and monthly workers frequently requested unpaid leave.[80] The employer's negotiator commented, "The majority of these persons are members of the Coast tribes who have shambas to attend to." That was precisely what the stabilization policy was intended to check. Rejecting the Union's request for longer leave to allow workers to travel to distant parts of Kenya, the PEA insisted, "regular dockers should become stabilised in Mombasa and really make this area their home."[81]

79. Notes of conciliation, 14–15 November 1957, LAB 9/1883.

80. Forty to forty-five workers were being deregistered each month for failing to work twenty shifts, while a hundred of the 1,600 stevedores and around a hundred of the 780 shorehandlers were away at any given time on unpaid leave at their own request. Ibid.

81. Conciliation hearings, 15 November 1957, LAB 9/1883.

The Union conceded high absenteeism among casual laborers but insisted that this stemmed not from their backward ways but from lack of incentives. They argued that the companies did not lose by nonattendance and should increase incentives if they wanted better attendance records. In particular, the lack of paid leave for casuals meant that workers helped themselves to leave by absenteeism. Most significantly, the union conceded that longer leaves should be accompanied by tighter control over illegitimate absences. The Union and the PEA, in a sense, were arguing over the best means to promote further stabilization.[82]

The problem of settling on some wage figure, meanwhile, was getting nowhere. The PEA refused to make any offer until the end of the year, when it could see what the Government was doing about wages for its employees. The Union refused to wait. Privately, the Labour Commissioner, as conciliator, told the employers that a small increase was justified on cost of living grounds and that industry was harming the advance of collective bargaining as a way of conducting industrial relations by throwing the problem to the Government.[83]

To the Union, the conciliator explained the ongoing pattern of wage increases for casuals: the current claim would send daily wages to Shs 11/25 plus Sh 1 attendance bonus, that is, an increase of 48 percent after increases of over 50 percent between 1955 and 1957. He suggested that if the momentum of previous increases was to be maintained, the dockers should receive more like a 20 percent raise, or Shs 1/45. If the PEA hoped Government figures would give the objective word on wage hikes, the Government's Labour Commissioner took refuge in the standards of precedent. The Union put forward a dual approach: it would drop its demand to Shs 2 during conciliation, but if the dispute went to arbitration, it would press for the full Shs 4 that it wanted. The employers would not agree and the conciliation proceedings deadlocked.[84]

The conciliation procedure had produced agreement on two of the eight items: injured casual workers would be paid at the full shift rate based on the individual's average earnings for the past six months, and monthly workers would be given a month's notice of termination if they had to be laid off (issues 2 and 3). Three issues were withdrawn from discussion and left for future consideration by the JIC: gratuities for dismissed workers (part of issue 3), housing for monthlies (5), and the size

82. Notes of discussion with conciliator with DWU, 16–17 November 1957, ibid. The PEA argued that fringe benefits monthly (but not daily) workers received, worth about Shs 14 to 15, provided an extra inducement for workers to accept permanent employment. The Union—ever trying to make casual work more like permanent work—argued instead that the imbalance should be made up. Conciliation hearings, 20 November 1957.

83. Notes of conciliator, 21 November 1957, ibid.

84. Ibid., 20 November 1957.

of work gangs (7). It is noteworthy that the one labor-process issue was held in abeyance by agreement of both parties. There remained four issues, all classics of bread-and-butter unionism: the part-shift payments (1), the length of leave for monthlies (4), wages (6), and overtime (8).[85]

The Union gave twenty-one days notice of a strike, although it could only strike if an arbitrator were not appointed under the Essential Services Act. The Government acted quickly and sent the four unresolved issues to Justice E. A. J. Edmonds, assisted by one assessor nominated by the workers (Ronald Ngala) and one by PLUB (S. Wharlow).[86]

As the seemingly inevitable course to arbitration was being followed, the DWU brought in its heaviest artillery, Tom Mboya. The hearings were conducted in the atmosphere in which Mboya functioned best, a state of tension over the possible spread of disorder. The *Mombasa Times* reported on 30 November the presence of "agitators" in Mombasa who were inciting people to strike on 3 December, when the twenty-one-day notice would be up. Francis Gathuna, General Secretary of the DWU, warned dockworkers not to strike while hearings went on. They did not. But Mboya warned pointedly at the hearings of the danger of "unrest and uneasiness among the whole working population of Mombasa."[87]

Mboya's argument at the arbitration hearing was consistent with one he was making in his political writing.[88] Migratory labor was the result of inadequate wages: that workers chose to keep one foot on the farm was not a defense of certain intrinsically desirable forms of rural life so much as the failure of capital and the state to live up to their stated goals of making urban life possible, goals which Mboya shared. So his appeal to Edmonds was based not only on the rising cost of living for workers, but on the need to take a broader view of the kind of life they had to support. He dismissed as irrelevant the argument that dockworkers were already better paid than most, insisting that the health of the industry concerned and the state of collective bargaining were the only relevant issues. The strike had begun in defense of a traditional way of employing a particular category of labor; in Mboya's final presentation, organized labor was pushing faster than management for the shared goal of modernizing work organization and society in Kenya.

The PEA argued back that it would agree to wage increases only if it could be proven that the cost of living had risen: they still hoped to objectify the wage-fixing process. Evidence was submitted that prices had

85. Ibid., 21 November 1957.

86. MT, 22 November 1957; LC to Permanent Secretary for Education, Labour and Land, 22 November 1957, and Permanent Secretary to Press Liaison Officer, 22 November 1957, LAB 9/63.

87. MT, 29, 30 November, 3, 4, 5 December 1957.

88. See, for example, his article published in the same year in *Africa South*, p. 82.

risen 3 percent since January. Justice Edmonds was persuaded by the argument that dockers were already well paid, calling the PEA "one of the best employers of labour in Kenya."[89]

His award was a modest one, a 5 percent wage increase rounded off and adjusted slightly to preserve a fifty-cent differential in shift work between ship and shore. Shorehandlers' shift rates went from Shs 6/75 to 7/10, stevedores from Shs 7/25 to 7/60. The monthly scale went from a range of Shs 145 to 175 to Shs 152/25 to 183/75. He recommended increasing the differential for long-service employees and the attendance bonus given casuals who attended twenty days per month, in order to encourage greater stability in the work force. On the other issues, he compromised. He gave workers who were dismissed after working the first half-shift five-eighths of the full-shift rate instead of half; he was willing to have monthly workers, but not casuals, paid overtime for Sunday and holiday labor. He raised monthly workers' leave from fourteen days to eighteen, instead of the twenty-four requested by the union. He had praise for the PEA and the DWU, but not for the workers who had gone out on strike. They had committed "a grave irresponsibility."[90]

The wage increase was small compared to the 30 percent achieved in the strike of 1955, when demands had been placed in a less coherent fashion but which had frightened the authorities a great deal more. The award was in fact less than some of the raises given without strikes in the two intervening years. But in the period as a whole the dockworkers had done quite well for themselves. Most important, the Union had handled the increasingly formal structure of industrial relations in Mombasa effectively; the performance was better than the results.

But the strike had not begun as a dispute over wages. In its earliest phases, the workers' anger over management's seemingly arbitrary control over who worked when and their unhappiness with the labor supervisor who personified the new style of authority had triggered their actions. Other incidents in the daily interaction of supervisors and men would touch off more sudden work stoppages in years to come.

Whether any other form of labor organization other than the one that existed could have articulated more clearly and forcefully the concern of dockers with what went on in the workplace is a matter of speculation. The Dockworkers Union was most effective in presenting grievances that concerned access to the workplace and what workers took away from the workplace. But the one demand centered on what went on *inside* the workplace was dropped, and the discontent with supervision that had

89. MT, 3, 4, 11 December 1957.
90. Text of judgment, 6 December 1957, LAB 9/63.

been so apparent at the beginning of the strike quietly disappeared as the dispute entered the Government's industrial relations system.

Confrontations: Work, Wages, and Union Autonomy, 1958–1959
Workers continued to confront their union, as much as their employers, with a variety of work issues during the following year.[91] In January 1958, some workers followed up their strike of the previous November with a four-hour-long unofficial stoppage. On 12 January, a Saturday, 1,200 shorehandlers struck, upset that the overtime provisions of the Edmonds award were resulting in a loss of pay for workers on the second shift. They returned to their jobs after a Labour Department official talked to them and promised prompt negotiations. The DWU demanded that the weekly hours of shorehandlers on monthly contracts be reduced from 39 to 35. The dispute was settled a few days later when both sides agreed to keep the old second-shift hours, 4 to 11 P.M. Monday through Friday and 4 to 8 P.M. on Saturday, but to give an extra "token" payment to workers who stayed beyond 8 P.M. on Saturday—Shs 6/75 for shorehandlers, 7/25 for stevedores, and 9/25 for stevedore specialists.[92]

Meanwhile, the employers revived their attack on the customary position of specialist workers by demanding to reduce the number of winchmen and serangs in the casual labor pool, reclassifying them as ordinary laborers. The union objected and was under pressure from its members to hold the line: a DWU officer had been shouted down by eighty casual laborers and winchmen at a meeting in Majengo. The employers offered to reduce the number of workers subject to reclassification to fifty, but the DWU rejected the offer and declared a dispute.[93] The Labour Commissioner accordingly appointed his deputy to conciliate under the Essential Services Act. The Union offered a counterproposal to the conciliation hearing: that surplus winchmen and serangs rotate into and out of their specialized and higher-paying positions. It argued that many of the men had twenty to twenty-five years service and were liable to lose the extra earnings to which they were entitled, while they stood to lose their atten-

91. In London as well, the partial moves toward decasualization during and after World War II were accompanied by management efforts to assert authority over the labor process and to end various customary work rules that lowered productivity. Union leadership accepted this, but unofficial strikes made the postwar decade one of most strike-filled in the history of the port. Peter Weiler, "British Labor and the Cold War: The London Dock Strike of 1946," in James Cronin and Jonathan Schneer, *Social Conflict and the Political Order in Modern Britain* (New Brunswick, N.J.: Rutgers University Press, 1982), pp. 156, 159, 166; Michael P. Jackson, *Labour Relations on the Docks* (Westmead, Eng.: Saxon House, 1973), pp. 41–72.

92. EAS, 13, 14, 15 January 1958; Convener, PEA, to Senior LO, Coast, 20 January 1958, and Senior LO to Chairman, JIC, 29 January 1958, LAB 9/1883.

93. EAS, 14, 17, 24 January 1958.

dance money if they would not accept their demotion. The Union was also suspicious of how specialists were to be chosen for demotion. The employers refused the proposal, insisting on their right to weed out "specialists with the worst records" when they reduced numbers. The principle of last in, first out, which had emerged in the previous dispute over a similar issue, applied only to monthly workers and not to casuals, who were entitled under the Casual Labour Rules to be kept on the list, not to a privileged position.[94]

The conciliator sided with the employers. He argued that the surplus of labor in the specialist categories was genuine and that paying their attendance money (Shs 4, compared to Shs 3 for ordinary casuals) was an excessive burden. The winchmen and serangs should work—and be paid—as specialists when their services were needed but work as ordinary laborers when specialists were in short demand. He was not impressed by the apparent preference of the specialists not to work for Shs 4 instead of working for Shs 7/60 as a laborer. And he accepted the argument of the companies that those demoted would be "habitual slackers." The conciliator considered the DWU position insufficiently based to justify arbitration. The Government in Nairobi agreed and the dispute ended. The DWU, defeated, did not press further.[95]

The dispute occurred in the context of the longer-range effort of management to gain tighter control over gang leaders and other special categories in the hierarchy of dock labor. This implied that the ratio of leaders to specialists to laborers should be fixed by the companies, not by the gangs, the make-up of the current pool, or custom. Employers, willing to compromise on payments for overtime, would not do so on the issue of control. Nor would the Government, which shared management's notions of authority in industrial organizations, see much reason to defend the older conventions of dock work and the special privileges the more senior dockers had acquired within it.

Neither the outcome of these disputes nor the wage increase of the previous November made the dockworkers satisfied with the performance of their union. In March of 1958, an election meeting attended by barely 510 of the 6,000 dockworkers voted the old leadership out of office. Members felt, according to Richard Sandbrook, that the officeholders were too close to management. Francis Gathuna, the General Secretary, was on leave of absence from a clerical job, and some felt he was too easily subject to company sanctions. The answer to this danger

94. Notes on conciliation meetings, 28 January, 7 February 1958, and Acting General Secretary, DWU, to LC, 23 January 1958, LAB 10/326.

95. Report on conciliation proceedings, 11 February 1958, and Ag. Permanent Secretary for Education, Labour, and Land to General Secretary, DWU, 14 February 1958, LAB 10/326.

was to bring in someone who had never seen the inside of a cargo shed. The militant slate in the 1958 election was led by Denis Akumu, Secretary General of the Nairobi People's Convention Party and an associate (and fellow Luo) of Mboya. With no ties to employers and strong ties to Mboya—whose reputation in Mombasa had remained high ever since 1955—plus an outgoing and militant style, Akumu was in a strong position to challenge the old leadership of the Union and add new vitality to its already significant organizational achievements.[96]

Akumu is well remembered among dockworkers, even after his fall from grace in 1965, both for his organizational skills and for his militance. It was he, for example, who developed the shop steward system on the docks, in the face of opposition from both employers and the older serangs; and the union budget jumped from under Shs 9,000 in 1955–56 to Shs 51,000 in 1959–60 and Shs 156,000 in 1963–64.[97] Nevertheless, a look at the way in which conflicts unfolded over the next few years suggests that the traditions of spontaneity and assertiveness among Mombasa's workers remained an equally important part of the picture. When it came to strikes, Akumu, like his predecessors, followed more than he led. But he followed in a way that not only put forth grievances in clear memoranda but enhanced the sense of collective power that dockers had.

This was not exactly what the Port Employers Association had had in mind when it professed a desire to foster trade unionism. Captain Williams, who has a rather exaggerated reputation as a progressive capitalist, told the head of an Asian trade union that he "treated the development of responsible trade unionism as a vocation."[98] But when face-to-face with a live trade unionist, his definition of responsibility tended to exclude anything that directly challenged management.

The situation in the port was rather typical of major industries in Kenya after 1955. As Alice Amsden argues, the Mau Mau Emergency, as well as the dock strike of 1955, undermined the confidence of business in its capacity to ignore discontent and repress disorder. The Association of Commercial and Industrial Employers, founded in 1956, slowly convinced its members of the need for a more forward trade-union policy and came to an agreement in 1958 with Mboya and the Kenya Federation of Labour that carefully set boundaries for union-management bargaining. Collective bargaining within a particular industry, as well as with

96. Sandbrook, *Proletarians and African Capitalism,* p. 150.

97. Ibid., p. 64; DLC, notes of meeting with representatives of DWU, 22 December 1958, LAB 10/345; interviews with Alex Nyakoko, David Amimo, Mohamed Shallo, and Hashi Hussein.

98. Williams, letter, May 1958, quoted in Sandbrook, p. 213, n. 16. Williams's admirers include Clayton and Savage, *Government and Labour in Kenya,* p. 392.

individual firms, was deemed acceptable; the jurisdictions of the unions were specified; general workers unions, as with the AWF a decade earlier, were an absolute taboo. With this modus vivendi, trade-union membership in Kenya rose from 17,000 in 1956 to 100,000 in 1963, although, to the employers' chagrin, strikes became more numerous, if usually less devastating than the 1955 dock strike. And as Amsden suggests, this kind of trade unionism proved a mixed blessing: the idea that all legitimate disputes were negotiable, and that all non-negotiable disputes were illegitimate, concealed the sources of conflict as often as it provided solutions to certain problems.[99]

The events of 1958 and 1959 in Mombasa illustrate how painful and uncertain was the process within a given industry of fitting a long-standing pattern of worker-employer conflict into the confines of industrial relations machinery and collective bargaining ideology. Union autonomy quickly became an issue. The new President of the DWU, elected along with Akumu, was fired from a clerical position, allegedly for incompetence. The Union charged victimization. Akumu's broadside reflected an entirely new style of disputation. He issued a leaflet in Swahili: "After getting rid of all your leaders, the employers' aim is to play tricks on you— he will sack you today, and engage someone else tomorrow. . . ." The PEA's response was to praise the old leaders of the DWU and denounce the new, calling Akumu "the new Secretary from Nairobi," and contending that he "does not know anything of Port working" and was acting only "to disturb good relationships by his words."[100] Akumu replied in kind, asking whether it was the employers or the employees who were to choose the union's leaders and offering them a choice of following Williams or him. At a general union meeting on 11 May, Akumu received a vote of confidence.

Having strengthened Akumu while trying to undermine him, the PEA moved toward reconciliation, and the Union issued more conciliatory statements as well. When 2,500 dockworkers struck on 20 June 1958 to protest the dismissal of a clerk by the KL&S Co., Akumu urged them to go back. Akumu went to several meetings to try to get workers to return to work, meanwhile negotiating with Williams about the clerk. It took him four days to succeed. The Mombasa Trades Council passed a resolution supporting the strikers and calling for a general sympathy strike if the dispute was not settled. The Council noted that Mombasa had 6,000 unemployed workers and feared that this might make employers feel too confident. When Akumu brought the dispute to the JIC, the dockworkers

99. Amsden, *International Firms and Labour*, pp. 67–76, 154–56, 165.
100. Sandbrook, p. 151.

went back to work and the Council sent loudspeakers around town saying
that the general strike was off.[101]

During the summer, tension existed in the port over a variety of issues:
the Union complained about abusive supervisors and the management
canceled the Union's right to collect dues within the port area. Akumu
issued a series of leaflets with new wage demands.[102]

On 30 September, the dockworkers went on strike—unofficially
again—not to return until 8 October. The strike started at 4 P.M. and had
spread all over the port by 5:15, shutting down all work.[103] This time,
Akumu refused to ask the workers to return, accusing management of
provoking the walkout and then making the Union the scapegoat for a
strike it had not called. The PEA then withdrew its recognition of the
Union "as it is presently represented." It insisted that it would only resume talking to the DWU if Akumu and Msanifu Kombo, its Vice-Presi-
dent, were out. The Union sought meetings, but the PEA kept insisting
that Akumu and Kombo not be there. Akumu charged in turn that the
employers were seeking to determine the Union's leadership for it. These
exchanges went on until December, when the DWU declared a dispute
with the recognition issue as the first priority, but with wage and working
condition claims too.[104]

The September-October strike had gone on for nine days. The employers and the Government brought in European, Asian, and Arab
volunteers, as well as prisoners from a nearby jail to do heavy labor. By the
end of the strike, 570 prisoners were in the port.[105] On 8 October, workers began to return, but when met with a pamphlet from the PEA inform-
ing them that they would not be paid for their days lost, they straggled
away again, loitering long enough for the police to charge at some bands
of them with batons and tear gas. The next day, half the monthly
shorehandlers, 70 percent of the casual shorehandlers, and four hundred
casual stevedores returned to work, and the strike gradually ended, with
all parties awaiting the next move from the negotiators, who were not
negotiating. The strike had hurt, producing a backlog of ships that lasted
until November, "illustrating the narrow margin of capacity still existing
at the port."[106]

101. EAS, 23, 24, 25 June 1958.

102. Sandbrook, p. 152.

103. EAS, 1 October 1958.

104. Akumu to PEA, 17 October 1958; PEA to Akumu, 20 October 1958; Akumu to PEA,
30 October 1958; PEA to Akumu, 5 November 1958; Akumu to PEA, 11 November 1958;
PEA to Akumu, 17 November 1958; Akumu to PEA, 24 November 1958; Akumu to LC, 9
December 1958; all in LAB 10/345; Sandbrook, pp. 152–53.

105. EAS, 8, 9 October 1958; Mombasa District, AR, 1958.

106. EAS, 8, 9 October 1958; EAR&H, AR, 1958.

From October through December, all negotiating machinery in the port was in shambles. Labour Department officials thought that the hostilities of the past six months in the port made the PEA's attitude to Akumu and Kombo "not unreasonable," but not very productive either. The Deputy Labour Commissioner was sent, following the Union's declaration of a dispute, to try to patch things up.[107] The two sides would only talk to the conciliator in each other's absence.

The Union argued that the issue behind the strike was supervision, and once again Bruce Minnis, Labour Supervisor of PLUB, was on the spot. The Union contended that the strike of 30 September had been caused by a quarrel between Minnis and the workers of No. 8 Shed. Akumu, according to his assistant, did not hear of the strike until the morning of 1 October. Hamis Zanzibar, Acting President, pointed out that the union had "never once called a strike. It was the Employers who provoked the dockers into spontaneous strikes." Other union representatives stressed several dimensions of conflict in the day-to-day work life of the docks: supervisors issued unjustified charge sheets and gave peremptory orders; they had introduced new work rules without consultation.[108]

In the next session, Akumu blamed the strike on Minnis for calling the workers in No. 8 Shed "wanawake," women. Akumu insisted that he had discussed the problem of abusive supervisors many times and raised the question at the JIC. Moreover, Minnis bypassed the Union by addressing workers without a shop steward being present. Akumu claimed not to have known until the next day that the incident had led to a strike, but he considered that, given his warnings of trouble, it was up to the employers to get the men back. He denied allegations of trying to stir up racial animosity in his accusations against Minnis, insisting that he wanted certain African supervisors (of whom there were few) removed as well.[109] The Union, this time, would not even try to play the role of ending spontaneous strikes as it had in the past. The port employers blamed Akumu for stirring up the strike and for refusing, at a JIC meeting on 2 October, to try to stop it. Kombo was accused of abetting Akumu. The PEA used the low attendance at the March meeting that had elected Akumu to try to deny his legitimacy.[110]

As the employers refused to meet with the DWU as long as Akumu was

107. IRO to LC, 12 December 1958, LC to Akumu, 19 December 1958, LAB 10/345.
108. Deputy LC, Notes of meeting with representatives of the DWU, 22 December 1958, LAB 10/345. Other sources claim that the cause of the strike was the victimization of a shop steward by the KL&S Co. (EAS, 1 October 1958) or reaction to a management decision to move a laborer from one shed to another because of insubordination (LD, AR, 1958, p. 16).
109. Deputy LC, Notes of 2d and 3d meetings with DWU, 23 December 1958, LAB 10/345.
110. Ibid., 3d meeting.

there, Akumu eventually agreed to absent himself.[111] That afternoon, a most unproductive meeting took place. Sammy Umari, from the old guard of the DWU, stood guard for the new. The Union refused to accept the PEA's demand that Akumu and Kombo resign. Umari asked that the JIC be reopened, but the PEA refused. The only point on which the two sides agreed was that a deadlock existed.[112]

On that same day, but by prior arrangement, the port was taken off the schedule of the Essential Services Ordinance, in effect legalizing strikes and ending the requirement for compulsory arbitration. The state had realized that the workers had used their ability to provoke disputes to insure that an arbitrator would be appointed who would give them a portion of what they wanted.[113] The new ruling would throw disputes into the arena of collective bargaining. Unfortunately, the long overdue reform came at a time when collective bargaining mechanisms were in total disarray.

The Reorganization of Work Consolidated

The unresolved disputes over supervision, hours, overtime, and other such issues during 1958 led the Government to try another of its favorite remedies again, the investigatory commission. In December 1958, a decision was made to appoint a board of inquiry to look into "Employment in the Port of Mombasa." Gazetted in January 1959, beginning work in March, and reporting in April, the commission was headed by Ian Parkin and included Brian Goord and S. N. Waruhiu as members. It was a departure from previous post-strike tribunals and commissions in that it was to examine not wages, but the organization of work and the conditions and terms of labor—precisely the problems that had led to so many unofficial disputes and resistance to discipline. The Parkin inquiry was told to decide how "to promote good labour relations within the Port area and to obtain maximum efficiency in Port working."[114] The two were at last seen to have something to do with one another.

The JIC, newly reconstituted, was held in abeyance awaiting the outcome of the report, which "gave our task a sense of urgency."[115] The DWU, the Harbour Asian Union, the European staff association, and representatives of the stevedoring, shorehandling, and shipping firms, as well as of the railway, made presentations to the Board. But even as the

111. Deputy LC, notes of meeting with representatives of the PEA, 11 A.M., 23 December 1958, Notes of 3d meeting with DWU, noon, 23 December 1958, LAB 10/345.
112. Notes of a joint meeting with delegations of the PEA and DWU, 3 P.M., 23 December 1958, LAB 10/345.
113. EAR&H, AR, 1958, p. 25.
114. Parkin Report, p. 1.
115. Ibid., p. 2.

Board was waiting to get started, yet another strike had occurred over a work issue in January (see below).

The Board, reviewing the first five years of the casual labor scheme, wholeheartedly endorsed not only the program, but the underlying assumption that African culture required a special approach to building a working class: "The need to encourage stability among labour is particularly important in the case of African workers who sometimes rate leisure more highly than the irksome discipline of regular work." To "discourage the large scale influx of labour into urban areas" and "to ensure a reasonable livelihood to the men to whom certificates were issued" were goals that required no reassessment. But it added a revealing note: "We understand that the casual labourers now in the pool are aware that vacancies in the monthly pool are open to them. There is a reluctance, however, to make the transfer, and much of this we consider to be due to the factors which we have outlined"—mainly the African preference for leisure.[116] Decasualization apparently remained a management initiative, not a choice of the workers.

The Board recommended tinkering a bit with the Casual Labour Scheme, above all shifting to weekly rather than daily labor in order to meet continuing fluctuations in labor requirements—a change that was implemented after negotiations with the DWU. Overall, the Board was so satisfied with progress toward stabilization that it concluded, "the use of the term 'casual' is incongruous. . . ."[117]

The Board termed "anomalies" two ways in which casual workers had entrenched advantages under the rules. Casual workers had greater job security than monthlies, since no casual who did his twenty shifts and was not specifically charged with misconduct could be made redundant; and employers were obligated to pay casuals wages or attendance money every day of the month if the workers chose to appear, while workers could choose to take off one day in three.[118] The Board did no more than note these anomalies. Like PLUB and the individual companies, it was still handling casual workers gingerly.

Time was again a subject of conflicting demands. The PEA wanted to replace the hour-long noon lunch break with staggered thirty-minute breaks; the DWU and the Harbour Asian Union went in the opposite direction, asking for a two-hour lunch break so that workers could eat at home. More clearly than major issues, this demand revealed how all sides

116. Ibid., pp. 10, 12, 13.
117. Ibid., pp. 13–14. Pending the advent of weekly labor, the Board recommended phasing the starting point of each casual laborer's monthly work quota so that the work force would not absent itself so much at the end of each month. It also wanted to combine ship and shore pools for greater managerial flexibility.
118. Ibid., p. 11.

now regarded time as divisible and negotiable. But time was also money, and control of it, the Board decided, was management's prerogative. The "requirements of the Port" outweighed the valid "human claims" to a more spread-out workday. The PEA's proposal for staggered lunch breaks allowing the continuous operation of the port in two shifts from 7 A.M. to 11 P.M. became the new standard for the port.[119]

The Board was somewhat firmer with cargo handlers' insistence that they could keep second-shift workers on after 11 P.M. if they thought they could finish a ship during the night. They deemed this long overtime— up to a fourteen-hour work-night—"obnoxious in the extreme," dangerous to health and safety, and the cause of a 50 percent drop in output during the overtime shift. The Board would not end the third shift, but regulated it: no more than twenty gangs, on three ships, could be used in a given night. The work should be done by fresh gangs, and since only large incentives would bring them out in the middle of the night, the Board recommended paying them double time and suggested that these men be on monthly terms and either alternate with the second shift or be assigned specifically to third-shift work.[120]

Overtime had become an expected and important part of the earnings of monthly dockworkers, a mark of how fully the time discipline of industrial capitalism had been internalized by workers.[121] In 1958, overtime contributed 23 percent to the total earnings of monthly stevedores, 24 percent to those of shorehandlers. Monthly workers' rights to overtime had been enshrined by the Edmonds tribunal; casual workers only received overtime for extended shifts. But the Board thought that the company's control of overtime had to be regulated for their own good. The Board's stand was consistent with thinking in advanced capitalist economies: it had thought a lot about time; it respected management's prerogatives to judge the flow of tasks and to stretch the working day; but it saw a need for state intervention to put outer limits on the working day in the name of objective standards of safety and efficiency.[122]

Parkin and his colleagues, like the authors of the Labour Efficiency Survey twelve years before, looked beyond the workday to the home life of workers. It approved the progress the companies were making in providing amenities at the port but thought that the big obstacle to its explicitly stated objective of building a permanent place for the dock-

119. The new shifts went from 7 A.M. to 3 P.M. and 3 P.M. to 11 P.M., instead of the previous pattern of 7 A.M. to 4 P.M. and 4 P.M. to 11 P.M. (with no break in the second shift). Ibid., pp. 3–7.

120. Ibid., pp. 6–7.

121. A point made by E. P. Thompson, "Time, Work-Discipline and Industrial Capitalism," *Past and Present* 38 (1967): 56–97.

122. Parkin Report, pp. 8–9.

worker near the docks was still housing (see chapter 4). Its suggestion for planned "neighborhood units" near the port was a reminder that the goal of restructuring the workplace was a more attainable one than restructuring the city.[123]

Implicit in the Board's belief that the workplace was amenable to rational planning was an idea that issues such as those it raised could be discussed rationally. Despite the fact that the JIC had been out of commission, it believed that the system of industrial relations was "well founded."[124] Its suggested improvement—yet another committee where employer and employee representatives could discuss hiring, registration, discipline, welfare work, training, and sports—was less significant than its recognition of a serious problem: the need to improve "the general relationship between the two sides."[125]

But the Board was having trouble grappling with the most critical issue behind the tensions of the past four years. It knew that something was wrong: "The Dockworkers' Union considered that many stoppages in the Port had resulted from a lack of human understanding. The importance of good personal management cannot be unduly stressed. On it depends, among other things, the attainment of efficiency and good relations between workers and employers."[126] But it was precisely this kind of problem that was so intractable within the notions of objectified industrial relations. The creation of new bodies to facilitate communications was a very limited answer. That the transformation of supervision and the new controls on time were above all an exercise of power—the redefinition of what choices people could make—was a point that the Board submerged beneath its tacit acceptance of a certain structure of work as socially rational.

All it could do, in these limits, was to suggest that the quality of supervisors be raised and that they should speak Swahili. The KL&S Co., it noted, already had a training "within industry" scheme, which the Board applauded. The Board realized that a wide gap had arisen between supervisors, who were generally white or Asian and whose authority came down from capital, and the serangs, who generally rose from the ranks of African dockworkers and whose previous basis of authority in their close relation to the men was being eroded. It proposed that the gap be nar-

123. Ibid., pp. 16–19.

124. The Board suggested that the racially defined joint committees be replaced by such categories as "supervisory," "clerical," and "non-clerical." But in the absence of equivalent nonracial unions, the Harbour Asian Union and the Dockworkers Union (with its exclusively African membership) would nominate people to these committees; the name changes were not likely to mean much in the near future.

125. Parkin Report, pp. 14, 15.

126. Ibid., p. 19.

rowed by introducing a classification of junior foreman between the two, and that the junior foremen be trained at the Labour Department's school.

Most seriously, supervisory grades generally demanded a school certificate, which had not previously been the case. This created high barriers to advancement even within clerical positions, let alone for manual laborers. The Board had no ready remedy except to wait until raised entrance requirements for clerks meant that the insufficiently educated would not even get to ground level. This was a problem being faced throughout the civil service, as Africanization policies often ended up replicating in the name of standards the same hierarchies that had previously been erected in the name of race. The Railway, with its more complex job hierarchy, was facing the problem more directly than were the docks, where manual labor predominated. For the moment, the contradiction between the aim of having good supervision and that of providing a ladder of increasingly responsible posts to which workers could aspire was passed over in the hope that education would one day make it go away.[127]

An almost offhand comment reveals the extent to which work issues had been redefined in the past decade and the ambivalence of the Union before conflicting conceptions of work: "the picturesque titles of *serang* and *tindal,* which came originally from Arabia, have been used in Mombasa for hundreds of years. . . . We are not satisfied that there is much substance in the submission of the union that the titles of *serang* and *tindal* are outmoded, and we offer no further comment."[128] The Union, having erected a system of shop stewards the previous year, was no more interested than management in preserving the authority of serangs and tindals, who were often the older, more conservative dockers. The Union had defended the rights of serangs and tindals to job security and extra pay as senior specialists, but it was not interested in them *as serangs* or *as tindals.* The past authority that these titles invoked did not fit in with the trade unionists world where shop stewards faced foremen. The Board apparently thought that the erosion of the authority of serangs and tindals had gone so far—maybe even too far beneath that of foremen—that they might as well keep their picturesque titles.

Such were the limits of the language in which change could be discussed. Issues like working hours and overtime could be the subject of specific demands by the DWU and the PEA, and a more or less independent Board could make rational and balanced decisions about them. The

127. Ibid., p. 20. For a discussion of the disputes over the shift to nonracial scales on the Railway and the development of new hierarchies through regrading posts, see R. D. Grillo, *Race, Class and Militancy: An African Trade Union, 1939–1965* (New York: Chandler, 1974).
128. Parkin Report, pp. 20–21.

changing meaning of power, however, could be broached only indirectly. The gangs had once been collectivities, recruited by serangs, presented to the companies as a group, supervised by the serangs themselves, and often paid as a group in accordance with their collective accomplishments. The gangs were now constituted each day by company employees, after direct recruitment through monthly hiring or a bureaucratized daily hiring operation; the serangs and tindals supervised the lowest level of work-group but had nothing to do with hiring men, constituting gangs, or paying wages. The centralization of authority and the racial divisions that so starkly separated different categories of dockers had, since 1955, been the cause of much abusive behavior, anger, incrimination, and several strikes. The Board hoped that training and sensitivity would make things better. There was not much more it could say.

The Board reported in April. During the next months, its recommendations became a key object of discussion in the recently revived JIC and formed the basis of important reforms in working hours and rules about shifts and overtime. The Parkin Report ratified the transformations of the 1950s and laid out the blueprint for the 1960s. The basic elements of its approach to hiring and supervising dockworkers remained largely intact even when the separate stevedoring and shorehandling companies were absorbed after independence into a single parastatal corporation.

The Union's Position Consolidated

The Union, no more than the Parkin Board, did not see the manifest tensions in the port as any reason to worry about the demise of gang-based supervision or decasualization. Its own vision of a stable, dues-paying membership and established ways of negotiating with or confronting management fit in with the basic directions of reform of the postwar years, even if the DWU played its part with vigor and a sense of its own autonomy. In 1959, the Union managed to stabilize its institutional position more effectively.

The recognition issue was pending even as the Parkin Board began its investigations. Captain Williams realized that the PEA had misplayed its hand. On 6 January 1959 he told a Labour Department official that the opposition to Akumu could not be maintained, since Union members had stuck by him and the PEA had prejudiced its case by interfering in the leadership choices of a union. His fellow port employers, however, remained adamant on Akumu. The Labour Department took advantage of this break in the ranks to send an Industrial Relations Officer to Mombasa to persuade the Union to withdraw its notice of dispute in order to improve the atmosphere. By mid-month, DWU and PEA representatives were haggling over the wording of a new recognition agreement, leaving the Akumu question in the background.[129] The Union agreed to discuss rerecognition with Akumu and Kombo absent, provided that after the agreement the union would hold elections and the PEA would accept whoever won. This proved to be the break needed to end a long dispute, and agreement was reached on recognition on 3 February.

Later that month, the Union held its annual election meeting. This time, 4,000 workers attended, compared to 510 the previous April. Akumu and his slate were returned unopposed. In June, a reorganized JIC began to function again. Coming after months of direct management attacks on Akumu—and a period when he had not acted very decisively in several strikes—the victory showed how much the PEA's attempt to choose the Union's leaders for it had done to assist the very leaders it opposed. For all its success in tightening its control over the labor process, the employers had been caught in the contradiction of needing a union that was simultaneously effective in controlling its men and tame in its relations with management.[130]

After the reestablishment of union–management contact, employers and employees met in a hierarchy of committees—with the JIC on top—to facilitate discussion of grievances and to negotiate contracts; the hierarchy was divided into segments for manual (subdivided between casual and monthly), clerical, and supervisory personnel. This was paralleled by a disciplinary hierarchy, beginning with the filing of a complaint sheet that a foreman had to fill out if he was dissatisfied with work performance, and ending in an appeal to the company manager in the case of monthly workers and to a series of officials of PLUB and an appeals tribunal for casuals. The day of the organization chart had come to labor relations in Mombasa.[131]

But even while these mechanisms were not yet in operation, another wildcat strike over a work issue had taken place, and the then unrecognized union had played about the same role that the recognized union had in such affairs the year before. On 19 January 1959, 839 monthly workers for the KL&S Co.—about two-thirds of the total—staged a sit-down strike in the sheds. They refused to accept the cards that were being issued preliminary to the introduction of a clocking-in system. Workers did not want to punch a clock—a part of work discipline so ingrained in

129. IRO to Dep. LC, 7 January, LC to Akumu, 8 January, Akumu to LC, 12 January 1959, IRO, Memorandum of joint meeting with PEA and DWU, 16 January 1959, LAB 10/345.

130. IRO to LC, 21 January, 5 February 1959; Sandbrook, *Proletarians and African Capitalism*, p. 153.

131. Chart of Industrial Machinery of the Landing and Shipping Co. of East Africa, Ltd., Mombasa Branch, c. 1960, EST 31 II.

the industrial societies that it has ceased to be an issue, but one that epitomized the regimentation newly brought to the docks of Mombasa. Clocking-in was due to start on 20 January, and the Union had already objected to its unilateral imposition. On the morning of 19 January, 420 men had accepted cards and gone to work, as had the casuals. The other monthlies had not, and in the afternoon shift, all monthly workers refused their new cards.

Denis Akumu had been out of town. The Assistant General Secretary was told by the Deputy Labour Commissioner to get the men back to work, and he reluctantly told them to do so, to no avail. The next day, Williams agreed to suspend the clocking-in system, although the new cards would be issued. Akumu returned from upcountry and persuaded the men to return to work after the noon break.[132]

The issue of clocking-in, significantly, was not dealt with by the Parkin Board. It was not Akumu's issue, so he would be unlikely to raise it, and the companies regarded it as no one's concern except their own—a point they made explicitly when another strike over the issue occurred in September.[133]

Management tried again in September. The morning shift monthly workers were told to punch in, and about half of them obeyed before a new sit-down strike began. According to the KL&S Co., 1,642 of its monthly employees struck, although other of its employees, including a few casuals, kept working. One port official commented: "If you as much as mention clocking-in everyone practically faints. It has been thought of before but never implemented."[134] Akumu, again, had been in Nairobi. Back in Mombasa, he told the workers to return to work and assured them that the issue would be taken up by the JIC. The company, he claimed, had chosen the "wrong time" to push the matter, for the port was tense over "other matters."[135] Perhaps it was Akumu who was concerned with the other matters, for he never seized an issue that had led to two sudden and angry strikes. Management stuck to its position and to its clocks.[136]

The militancy of the union leadership was geared above all to the wages/hours/benefits issue—always an important, but not an exclusive, concern of the rank and file. Sandbrook calls this pattern "militant economism." Needing to maintain a dues-paying membership with no long tradition of trade unionism, often lacking the check-off (until 1960 in the

132. Deputy LC, Note on stoppage of work, 20 January 1959, LAB 10/345; EAS, 20, 21 January 1959.

133. IRO to LC, 15 September 1959, LAB 9/63.

134. EAS, 16 September 1959.

135. EAS, 16, 17 September 1959.

136. Mombasa District, AR, 1959.

case of the DWU) and thus having to collect dues each year, union leaders concentrated on the immediate and continual delivery of better wages.[137]

In the case of the DWU, Akumu—not himself a dockworker—fought vigorously for the integrity of the union, and he focused on issues that made the most sense from his perspective. On questions such as the style of management or clocking-in, he responded to ongoing disputes but neither initiated nor controlled the action. And when it came to the overall framework in which on-the-job disputes arose—the transition from a gang-based structure to centralized management—Akumu had neither the personal experience to make him sensitive to tensions in the workplace nor an organizational interest distinct from that of management. He had little reason to value the leadership of serangs over the shop stewards he had been instrumental in introducing into his union or to stand in the way of the long-term trend toward stabilizing employment and regularizing work rhythms, a pattern which also tended to stabilize the organizational base of the union.[138] All this said, it remains important to observe that the leadership of the DWU did defend workers who engaged in wildcat strikes and did negotiate on a number of positions raised by the workers' actions. This testifies to the substantial give-and-take within the dockworking community and to a situation in which assertive workers could at least push the DWU leadership a step or two beyond structurally logical positions.

Although the Union failed to join effectively the clocking-in dispute, it did negotiate in the JIC on a number of issues raised by the Parkin Report. Its role in moving from daily to weekly temporary labor was important, but it basically accepted the framework established by Parkin. Union officials agreed to new hours and new overtime rates. They agreed as well that the Union would support disciplinary action against any worker who refused to put in up to three hours overtime if so asked.[139]

The one issue over which Akumu issued an official fourteen-day notice of intent to strike was wages. In fact, the notice did not apply to the other questions springing from the Parkin Report that the union was discussing in the JIC at the same time. The ultimatum was issued on 3 July 1959, but the issue was settled within the JIC with little help from the Labour Department. The Union won pay hikes of Shs 12 per month for certain categories of workers—in exchange for a one-year wage freeze. Other disputed questions were dropped, and Akumu issued a statement prais-

137. Sandbrook, pp. 144–80. On the checkoff, see L&S Co., AR, 1960, p. 8.

138. According to Minnis (interview), conflict between the serangs and the union had been noticeable. From the point of view of the serangs, the "union with its shop stewards was taking power from them. They considered themselves the arbitrators of labor, and not shop stewards or union."

139. MT, 21 November 1959; EAS 24 November 1959.

FIGURE 5:1

AVERAGE CASH WAGES PAID TO ADULT AFRICANS IN KENYA, 1954–1960

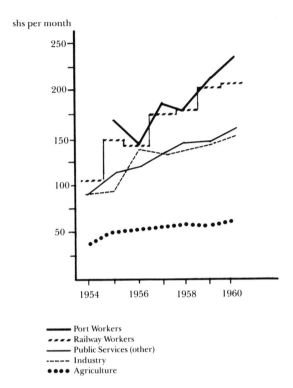

— Port Workers
- - - Railway Workers
— Public Services (other)
----- Industry
•••• Agriculture

SOURCE: EAR&H, AR, 1960, p. 32

ing Captain Williams and the Labour Department. Williams in turn praised the "orderly" nature of the negotiations.[140] The procedures, boundaries, and spirit of labor–management bargaining had been reestablished.

By then, the dockworkers had pushed their wages clearly ahead of railway workers and well ahead of industrial workers and laborers in the public services, as figure 5.1 shows. Their wages were vastly higher than those in the agricultural sector, and the gap was widening.

In the next round of contract talks, the workers got another modest raise, bringing the minimum wage for monthly workers to Shs 178. Perhaps more important, the provident fund system—under which retiring workers received a lump sum accumulated through employer and employee contributions over the years—was revamped and improved. Under the old system, a fifteen-year veteran received £50–75; under the new

140. MT, 3, 14, 15 July 1959; EAS, 15 July 1959; EAR&H, AR, 1959.

provident fund, he would get £162–200. Williams was again full of praise for the "rational" negotiations and the absence of a work stoppage.[141]

So it continued. When the General Manager referred to the dock-workers as "the highest paid group of industrial workers in Kenya and Uganda," Akumu accused him of being "provocative." Negotiations were on again.[142] By 1963, the year of Kenya's independence, dockworkers had pushed their minimum pay to Shs 254/13, and the average gross monthly earnings of ship and shore workers were around Shs 350, plus fringe benefits worth Shs 67 more. This was about three times the mini-mum wage for adult males in Mombasa. The Port Manager, meanwhile, complained that the productivity index—tons of dry cargo moved per hour—had dropped to 5.16, its lowest ever.[143] The wages were new, the managerial techniques were new. The results were still in question.

The increasing wages, the growing power of the Union, and the new dichotomy between having and not having a job, as well as the develop-ment of party politics in Mombasa in the late 1950s, politicized the job question in a way it had not been before. For aspiring politicians, the DWU was becoming by 1958 an important base; for workers, politics was becoming part of the quest for jobs. Denis Akumu, Msanifu Kombo, and Sammy Umari were among the DWU leaders who ran for office in Mom-basa; Kombo eventually became mayor.[144]

The questions of jobs and power were part of what was becoming the most divisive issue in Mombasa's politics: the growing tension between its residents who came from the coastal region and those who came from upcountry. The most powerful political party in the colony, the Kenya African National Union (KANU), was widely perceived on the coast as supporting upcountry interests. Its rivals—themselves divided—made this their main issue, and a movement for regional autonomy contributed to political tensions in the years before independence.

On the labor front, regional tensions were not exactly new, but the postwar transformation of work changed the nature of job competition. There had been a rough modus vivendi on the docks: casual workers were largely coastal in origin and protected themselves through their serangs and the Swahili milieu in which the gang system operated; monthly work-ers tended to come from upcountry. But such a division of labor was eliminated by decasualization and the rising stakes of acquiring perma-nent jobs. Competition for jobs was no longer mediated by the particular institutions of Mombasa: coastal and upcountry workers faced more cen-

141. MT, 5 August 1960.

142. MT, 14 February 1961.

143. MT, 5 April 1963; LD, AR, 1963, pp. 4–5; PM, AR, 1963, p. 3.

144. Richard Stren, *Housing the Urban Poor in Africa: Policy, Politics, and Bureaucracy in Mombasa* (Berkeley, Calif.: Institute of International Studies, 1978), p. 79. Richard Luyt had predicted in 1949 that trade-union leadership would play such a role in politics (see above, pp. 133–34). For background, see A. I. Salim, *The Swahili-Speaking Peoples of Kenya's Coast, 1895–1965* (Nairobi: East African Publishing House, 1973).

tralized systems of hiring as individuals, and without feeling that they knew the rules of the game. The change in work structure exposed ethnic cleavages, rendering city officers, labor leaders, and anyone perceived to be in a position to influence hiring or access to other resources liable to charges of ethnic favoritism. The rapid expansion of jobs requiring educational qualifications, which placed coastal people at a disadvantage, exacerbated anxiety throughout the city. The issue was raised in Municipal and other elections in the late 1950s. Denis Akumu, trying to use his Union base and his KANU connections to enter Mombasa politics, foundered on the accusation that he was pushing his fellow Luo into jobs on the docks and elsewhere at the expense of coastal people. Some coastal politicans went so far as to arrange for scab labor when a largely upcountry work force struck the Municipality in 1961.[145]

The issue spilled over into the internal politics of the DWU. Akumu was repeatedly accused of favoring upcountry over coastal workers on the docks and in the union; Sammy Umari, once in the old guard of DWU leadership and later a leader of the Coast African Peoples Union, began a campaign against him in 1961. An unsuccessful attempt was made to start a rival union with a coastal base. In fact, Akumu went to some lengths to diversify his base within the Union, and held onto his office until 1965, when the ethnic issue and his falling out with Mboya led to his defeat by a Taita (from the inland port of Coast Province), who was in turn quickly replaced by a Mijikenda, Juma Boy. The divisions within the Union were the other side of its strength: for ordinary workers and for politicans in Mombasa, it was an institution worth battling to control.[146]

The rise of ethnic competition within the city and within the Dockworkers Union was in part a consequence of the efforts of the state and capital to "modernize" the organization of work. With the destruction of the complex social structures that had intervened between workers and jobs in Mombasa, individuals sought to enlist the new institutions of union and political party to find patronage and support. They feared that others were doing likewise, and the tensions increasingly fostered clientalistic and factional politics within these institutions. The broad web of ethnicity began to replace the specific webs of affiliation that had once meant so much in the struggle for employment in Mombasa.

With independence, the DWU, like unions throughout Africa, became subject to governmental pressures to contain the autonomy of labor organizations and to slow the pace of wage increases in the name of national development. The Railway's General Manager—not a Kenyan—assimilated the new language of industrial relations very quickly, writing in 1963: "The dockworkers are no longer to be a separate body of men looking largely for their own good in a struggle against private employers.

145. Stren, pp. 79–87.
146. Sandbrook, *Proletarians and African Capitalism*, pp. 116–17, 135–36; Stren, pp. 85–86.

They are to be key workers—respected and paid as such—in the wider national struggle to build up the wealth of the territories."[147] This argument, even when made by leaders with more plausible nationalist credentials, was not always taken to heart; but that is another subject. The dockworkers had already given themselves a strong position—in terms of their current base pay and their organizational strength and spirit—from which to defend and extend the gains of the late colonial era. Their union, like others, would have its internal dissensions and its external pressures, but there was no going back to the days when dockers were part of an urban mass living on the edge of poverty.[148]

A small incident offers an important insight into the atmosphere that had developed in Mombasa by 1959. Railway management had decided that it should reduce the soap ration for its employees—one of several in-kind payments railwaymen still received—but the Port Manager was afraid that such a momentous action would cause trouble in Mombasa. He warned that this might lead to a "deterioration in staff relations and will prejudice our claim to being a good employer." The Industrial Relations Officer replied, "I know that the situation at Mombasa is very touchy, but heavens, it's been touchy for years and I doubt giving up is likely to improve the situation."[149]

The relations among workers, bosses, and state officials in Mombasa had become touchy in an era when unions and industrial relations machinery did not exist. In a transformed work situation, something of the spirit of those times remained in the feistiness of workers, in the pressures that workers put on their own leaders, and in the sensitivity of managers to the volatility of workers in the port. The spirit of the port workers had once engulfed an entire city. Now, it contributed to an atmosphere in which workers in the port negotiated, above all, about wages, hours, and fringe benefits. Dockers, along with much of Mombasa's working class, had at one time stood in the Kiwanja cha Maskini to hear Chege Kibachia speak of their common struggle; hardly more than a decade later, Denis Akumu and other union leaders carried forward the struggle by writing memoranda about overtime and the duration of paid leave. Workers' anger over arbitrary discipline could still quickly lead to walkouts, but such actions no longer embraced the city's working class as a whole. By the time of independence, dockers were the best-paid African manual workers in Kenya. Meanwhile, capital and the state had succeeded in transforming the meanings of time and supervision on the docks, and they had done much to shape the organizations through which Africans would fight for a better life, and even the objectives they would pursue.

147. G. M. MacKay, article in *Spear* 6, no. 1 (February 1963): 18.
148. On the union in independent Kenya, see Sandbrook.
149. PM to GM, 18 February 1959, IRO to CEO, 23 February 1959, EST 1/22/1/5.

6 Work, Disorder, and the Crisis of Colonialism in Africa

This book has been about a turning point in African labor history, a period when old structures crumbled and colonial states, capitalists, and workers groped and pushed toward new ways of thinking about work and new forms of action. The casual labor system of Mombasa carried to an extreme the contradictions of work organization in most of Africa before the 1940s: anonymous laborers, paid barely enough to keep a single man alive, circulated into and out of jobs. They were largely immune to the incentives and discipline that, in industrial Europe, had gone some way toward creating orderly, diligent, and responsible—if still militant— working classes. Colonial officials, managers, and the guardians of civic order had long seen port work and urban life through Victorian lenses: casual work led to a casual life; it created a dangerous class. The myth had concealed an even more frightening reality: the colonial state had not fully penetrated the workplace or the living space of African workers, who could communicate and act decisively and with unity through mechanisms that the state could not understand, let alone control. The casual workers, through their daily decisions about whether or not to work and through the social bonds that existed among the work gangs, asserted power over the rhythm of their working lives, and—through the strikes of 1934, 1939, and 1947—they demonstrated that they could use that power collectively as well as individually.

The postwar discussion of the labor question in Mombasa was carried on with words like *stabilization, productivity, welfare,* and *industrial relations,* but beneath it was a reassertion of the power of capital and state. The port firms, after some hesitation, seized control over workers' time: they had to work steadily or not at all. And they asserted their authority within the workplace, replacing the self-discipline of piecework gangs and the subtle give-and-take of worker-leader relationships with the top-down authority of foremen and supervisors who were starkly separated by education, culture, and race from the dockers. The state—through the influence of the Labour Department, the economic muscle of the Railway, and the use of commissions and boards—had done much to line up stevedoring and shorehandling firms behind a new approach to labor. It asserted its power directly in trying to plan a city consistent with its vision of a stable and differentiated working class, living as families in their small rooms, learn-

ing the value of modern nutrition, modern education, and modern sanitation, and protected from the atavism of their own rural past, from the
contagion of the idle and the criminal, and from the worst side effects of
industrial development.

But though capital and the state could alter the meanings of time,
authority, and space, they did not fully dominate the workplace, and even
less the city. Workers figured out how to evade some of the new rules, and
challenged others by wildcat strikes. The dockworkers had reasserted
their tradition of militancy on a larger scale in 1955, and later the union
that the Kenya Labour Department hoped would channel such cata-
clysmic city-wide strikes into a more predictable form of industrial dispute proved itself to be more autonomous and militant than expected.
The price of capital's assertion of power within the workplace was its
implicit admission that power over the pay packet would have to be
shared, not just with a state anxious to impose objectified standards and
new notions of social engineering on African life, but with African workers building new institutions out of old traditions. The state, at the same
time, had to accept that its own attempt to shape institutions capable of
participating in acceptable ways in industrial and political processes also
gave power to those institutions and to the people, like Tom Mboya, who
could use them effectively, and that this power would also be used in ways
that it could not entirely define.

The experience of disorder was a blow to a conception of African
society that saw urban workers as so many interchangeable units of labor
power and rural society as the repository of the true Africa, naturally
tranquil and immutable. Whatever the currents in imperial thinking that
were already running against this tendency, the actions of African workers showed that such an approach simply did not work. Workers had
come to the city; they lived there; and they raised their voices there. By
1945, with the Report of the Committee to Investigate Labour Unrest at
Mombasa, the labor problem was explicitly defined as a problem of class.
The urban working class had come into being before its place in the city
had been blessed by the colonial state. The choice was between forcefully
pushing it out while ruthlessly containing it during its necessary sojourns
in the workplace, or else moving toward a new structure of labor that
would tame and incorporate that class into a pattern of stable jobs, stable
family life, stable housing, a stable community life, and eventually a stable
political system.

The transition meant something quite different to workers. What officials called casualism was, for workers, part of a complex web of social
relations and culture connecting workplace, urban residence, and farms.
From their standpoint, the transformations of the 1950s made them more
isolated and anonymous rather than less, above all in the workplace itself.

The hiring process was bureaucratized; supervision became more authoritarian; the gangs lost the basis of their group identity; and the fact that housing did not badly fragment the old neighborhoods reflected, not the intent of postwar housing policy, but the shortcomings of its implementation. The community and the institutions that the state hoped to create were at first only abstractions to the workers. Gradually, they became concrete, and the workers' traditions of unity and militance—as much as the divisions among them—helped to give them shape.

The creation of a stark contrast between a job and no job, the changed meaning of work over the course of a lifetime, the undermining of the solidarity of work gangs, and the development of the solidarity of the union implied a great change in the world of the dockers by the end of the 1950s. It did not imply—whatever the intentions of the state—that the web of connection between city and countryside, between different kinds of workers in the city, between workers and their compatriots who could not find work or engaged in other sorts of economic activities was altogether shattered. What this new world was like requires a detailed sociological study that I have not attempted here. It must be studied not merely where dockers worked, but where they lived, where they talked, where they engaged in politics, where they grew up, where they retired to, and where they participated in old, new, or changed relationships.[1]

The transformations of the postwar era have a global dimension as well. Following up their implications would not only take us into different regions of Kenya—from Majengo to coastal districts to Nyanza—it would also take us to London and Paris, to Accra and Dakar, to Jamaica and Indochina. The new ideas and the new policies that the colonial state put into practice in one African port city reflected empire-wide processes; and the complexities and contradictions that the state encountered in that city and in others like it in turn influenced the unfolding of the history of the colonial empires in the final decades of their existence. By focusing specifically on the transformations and confrontations in a single city during this critical conjuncture, the coming together of complex pro-

1. It would be difficult, in any case, for a historian to develop such a portrayal of a work force as it existed around 1960, barring the good fortune of falling across someone else's survey. But contemporary studies using surveys and interviews are a natural complement to historical methods. See, for example, the way in which R. D. Grillo studied the lives of railway workers in Kampala. He argues that, given the relatively high pay of railwaymen and the dearth of other jobs, "leaving the EARH would be a disastrous step." Hence the mean length of service in his sample was nearly thirteen years, with unskilled workers slightly above average. Grillo shows that such a workforce nevertheless developed a variety of strategies to maintain rural ties and access to land. *African Railwaymen: Solidarity and Opposition in an East African Labour Force* (Cambridge: Cambridge University Press, 1973), esp. pp. 38, 40, 62.

cesses becomes apparent. But seeing this should encourage scholars to look outward again and think anew about the history of labor and the history of empire in a global perspective.

What happened in Mombasa can be reexamined in three contexts. First was the social crisis in African cities and in the colonial world generally—the frequent, intense, and critically important strikes in towns and mines across the continent between roughly 1935 and the early 1950s which forced a reexamination of the labor question. Second was the crisis in empire itself. The labor problem was part of a wider dynamic: new imperatives to solve long-standing structural failures in colonial economies; a search for political formulas to allow the imperial connection to endure in a new form; and, perhaps most important of all, a crisis of ideology among the imperial powers. The most basic conceptions of African society and of how Europe could change it proved inadequate to understand the present and provided little help for the future. The ferment led principal officials to work toward establishing a new ideological framework for the postwar period, a framework that collapsed barely after it was wrought. Third was the temporal context, especially the relation of the urban crisis of the 1940s to that of the 1960s and 1970s. The origins of the new crisis lay largely in the efforts of capital and the state to resolve the old, in the partial success and partial failure of their attempts to recast the workplace and the city. What follows is a preliminary and impressionistic view of these contexts (with emphasis on British Africa), which I, and many others, hope to study in the future.[2] Even an overview lends a different perspective to a study of a city such as this, for one should keep in mind the relationship of change in the smallest of microcosms to transformations on the largest scale. The local may be more than a case study of global processes or an indication of their universal power; the local and the peripheral may in some ways shape the global.

STRIKES AND THE LABOR QUESTION

The strike wave of the post-Depression, wartime, and early postwar era needs further study, quantitative and otherwise, but a rapidly growing and exciting series of studies by African labor historians is already shedding considerable light on it. The strikes stand out not just for their frequency, but for their nature, and in both senses they represent a vivid contrast to the stultifying lack of urban labor protest during the height of

---

2. A preliminary version of a comparison between the labor question in British and French Africa will appear in Frederick Cooper, "La Question du travail et les luttes sociales en Afrique britannique et française, 1935–1955," in Michel Agier, Jean Copans, and Alain Morice, eds., *Les Classes ouvrières d'Afrique Noire* (Paris: Karthala, forthcoming).

the Depression before 1935.[3] As in Mombasa in 1939 and 1947, the strikes in Dakar in 1946, Dar es Salaam in 1947, Zanzibar in 1948, and Nairobi in 1950 were general strikes, convulsing entire cities. The Nigerian general strike of 1945 spread along the railway from Lagos to major towns throughout the colony, lasted over a month, and was resolved only by the appointment of a commission to raise wages throughout the government service. It involved mass processions as well as picketing, the cooperation of market women, and solidarity among government workers across departments, positions, and towns.[4] There were also strike waves that rolled through cities, bringing out dockers or municipal workers or industrial workers in different plants one after another; this happened, for example, in Dakar in 1936 and Mombasa in 1942.[5] In the Rhodesias, there had been occasional mine strikes over many years, but the Northern Rhodesia strikes of 1935 and 1940 acquired another dimension: they spread from mine to mine and reflected widespread reactions to prices, taxes, and other elements of urban life—the costs of being a worker—as much as they entailed specific disputes between workers and employers.[6] In the Gold Coast, authorities reported "a series of strikes" in 1941–42 and a "wave of strikes" in 1947–48; mine and railway workers, both well-organized, took the lead in a colony-wide trend.[7] The great

3. Quantitative study of strike rates across Africa as a whole is obviously useful, but perhaps impossible. As Peter Kilby notes in regard to Nigeria, strike statistics before the late 1940s are bad, and even worse are the employment statistics needed as a reference point for the number of strikers or man-hours lost. "A Reply to John Weeks's Comment," *Journal of Developing Areas* 1 (1967): 20–21. For whatever they are worth, however, Robin Cohen's figures on man-days lost in Nigeria since 1940 show the overwhelming importance of general strikes (as in 1945) and nation-wide strike movements as compared to industry-specific disputes. *Labour and Politics in Nigeria, 1945–1971* (London: Heinemann, 1974), p. 195.

4. John Iliffe, "The Creation of Group Consciousness: A History of the Dockworkers of Dar es Salaam," in Robin Cohen and Richard Sandbrook, *Development of an African Working Class* (London: Longman, 1975), pp. 49–72; Anthony Clayton, "The General Strike in Zanzibar, 1948," *Journal of African History* 17 (1976): 417–34; Cohen, *Labour and Politics in Nigeria;* Wale Oyemakinde, "The Nigerian General Strike of 1945," *Journal of the Historical Society of Nigeria* 7 (1975): 693–710.

5. Nicole Bernard-Duquenet, "Les Débuts du syndicalisme au Sénégal au temps du Front Populaire," *Le Mouvement Social* 101 (1977): 37–59.

6. Ian Henderson, "Early African Leadership: The Copperbelt Disturbances of 1935 and 1940," *Journal of Southern African Studies* 2 (1973): 83–97; Charles Perrings, *Black Mineworkers in Central Africa* (New York: Africana, 1979); Jane Parpart, *Labor and Capital on the African Copperbelt* (Philadelphia: Temple University Press, 1983).

7. Not long before the first strike wave the Gold Coast Labour Department had predicted that "upheaval in labour is unlikely." AR, 1938–39, 1941–42, 1947–48; Jeff Crisp, *The Story of an African Working Class: Ghanaian Miners' Struggles, 1870–1980* (London: Zed, 1984); Richard Jeffries, *Class, Power, and Ideology: The Railwaymen of Sekondi* (Cambridge: Cambridge University Press, 1978).

railway strike in French West Africa extended across the entire region between October 1947 and March 1948, paralyzed the economy, and left the French on edge for years.[8] South Africa faced a similar burst of strikes in cities during the war years, extending from the rapidly growing manufacturing sector to the docks in Durban and culminating in the mine strike of 1946 that brought out over 70,000 black workers.[9]

Other kinds of disturbances fit the pattern of these years: the invasions of squatters who seized urban land to build their own shacks and houses in Johannesburg and Durban in the 1940s, the shop boycott and ex-servicemen's march, leading up to riots and looting in the Gold Coast in 1948, the sans-travail riots in the Camerouns in 1945.[10] The crises were not just industrial actions but crises of the city.

These upheavals revealed how narrow and vulnerable the colonial economy in fact was. In the Depression, colonial states had sloughed their social problems off into the countryside. But the problems of production were tougher than the problems of nonproduction. With recovery in the mid-1930s, and even more clearly with the imperial drive throughout British Africa to produce more commodities for the war effort and to earn foreign exchange, and then with the equally acute imperatives to expand dollar-earning colonial exports and take full advantage of favorable world markets in the postwar years, the strain on feeble infrastructures, inadequate housing stocks, and almost nonexistent facilities for urban social services was severe, while capital resources to improve them were insufficient.[11] The pressure on social resources—forms of labor

8. The best treatment of the strike is in fictional form: Sembene Ousmanne, *God's Bits of Wood*, trans. Francis Price (London: Heinemann, 1981).

9. Dan O'Meara, "The 1946 African Mine Workers' Strike and the Political Economy of South Africa," *Journal of Commonwealth and Comparative Politics* 13 (1975): 146–73; David Hemson, "Dock Workers, Labour Circulation, and Class Struggles in Durban, 1940–59," *Journal of Southern African Studies* 20 (1977): 88–124.

10. A. W. Stadler, "Birds in the Cornfield: Squatter Movements in Johannesburg, 1944–1947," *Journal of Southern African Studies* 6 (1979): 93–123; Paul Maylam, "The 'Blackbelt': African Squatters in Durban 1935–1950," *Canadian Journal of African Studies* 17 (1983): 413–27; Joseph Engwenyu, "Labour and Politics in Ghana: The Militant Phase 1947–1950," paper presented to the meeting of the Canadian Association for African Studies, 1982; Richard Joseph, "Settlers, Strikers and Sans-Travail: The Douala Riots of 1945," *Journal of African History* 15 (1974): 669–81.

11. Along with the restructuring of labor systems, the efforts to recapitalize African economies in both French and British empires represent one of the major new departures after the 1930s. This process needs careful attention, but for now see J. M. Lee and Martin Petter, *The Colonial Office, War, and Development Policy: Organisation and the Planning of a Metropolitan Initiative, 1939–1945*, Commonwealth Papers No. 22 (London: Maurice Temple Smith, 1982), and—for a stimulating interpretation of a broader question—Jacques Marseille, *Empire coloniale et capitalisme française: histoire d'un divorce* (Paris: Albin Michel, 1984).

management, marketing mechanisms, agricultural systems—quickly proved to be so great that the colonial powers soon concluded that all had to be thoroughly reconstructed.

The shortcomings of prior development had a double implication: the inability of economic systems to respond in an effective and balanced manner to rapid expansion, and the extreme vulnerability of the economies to the actions of relatively small groups of workers. The former condition helps to explain the grievances of workers and the burst of agitation in this period; the latter, why these actions so badly shook the British Empire. For the same reason, French West Africa, where the isolation of the Vichy period led to drastic declines in export production, experienced little such disorder until, after the war, economic growth, a development drive, and labor unrest all began apace.[12]

With colonial economies relying on workers circulating into and out of jobs, to increase the output of wage labor meant piling on more workers. The growth of Kenya's workforce from 150,000 to 250,000 between 1935 and 1945 was echoed, for example, by a growth from 183,000 to 300,000 in Nigeria during the war years.[13] The additional workers strained already inadequate urban resources, especially housing. The shortages of imported commodities in the war and early postwar years not only added directly to this Africa-wide inflation but removed the one incentive that food producers had to grow more crops to feed the workers, even while the alternative of cash-crop production was becoming more attractive. Still fragmentary studies of real wages in various parts of Africa suggest that economic expansion made life worse, not better, for wage laborers.[14] Wage increases often came in bursts, following agitation, and only after the pace of inflation cooled in the 1950s did those groups that had gained in this uneven process consolidate their advantages.

Given a labor system that bunched African workers closely together at the bottom of the scale, workers had little stake in obedience, not to mention in regularity, sobriety, effort, and learning. The casual workers of Mombasa, blamed by officials for cluttering up the city and exacerbating pressures on scarce urban resources, epitomized a more general problem. In Northern Rhodesia and Sierra Leone as well as Mombasa, officials thought that much trouble resulted from the overlap of the idle and the criminal with regular workers. The man struggling to get from one day to

12. Cooper, "La Question du travail."

13. Chapter 3, table 3.1; Cohen, *Labour and Politics,* p. 159.

14. Elliot Berg, "Real Income Trends in West Africa 1939–1960," in Melville J. Herskovits and Mitchell Harwitz, eds., *Economic Transition in Africa* (Evanston, Ill.: Northwestern University Press, 1964), pp. 199–238; Michael Cowen and J. R. Newman, "Real Wages in Central Kenya," unpublished paper, 1975; Bill Freund, *Capital and Labour in the Nigerian Tin Mines* (London: Longman, 1981).

the next and the man trying to build a life and support a family experienced their frustrations together.[15]

The cheap labor system thus created a danger that disorder, if it occurred, would know no limits. The first rumblings in the Gold Coast in 1939 led the Governor to call for an immediate solution, since the problem affected "unskilled labour throughout the Colony." Eight years later, another Governor found himself faced with "almost daily threats of strikes" (and some actual ones) and "a spontaneous, widespread and barely coherent demand for more money." As agitation among Nigeria's government workers grew over several months in 1942, Acting Governor Burns noted the "solidarity of all classes of Government servants in the demand for an improvement in their living conditions generally." Despite fears of "appeasement" and of fueling inflation even further, the government conceded substantial wage increases. The Governor of nearby Sierra Leone quickly saw that such demands would spread "and I do not see how they could be resisted."[16] Three years later, the Nigerian General Strike unleashed another round of concessions and demands, with a radical union leadership coming to the fore. "There is very little more I can do," wrote the Governor, since the "mood of the people of Lagos in general is such that there are few lengths short of violence to which they would not go to secure greatly increased wages." That was what the workers secured, as they did after strikes in the Gold Coast after the war and in Mombasa in 1942, 1945, and 1947.[17]

If the cheap labor system presented colonial states with a singular demand coming from or affecting the vast majority of the working population, the narrowness of the colonial economy compounded its vulnerability. The small size of African wage-labor forces was no indiciation of their

15. The "shifting population of labourers" is cited as "a fertile ground for subversive doctrines" and "ground for discontent"—and specified as cause of the Copperbelt strike and West Indian disorders—in Report of the Commission appointed to Enquire into the Disturbances in the Copperbelt, Northern Rhodesia (Lusaka, 1935), p. 38, and Lord Hailey, draft of confidential report (after a visit to Sierra Leone), September 1941, CO 847/22/47100/8, para. 7, 54.

16. Governor, Gold Coast, to Secretary of State, 31 May 1939, and to Arthur Dawes, 27 May 1939, CO 96/760/31312; Governor, Gold Coast, to Creech Jones, 30 October 1947, CO 96/795/31312; Burns to Secretary of State, 9 June 1942, CO 554/129/33669; Governor, Nigeria, to Moyne, 24 January 1942, CO 583/262/30519; Governor, Sierra Leone, to Secretary of State (telegram), 28 June 1942, CO 554/129/33669. In London, Frederick Pedler noted that some of the Governor's concessions were followed by more demands from unions—a "classic instance of the effects of appeasement"—but he had earlier minuted, "if concessions are necessary to keep African labour from striking etc they will have to be made." Minutes, 9, 28 May 1942, ibid.

17. Acting Governor Whiteley to Stanley, 13 July 1945, CO 583/275/30647/1; Governor Richards to Hall, 21 November 1945, ibid; Cohen, Labour and Politics; Oyemekinde, "Nigerian General Strike."

power and importance. On the contrary, Mombasa's 4,000 to 6,000 dock-workers could as effectively—and much more readily—shut down the export economy of East Africa as could the simultaneous refusal to produce of millions of peasants. Not only did mineworkers in Northern Rhodesia or railwaymen in the Gold Coast or French West Africa live within spatial systems narrow enough to give them an opportunity to develop an understanding among themselves, but they could also exercise an effect on the export economy altogether disproportionate to their numbers.

This raises another question that requires further comparative study: why was such power not always exercised? In Kenya, the dockers did exert it, while the railwaymen, who were an equally vulnerable communications link, did not until the very end of the 1950s; in Nigeria, however, the railway was the locus of militancy, while the docks were relatively quiet except during nation-wide movements whose heart was elsewhere.[18] The militance of Mombasa's workers in the 1930s and 1940s was rooted in the structure of the work gangs and in the political culture of the city in general and Majengo in particular, in a dense network of communications, and in workers' acceptance of other workers' niches in the job structure. It was facilitated by a port layout that sent workers through a limited access point with each shift, allowing strikers to pass on strike orders and observe compliance; but informal networks in Majengo and mass meetings gave a city-wide dimension to the major strikes. Mombasa had only a few port companies and standardized conditions in contrast to the more decentralized and personal contractor system of Lagos. Out of the interplay of specific patterns of social relations and the structural tendencies of colonial labor systems in the post-Depression era, arose complex, uneven, but powerful pressures for fundamental change.

Immediately after the first of the great central African mine strikes in 1935, Governor Hubert Young had written that industrialization and detribalization were "the most important problems that confront not only Northern Rhodesia but other parts of Africa."[19] A second vast mine strike in 1940 kept the problem to the fore. As a number of able studies of the Copperbelt have made clear, the mine companies and the state (with

18. Peter Waterman, *Division and Unity amongst Nigerian Workers: Lagos Port Unionism, 1940s–60s* (The Hague: Institute for Social Studies, 1982), p. 102. As Hemson ("Dock Workers") shows, even in a more ruthlessly repressive state, resistance could still be vigorous. See also Iliffe, "Group Consciousness."

19. The Secretary of State, J. H. Thomas, replied that he hoped that enough workers would return regularly to their home districts for tribal authority to be preserved, but that the mines had indeed brought others to the mine towns for good: "it will be necessary to accept a degree of detribalization." Young to Thomas, 23 October 1935, and Thomas to Young, 24 December 1935, CO 795/76/45083.

provincial officials stubbornly resisting) moved not only to accept but to promote a degree of stabilization of mine labor. They came to regard stabilization as a way out of the binds of cheap, migratory labor.[20] As in Mombasa, the compact labor force, capable of being educated, socialized, and distinguished by better pay and distinct career lines from its idle and disorderly fellows, seemed to offer the only escape from a conundrum whose social costs emerged clearly in the Africa-wide strike wave.

This rethinking of the labor question, and in a broader sense of African society, was not simply the consequence of strikes: an intellectual history of British or French conceptions of African society and social change remains to be written.[21] But the significant moves to translate earlier concerns into actual urban and labor policies began, rather tentatively, in Northern Rhodesia after the 1935 mine strike, in Kenya after the 1939 general strike, and more decisively after the unrest of 1942 and 1945. The Colonial Office, from the mid-1930s, had been telling colonial governments to create labor departments, to pass legislation to protect workers, to promote trade-union organization, and to take other moderate actions to improve and regulate the labor situation. But as a study of Nigeria clearly shows, the Administration did virtually nothing, except in the aftermaths of major strikes in 1937–38, 1942, and 1945, when action occurred rapidly and in a state of panic.[22]

Most important was the sudden transition within the colonial state from complacent ignorance about the lives of workers to obsession with their social conditions.[23] The Willan Commission following the strike of 1939 was the first study of work and of working lives—as opposed to investiga-

20. Parpart, *Labor and Capital;* Perrings, *Black Mineworkers;* Helmuth Heisler, *Urbanisation and the Government of Migration: The Inter-relation of Urban and Rural Life in Zambia* (London: Hurst, 1974); George Chauncey, Jr., "The Locus of Reproduction: Women's Labour in the Zambian Copperbelt, 1927–1953," *Journal of Southern African Studies* 7 (1981): 135–64.

21. For example, Godfrey and Monica Wilson drew on their anthropological training, which emphasized societies as complex wholes whose integrity could be protected or shattered, as well as their Christian ideology to criticize migratory labor as inhumane and destructive. They argued that rural and urban societies both needed to be stabilized in their own ways. Such an approach thus had its own root systems but came to a conclusion not incompatible with that being reached by those with distinctly managerial interests. See Godfrey Wilson, *An Essay on the Economics of Detribalisation in Northern Rhodesia* (Livingstone, Rhodesia: Rhodes-Livingstone Institute, 1941), and Godfrey and Monica Wilson, *The Analysis of Social Change* (Cambridge: Cambridge University Press, 1945), as well as the useful comments on this literature in Bill Freund, "Labor and Labor History in Africa," *African Studies Review* 27, no. 2 (1984): 3–6.

22. David Norman Souter, "Colonial Labour Policy and Labour Conditions in Nigeria, 1939–1945," D. Phil. diss., Oxford University, 1980, esp. p. 387. The Colonial Office was well aware of how sluggish most colonies were in undertaking any reexamination of labor policy, until they rapidly began to act around 1939 and 1940. Minutes of J. G. Hibbert and Malcolm Macdonald, 20 February and 2 March 1940, CO 859/28/12259.

tions of labor shortages and the difficulties of recruitment—undertaken by the Kenyan state.[24] It was followed in quick and anxious succession by a spate of investigations of African diets and budgets during the war, and more commissions, social surveys, and studies after it—a veritable plague of sociologists. The appointment of Orde Browne as the Colonial Office's first Labour Advisor in 1938 was another part of the sudden discovery of the labor problem, and he promptly began the first of a series of investigations into African labor, not coincidentally in the post-strike Copperbelt, with the observation that "The whole group of problems connected with labour was thus ignored or treated only in conjunction with other matters."[25] The Colonial Office's effort to make the colonies found labour departments was another response to unrest throughout the empire, and the Kenya Government's acceptance of this directive was, as officials said, a direct consequence of the 1939 strike.[26] The Government's role in promoting the beginnings of urban research at the Rhodes-Livingstone Institute in Rhodesia after 1937, and its new support for social science research generally, also represented a new departure.[27]

But although the urgency to reexamine and rethink the African labor problem emerged suddenly in the era of strikes, the British state's experience with its own working class provided a ready store of diagnoses and remedies. At a minimum, Colonial Office policy was regulatory and institutional, stressing legislation along the lines of British factory acts,

23. In French Africa, ignorance of labor conditions was as striking, until it too began to be remedied in the mid-1930s. Monique Lakroum, *Le Travail inégal: paysans et salariés sénégalais face à la crise des années trentes* (Paris: Harmattan, 1982), pp. 33–34.

24. The main precedent for study came from the work of the Medical Officer of Health in Nairobi, whose findings did not lead to a generalized reconsideration of the "labor problem," since they could be defined as a "health problem." Authorities in Nairobi tried above all to contain and sanitize urban poverty by removing "undesirables," enforcing pass laws, and segregating and controlling urban space. When they became more concerned later on with making the poor into better workers, things became more complicated. See Roger van Zwanenberg, "History and Theory of Urban Poverty in Nairobi: The Problem of Slum Development," *Journal of East African Research and Development* 2, no. 2 (1972): 167–203. Luise White's forthcoming research should shed more light on this transition.

25. Major G. St. J. Orde Browne, Labour Conditions in Northern Rhodesia, Colonial No. 150 (1938), p. 4; Labour Conditions in West Africa, Parliamentary Papers, 1940–41, IV, 1; Labour Conditions in East Africa, Colonial No. 193 (1946).

26. In 1935, several governors had explicitly rejected the idea of founding Labour departments and insisted that machinery for supervising labor was adequate. In the empire as a whole, there were eleven Labour departments in 1937, 33 in 1941. Replies to Colonial Office circular of 9 November 1935, Co 323/1319/1766/2; "Labour Supervision in the Colonial Empire, 1937–1943," Colonial No. 185 (1943), p. 4.

27. Richard Brown, "Passages in the Life of a White Anthropologist: Max Gluckman in Northern Rhodesia," *Journal of African History* 20 (1979): 525–42. As this fascinating study suggests, examining the relationship of social conflict and change in colonial Africa to the development and funding of social science is an important topic for further investigation.

workers' compensation laws, trade-union laws, and machinery to regulate wages, as well as the creation of labour departments to "supervise" labor.[28]

Even more important, the Office became an advocate of higher wages. With the disturbances in the West Indies very much in mind, Lord Moyne, as Secretary of State for the Colonies, told his governors in 1941 that most of the empire would have to make sacrifices during the war, but that it was "the obligation to raise the standard of living of all those classes in the Colonial Empire whose standard is at present below the minimum that can be regarded as adequate" even during wartime.[29] Frederick Pedler later argued that this meant not just a small increase—which would be rapidly eaten up—but a big enough one (fourfold perhaps) to bring about a structural change, notably allowing the worker to bring his family to the city and avoid the evils of bachelor existence.[30] The wartime reality was more mundane: endless investigations of budgets but a pattern of wage increases, as in Mombasa, that had more to do with fear of strikes than objective study of the standard-of-living question. A Nigerian union might have spoken for its Kenyan brothers when it called a 1945 budget study, "a mysterious jumble of metaphysical figures"; Nigerians' real wages declined during the war, except when they forced the administration's hand.[31]

But after the war, the argument resumed: the Colonial Office again advocated systematic efforts to increase African wages: "we cannot condone colonial economies which are based on cheap labour," Creech Jones told his officials.[32] But the problem was structural as well. In a paper on "Labour Productivity in Africa" in 1953, the Colonial Office made "stabilization" the first topic and concluded; "The answer lies not only in

28. For an overview, see B. C. Roberts, *Labour in the Tropical Territories of the Commonwealth* (London: London School of Economics, 1964).

29. Moyne, Circular, 5 June 1941, CO 852/482/6. The head of the Africa Department, Sir Arthur Dawe, interpreted this as meaning that basic wages—not just cost of living allowances—should be raised, but the head of the new Economics Department, Sidney Caine, thought this impossible. The two compromised on a circular despatch that pointed out the desirability of increasing colonial peoples' real standard of living, but also the necessity of preventing its decrease during wartime inflation. Minutes, 17, 20 December 1941, 17 January 1942, despatch 9 February 1942, CO 852/506/15.

30. The economic experts disagreed, arguing that in present circumstances African workers would produce less rather than more with such wages. Pedler, Minute, 17 April 1942, and S. Caine, Minute, 26 August 1942, CO 852/503/17.

31. African Civil Servants' Technical Workers Union, cited in Souter, "Labour Policy," p. 306; Berg, "Wages," p. 205.

32. Minute by Creech Jones, 3 November 1948, CO 859/150/12284/1946–48. The minutes in this file suggest the difficulties the Colonial Office had in translating the sensibility of the Secretary of State into a wage policy.

monetary inducements, important as these may be, for one of the effects of a general wage increase may be to enable the target worker to reach his target quicker and leave work sooner. The solution must be found in a variety of incentives. . . ."[33] The broad approach was hard to implement, and advisors in London came back to promoting stabilization through raising wages to a level sufficient to support a family; they repeatedly chastised East African governments for paying Africans too little.[34]

The problem, at base, was one of class, and Kenyan officials like Phillips and Mitchell posed it in exactly that way. Poverty, as such, was not their main concern: impoverished nonworkers, they thought, could be banished from the city; but the poverty of workers made them inefficient and dangerous. Nor, at the other end of the scale, were they solely concerned with the demands for greater skill that a more complex economy was beginning to raise; they had yet to learn how to get unskilled workers to obey orders, produce steadily, and maintain order. Their concern was more general: could they shape a working class that was well enough fed and housed to be efficient, motivated enough to meet the escalating demands of the postwar era, involved enough in city life and modern enterprises to assimilate the cultural values appropriate to a life of labor, and integrated well enough into the institutions of workplace and residence so that it would end its pattern of drifting into and out of jobs and its tendency to join in mass unrest?

In a general sense, the new approach to the labor problem that slowly emerged during the 1940s was an application of the lessons of the European industrial revolution to Africa: a stable and growing capitalist order was impossible if workers were treated solely as units of labor power to be used and discarded. More specifically, the task recalled that of taming the residuum of Victorian England—only in Africa virtually the entire working class was footloose and untamed. That was precisely why so much of the discussion in the 1940s centered on casual labor, as in Mombasa, or the more general problem of migratory labor, as in the Copperbelt. All the hoped-for processes that might mold a more respectable working class were vitiated by these part-time proletarians: they themselves could not be acculturated and pacified, and they cluttered up the city, consuming its scarce resources and providing a dangerous example of immunity from time discipline. In Mombasa, a diagnosis and a remedy were avail-

33. Paper prepared for the Third Inter-African Labour Conference, Bamako, 1953, CO 859/304.

34. Report by Labour Advisor on a visit to Kenya, 9 December 1952, CO 822/657; draft paper on "Wage Fixing and Family Responsibilities," for Colonial Labour Advisory Committee, 9 May 1953, Minutes of meeting, 18 June 1953, Minutes of meeting of subcommittee on Wage-Fixing and Family Responsibilities, 28 July 1953, LC, Tanganyika, to Labour Advisor, 21 September 1953—all in CO 859/257.

able as soon as the evidence of illness was unmistakable: the call for decasualization received official blessing from the Willan Report within months of the 1939 strike, although only more disorder and uncertainty evoked remedial action.[35]

If capital and the state could seize control of time and separate a finite group of workers from the vastness of uncivilized Africa, they could begin to shape the formation and reproduction of an urban working class. Again, they could turn to a preexisting discourse in academic, managerial, and government circles that placed the minimal biological and social needs of workers in a scientific and objective context.[36] As the need for greater efficiency in the critical bottlenecks of the Kenyan economy became clear, the Railway could import an expert from a British firm, with his notions of what good management looked like, to tell them that Africans could be good workers too, if only they were well nourished, well managed, and socialized to the job.[37]

Shaping a respectable working class required another step. Workers, officials knew all too well, would engage in collective action. The question was in what form. Discussing trade-union legislation, officials in London debated, in so many words, the question of whether the "British model" was relevant to Africa, and decided that it was. This approach to labor organization would—in the language of a Colonial Office report from 1951—"guide this inevitable development into a sound and responsible movement, able to play its proper organic part in the democratic structure of the territory."[38]

35. The critique of casual labor in the docks in Mombasa was paralleled by a vigorous program of decasualization (also following strikes) in Dar es Salaam, and by less far-reaching attempts to register dockworkers and restrict pools in the Gold Coast, Nigeria, and Sierra Leone. The history of African dock labor requires more specific attention before one can attempt comparisons, but the registration schemes are mentioned in Secretary of State to Governor Macpherson, 24 June 1950, CO 583/310/30647/1F, which discusses the just completed report of a Commission of Enquiry into Coastal Dock Labour in West Africa, and at a meeting of the Colonial Labour Advisory Committee, 5 April 1951, CLAC(51)13, CO 888/8. See also Waterman, *Lagos Port Unions;* and, on Dar es Salaam, Iliffe, "Group Consciousness."

36. This came to Kenya via South Africa, mainly (as the references in the Phillips Committee indicate) through the work of Edward Batson. See his discussion of his work in Cape Town in *Towards Social Security* (Cape Town: Koston, 1943).

37. Belinda Bozzoli and Jeff Crisp discuss the importation of the idea of scientific management to South Africa and the Gold Coast. Crisp emphasizes that it was only after a major strike and wage hikes made efficient production into a new imperative that mine owners came to believe management should be scientific. Belinda Bozzoli, "Managerialism and the Mode of Production," *South African Labour Bulletin* 3, no. 8 (1977): 6–49; Jeff Crisp, "Productivity and Protest: Scientific Management in the Ghanaian Gold Mines, 1947–56," in Frederick Cooper, ed., *Struggle for the City: Migrant Labor, Capital, and the State in Africa* (Beverly Hills, Calif.: 1983), pp. 91–130.

38. Colonial Labour Advisory Committee, Memorandum on "Trade Unionism in the Colonies," 1951, CLAC(51)11, CO 888/8. The issue of institutional transfer is discussed in

The idea of a stable wage-labor force, guaranteed certain rights and incorporated into a system of institutions, soon came to be a dogma of international discourse on labor, replacing the more modest International Labor Organization conventions directed above all against compulsory methods of recruitment. A United Nations report in 1952 argued, as British Colonial Officials had before, that the migrant worker, with one foot in his village economy, responded to incentives in a fundamentally different way from the permanent worker—he might take advantage of a wage increase to work less. But "permanent workers, on the contrary, generally react in the same way as workers in industrial countries." The need to raise productivity thus implied that workers should cease to lead their double lives and become like other citizens of the modern world. A follow-up report concluded, "migratory labor is not only inefficient on account of the high labour turnover and the need continuously to recruit and train new workers. The worker, shuttling back and forth between two modes of life, may in fact make a satisfactory adjustment to neither." Trade unions had an "indispensable role in educating other workers to accept changes" needed to raise productivity, and adequate wages and conditions were essential to giving workers a stake in improving output.[39]

The new language of international agencies and economic experts rarely discussed the structures that were being created in the factories, mines, and dockyards of Africa as products of the confrontation of labor and capital; they were part of a universal "logic of industrialism" whose basic nature was part of the modern order of things toward which all Africans could aspire.[40] Increasing production, meanwhile, was not to be taken as a sign of intensified colonial exploitation but as a universal goal, a blow struck against world poverty.

But the universals of social science and the European experience of labor were the roughest of guidelines for facing the ferment and confrontations in Africa. The same British report that eloquently expressed the

---

William H. Friedland, *Vuta Kamba: The Development of Trade Unions in Tanganyika* (Stanford, Calif.: Hoover, 1969).

39. UN, General Assembly, paper prepared by the ILO, "Preliminary study on wages and productivity of labour in non-self-governing territories," A/AC.35/L.108, 3 September 1952; UN, Economic and Social Council, paper prepared by the ILO on "Economic development of under-developed countries: question of methods to increase world productivity," E/2440, 22 May 1953, copies in CO 859/304. This international dimension of ideological change also deserves detailed examination.

40. Clark Kerr, John T. Dunlop, Frederick Harbison, and Charles A. Myers, *Industrialism and Industrial Man* (Cambridge, Mass.: Harvard University Press, 1960). See also UNESCO, *Social Implications of Industrialization and Urbanization in Africa South of the Sahara* (Paris: UNESCO, 1956), and, for a critical study of writing on this subject, Michael Burawoy, "The Anthropology of Work," *Annual Review of Anthropology* 8 (1979): 131–66.

corporatist ideal of workers' finding their place in democratic society through their proper institutions went on to worry that 90 to 95 percent of workers in the colonies were not organized. It was equally important, for the preservation of peace and production, that their wages be adequate; but the state-run wage-fixing machinery, officials feared, might actually compromise the growth of collective bargaining. Wage-fixing by tribunal, as in Mombasa, posed the danger that such state action would recreate, through overbroad standards, a unified laboring mass that would agitate for government attention and undermine the kind of differentiated and ordered society that collective bargaining promoted.[41] Meanwhile, faced with actual African trade unionists, officials—in Nigeria, the Gold Coast, and Sierra Leone as well as Kenya—found trade-union practice less appealing than the theory, and put obstacles in the path of trade unions seeking that organic place in democratic society which officials in London had pointed out to them.[42]

The restructuring of the colonial labor system would go through many trials and many errors. The long and conflict-ridden process which had defined the place of British workers in society and politics—through welfare systems, trade unions, industrial relations machinery, the rational organization of the shop-floor, urban planning, and party politics—offered an inspiration to colonial officials. But it was not clear what lay between this vision of the modern world and the realities of postwar Africa. African cities, and the African countryside, were proving themselves in a period of economic growth to be as inchoate, as hard to comprehend, as hard to control as ever. The universalism of imperial discourse contrasted with the unevenness of practice and the social fragmentation postwar policies in fact fostered. The idea that African trade unions and labor organization generally could be assimilated into the institutional structure of modern government and modern economies was less an observation of an ongoing process than a desperate hope that things would turn out that way. What officials knew was that the older vision of Africa as a repository of infinitely replaceable labor, kept alive at minimal levels while working in the city and stored in a tranquil and backward countryside when not, was now useless. And the pressure of disorder and the demands for increased production were too acute to guard the old hope that a uniquely African society could be protected and slowly modified on its own terms. A reversal of this view of Africa, a ready-made and

41. See "Trade Unionism in the Colonies," CLAC(51)11, and the discussion of this and related reports during 1951, all in CO 888/8.

42. Cohen, *Labour and Politics;* Jeffries, *Class, Power and Ideology;* Milcah Amolo, "Trade Unionism and Colonial Authority: Sierra Leone, 1930–1945," *Transafrican Journal of History* 8, no. 1 (1979): 36–52.

ethnocentric vision of all the institutions of the modern world being replicated on the African continent, defined a vague and ultimately unrealiza-
ble alternative.[43]

IMPERIAL PERSPECTIVES: PRODUCTION AND POLITICS

For all the unevenness of its implementation, the language of labor reform lent itself not only to restructuring the workplace and industrial
relations machinery, not only to social planning for cities, but also to
politics. The imperial context added great urgency to the series of labor
disputes of the late 1930s and 1940s and to the rethinking of the problem
which they stimulated. The labor problem had powerful implications,
first, for the productionist ethos of the war and postwar eras—the obsession with raising Africa's output—and second, for the growing crisis of
imperial rule itself.

The war and its aftermath enhanced the economic importance of Africa to England as never before. Its minerals were needed for weapons, its
cocoa and oil products, to keep the strapped British population fed;
alternative tropical sources of supply in Asia had been lost. Postwar England—desperate for foreign exchange, faced with American demands
for its debts to be repaid in hard currency, its own industry damaged and
its long-term ability to compete in international markets doubtful, on the
verge of losing India—saw the unrealized potential of Africa as that
continent's greatest attraction: it promised to be the only place where a
breakthrough in export production could possibly be achieved.

This was the gist of what the postwar government was saying after the
war. Sir Stafford Cripps, Minister for Economic Affairs, told a conference
of African governors in 1947, "the whole future of the sterling group and
its ability to survive depends in my view upon a quick and extensive
development of our African resources." Frederick Pedler put it even
more strongly in private, "Africa is now the core of our colonial position;
the only continental space from which we can still hope to draw reserves
of economic and military strength."[44] Ernest Bevin, the Foreign Secretary, thought, "If only we pushed on & developed Africa we could have
U.S. dependent on us, and eating out of our hand in four or five years."
Bevin's belief that Africa held "mountains of manganese" and possessed
the ability to supply a long list of minerals and agricultural products was

---

43. Now that "modernization theory" has lost most of its lustre as an analytic tool, it
deserves reexamination as part of the history of ideology in the postwar world.

44. Transcript of African Governors' Conference, 12 November 1947, p. 40 (copy in
Rhodes House); Pedler, Minute, 1 November 1946, CO 847/35/47234/1/1947.

both fanciful and desperate.[45] And these hopes could be shattered by small groups of dockers, miners, railwaymen, and urban mobs.

The productionist ethos of the war and postwar eras empowered African workers. It empowered them as individuals: officials during the first postwar decade feared not only labor shortages but resistance to work discipline on the part of workers whose rural base provided them with alternatives. It empowered them as collectivities, for the key points in the production process were narrow enough to be blocked by a modest level of worker organization.[46] Workers used this power often enough to shape a context in which officials not only made concessions but sought to build new structures that would reassert power within the workplace and the city, and contain conflict.

The dynamics of postwar politics can perhaps best be understood in terms of the ultimate irreconcilability of the objectives of intensified production and social order. What D. A. Low and John Lonsdale call the "second colonial occupation"—the new effort of the imperial powers finally to make Africa productive, controllable, and stable—quickly unleashed forces that shook the viability of the colonial system even more than what had gone before.[47]

The production drive led to conflict as much by its successes as by its failures. High export crop prices discouraged food production, while the rapid pace of commerce in major ports stimulated an upsurge in migration of workers to cities. Trying to minimize imports from outside of the sterling area and unable to supply them from within, the British government saw prices soar and feared that an enriched farming class would sell less food and consume more scarce imports, driving urbanites into rebellion. The desire to maintain urban stability was one of the most important reasons why states felt impelled to use marketing boards to keep much of the new agricultural wealth out of the countryside and in government accounts, leading—not surprisingly—to much rural anger.[48]

45. Quoted in Hugh Dalton diaries, 15 October 1948, cited in R. D. Pearce, *The Turning Point in Africa: British Colonial Policy 1938–1948* (London: Cass, 1982), pp. 95–96. Great Britain's need to exploit Africa's foreign exchange surpluses to save metropolitan finances is stressed in Yusuf Bangura, *Britain and Commonwealth Africa: The Politics of Economic Relations, 1951–75* (Manchester, Eng.: Manchester University Press, 1983).

46. The CO invoked just this argument to get the Gold Coast government to settle the railway strike of 1947 with speed, and the governor replied sadly that the unions were equally well aware of officials' desperation. Lloyd to Acting Governor, 23 October 1947, and Acting Governor to Lloyd, 24 October 1947, CO 96/795/31312.

47. D. A. Low and John M. Lonsdale, "Introduction: Towards the New Order 1945–1963," in D. A. Low and Alison Smith, eds., *The Oxford History of East Africa. Vol. 3* (Oxford: Oxford University Press, 1976), p. 12.

48. In 1951, a Cabinet Paper posed the dilemma: to continue to "cream off" the high export earnings of farmers, thus encouraging food production and lowering urban food

The productionist ethos also shaped the willingness of the state to recast its vision of African society. Not only did the critical urban workers have to be made more efficient and content, but rural society had to be stabilized too. The primitive subsistence producer had been the other incarnation of the migrant worker: both worked cheaply but badly. As officials pondered their postwar policies, they insisted that both had to go. There was no point, they argued, in assisting part-time food producers, for this was "not progress, but rather a reversion to the subsistence economy of primitive man." Pedler saw clearly the implications of such a policy: "In application, it means abandoning all idea of stabilising entire populations on the basis of peasant production; consequently urbanisation and industry."[49] Subsistence production might in effect provide for the social reproduction of rural cash-crop producers as well as urban workers— feeding children, nonworkers, and the aged without adding to the cost of the product—but they were reproducing the wrong kind of society for the postwar era. Workers must be workers, and farmers, farmers. The older approach of encouraging workers to maintain ties to the farm implied, to borrow Marx's famous phrase, the ruralization of the city. The new orientation implied the urbanization of the countryside.

As with urban production, improving agricultural output, protecting against soil erosion and crop diseases, incorporating new techniques into agriculture, improving access to credit, and raising incentives—all implied more than technological changes but substantial social change as well.

> There is today general agreement that African agriculture can not secure the improvements in productivity which are necessary by continued dependence on the efforts of the individual family working with primitive tools and that radical changes in the system of agriculture are required to permit operations on a larger scale, with increased use of mechanical assistance and with the basic object of increased productivity.

---

prices at the expense of creating rural discontent, or else to let farmers benefit fully from world markets, thus fostering urban inflation and disorder; Memorandum on the Implications of the Colonial Balance of Payments Position, CAB 129/48, C.(51) 22. High prices for locally grown food were seen as a cause of the Gold Coast disturbances of 1948, while West African governors argued that this danger was a reason to limit farmers' earnings from export crops. Report of the Commission of Enquiry into Disturbances in the Gold Coast 1948, Colonial No. 231 (1948), p. 38; Governor of Nigeria to Secretary of State, 15 September 1950, CO 583/303/30585; Governor to A. Cohen, 29 January 1951, CO 583/311/30647/15; Officer Administering the Government, Gold Coast, to Secretary of State, 3 June 1949, CO 537/4638.

49. Memorandum by G. Clauson, 8 March 1942, and Minute by F. J. Pedler, 17 April 1942, CO 852/503/17.

Only officials—as their reports reveal—were much less sure than in the case of urban Africa what those changes should be.[50] They dismissed the peasant as backward but distrusted the plantation owner as likely to instigate class conflict. Some plans leaned toward master farmers—freed from the constraints of African land tenure, individualistic, fully committed to the market, hard-working, but not exploiters of others' labor. But however unsure the vision of agricultural reform, officials were convinced that it was so vital for Africans and for the metropole that it had to be imposed. Rural resistance—from violence to participation in national political movements to the peasant's old defense of nonproduction—was widespread and important in this period, rural Africa's greatest era of prosperity.[51]

But the very unevenness of rural progress affected colonial perceptions of the city. Each sector had to be stabilized in its own way, and the city was too vulnerable to be held back by the enormous expanse and social complexity of rural Africa. For the time being, at least, the young urban working class had to be protected from rural contagion. In the city, it seemed, was a struggle that the colonial state could win.

To a significant extent, as the case of Mombasa illustrates, the state did succeed in remaking the workplace within a limited range of industries. It did not succeed so well in pacifying the city, in large part because it had fallen far short in the countryside. Unable to stop migration forcibly in the early 1950s, toward the end of the decade Kenyan officials realized the alarming implications of the narrowness of the terrain it had reconquered.

Uncontrollable urban migration was one of the intractable problems that colonial powers bequeathed to their successors. The decolonization process itself took place in a context influenced by the anxiety over urban unrest. The thinking of the rulers of empire in the 1940s and 1950s was not only shaped by their need for uninterrupted, expanding production, but by anxiety about political challenges to the colonial system. This gave a heightened meaning to every confrontation; the major upheavals in the empire had all started small.

The scene had been set in the West Indies. A series of strikes, most dramatically in the oil fields of Trinidad and the plantations and cities of

50. Report of the Committee on the Conference of African Governors, 22 May 1947, appendix 6: "The Economic Development of Agricultural Production in the African Colonies," CO 847/36/47238.

51. Two particularly fine articles on this elusive topic are William Beinart, "Soil Erosion, Conservationism and Ideas about Development: A Southern African Exploration, 1900–1960," *Journal of Southern African Studies* 11 (1984): 52–83, and Michael Cowen, "The British State and Agrarian Accumulation in Kenya after 1945," in Martin Fransman, ed., *Industry and Accumulation in Africa* (London: Longman, 1981), pp. 142–69.

Jamaica between 1935 and 1938, had turned into riots and island-wide clashes. They shocked the Colonial Office and Parliament.[52] The famous commission under Lord Moyne that studied the problem and the Colonial Development and Welfare Act of 1940 were direct responses. By 1950, perceptions were being shaped in an equally important way by the events in Malaya.[53] Labor unrest in Malayan plantations, labor organizing by communist unions, and strikes had become a guerrilla war by 1948, a severe challenge which the British government met with great difficulty, and eventually with success. The references to the West Indies and Malaya that have been cited at various points in this study—from Colonial Office reactions to the 1939 strike to the Kenya Government's decision to suppress the AWF in 1947—made clear the fear of officials that any pattern of labor unrest could become a revolution. The Malayan analogy also weighed heavily in the Gold Coast, and the Governor who presided over its most critical crises compared the two at length.[54]

In this context, the most effective strikes—those in Mombasa, the French West African and Gold Coast railway strikes—were perceived not only as economic dangers but as political threats. The Phillips Committee in 1945 had seen the danger of the potential unity of workers who were all poor and all black: "the beginnings of class-consciousness, complicated by race-consciousness." After strikes in Northern Rhodesia in 1940, in the Gold Coast in 1947, and above all after the riots in the Gold Coast in 1948, similar points were made.[55]

The danger transcended urban riots. Officials, with the examples of India and Malaya in mind, feared the mob would acquire a leader, that it would become a movement. As Orde Browne put it, "a discontented labour force is a constant danger as affording a permanent basis for political agitation of the unscrupulous type."[56] This fear lay behind the

52. They had been warned. W. M. Macmillan had written just before the strikes that the British had allowed a severe social problem to fester in its colonies, and predicted that things would come to a head in the West Indies. He was able to write an "I told you so" preface to the second edition of his book. *Warning from the West Indies: A Tract for the Empire*, 2d ed. (London: Penguin, 1938).

53. In between came the war. As Frederick Pedler later put it, "you just couldn't afford to have disorders in the colonies while you were fighting Hitler." Interview for Colonial Records Project, Rhodes House, pp. 26–27.

54. Governor Arden-Clarke, Draft Report on Disturbances in the Gold Coast in Early 1950, sent to CO on 29 June 1950, pp. 19–27, CO 537/5812. This analogy seemed to interest the CO more than anything else in the report; Arden-Clarke was asked to develop it into a separate despatch. Gorsuch to Arden-Clarke, 23 September 1950, ibid.

55. Minute by A. Dawes (on Northern Rhodesia), 15 May 1940, CO 795/122/45109/7; Governor, Gold Coast, to Creech Jones, 30 October 1947, CO 96/795/31312; Commission of Enquiry into Disturbances in the Gold Coast. On Phillips, see above, p. 73.

56. Minute, 31 March 1943, CO 554/132/33178.

vehement attack on Chege Kibachia after the 1947 general strike. Similarly, after the Nigerian general strike of 1945, a member of the Legislative Council fulminated about the role of "politico-press demagogues" in encouraging this widespread movement. He was referring to Nnamdi Azikiwe. In London the next year, Pedler argued that Azikiwe was stirring up the masses, and that "racial conflict deliberately fomented by Azikiwe in Nigeria, and the Messianic fervour with which he is regarded by many Nigerians, raise a serious danger that we may come to blows with Africans in Nigeria."[57]

The state had to separate the mob from the demagogue. The Governor of the Gold Coast used this argument in justifying the detention of the leading politicians after the 1948 riots: the detentions "are like the quarantine which is imposed on people who have caught a dangerous infectious disease."[58] The Secretary of State for the Colonies, noting that the "illiterate and semi-literate population in the towns and urban areas" had supplied the "followers" of the irresponsible political leaders of the Gold Coast, saw a still wider danger: "It has seemed to me for some time that many of our most serious difficulties in Africa are going to lie in our relations with these detribalised urban people." The greatest danger of all was that the urban mob and organized labor might act together; the Governor thought Nkrumah was trying "to forge organised labour into the spear-head of his attack on ordered government."[59]

Political concerns thus reinforced the economic and social imperatives to break up the urban mass into distinct elements, with their own career lines, their own interests, their own institutions, and their own spokesmen. A more complex African class structure—with landowners, shopkeepers, factory managers, and skilled mechanics—would further differentiate and balance the bottom-heavy African social structure.[60] Bringing about such a class structure meant paying a respectable working class a respectable wage and being sure that the moderate institutions appropriate to it had something to show for themselves. Just these reasons were used to justify wage increases.[61]

57. J. F. Winter in proceedings of the Legislative Council, Nigeria, 23d session, 13 December 1945, pp. 140–41; Pedler, Minute, 1 November 1946, CO 847/35/47234/1/1947.

58. Broadcast speech by Gerald Creasy, text incl. Creasy to Creech Jones, 13 March 1948, CO 96/795/31312/2.

59. Creech Jones to Creasy, 9 April 1948, CO 537/3558; Acting Governor to Creech Jones, 3 June 1949, CO 96/797/31312/4.

60. "The development of this class would go far to give the African the feeling that he owned his country and exploited its resources, instead of seeing these constantly in the hands of the white man." Orde Browne, Minute, 31 March 1943, CO 554/132/33178.

61. The governor of Nigeria wrote in 1946, after complaining that a commission had recommended excessive wage increases, "political considerations alone dictate acceptance"

It was equally essential to foster a class of respectable politicians, who would be the political counterparts of the respectable working class. This meant, as Pedler put it in 1946, slowly developing institutions of local government that would "bring literates and illiterates together, in balanced and studied proportions, for the management of local finances and services. Failing this, we shall find the masses apt to follow the leadership of demagogues who want to turn us right out very quickly."[62] Not only did the Kibachias, the Kenyattas, the Azikiwes, the Nkrumahs, and the Wallace-Johnsons of Africa have to be checked, but more reasonable, moderate, respectable politicans had to be encouraged. Creech Jones pulled together the concern with the past disturbances, the fear of demagoguery, and the need to encourage moderation when he presented a plan for constitutional reform in the Gold Coast to the British Cabinet in 1949. The "extremists" had led "the less responsible elements" in "political agitation." "There is, however, a large body of moderate opinion which, while recognizing that the country is not yet ready for full responsible government, is convinced, as the Governor and I myself are, that immediate constitutional advance is necessary." Not to encourage such an advance risked alienating the moderates, encouraging the extremists, and fostering "serious trouble."[63]

It was precisely the threat of the masses that made the concessions to the moderates so necessary. The irony of the era was that the greatest of all the apostles of disorder, Kwame Nkrumah, went almost directly from jail to the statehouse in 1951, from being the epitome of the demagogue to being the one man that the colonial state hoped could lead the peaceful transformation of politics.[64]

---

of the commission's award; Governor to Secretary of State, 25 May 1946, CO 583/276/30647/6A. Later, noting encouraging developments in the trade-union movement in the Gold Coast, an official wrote: "here we have a trade union movement which has been wrested from the hands of extremists and appears to be following a reasonable line which promises well for the future. But its hold on its membership will be measured by its successes. . . ." G. Foggin, Minute, 1 March 1951, CO 96/819/31312/9A.

62. F. J. Pedler, Minute, 1 November 1946, CO 847/35/47234/1/1947.

63. Cabinet Paper CP(49) 199, 8 October 1949, ACJ 55/1. Once the hopefully moderate politicans had been given responsible positions, "it is essential that that Government should be able to show results in the sphere of economic and social development. Otherwise it was bound to disappoint the people and likely to lead . . . to the transfer of power to irresponsible extremists." This reasoning thus established the political necessity of strong British support for development plans in the closing years of colonial rule. Minute by Andrew Cohen, 14 April 1951, CO 96/826/31596, and other papers in this file.

64. Officials were sensitive to this irony, but felt they had no choice. Nkrumah had demonstrated his mass support through the test officials themselves devised—elections— and the masses had repeatedly demonstrated their anger in the streets between 1948 and 1950. Not accepting the result would lead to "widespread agitation." Gold Coast, Political

Why could colonial governments not wait for the emergence of African leaders more respectable than the Nkrumahs or Kenyattas whom they had seen fit to jail? The very concessions they made to the mythical "moderate element" which they sought to promote against the "extremists"—including fuller political roles and extensions of the franchise—provided new mechanisms for the extremists to use to demonstrate their popularity. The fact was, no relationship of a colonial government with an African leader—whether collaboration, cooptation, or mere tolerance—did much to help the imperial government's cause unless that leader had a following. States could try to set limits—as the British did in their assault on the African Workers Federation in Mombasa, or the French in a long and bloody confrontation with a nationalist movement in the Camerouns—but the ways in which the much-denounced African masses personified their aspirations set some limits too. The state could try to fracture mass power by fostering a more differentiated and balanced social structure—to the considerable advantage of crucial workers like the dockers of Mombasa—but that method was slow, and the very process created other sorts of interests and political relationships not always easy to predict.

The atmosphere of uncontrollable urban disorder, crossing the continent and reaching to the Caribbean and East Asia, was an important element in understanding the dynamics of political change in postwar Africa. In a more specific and mundane way, the experience of strikes contributed also to colonial officials' self-doubt and a feeling that they themselves could not control the forces that the rapid changes of the postwar era had suddenly unleashed. In the midst of the 1947 Mombasa strike, the Government had sent a white missionary officially representing African interests in the Legislative Council to Mombasa to reason with the strikers; they had ignored him. But an African member, Eliud Mathu, had succeeded at the same task and had been profusely thanked by the Attorney General for having at last persuaded the men to return to work (see chapter 3). In the same year, almost the same process occurred during a railway strike in the Gold Coast. Two African members of the Legislative Council had talked the men into going back, on terms reasonably favorable to the government. Years later, two officials who had been there at the time told an interviewer that it was "a quite extraordinary thing that a major strike in a nationalized industry should be settled by a

<hr>

Intelligence Report, 12 February 1951, CO 537/7233. In Kenya, not only was the state unable to find any remotely plausible African leader more conservative than Kenyatta, but Kenyatta himself was in acute danger by 1950 of being pushed to the sidelines by more militant leaders in better touch with the masses in Nairobi. David Throup, "The Origins of Mau Mau," *African Affairs* 84 (1985): 420.

back-bench member of Parliament." This perception had gone straight to the top. Creech Jones wrote, "The African members of the Legislative Council there have shown ability and a real sense of responsibility and the settlement of the recent railway and mining strikes in the Gold Coast was largely due to their efforts."[65]

Black politicians had done what whites could not. It happened again in Mombasa in 1955, when Tom Mboya took a tense and spreading strike situation in hand, used his influence with whites to break their intransigence and his ability to convince blacks that his knowledge of the ways of government would work to their interest, and obtained a settlement. But there was a price to be paid to individuals like Mboya and to the institutions—those "responsible" trade unions—that the state came to see as essential. The leaders and the unions needed something to show for their willingness to carry out their struggles within boundaries acceptable to the state.

The dynamics of the late colonial era were as rapid and as cathartic as they were precisely because the Mboyas were not tools of the state. Mboya had indeed been a protégé of leading officials at a time when they needed an antidote to Makhan Singh and others regarded as trade union demagogues, just as the Sierra Leone government had cultivated Siaka Stevens as an alternative to I. T. A. Wallace-Johnson.[66] But Mboya had used his credibility with Government officials to gain a good settlement for Mombasa's workers and to build his power base among them. He later proved an effective nationalist leader while Kenyatta remained in jail. His own sense of the frightening quality of urban disorder enabled him to argue to great effect—in labor negotiations or at a constitutional conference—if not me, the rabble.

It was no coincidence that imperial powers faced the problem of finding new ways of involving Africans in political processes at the same time that they faced the social consequences of the intensification of production. The preceding passages have done little more than hint at the connections of the politics of decolonization to the problems of mass unrest, labor movements, and the restructuring of urban life; they are no sub-

---

65. Transcript of discussion between G. N. Burden and Sir Kenneth Bradley, 7 August 1971, Colonial Records Project, Rhodes House, pp. 9–10; Creech Jones, Memorandum by the Secretary of State for the Colonies on the memorandum by the Chief of the Imperial General Staff on his tour of Africa, 6 January 1948, PREM 8/923 (Public Record Office).

66. Goldsworthy, *Tom Mboya*. E. Parry, the CO's labor specialist in Sierra Leone, called Stevens "my principal discovery," contrasting him to Wallace-Johnson, "the most objectionable and unscrupulous person I have met in political life"; Parry to Rita Hinden, 23 September, 29 December 1945, FCB 86/2, ff. 114–15, 118. See also Leo Spitzer and LaRay Denzer, "I. T. A. Wallace-Johnson and the West African Youth League," *International Journal of African History* 6 (1973): 413–52, 565–601, as well as studies of splits between "moderate" and "extremist" trade unionists in other colonies.

stitute for the many studies needed to decipher these topics.[67] But the experience of Mombasa is suggestive: the colonial state faced an unprecedented challenge originating within an African city, a serious loss of control over African workers at a time when colonial states needed their time and their effort more than ever, and the loss of their own confidence in themselves as an unchallenged force for progress in Africa.

The disturbances in African cities were important precisely because they were, above all, labor uprisings. Colonial states in Africa, without question, had the power to quell riots. What was less clear was that they had the power to make men work, and especially to work well. The problem could not be banished to the countryside, eased by a fanciful recreation of traditional African authority. It could—with great repression and great difficulty—be solved the way the South Africans did it, through a bureaucracy capable of following laborers through all phases of their lives. The South African experience is a reminder that the transformations of colonial labor systems were social choices, not automatic consequences of economic change, but it is a reminder as well of the consequences of such choices.[68] Rapid expansion and industrialization with a migrant labor force excluded from the institutions of an industrial society required not only enormous manpower and money to enforce pass laws and contain dissent, but a sense of collective will among the dominant group that set South Africa apart from the colonial metropoles in a way it had not been before the war.[69]

67. It is insufficient to suggest, as have Ronald Robinson and R. D. Pearce, that the Colonial Office made the basic decisions about devolving power in advance of and in anticipation of a challenge from African nationalists in the late 1940s. This assumes that nationalism is indeed the central question, as opposed to the dilemmas of the colonial state's exercising effective control over economic and social change in the face of complex and varied challenges. See Robinson, "Andrew Cohen and the Transfer of Power in Tropical Africa, 1940–1951," in W. H. Morris-Jones and Georges Fischer, eds., *Decolonization and After: the British and French Experience* (London: Cass, 1980), pp. 50–72, and Pearce, *Turning Point.* One should note, however, that the historiography of decolonization is in its infancy, although rapidly growing. For a beginning—most notable for its bibliographical material— see Prosser Gifford and Wm. Roger Louis, eds., *The Transfer of Power in Africa: Decolonization 1940–1960* (New Haven: Yale University Press, 1982).

68. The election of 1948 in South Africa was to a significant extent fought over the issue of whether or not to foster a stable working class in the rapidly expanding cities, or to reinforce the existing policies of rigid influx control and rigid exclusion of Africans from urban institutions. See Stanley Greenberg, *Race and State in Capitalist Development* (New Haven: Yale University Press, 1980), and Dan O'Meara, *Volkskapitalisme: Class, Capital and Ideology in the Development of Afrikaner Nationalism, 1934–1948* (Cambridge: Cambridge University Press, 1984).

69. That the Kenya Government turned to South African welfare studies in the 1940s suggests that up to then it could serve as a model for progressive labor policies. Afterward, South Africa came to symbolize retrograde labor policies, and Europe itself would provide the models for labor and welfare policies in African colonies.

In the 1940s, British officials thought that expanding production, building better transport facilities and capital resources, improving wages and living conditions, promoting trade unions, and gradually giving Africans a greater voice in political affairs all went together. All were, in one sense or another, reform. It was precisely the relationship among these processes that caused the African empire rapidly to come apart. Development, after the West Indian riots, was presented to Parliament as the cure for disorder. Ten years later, the strains which expansion induced on tottering economic structures, the coerciveness of the state's intervention in rural areas, and the complex and varied demands that came from new and old social groups made it seem as if development caused as much disorder as it cured.

The Contradictions of Labor Control

In the connection of these economic crises with a crisis of urban order lies a clue not only to the dynamics of decolonization but to some of the most acute problems that faced newly independent African countries, problems that also appeared simultaneously as crises of poverty, political stability, and social structure. When Tom Mboya became Minister of Labour in the Government of Kenya just before independence, he told the Legislative Council that no problem was graver than unemployment, and it was growing. Like some of his colonial predecessors, Mboya admitted that the policy of stabilizing urban labor and paying relatively good wages contributed to job shortages.[70] Like them, he argued that it was worth it, and his answer revealed how deeply in the social and economic structure of the colonial era the dilemma lay:

> I am of the opinion that we are better off with a more satisfied labour force than with a totally dissatisfied labour force, and it is no use paying so many people wages on which they cannot live in order to have many more employed. I think that it is better to pay a few people wages on which they can live and work to maximum production; at least that way you go much further economically than the other way with its frustration and exploitation that would attend it. . . .[71]

Mboya was not merely saying that low wages were politically risky. They were an economic danger as well. A ragtag army of miserably paid workers could not lead a nation to development.

70. Legislative Council Debates, 89 (18 July 1962), c. 1004; C. H. Hartwell to P. Rogers, 29 January 1953, CO 822/657; East Africa Royal Commission, Report, 1955, pp. 147–48.
71. Legislative Council Debates, 89 (18 July 1962), c. 1030. His argument was particularly close to that of A. G. Dalgleish's important report of 1960 that saw unemployment as the side effect of the correct policy of stabilizing African family life. See above, p. 180.

Mboya's experience had also led him to accept what the Secretary of State for the Colonies, Oliver Lyttleton, had argued in 1954: that workers might have to be paid more than their market price to make them productive (see above, p. 128). Production was a social process—it could be done badly or well—and the conditions that promoted stable family life, commitment to urban society, and regular participation in trade unions also promoted productivity. The compact, efficient working class was the key not only to social peace but to economic growth.

The consequences of such a policy, however, were difficult for a government to shape. The stark dichotomy of job and no job attracted people to gamble on finding an urban job, and many would not win. The problem of "labor shortage" at the end of the war became the problem of "unemployment" by the time of independence. This unemployment coexisted with relatively high wages in the city—which did not fall with the labor surplus—and with labor shortages in such activities as plantation production. Officials at first welcomed the forging of distinct and self-conscious bodies of workers committed to their careers and their places of work; they later learned that this form of segmentation in the labor market juxtaposed such workers in the city against larger bodies of workers who stood little chance of penetrating the bastions of high wages, creating in another form the problem of contagion that the colonial state had tried to solve.[72]

Diagnosing these social problems has since become a favorite activity of social scientists, and a concern of government. Some have produced denunciations of "urban bias" on the part of African and Asian governments and of wage/price policies that give too much to those urban workers lucky enough to have "formal" jobs and too little to farmers or the irregular army of urban jobseekers.[73]

The bias of colonial states was not an urban bias per se but a concern with creating a differentiated urban working class in contrast to the dan-

72. John R. Harris and Michael P. Todaro, "Migration, Unemployment, and Development: A Two-Sector Analysis," *American Economic Review* 60 (1970): 126–42; John Weeks, "Wage Policy and the Colonial Legacy—a Comparative Study," *Journal of Modern African Studies* 9 (1971): 361–87; William House and Henry Rempel, "Labour Market Segmentation in Kenya," *East African Economic Review* 8 (1976): 35–54; Gavin Kitching, *Class and Economic Change in Kenya: The Making of an African Petite Bourgeoisie, 1905–1970* (New Haven: Yale University Press, 1980), pp. 375–410.

73. Michael Lipton, *Why Poor People Stay Poor: Urban Bias in World Development* (Cambridge, Mass.: Harvard University Press, 1977); Michael P. Todaro with Jerry Stilkind, *City Bias and Rural Neglect: The Dilemma of Urban Development* (New York: The Population Council, 1981); Robert Bates, *Markets and States in Tropical Africa* (Berkeley: University of California Press, 1981). A thorough review of the literature on poverty, class, and conflict in contemporary African cities is included in Richard Sandbrook, *The Politics of Basic Needs: Urban Aspects of Assaulting Poverty in Africa* (London: Heinemann, 1982).

gerous urban mass. Those fears were not so distant when Mboya spoke in 1962, and they are not so distant now. In much of Africa, the channels of communication remain narrow, the strain on urban resources is often acute, and above all the compact, disciplined work force created within the islands of labor reform has rarely been generalized throughout society. Mboya's concern was with control. Was the grudging, malnourished worker, with little stake in the continuity or results of his job, the true answer to the problems of African economic development or social order? The answer Mboya gave in 1962 and other African leaders have given since was not just rooted in faith in the modern corporation, with its rationalized management and stabilized work force, but in a profound distrust of the vast portion of African society that lay outside the small but potentially controllable "modern" workplace and "modern" city. The lavishing of resources on this sector made sense above all in terms of power: it was the one part of African society where policymakers could bring mechanisms of control to bear with some predictable response. To someone in Mboya's position in 1962, outside the city with its corporate capital and unionized workers lay an "uncaptured" peasantry and workers whose captivity was at best temporary and unproductive.[74]

There have been those who saw capturing this peasantry as the best alternative to either the segmented structure created in the 1950s and defended by Mboya or the circulating mass of labor power it was intended to replace. Even some leftist scholars have argued that peasant production is necessarily a brake on progress, and its displacement in favor of wage-labor agriculture is a necessary step to any more positive future.[75] But colonial states, Kenya included, have previously stumbled before the awesome difficulties of taking away the autonomy—even the impoverished, miserable autonomy—of the rural cultivator. It is far from clear whether these cultivators would gain the benefits, or merely suffer the pains, of such a process. To a large extent, officials' fanciful

74. Goran Hyden, *Beyond Ujamaa in Tanzania: Underdevelopment and an Uncaptured Peasantry* (London: Heinemann, 1980). Even scholars who are frank enough to say, in so many words, that "unequal bargaining and cheap labor—in its potential for low-cost production and enlarged reinvestable surpluses—represents the underdeveloped country's primary resource for accelerating economic growth" have shied away from examining what cheap labor would look like in concrete social, political, and economic terms. The above phrase comes from Peter Kilby, "Further Comments on the Kilby/Weeks Debate: Final Observations," *Journal of Developing Areas* 5 (1971): 176.

75. For some perspectives on this argument from varying positions in the political spectrum, see Keith Hart, *The Political Economy of West African Agriculture* (Cambridge: Cambridge University Press, 1982); Goran Hyden, *No Shortcuts to Progress: African Development and Management in Perspective* (London: Heinemann, 1983); Kitching; and an uncommonly sensible review of this and related issues by Sara Berry, "The Food Crisis and Agrarian Change in Africa: A Review Essay," *African Studies Review* 27, no. 2 (1984): 59–112.

invocation since the early 1950s of a "modern" society springing up in Africa reflects their unwillingness to pursue to the end the question of exactly how a working class is made, a question they themselves had tentatively broached.

Meanwhile, the experience of the docks of Mombasa remains instructive: by paying dockers more, by increasing their stakes in their jobs and weakening their involvement in other kinds of economic structures, by concentrating resources and supervisory authority on a compact labor force, management has been able to rule the docks in a way it could not before the 1950s. The fact that modern capitalism and the modern state do not rule the city, let alone the countryside, in the same way has been an incentive to maintain the gap—a gap in structure even more than in differential wages—rather than to bridge it. In the case of a valuable and vulnerable port, the alternative of low wages—of plunging dockers unprotected into a harsh labor market swollen by rural migrants—promised and promises questionable rewards for a cost that, since the general strike of 1939, has had an all too familiar meaning.

The high-wage policy explicitly defended by Mboya has been attacked not just from the right on free market grounds, but from the left on the grounds that it produces a privileged and coopted "labor aristocracy" clearly set off from the rest of society. Both arguments say something rather similar, and both—in the abstract—make a reasonable case. But the wonderfully ironic nineteenth-century term for the best-paid workers does not have the kind of analytic precision it has been assumed to possess in a long and largely tiresome debate.[76] As critics have pointed out, the so-called aristocrats are often not so well off after all and often have fluid, complex, and close relations with the plebians; they can be on the same side of the barricades. But a working class can be divided into more sections than two, and the tendencies toward unity and division must be analyzed with historical specificity. The colonial state did, in fact, succeed to a significant extent in fracturing the unity of a mass of similarly paid, impoverished workers. That no such unity has reappeared in Kenya may indeed reflect the willingness of the state and capital to continue to pay the price of a differentiated labor force.[77] Where governments in the

76. The debate has had the beneficial effect of encouraging specific social studies of relationships among different categories of workers. For an introduction to it, see Sandbrook and Cohen, *Development of an African Working Class*. A Europeanist version, raising a number of interesting points, has been going on in the pages of *Social History* for several years. See in particular H. F. Moorhouse, "The Marxist Theory of the Labor Aristocracy," *Social History* 3 (1978): 61–82.

77. African governments in the 1950s found that Africanization of positions in the civil service and in corporations that once used extensive non-African labor in skilled or managerial positions gave them a one-time-only chance to move people rapidly upward in job

name of equality or development—or because of lack of money—have tried policies of leveling wages downward, the aristocrats of labor have at times acted like the vanguard of the proletariat in leading movements that became widespread and serious challenges to the state. The strikes in Ghana in 1961 and 1971, and in Nigeria in 1964 and 1973 recall, in some ways, the type of strike that occurred in the 1940s.[78] The South African government, unwilling to seek consent in the workplace by the means pursued by the colonial powers after the war, and despite efforts to destroy African political and labor organization, has faced a resurgent labor movement and waves of urban rioting, especially since the Durban strikes of 1972–73.

Labor movements—like production—are social processes. Between the conditions that stimulate collective struggles, the organizing of the people who carry them out, and the dynamics of the confrontations themselves is a wide terrain that requires careful exploration. Struggles took place within workplaces, cities, states, and empires. In the process of confrontation, the range of issues that could be contested and the forms in which contestation could take place were as much at issue as wage rates; conceptions of society were affected as deeply as working conditions and profits.

This book has examined a profound transformation in the way dock-work was done, in the nature of social groups and social action in a city, and in ways of thinking about work and about workers in colonial society. The efforts of African workers in the 1930s and 1940s to find food and housing and to win wages that would allow them to marry and to raise children in the conditions of a rapidly growing city touched a nerve in colonial society. As much as the theorists of empire had tried to think of themselves as the trustees of a slowly evolving primitive society, African workers made them face—with little preparation, and with a great deal at stake—the realities of an African urban working class. If the unified challenge of the dangerous urban masses and the vitally necessary working class—all rolled into one—were to be met, colonial officials had to rethink in a systematic way the most fundamental questions about colonial society. As the colonial state and colonial capital reexamined the work-

---

hierarchies; this process, not without much contestation, gave managers a decade or two in which differential mobility was a much more manipulatable mechanism than in a more static situation. But it became less so as soon as relatively young people had made their way into the better positions and risked a correspondingly serious resurgence of a conception of society as divided into haves and have-nots.

78. The comparison of 1945 and 1964 in Nigeria is made by Cohen, *Labour and Politics*, p. 164. The politics of labor in independent Africa has been discussed especially well by Jeffries, *Class, Power and Ideology in Ghana*, and Adrian Peace, *Choice, Class and Conflict: A Study of Nigerian Factory Workers* (Brighton, Eng.: Harvester, 1979).

place, the city, and rural Africa, and as they slowly groped toward new theories and new practices, they encountered and often stimulated still other challenges and contradictions. Capital and the state have tried to make and remake the workplace and the city, and they have found that the new world which emerged was no more theirs to forge than the one before.

Note on Sources

The most important sources for this book are archives in Nairobi. The Kenya Railway (formerly East African Railways and Harbours) houses in a basement archive a rich body of materials. Before 1940, relevant material is in class SPG, and the files that do exist on labor suggest that the administration knew very little about the subject. After 1940, there is a new filing system and much information. Most material on labor is under EST (Establishment), including the heading EST/13 and its subheadings, on strikes and labor unrest. Also useful is the category HBR, Harbours. I also found an unclassified, but very rich, file on the dock strike of 1955. There is (in a different room) a list of file classifications, but no true index. I worked in the archives room directly by going along the shelves and extracting files from a cloud of dust.

The Kenya National Archives is well indexed. The most important files there are in the LAB (Labour) class, records of the Labour Department. Also important are the Provincial and District records, available as well on microfilm, including annual reports and other records. The Coast Province Deposit is also microfilmed, and is useful for the 1920s and earlier.

In Mombasa, the Provincial Commissioner's Archives contain the same kind of material as the Coast Province Deposit in the Kenya National Archives, but for more recent dates. I used series LAB (Labour), L&O (Law and Order), and PUB (Public Relations). The City Council archives, when I was in Kenya, were apparently in the process of being moved to Nairobi and were unavailable. Inquiries at the Kenya Cargo Handling Service (the successor to the stevedoring and shorehandling companies in the port) did not produce any archival material, but that does not mean it does not exist.

As the question of changing imperial views on the labor question became more important to me during the course of this research, I made repeated visits to English archives. The most relevant files in the Public Record Office are CO 533 (Kenya), CO 822 (East Africa), CO 859 (Social Services), CO 888 (Colonial Labour Advisory Committee), plus the transcript of Chege Kibachia's deportation hearing, CO 537/2109. Rhodes House library at Oxford University houses the papers of Major G. St. J. Orde Browne, Arthur Creech Jones, and the Fabian Colonial Bureau, which had correspondence with important figures in, or interested in, Kenya. James Patrick's memorandum on his work as a trade-union organizer in Kenya is there (FCB 118/1).

The discovery of the labor problem produced an outpouring of printed material. The most revealing (published by the Government Printer in Nairobi except as noted) are: Report of the Commission of Inquiry appointed to Examine the Labour Conditions in Mombasa (1939) [Willan Report]; Report of the Warren Wright Board of Inquiry (1944); Report of the Committee of Inquiry into Labour Unrest at Mombasa (1945) [Phillips Report]; H. S. Booker and N. M. Deverell, Report on the Economic and Social Background of the Mombasa Labour Dispute (cyclostyled, 1947); C. H. Northcott, ed., *African Labour Efficiency Survey*, Colonial Research Publications No. 3 (London, 1949); E. A. Vasey, Report on African Housing in Townships and Trading Centers (1950); Report of the Committee on African Wages (1954) [Carpenter Report]; East Africa Royal Commission (London, 1953–55); the Mombasa Social Survey (cyclostyled, 1958); Report of a Board of Inquiry Appointed to Inquire into Employment in the Port of Mombasa (1959) [Parkin Report]; A. G. Dalgleish, Survey of Unemployment (1960).

Routine Kenyan publications include the Legislative Council Debates and the annual reports of the Labour Department, of the Native Affairs (later African Affairs) Department, and of the Kenya and Uganda Railway and Harbours Administration (later East African Railway and Harbours Administration). In England, the House of Commons Debates, the Parliamentary Papers, and the Colonial Reports series proved useful. See especially Major G. St. J. Orde Browne, "Labour Conditions in East Africa," Colonial No. 193 (1946). The two most relevant newspapers are *The East African Standard* and the *Mombasa Times*. Other important primary sources were Lord Hailey, *An African Survey*, 2d ed. (London: Oxford University Press, 1945), Richard E. Luyt, *Trade Unionism in African Colonies*, New Africa Pamphlet No. 119 (Johannesburg: Institute of Race Relations, 1949), Tom Mboya, "Trade Unionism in Kenya," *Africa South* 1, no. 2 (1957), and Tom Mboya, *Freedom and After* (Boston: Little, Brown, 1963).

Among the interviews I did in Mombasa during my research there in 1978–79, the following were used in this book: David Amimo, now Superintendant in Charge of Labour Pool, Kenya Cargo Handling Service (KCHS), and a clerical worker in the port since 1953; Salim Ferunzi, Director of Social Services and Housing for the Mombasa City Council, a worker for the council since 1954, and a Mombasa native well informed about city life during his youth in the late 1940s and early 1950s; Hashi Hussein, Labour Officer for KCHS, and a dockworker (a former tindal) since 1956; Bruce Minnis, now stores manager for African Marine and

General in Mombasa, and former Labour Manager for the Mombasa Port Labour Utilisation Board, the "front line" managerial position for the Landing and Shipping Co. during the transformation of labor control during the mid-1950s; Alex Nyakoko, now Industrial Relations Officer of KCHS, a former clerical worker in the port (since 1953) and an activist in the Dockworkers Union during its early years; Hussein Ramadan, Staff Officer for KCHS, who worked for Shell Oil Company in the port since the 1940s and on the docks since 1959; Mohamed Shallo, Welfare Officer for KCHS, long-time Mombasa resident and staff member in welfare and other administrative positions with the Landing and Shipping Co.

African labor history has in recent years produced a wealth of fine studies. Fortunately, the need to review it has been met in an excellent article by William Freund, "Labor and Labor History in Africa," *African Studies Review* 27, no. 2 (1984): 1–58. I have spelled out my own approach to the theoretical issues most germane to this study in "Urban Space, Industrial Time, and Wage Labor in Africa," in Frederick Cooper, ed., *Struggle for the City: Migrant Labor, Capital, and the State in Urban Africa* (Beverly Hills, Calif.: 1983), pp. 7–50. I have also been much influenced by studies of labor and class and England and other advanced capitalist societies. This and other theoretical and comparative work have been cited in the notes, as relevant.

Two aspects of the literature on labor, the state, and social and economic change in Africa do deserve special mention. One is that on Kenya, one of the best served parts of Africa. The reader might profit in particular from: Alice H. Amsden, *International Firms and Labour in Kenya, 1945–70* (London: Cass, 1971); Anthony Clayton and Donald Savage, *Government and Labour in Kenya, 1895–1963* (London: Cass, 1974); Michael Cowen, "The British State and Agrarian Accumulation in Kenya after 1945," in Martin Fransman, ed., *Industry and Accumulation in Africa* (London: Heinemann, 1982), pp. 142–69; David Goldsworthy, *Tom Mboya: The Man Kenya Wanted to Forget* (London: Heinemann, 1982); David Gordon, *Decolonization and the State in Kenya* (Boulder, Col.: Westview, 1986); R. D. Grillo, *Race, Class, and Militancy: An African Trade Union, 1939–1965* (New York: Chandler, 1974); Karim K. Janmohamed, "A History of Mombasa, c. 1895–1939: Some Aspects of Economic and Social Life in an East African Port Town during Colonial Rule," Ph.D. diss., Northwestern University, 1977; Gavin Kitching, *Class and Economic Change in Kenya: The Making of an African Petite Bourgeoisie, 1905–1970* (New Haven: Yale University Press, 1980); Colin Leys, *Underdevelopment in Kenya* (Berkeley: University of California Press, 1975); Richard Sandbrook, *Proletarians and African Capitalism: The Kenyan Case, 1960–1972* (Cambridge: Cambridge University Press, 1975); (in a rather special category) Makhan Singh, *History of Kenya's Trade Union Movement to 1952* (Nairobi: East

African Publishing House, 1969), and Makhan Singh, *1952–56 Crucial Years of Kenya Trade Unions* (Nairobi: Uzima, 1980); Sharon Stichter, *Migrant Labour in Kenya: Capitalism and African Response 1895–1975* (London: Longman, 1982); Richard Stren, *Housing the Urban Poor in Africa: Policy, Politics, and Bureaucracy in Mombasa* (Berkeley, 1978). Of particular importance has been the work on the Kenyan state of John Lonsdale and Bruce Berman. Most of their studies on the postwar period are still unpublished, and I am grateful to both these scholars for sharing so many ideas with me. Meanwhile, see their "Coping with the Contradictions: The Development of the Colonial State in Kenya," *Journal of African History* 20 (1979): 487–506, and "Crises of Accumulation, Coercion and the Colonial State: The Development of the Labour Control System in Kenya, 1919–1929," *Canadian Journal of African Studies* 14 (1980): 37–54, plus John Lonsdale, "The Depression and the Second World War in the Transformation of Kenya," in Richard Rathbone and David Killingray, eds., *Africa and the Second World War* (London: Macmillan, 1984).

Also of relevance to this topic is the literature on dockworkers. We are well short of having sufficient information to write a comparative study of dockwork. But Africanists have already made a beginning to join a still insufficient body of literature on other ports of the world (see chapter 2 for some studies on England): M. A. Hermassi, "Sociologie du Milieu Docker," *Revue tunisienne de sciences sociales* 7 (1960): 153–79; David Hemson, "Dock Workers, Labour Circulation, and Class Struggles in Durban, 1940–59," *Journal of Southern African Studies* 4 (1977): 88–124; John Iliffe, "The Creation of Group Consciousness: A History of the Dockworkers of Dar es Salaam," in Richard Sandbrook and Robin Cohen, eds., *The Development of an African Working Class* (London: Longman, 1975), pp. 49–72; Monique Lakroum, "Les Salaires dans le port de Dakar," *Revue française d'histoire d'outre-mer* 63 (1976): 640–53; and Peter Waterman, *Division and Unity amongst Nigerian Workers: Lagos Port Unionism, 1940s–60s* (The Hague: Institute for Social Studies, 1982).

Index

Abdur Rehman bin Naaman, 44
Africa, economic importance of, 263–64
African economies: and capitalist develop-
    ment, 9–10, 23–26, 116–17, 129–30,
    265–66; and wage labor, 28, 119, 124,
    126, 261
African Labour Efficiency Survey, 120–
    21, 125–26, 133, 135–36n67, 142, 164
African society (traditional): British views
    of, 8, 34, 119, 129, 134, 248, 262, 265–
    66; incompatibility with wage labor,
    119, 121, 126–27, 138, 235; backward-
    ness of, 121, 129, 169, 265, 277
African Wharfage Company, 37, 56, 148.
    See also stevedoring companies
African Workers Federation: in 1947
    strike, 83–87; and working-class unity,
    87, 99, 106, 134; in coastal region, 98;
    after strike, 98–113, 195–96; and
    Thacker awards, 99–106; repression of,
    104–11, 134, 195–97, 270; in Nairobi,
    107
Africanization, 165, 170, 172, 233, 238,
    276–77n77
Agoi, Chief Paul, 69–70
Agriculture, workers in. See workers,
    agricultural
Akumu, Denis, 230–34, 239–46
Allen, P. deV., 45, 55
Alliance High School, 84, 87
Amoth, Chief, 69–70
Amsden, Alice, 230
Arabs: in coastal region, 15, 16; as dock-
    ers, 26–29 passim, 40, 44, 149–50, 157
Association of Commercial and Industrial
    Employers, 116n2, 230
attendance money, 150, 152–53, 219; in
    Britain, 19–20
Azikiwe, Nnamdi, 268

bachelor wages. See workers—and family
    life
Beecher, Archdeacon, 86, 93
Beni, 38–40, 42–46
Bevin, Ernest, 19, 263
Booker, H. S., 91, 138
Boy, Juma, 245

Braverman, Harry, 163, 174
Brewery, strikes at, 207, 220
Budgets. See standard of living, measures
    of
Burns, Alan, 254
Bury, Jim, 212, 215, 217

Camerouns, riots in, 252
capitalism, and development in Africa, 9–
    12, 115, 265, 275–76. See also African
    economies, and capitalist development
cargo handling statistics, 136–38, 173–74.
    See also port, traffic in
Carpenter Report (Committee on African
    Wages, 1954), 115, 130–31, 158, 162,
    200, 201, 209, 218
Carrier Corps, 29
casual labor: and living conditions, 17–19,
    21, 34–35; in Britain, 18–21; and ex-
    slaves, 25; reliance on, 25, 29, 145–46;
    criticism of, 25, 29, 34–36, 49–52, 88,
    113, 124–36, 144, 259; workers' atti-
    tudes toward, 28, 31, 88, 143–52, 155,
    235; and housing, 34, 52, 184, 190–91;
    and strikes, 46, 50, 51, 61, 64, 80, 83–
    84, 139, 205; port firms' defense of,
    56–57, 78; working patterns of, 58, 77–
    78, 94, 144–57; and weekly labor, 162,
    235. See also decasualization; workers—
    docks
Chadwick, J. T., 50, 51
Changamwe (Mombasa), 80, 189
cheap labor system, and disorder, 50, 73,
    105, 123, 129, 132, 254, 258
Clarke, Hilda Selwyn, 199
class: consciousness, 7, 73, 75, 267; con-
    flict, 7–8, 17, 129, 266; and social
    stability, 16–17, 35, 129, 186–88, 268–
    69. See also dangerous classes; working
    class
clocking-in, 240–41
Closer administration, 186–87
Coast African People's Union, 245
Coast Employers Association, 213
Coast Labour Committee, 101, 103, 111,
    180